KEITH A. MAYES

Managerial Economics and Operations Research

FIFTH EDITION

Managerial Economics
and
Operations Research

Techniques, Applications, Cases

FIFTH EDITION

EDITED BY

Edwin Mansfield

UNIVERSITY OF PENNSYLVANIA

W · W · NORTON & COMPANY
New York · London

Library of Congress Cataloging-in-Publication Data
Managerial economics and operations research, second edition.
Bibliography; p.
1. Managerial economics. 2. Operations research.
I. Mansfield, Edwin.
HD30.22.M355 1987   338.5'024658   86-21746

ISBN 0-393-95590-7

W. W. Norton & Company, Inc., 500 Fifth Avenue, New York, N.Y. 10110
W. W. Norton & Company Ltd., 37 Great Russell Street, London WC1B 3NU

1 2 3 4 5 6 7 8 9 0

Acknowledgments

"Managing Our Way to Economic Decline," by Robert Hayes and William Abernathy from *Harvard Business Review*, July–August 1980, pp. 67–77.

"The Japanese Cost and Quality Advantages in the Auto Industry," by the National Research Council, reprinted from *The Competitive Status of the U.S. Auto Industry: A Study of the Influences of Technology in Determining International Industrial Competitive Advantage*, 1982, with permission of the National Academy Press, Washington, D.C.

"Industrial Robots in the United States and Japan," by Organization for Economic Cooperation and Development, from *Industrial Robots: Their Role in Manufacturing Industry*. Copyright 1983 by Organization for Economic Cooperation and Development.

"The Decision-making Process," by Herbert A. Simon, from "The Executive as Decision Maker" in *The New Science of Management Decision*, by Herbert A. Simon. Copyright © 1960 by School of Commerce, Accounts, and Finance, New York University. Reprinted by permission by Harper & Row, Publisher.

"The Comparison of Alternatives," by Eugene L. Grant and W. Grant Ireson, from *Principles of Engineering Economy*, Fourth Edition, Revised Printing. Copyright © 1964 by The Ronald Press Company.

"Parkinson's Law," by C. Northcote Parkinson, from *The Economist*, London, November 19, 1955. Reprinted by permission of *The Economist* and Houghton Mifflin Company.

"Cost Analysis," by Neil Harlan, Charles Christenson, and Richard Vancil, from *Managerial Economics: Text and Cases* (Homewood, Ill.: Richard D. Irwin, Inc.), 1962.

"Production Functions and Cost Functions: A Case Study," by Leslie Cookenboo, from *Crude Oil Pipe Lines and Competition in the Oil Industry*. Copyright © 1955 by the President and Fellows of Harvard College. Reprinted by permission of Harvard University Press.

"How Cars Are Manufactured," by the National Research Council, reprinted from *The Competitive Status of the U.S. Auto Industry: A Study of the Influences of Technology in Determining International Industrial Competitive Advantage*, 1982, with permission of the National Academy Press, Washington, D.C.

To Charity L.

A GREAT WOMAN AND A GREAT HORSE

CONTENTS

Preface

Recent decades have witnessed exciting and important developments in economics and related disciplines with the invention or adaptation of new techniques and concepts for solving major managerial problems of business firms, government agencies, and other organizations. In the process of extending economic analysis to meet the need for greater precision in the management of the business enterprise, a major field, managerial economics, has emerged. Managerial economics draws upon economic analysis for such concepts as cost, demand, profit, and competition. It attempts to bridge the gap between the purely analytical problems that intrigue many economic theorists and the problems of policy that management must face. It now offers powerful tools and approaches for managerial policy making.

Another related field—operations research or management science—has also been opened up in recent decades. Its boundaries are not easy to define. According to one definition, operations research involves "the use of systematic quantitative analysis to aid in the making of management decisions."[1] Emphasis is placed on a scientific approach to decision making, with considerable reliance on advanced mathematical techniques and computer-based technology. First used on a sustained and significant scale in connection with military activities during World War II, operations research has spread throughout American industry, and is now a very important managerial tool.

This book provides an elementary description of important facets

1. Charles Hitch, "Economics and Military Operations Research," *Review of Economics and Statistics*, August 1958, p. 200.

of managerial economics, as well as relevant aspects of operations research. Aimed primarily at students of economics and business administration with modest training in mathematics, it provides a general introduction to the nature, purpose, and potential useful-ness of various concepts and techniques in managerial economics (and operations research) without going far into their technical details. Much published material is available for the advanced student with some mathematical sophistication, but little is available for the beginner. Hopefully, this book will help fill the gap.

The papers in Part One explore the problems of American indus-try in the 1980s. The papers in Part Two deal mainly with costs and production, while those in Part Three are concerned with demand, pricing, and corporate strategy. Part Four takes up capital budget-ing and investment, and Part Five deals with business and economic forecasting. In Part Six, linear programming, decision theory, and scheduling techniques are examined in theory and in practice. Part Seven deals with game theory, inventory policy, and queuing analy-sis. The papers in Part Eight focus on the relationships between business and government, and the use of economics in solving important problems in the public sector of the economy.

In this fifth edition, I have tried to alter the book's contents in the light of the reactions of the many instructors who have used the book in their courses. An important feature of this edition is the emphasis on the manufacturing function and on the competitiveness of American industry. In view of the growing importance of these topics to firms, and their place in many courses in managerial eco-nomics, this should be a welcome addition. Also, I have expanded and updated the parts of the book dealing with forecasting and with corporate strategy and rivalry. Other parts have also been altered, and about 40 percent of this edition is new. Once again, I want to thank the many teachers and students who have given me (and the book) the benefit of their comments and suggestions.

E.M.

Part One

American Managerial Problems of the 1980s

MANAGERIAL economics is concerned with problems as well as techniques. Indeed, to understand how the techniques of managerial economics can and should be applied, it is important to be aware of the major problems of American industry. Traditionally, the United States has been admired throughout the world for the proficiency and ingenuity of its industrial managers, but the past decade has seen a great deal of criticism and soul-searching on this score.

The opening article, by Robert Hayes and the late William Abernathy, is a well-known diagnosis of the problems of American industry. In their view, "Our managers still earn generally high marks for their skill in improving short-term efficiency, but their counterparts in Europe and Japan have started to question America's entrepreneurial imagination and willingness to make risky long-term competitive investments. . . By their preference for servicing existing markets rather than creating new ones and by their devotion to short-term returns and "management by the numbers," many of them have effectively forsworn long-term technological superiority as a competitive weapon." This is a controversial view, but one that has received an enormous amount of attention in recent years.

1

The following article, published by the National Research Council, provides detailed information concerning the cost and quality advantages of Japanese over American producers in the automobile industry. The authors conclude that the Japanese have a landed-cost advantage of between $700 and $1500 per small vehicle, which is attributable in large part to their "commitment to manufacturing excellence and a strategy that uses manufacturing as a competitive weapon." The final article in this introductory section deals with the fascinating and important field of robotics, and points out that Japan "is now the foremost producer and user of robots, as well as the world's leading producer of computerized automation in general."

Clearly, American industry is being challenged both in international and domestic markets. The clear-cut dominance of American firms that characterized the period following World War II is long gone. To respond to this challenge, it is essential that the basic principles of managerial economics be properly understood and effectively employed. The articles contained in subsequent sections of this volume should be of considerable help to the student or practitioner in this regard.

Managing Our Way to Economic Decline

ROBERT H. HAYES AND WILLIAM J. ABERNATHY

Robert Hayes is Professor of Business Administration at the Harvard Business School. The late William Abernathy also was a professor there. This article appeared in the Harvard Business Review *in 1980.*

During the past several years American business has experienced a marked deterioration of competitive vigor and a growing unease about its overall economic well-being. This decline in both health and confidence has been attributed by economists and business leaders to such factors as the rapacity of OPEC, deficiencies in government tax and monetary policies, and the proliferation of regulation. We find these explanations inadequate.

They do not explain, for example, why the rate of productivity growth in America has declined both absolutely and relative to that in Europe and Japan. Nor do they explain why in many high-technology as well as mature industries America has lost its leadership position. Although a host of readily named forces—government regulation, inflation, monetary policy, tax laws, labor costs and constraints, fear of a capital shortage, the price of imported oil—have taken their toll on American business, pressures of this sort affect the economic climate abroad just as they do here.

A German executive, for example, will not be convinced by these

Note: Some footnotes have been omitted from the original article.

explanations. Germany imports 95 percent of its oil (we import 50 percent), its government's share of gross domestic product is about 37 percent (ours is about 30 percent), and workers must be consulted on most major decisions. Yet Germany's rate of productivity growth has actually increased since 1970 and recently rose to more than four times ours. In France the situation is similar, yet today that country's productivity growth in manufacturing (despite current crises in steel and textiles) more than triples ours. No modern industrial nation is immune to the problems and pressures besetting U.S. business. Why then do we find a disproportionate loss of competitive vigor by U.S. companies?

Our experience suggests that, to an unprecedented degree, success in most industries today requires an organizational commitment to compete in the marketplace on technological grounds—that is, to compete over the long run by offering superior products. Yet, guided by what they took to be the newest and best principles of management, American managers have increasingly directed their attention elsewhere. These new principles, despite their sophistication and widespread usefulness, encourage a preference for (1) analytic detachment rather than the insight that comes from "hands on" experience and (2) short-term cost reduction rather than long-term development of technological competitiveness. It is this new managerial gospel, we feel, that has played a major role in undermining the vigor of American industry.

American management, especially in the two decades after World War II, was universally admired for its strikingly effective performance. But times change. An approach shaped and refined during stable decades may be ill suited to a world characterized by rapid and unpredictable change, scarce energy, global competition for markets, and a constant need for innovation. This is the world of the 1980s and, probably, the rest of this century.

The time is long overdue for earnest, objective self-analysis. What exactly have American managers been doing wrong? What are the critical weaknesses in the ways that they have managed the technological performance of their companies? What is the matter with the long-unquestioned assumptions on which they have based their managerial policies and practices?

A FAILURE OF MANAGEMENT

In the past, American managers earned worldwide respect for their carefully planned yet highly aggressive action across three different time frames:

> *Short term*—using existing assets as efficiently as possible.

> *Medium term*—replacing labor and other scarce resources with capital equipment.

> *Long term*—developing new products and processes that open new markets or restructure old ones.

The first of these time frames demanded toughness, determination, and close attention to detail; the second, capital and the willingness to take sizable financial risks; the third, imagination and a certain amount of technological daring.

Our managers still earn generally high marks for their skill in improving short-term efficiency, but their counterparts in Europe and Japan have started to question America's entrepreneurial imagination and willingness to make risky long-term competitive investments. As one such observer remarked to us: "The U.S. companies in my industry act like banks. All they are interested in is return on investment and getting their money back. Sometimes they act as though they are more interested in buying other companies than they are in selling products to customers."

In fact, this curt diagnosis represents a growing body of opinion that openly charges American managers with competitive myopia: "Somehow or other, American business is losing confidence in itself and especially confidence in its future. Instead of meeting the challenge of the changing world, American business today is making small, short-term adjustments by cutting costs and by turning to the government for temporary relief. . . . Success in trade is the result of patient and meticulous preparations, with a long period of market preparation before the rewards are available. . . . To undertake such commitments is hardly in the interest of a manager who is concerned with his or her next quarterly earnings reports."[1]

More troubling still, American managers themselves often admit the charge with, at most, a rhetorical shrug of their shoulders. In established businesses, notes one senior vice president of research:

1. Ryohei Suzuki, "Worldwide Expansion of U.S. Exports—A Japanese View," *Sloan Management Review*, Spring 1979, p. 1.

"We understand how to market, we know the technology, and production problems are not extreme. Why risk money on new businesses when good, profitable low-risk opportunities are on every side?" Says another: "It's much more difficult to come up with a synthetic meat product than a lemon-lime cake mix. But you work on the lemon-lime cake mix because you know exactly what that return is going to be. A synthetic steak is going to take a lot longer, require a much bigger investment, and the risk of failure will be greater."[2]

These managers are not alone; they speak for many. Why, they ask, should they invest dollars that are hard to earn back when it is so easy—and so much less risky—to make money in other ways? Why ignore a ready-made situation in cake mixes for the deferred and far less certain prospects in synthetic steaks? Why shoulder the competitive risks of making better, more innovative products?

In our judgment, the assumptions underlying these questions are prime evidence of a broad managerial failure—a failure of both vision and leadership—that over time has eroded both the inclination and the capacity of U.S. companies to innovate.

FAMILIAR EXCUSES

About the facts themselves there can be little dispute. Exhibits 1–4 document our sorry decline. But the explanations and excuses commonly offered invite a good deal of comment.

It is important to recognize, first of all, that the problem is not new. It has been going on for at least 15 years. The rate of productivity growth in the private sector peaked in the mid-1960s. Nor is the problem confined to a few sectors of our economy; with a few exceptions, it permeates our entire economy. Expenditures on R&D by both business and government, as measured in constant (noninflated) dollars, also peaked in the mid-1960s—both in absolute terms and as a percentage of GNP. During the same period the expenditures on R&D by West Germany and Japan have been rising. More important, American spending on R&D as a percentage of sales in such critical research-intensive industries as machinery, professional and scientific instruments, chemicals, and aircraft had dropped by the mid-1970s to about half its level in the early 1960s. These are the very industries on which we now depend for the bulk of our manufactured exports.

2. *Business Week*, February 16, 1976, p. 57.

EXHIBIT 1

GROWTH IN LABOR PRODUCTIVITY SINCE 1960
(United States and abroad)

	Average annual percent change	
	Manufacturing 1960–1978	All industries 1960–1976
United States	2.8%	1.7%
United Kingdom	2.9	2.2
Canada	4.0	2.1
Germany	5.4	4.2
France	5.5	4.3
Italy	5.9	4.9
Belgium	6.9[a]	—
Netherlands	6.9[a]	—
Sweden	5.2	—
Japan	8.2	7.5

[a] 1960–1977.

SOURCE: Council on Wage and Price Stability, *Report on Productivity*. Washington, D.C.: Executive Office of the President, July 1979.

EXHIBIT 2

GROWTH OF LABOR PRODUCTIVITY BY SECTOR, 1948–1978

Time sector	Growth of labor productivity (annual average percent)		
	1948–65	1965–73	1973–78
Private business	3.2%	2.3%	1.1%
Agriculture, forestry, and fisheries	5.5	5.3	2.9
Mining	4.2	2.0	−4.0
Construction	2.9	−2.2	−1.8
Manufacturing	3.1	2.4	1.7
Durable goods	2.8	1.9	1.2
Nondurable goods	3.4	3.2	2.4
Transportation	3.3	2.9	0.9
Communication	5.5	4.8	7.1
Electric, gas, and sanitary services	6.2	4.0	0.1
Trade	2.7	3.0	0.4
Wholesale	3.1	3.9	0.2
Retail	2.4	2.3	0.8
Finance, insurance, and real estate	1.0	−0.3	1.4
Services	1.5	1.9	0.5
Government enterprises	−0.8	0.9	−0.7

SOURCE: Bureau of Labor Statistics.

NOTE: Productivity data for services, construction, finance, insurance, and real estate are unpublished.

EXHIBIT 3

National Expenditures for Performance of R&D as a Percent of GNP by Country, 1961–1978[a]

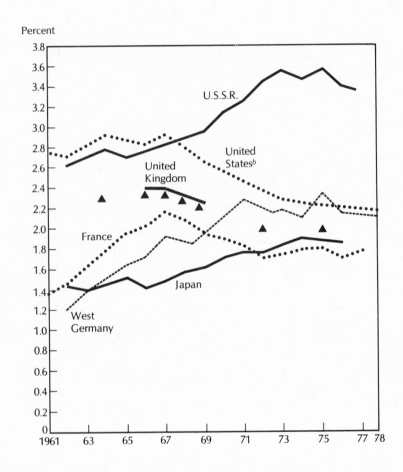

Percent

U.S.S.R.

United States[b]

United Kingdom

France

West Germany

Japan

SOURCE: *Science indicators—1978.* (Washington, D.C.: National Science Foundation, 1979), p. 6.

NOTE: The latest data may be preliminary or estimates.

[a] Gross expenditures for performance of R&D including associated capital expenditures.

[b] Detailed information on capital expenditures for R&D is not available for the United States. Estimates for the period 1972–1977 show that their inclusion would have an impact of less than one-tenth of 1% for each year.

EXHIBIT 4

INDUSTRIAL R&D EXPENDITURES FOR BASIC RESEARCH, APPLIED RESEARCH, AND DEVELOPMENT, 1960–1978 (in $ millions)

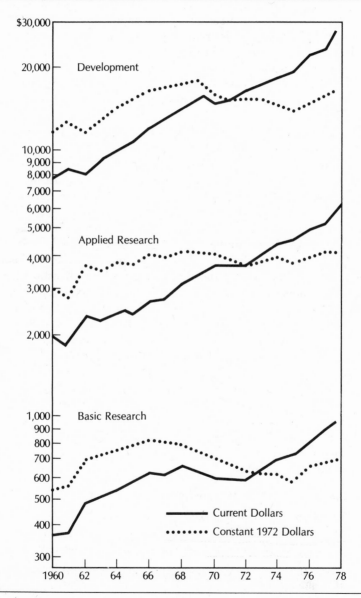

SOURCE: *Science indicators—1978*, p. 87.
NOTE: Preliminary data are shown for 1977 and estimates for 1978.
ᵃGNP implicit price deflators used to convert current dollars to constant 1972 dollars.

[handwritten: NOT MANAGERS, MAYBE HIDDEN GOVERNMENT ?]

Investment in plant and equipment in the United States displays the same disturbing trends. As economist Burton G. Malkiel has pointed out: "From 1948 to 1973 the [net book value of capital equipment] per unit of labor grew at an annual rate of almost 3%. Since 1973, however, lower rates of private investment have led to a decline in that growth rate to 1.75%. Moreover, the recent composition of investment [in 1978] has been skewed toward equipment and relatively short-term projects and away from structures and relatively long-lived investments. Thus our industrial plant has tended to age. . . ."[3]

Other studies have shown that growth in the incremental capital equipment-to-labor ratio has fallen to about one-third of its value in the early 1960s. By contrast, between 1966 and 1976 capital investment as a percentage of GNP in France and West Germany was more than 20% greater than that in the United States; in Japan the percentage was almost double ours.

To attribute this relative loss of technological vigor to such things as a shortage of capital in the United States is not justified. As Malkiel and others have shown, the return on equity of American business (out of which comes the capital necessary for investment) is about the same today as 20 years ago, *even after adjusting for inflation*. However, investment in both new equipment and R&D, as a percentage of GNP, was significantly higher 20 years ago than today.

The conclusion is painful but must be faced. Responsibility for this competitive listlessness belongs not just to a set of external conditions but also to the attitudes, preoccupations, and practices of American managers. By their preference for servicing existing markets rather than creating new ones and by their devotion to short-term returns and "management by the numbers," many of them have effectively forsworn long-term technological superiority as a competitive weapon. In consequence, they have abdicated their strategic responsibilities.

THE NEW MANAGEMENT ORTHODOXY

We refuse to believe that this managerial failure is the result of a sudden psychological shift among American managers toward a "super-safe, no risk" mind set. No profound sea change in the char-

3. Burton G. Malkiel, "Productivity—The Problem Behind the Headlines," HBR May–June 1979, p. 81.

acter of thousands of individuals could have occurred in so organized a fashion or have produced so consistent a pattern of behavior.
Instead we believe that during the past two decades American managers have increasingly relied on principles which prize analytical
detachment and methodological elegance over insight, based on
experience, into the subtleties and complexities of strategic decisions. As a result, maximum short-term financial returns have become
the overriding criteria for many companies.

For purposes of discussion, we may divide this *new* management
orthodoxy into three general categories: financial control, corporate
portfolio management, and market-driven behavior.

Financial Control · As more companies decentralize their organizational structures, they tend to fix on profit centers as the primary
unit of managerial responsibility. This development necessitates,
in turn, greater dependence on short-term financial measurements
like return on investment (ROI) for evaluating the performance of
individual managers and management groups. Increasing the structural distance between those entrusted with exploiting actual competitive opportunities and those who must judge the quality of their
work virtually guarantees reliance on objectively quantifiable short-
term criteria.

Although innovation, the lifeblood of any vital enterprise, is best
encouraged by an environment that does not unduly penalize failure, the predictable result of relying too heavily on short-term
financial measures—a sort of managerial remote control—is an environment in which no one feels he or she can afford a failure or even
a momentary dip in the bottom line.

Corporate Portfolio Management · This preoccupation with control
draws support from modern theories of financial portfolio management. Originally developed to help balance the overall risk and
return of stock and bond portfolios, these principles have been applied
increasingly to the creation and management of corporate portfolios—that is, a cluster of companies and product lines assembled
through various modes of diversification under a single corporate
umbrella. When applied by a remote group of dispassionate experts
primarily concerned with finance and control and lacking hands-on
experience, the analytic formulas of portfolio theory push managers

even further toward an extreme of caution in allocating resources.

"Especially in large organizations," reports one manager, "we are observing an increase in management behavior which I would regard as excessively cautious, even passive; certainly overanalytical; and, in general, characterized by a studied unwillingness to assume responsibility and even reasonable risk."

Market-driven Behavior · In the past 20 years, American companies have perhaps learned too well a lesson they had long been inclined to ignore: businesses should be customer oriented rather than product oriented. Henry Ford's famous dictum that the public could have any color automobile it wished as long as the color was black has since given way to its philosophical opposite: "We have got to stop marketing makeable products and learn to make marketable products."

At last, however, the dangers of too much reliance on this philosophy are becoming apparent. As two Canadian researchers have put it: "Inventors, scientists, engineers, and academics, in the normal pursuit of scientific knowledge, gave the world in recent times the laser, xerography, instant photography, and the transistor. In contrast, worshippers of the marketing concept have bestowed upon mankind such products as new-fangled potato chips, feminine hygiene deodorant, and the pet rock. . . ."[4]

The argument that no new product ought to be introduced without managers undertaking a market analysis is common sense. But the argument that consumer analyses and formal market surveys should dominate other considerations when allocating resources to product development is untenable. It may be useful to remember that the initial market estimate for computers in 1945 projected total worldwide sales of only ten units. Similarly, even the most carefully researched analysis of consumer preferences for gas-guzzling cars in an era of gasoline abundance offers little useful guidance to today's automobile manufacturers in making wise product investment decisions. Customers may know what their needs are, but they often define those needs in terms of existing products, processes, markets, and prices.

Deferring to a market-driven strategy without paying attention to

4. Roger Bennett and Robert Cooper, "Beyond the Marketing Concept," *Business Horizons*, June 1979, p. 76.

its limitations is, quite possibly, opting for customer satisfaction and lower risk in the short run at the expense of superior products in the future. Satisfied customers are critically important, of course, but not if the strategy for creating them is responsible as well for unnecessary product proliferation, inflated costs, unfocused diversification, and a lagging commitment to new technology and new capital equipment.

THREE MANAGERIAL DECISIONS

These are serious charges to make. But the unpleasant fact of the matter is that, however useful these new principles may have been initially, if carried too far they are bad for U.S. business. Consider, for example, their effect on three major kinds of choices regularly faced by corporate managers: the decision between imitative and innovative product design, the decision to integrate backward, and the decision to invest in process development.

Imitative vs. Innovative Product Design · A market-driven strategy requires new product ideas to flow from detailed market analysis or, at least, to be extensively tested for consumer reaction before actual introduction. It is no secret that these requirements add significant delays and costs to the introduction of new products. It is less well known that they also predispose managers toward developing products for existing markets and toward product designs of an imitative rather than an innovative nature. There is increasing evidence that market-driven strategies tend, over time, to dampen the general level of innovation in new product decisions.

Confronted with the choice between innovation and imitation, managers typically ask whether the marketplace shows any consistent preference for innovative products. If so, the additional funding they require may be economically justified; if not, those funds can more properly go to advertising, promoting, or reducing the prices of less-advanced products. Though the temptation to allocate resources so as to strengthen performance in existing products and markets is often irresistible, recent studies by J. Hugh Davidson and others confirm the strong market attractiveness of innovative products.

Nonetheless, managers having to decide between innovative and imitative product design face a difficult series of marketing-related trade-offs. Exhibit 5 summarizes these trade-offs.

By its very nature, innovative design is, as Joseph Schumpeter observed a long time ago, initially destructive of capital—whether in the form of labor skills, management systems, technological processes, or capital equipment. It tends to make obsolete existing investments in both marketing and manufacturing organizations. For the managers concerned it represents the choice of uncertainty (about economic returns, timing, etc.) over relative predictability, exchanging the reasonable expectation of current income against the promise of high future value. It is the choice of the gambler, the person willing to risk much to gain even more.

Conditioned by a market-driven strategy and held closely to account by a "results now" ROI-oriented control system, American managers have increasingly refused to take the chance on innovative product market development. As one of them confesses: "In the last year, on the basis of high capital risk, I turned down new products at a rate at least twice what I did a year ago. But in every case I tell my people to go back and bring me some new product ideas."[5] In truth, they have learned caution so well that many are in danger of forgetting that market-driven, follow-the-leader companies usually end up following the rest of the pack as well.

EXHIBIT 5

TRADE-OFFS BETWEEN IMITATIVE AND INNOVATIVE DESIGN FOR AN
ESTABLISHED PRODUCT LINE

Imitative design	*Innovative design*
Market demand is relatively well known and predictable.	Potentially large but unpredictable demand; the risk of a flop is also large.
Market recognition and acceptance are rapid.	Market acceptance may be slow initially, but the imitative response of competitors may also be slowed.
Readily adaptable to existing market, sales, and distribution policies.	May require unique, tailored marketing distribution and sales policies to educate customers or because of special repair and warranty problems.
Fits with existing market segmentation and product policies.	Demand may cut across traditional marketing segments, disrupting divisional responsibilities and cannibalizing other products.

5. *Business Week*, February 16, 1976, p. 57.

Backward Integration · Sometimes the problem for managers is not their reluctance to take action and make investments but that, when they do so, their action has the unintended result of reinforcing the status quo. In deciding to integrate backward because of apparent short-term rewards, managers often restrict their ability to strike out in innovative directions in the future.

Consider, for example, the case of a manufacturer who purchases a major component from an outside company. Static analysis of production economies may very well show that backward integration offers rather substantial cost benefits. Eliminating certain purchasing and marketing functions, centralizing overhead, pooling R&D efforts and resources, coordinating design and production of both product and component, reducing uncertainty over design changes, allowing for the use of more specialized equipment and labor skills— in all these ways and more, backward integration holds out to management the promise of significant short-term increases in ROI.

These efficiencies may be achieved by companies with commoditylike products. In such industries as ferrous and nonferrous metals or petroleum, backward integration toward raw materials and supplies tends to have a strong, positive effect on profits. However, the situation is markedly different for companies in more technologically active industries. Where there is considerable exposure to rapid technological advances, the promised value of backward integration becomes problematic. It may provide a quick, short-term boost to ROI figures in the next annual report, but it may also paralyze the long-term ability of a company to keep on top of technological change.

The real competitive threats to technologically active companies arise less from changes in ultimate consumer preference than from abrupt shifts in component technologies, raw materials, or production processes. Hence those managers whose attention is too firmly directed toward the marketplace and near-term profits may suddenly discover that their decision to make rather than buy important parts has locked their companies into an outdated technology.

Further, as supply channels and manufacturing operations become more systematized, the benefits from attempts to "rationalize" production may well be accompanied by unanticipated side effects. For instance, a company may find itself shut off from the R&D efforts of various independent suppliers by becoming their competitor. Similarly, the commitment of time and resources needed to master technology back up the channel of supply may distract a company from doing its own job well. Such was the fate of Bowmar, the pocket calculator pioneer, whose attempt to integrate backward into semiconductor production so consumed management attention that final assembly of the calculators, its core business, did not get the required resources.

Long-term contracts and long-term relationships with suppliers can achieve many of the same cost benefits as backward integration without calling into question a company's ability to innovate or respond to innovation. European automobile manufacturers, for example, have typically chosen to rely on their suppliers in this way; American companies have followed the path of backward integration. The resulting trade-offs between production efficiencies and innovative flexibility should offer a stern warning to those American managers too easily beguiled by the lure of short-term ROI improvement. A case in point: the U.S. auto industry's huge investment in automating the manufacture of cast-iron brake drums probably delayed by more than five years its transition to disc brakes.

Process Development · In an era of management by the numbers, many American managers—especially in mature industries—are reluctant to invest heavily in the development of new manufacturing processes. When asked to explain their reluctance, they tend to respond in fairly predictable ways. "We can't afford to design new capital equipment for just our own manufacturing needs" is one frequent answer. So is: "The capital equipment producers do a much better job, and they can amortize their development costs over sales to many companies." Perhaps most common is: "Let the others experiment in manufacturing; we can learn from their mistakes and do it better."

Each of these comments rests on the assumption that essential advances in process technology can be appropriated more easily through equipment purchase than through in-house equipment design and development. Our extensive conversations with the managers of European (primarily German) technology-based companies have convinced us that this assumption is not as widely shared abroad as in the United States. Virtually across the board, the European managers impressed us with their strong commitment to increasing market share through internal development of advanced process technology—even when their suppliers were highly responsive to technological advances.

By contrast, American managers tend to restrict investments in process development to only those items likely to reduce costs in the short run. Not all are happy with this. As one disgruntled executive told us: "For too long U.S. managers have been taught to set low priorities on mechanization projects, so that eventually divestment appears to be the best way out of manufacturing difficulties. Why?

"The drive for short-term success has prevented managers from looking thoroughly into the matter of special manufacturing equipment, which has to be invented, developed, tested, redesigned, reproduced, improved, and so on. That's a long process, which needs experienced, knowledgeable, and dedicated people who stick to their jobs over a considerable period of time. Merely buying new equipment (even if it is possible) does not often give the company any advantage over competitors."

We agree. Most American managers seem to forget that, even if they produce new products with their existing process technology (the same "cookie cutter" everyone else can buy), their competitors will face a relatively short lead time for introducing similar products. And as Eric von Hipple's studies of industrial innovation show, the innovations on which new industrial equipment is based usually originate with the user of the equipment and not with the equipment producer. In other words, companies can make products more profitable by investing in the development of their own process technology. Proprietary processes are every bit as formidable competitive weapons as proprietary products.

THE AMERICAN MANAGERIAL IDEAL

Two very important questions remain to be asked: (1) Why should so many American managers have shifted so strongly to this new managerial orthodoxy? and (2) Why are they not more deeply bothered by the ill effects of those principles on the long-term technological competitiveness of their companies? To answer the first question, we must take a look at the changing career patterns of American managers during the past quarter century; to answer the second, we must understand the way in which they have come to regard their professional roles and responsibilities as managers.

The Road to the Top · During the past 25 years the American manager's road to the top has changed significantly. No longer does the typical career, threading sinuously up and through a corporation with stops in several functional areas, provide future top executives with intimate hands-on knowledge of the company's technologies, customers, and suppliers.

Exhibit 6 summarizes the currently available data on the shift in functional background of newly appointed presidents of the 100 largest U.S. corporations. The immediate significance of these figures is clear. Since the mid-1950s there has been a rather substantial increase in the percentage of new company presidents whose primary interests and expertise lie in the financial and legal areas and not in production. In the view of C. Jackson Grayson, president of the American Productivity Center, American management has for 20 years "coasted off the great R&D gains made during World War II, and constantly rewarded executives from the marketing, financial, and legal sides of the business while it ignored the production men. Today [in business schools] courses in the production area are almost nonexistent."[6]

In addition, companies are increasingly choosing to fill new top management posts from outside their own ranks. In the opinion of foreign observers, who are still accustomed to long-term careers in the same company or division, "High-level American executives . . . seem to come and go and switch around as if playing a game of musical chairs at an Alice in Wonderland tea party."

Far more important, however, than any absolute change in numbers is the shift in the general sense of what an aspiring manager has to be "smart about" to make it to the top. More important still is the broad change in attitude such trends both encourage and express. What has developed, in the business community as in academia, is a preoccupation with a false and shallow concept of the professional manager, a "pseudo-professional" really—an individual having no special expertise in any particular industry or technology who nevertheless can step into an unfamiliar company and run it successfully through strict application of financial controls, portfolio concepts, and a market-driven strategy.

6. *Dun's Review*, July 1978, p. 39.

EXHIBIT 6

CHANGES IN THE PROFESSIONAL ORIGINS OF CORPORATE PRESIDENTS
(percent changes from baseline years [1948–1952] for 100 top
U.S. companies)

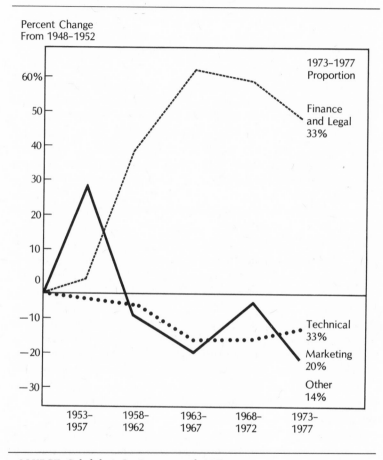

SOURCE: Golightly & Co. International, 1978.

The Gospel of Pseudo-professionalism · In recent years, this ideal-
ization of pseudo-professionalism has taken on something of the quality
of a corporate religion. Its first doctrine, appropriately enough, is
that neither industry experience nor hands-on technological exper-

tise counts for very much. At one level, of course, this doctrine helps to salve the conscience of those who lack them. At another, more disturbing level it encourages the faithful to make decisions about technological matters simply as if they were adjuncts to finance or marketing decisions. We do not believe that the technological issues facing managers today can be meaningfully addressed without taking into account marketing or financial considerations; on the other hand, neither can they be resolved with the same methodologies applied to these other fields.

Complex modern technology has its own inner logic and developmental imperatives. To treat it as if it were something else—no matter how comfortable one is with that other kind of data—is to base a competitive business on a two-legged stool, which must, no matter how excellent the balancing act, inevitably fall to the ground.

More disturbing still, true believers keep the faith on a day-to-day basis by insisting that as issues rise up the managerial hierarchy for decision they be progressively distilled into easily quantifiable terms. One European manager, in recounting to us his experiences in a joint venture with an American company, recalled with exasperation that "U.S. managers want everything to be simple. But sometimes business situations are not simple, and they cannot be divided up or looked at in such a way that they become simple. They are messy, and one must try to understand all the facets. This appears to be alien to the American mentality."

The purpose of good organizational design, of course, is to divide responsibilities in such a way that individuals have relatively easy tasks to perform. But then these differentiated responsibilities must be pulled together by sophisticated, broadly gauged integrators at the top of the managerial pyramid. If these individuals are interested in but one or two aspects of the total competitive picture, if their training includes a very narrow exposure to the range of functional specialties, if—worst of all—they are devoted simplifiers themselves, who will do the necessary integration? Who will attempt to resolve complicated issues rather than try to uncomplicate them artificially? At the strategic level there are no such things as pure production problems, pure financial problems, or pure marketing problems.

Merger Mania · When executive suites are dominated by people with financial and legal skills, it is not surprising that top management should increasingly allocate time and energy to such concerns as cash management and the whole process of corporate acquisitions and mergers. This is indeed what has happened. In 1978 alone there were some 80 mergers involving companies with assets in excess of $100 million each; in 1979 there were almost 100. This represents roughly $20 billion in transfers of large companies from one owner to another—two-thirds of the total amount spent on R&D by American industry.

In 1978 *Business Week* ran a cover story on cash management in which it stated that "the 400 largest U.S. companies together have more than $60 billion in cash—almost triple the amount they had at the beginning of the 1970s." The article also described the increasing attention devoted to—and the sophisticated and exotic techniques used for—managing this cash hoard.

There are perfectly good reasons for this flurry of activity. It is entirely natural for financially (or legally) trained managers to concentrate on essentially financial (or legal) activities. It is also natural for managers who subscribe to the portfolio "law of large numbers" to seek to reduce total corporate risk by parceling it out among a sufficiently large number of separate product lines, businesses, or technologies. Under certain conditions it may very well make good economic sense to buy rather than build new plants or modernize existing ones. Mergers are obviously an exciting game; they tend to produce fairly quick and decisive results, and they offer the kind of public recognition that helps careers along. Who can doubt the appeal of the titles awarded by the financial community; being called a "gunslinger," "white knight," or "raider" can quicken anyone's blood.

Unfortunately, the general American penchant for separating and simplifying has tended to encourage a diversification away from core technologies and markets to a much greater degree than is true in Europe or Japan. U.S. managers appear to have an inordinate faith in the portfolio law of large numbers—that is, by amassing enough product lines, technologies, and businesses, one will be cushioned against the random setbacks that occur in life. This might be true for portfolios of stocks and bonds, where there is considerable evidence that setbacks *are* random. Businesses, however, are subject not only to random setbacks such as strikes and shortages but also to carefully orchestrated attacks by competitors, who focus all their resources and energies on one set of activities.

Worse, the great bulk of this merger activity appears to have been absolutely wasted in terms of generating economic benefits for stockholders. Acquisition experts do not necessarily make good managers. Nor can they increase the value of their shares by merging two companies any better than their shareholders could do individually by buying shares of the acquired company on the open market (at a price usually below that required for a takeover attempt).

There appears to be a growing recognition of this fact. A number of U.S. companies are now divesting themselves of previously acquired companies; others (for example, W.R. Grace) are proposing to break themselves up into relatively independent entities. The establishment of a strong competitive position through in-house technological superiority is by nature a long, arduous, and often unglamorous task. But it is what keeps a business vigorous and competitive.

THE EUROPEAN EXAMPLE

Gaining competitive success through technological superiority is a skill much valued by the seasoned European (and Japanese) managers with whom we talked. Although we were able to locate few hard statistics on their actual practice, our extensive investigations of more than 20 companies convinced us that European managers do indeed tend to differ significantly from their American counterparts. In fact, we found that many of them were able to articulate these differences quite clearly.

In the first place, European managers think themselves more pointedly concerned with how to survive over the long run under intensely competitive conditions. Few markets, of course, generate price competition as fierce as in the United States, but European companies face the remorseless necessity of exporting to other national markets or perishing.

The figures here are startling: manufactured product exports represent more than 35% of total manufacturing sales in France and Germany and nearly 60% in the Benelux countries, as against not quite 10% in the United States. In these export markets, moreover, European products must hold their own against "world class" competitors, lower-priced products from developing countries, and American products selling at attractive devalued dollar prices. To survive this competitive squeeze, European managers feel they must place central emphasis on producing technologically superior products.

Further, the kinds of pressures from European labor unions and national governments virtually force them to take a consistently long-term view in decision making. German managers, for example, must negotiate major decisions at the plant level with worker-dominated works councils; in turn, these decisions are subject to review by supervisory boards (roughly equivalent to American boards of directors), half of whose membership is worker elected. Together with strict national legislation, the pervasive influence of labor unions makes it extremely difficult to change employment levels or production locations. Not surprisingly, labor costs in Northern Europe have more than doubled in the past decade and are now the highest in the world.

To be successful in this environment of strictly constrained options, European managers feel they must employ a decision-making apparatus that grinds very fine—and very deliberately. They must simply outthink and outmanage their competitors. Now, American managers also have their strategic options hedged about by all kinds of restrictions. But those restrictions have not yet made them as conscious as their European counterparts of the long-term implications of their day-to-day decisions.

As a result, the Europeans see themselves as investing more heavily in cutting-edge technology than the Americans. More often than not, this investment is made to create new product opportunities in advance of consumer demand and not merely in response to market-driven strategy. In case after case, we found the Europeans striving to develop the products and process capabilities with which to lead markets and not simply responding to the current demands of the marketplace. Moreover, in doing this they seem less inclined to integrate backward and more likely to seek maximum leverage from stable, long-term relationships with suppliers.

Having never lost sight of the need to be technologically competitive over the long run, European and Japanese managers are extremely careful to make the necessary arrangements and investments today. And their daily concern with the rather basic issue of long-term survival adds perspective to such matters as short-term ROI or rate of growth. The time line by which they manage is long, and it has made them painstakingly attentive to the means for keeping their companies technologically competitive. Of course they pay attention to the numbers. Their profit margins are usually lower than ours, their debt ratios higher. Every tenth of a percent is critical to them. But they are also aware that tomorrow will be no better unless they constantly try to develop new processes, enter new markets, and offer superior—even unique—products. As one senior German executive phrased it recently, "We look at rates of return, too, but only after we ask 'Is it a good product?' "[7]

CREATING ECONOMIC VALUE

Americans traveling in Europe and Asia soon learn they must often deal with criticism of our country. Being forced to respond to such criticism can be healthy, for it requires rethinking some basic issues of principle and practice.

We have much to be proud about and little to be ashamed of relative to most other countries. But sometimes the criticism of others is uncomfortably close to the mark. The comments of our overseas competitors on American business practices contain enough truth to require our thoughtful consideration. What is behind the decline in competitiveness of U.S. business? Why do U.S. companies have such apparent difficulties competing with foreign producers of established products, many of which originated in the United States?

For example, Japanese televisions dominate some market segments, even though many U.S. producers now enjoy the same low labor cost advantages of offshore production. The German machine tool and automotive producers continue their inroads into U.S. domestic markets, even though their labor rates are now higher than those in the United States and the famed German worker in German factories is almost as likely to be Turkish or Italian as German.

The responsibility for these problems may rest in part on government policies that either overconstrain or undersupport U.S. producers. But if our foreign critics are correct, the long-term solution to America's problems may not be correctable simply by changing our government's tax laws, monetary policies, and regulatory practices. It will also require some fundamental changes in management attitudes and practices.

7. *Business Week,* March 3, 1980, p 76.

It would be an oversimplification to assert that the only reason for the decline in competitiveness of U.S. companies is that our managers devote too much attention and energy to using existing resources more efficiently. It would also oversimplify the issue, although possibly to a lesser extent, to say that it is due purely and simply to their tendency to neglect technology as a competitive weapon.

Companies cannot become more innovative simply by increasing R&D investments or by conducting more basic research. Each of the decisions we have described directly affects several functional areas of management, and major conflicts can only be reconciled at senior executive levels. The benefits favoring the more innovative, aggressive option in each case depend more on intangible factors than do their efficiency-oriented alternatives.

Senior managers who are less informed about their industry and its confederation of parts suppliers, equipment suppliers, workers, and customers or who have less time to consider the long-term implications of their interactions are likely to exhibit a noninnovative bias in their choices. Tight financial controls with a short-term emphasis will also bias choices toward the less innovative, less technologically aggressive alternatives.

The key to long-term success—even survival—in business is what it has always been: to invest, to innovate, to lead, to create value where none existed before. Such determination, such striving to excel, requires leaders—not *just* controllers, market analysts, and portfolio managers. In our preoccupation with the braking systems and exterior trim, we may have neglected the drive trains of our corporations.

The Japanese Cost and Quality Advantages in the Auto Industry

National Research Council

This article comes from The Competitive Status of the U.S. Auto Industry, *published by the National Research Council in 1982.*

Over the last several years, information on foreign and domestic productivity and factor prices has been developed that implies a slight advantage for Japanese products and a disadvantage for producers in West Germany and the United Kingdom. These comparisons are for vehicles available for sale in the United States and thus include the costs of ocean freight and applicable tariffs for imported products.

One of the most careful studies of relative costs was conducted by Eric Toder and his colleagues at Charles River Associates. Using data for 1974, Toder found a Japanese disadvantage of 3 percent. If Toder's analysis were revised to reflect more realistic transportation costs, the data would imply a Japanese advantage of about 7 percent.

In 1978, additional U.S.–Japanese cost comparisons were published by Ford in a white paper entitled *State of the U.S. Automotive Industry*. Ford estimated the net Japanese cost advantage per vehicle to be $525 on a subcompact-size car landed in the United States. Although methods and sources were not identified, higher U.S. costs were largely due to higher wage rates, a result generally

Note: All footnotes have been omitted from the original article.

consistent with the analysis of Toder. The difference in the two analyses could be explained by differences in time period, intervening inflation, and changes in productivity.

The notion that the landed-cost differential between U.S. and Japanese products is $500–$600 recently found its way into congressional testimony. Speaking before the Subcommittee on Trade of the House Ways and Means Committee, Abraham Katz, Assistant Secretary of Commerce for International Economic Policy, summarized what appears to be a concensus view:

> Average hourly compensation (including fringe benefits) in the Japanese auto industry in 1979 was $6.85—half of the $13.72 hourly compensation in the U.S. auto industry. Present indications are that productivity in the U.S. and Japanese auto industries may be roughly equal. On this basis Japanese producers appear to have had an $860 labor cost advantage per car in 1979. Other differential costs (principally the higher cost of steel in the United States) may have added $100 per car to the U.S. cost. As freight and insurance on Japanese cars averages $400, the apparent cost advantage to Japanese producers may have been $560 per car in 1979. The actual advantage may have been considerably less, for the above calculations do not take into account energy costs, capital costs, and the costs of other production factors—some of which are cheaper in the United States than in Japan.

It is our view that the estimates presented by Katz and his suggestion that actual differences might be even lower constitute an understatement of the current cost advantage of the Japanese. Not only do the estimates fail to reflect current rates of compensation but they also fail to capture important differences in production processes that result in higher productivity in Japan. Estimates that reflect these differences have been developed using a variety of methods. We have estimated the productivity and cost differential using both a macro, economy-wide approach and a "bottom up" approach with microdata. We have taken an industry-wide perspective, using publicly available sources, and we have analyzed annual reports. Comparisons of this sort involve several difficulties. The automobile manufacturers of the United States and Japan produce a different mix of products and have organized production in different ways, particularly in terms of vertical integration. Productivity comparisons are also significantly affected by differences in capacity utilization that have been substantial in recent years. While attempts have been made to correct for these factors, even the most careful comparison requires judgements and assumptions that affect the results.

Evidence from Alternative Perspectives · Table 1 outlines the various perspectives taken and summarizes the basic results. The analysis suggests that the Japanese enjoy a landed-cost advantage of between $700 and $1500 per small vehicle. These estimates are larger than those used in congressional hearings during 1980. Furthermore, the immediate sources of the Japanese advantage may be quite different. Those analyses that focused on the auto sector found sizeable differences in labor hours per vehicle (a measure of productivity) along with differences in employee costs and other prices. The industry level analysis (which includes suppliers) found a 20–25 percent Japanese advantage in productivity, while examination of specific plants and processes revealed an even larger productivity gap.

The wide disparity in estimates of the Japanese productivity advantage underscores the difficulty of making precise calculations, particularly in this context, where the industry structure is different and hard data are relatively scarce. Indeed, precise order of magnitude and the confidence which industry panel members place in the estimated cost difference (i.e., $1200–$1500) comes from internal studies, using confidential and proprietary data.

ASPECTS OF PRODUCT QUALITY

When VW first made significant penetration into the U.S. market, its strategy established a formula for success that has been refined and extended by the Japanese. A critical element in that strategy was the production of a vehicle that the market perceived to be of high quality. Beginning with the VW Beetle in the late 1950s, the word used most often to describe the character of imported products has been "workmanship," which connotes attention to detail and care in production and quality appearance. The view is now widespread that quality defined in these terms has been a significant factor in the recent success of the Japanese. It seems clear from recent statements of industry executives that an improvement in quality will be an important aspect of any improvement in the U.S. competitive position. In this essay we identify dimensions of quality that appear to be significant and present evidence about the relative U.S. position.

TABLE 1

ESTIMATES OF U.S.–JAPANESE RELATIVE COSTS: ALTERNATIVE PERSPECTIVES AND APPROACHES

Category	Industry/Macro	Industry/Micro	Company	Plant
Approach	Estimates productivity and costs using input/output model of whole industrial economy; thus, compares U.S. economy and Japanese; uses published data on wages and input/output matrices.	Examines relative productivity and costs in the auto industry as a whole, including suppliers; uses published data on productivity growth, cost structure, wage rates, and labor hours.	Estimates productivity and costs at the assembler level (Ford, GM, etc.); corrects for difference in product mix and vertical integration; uses data in annual reports.	Productivity and cost estimates based on plant-by-plant comparisons; uses public information on Japanese firms and consultant reports for U.S. firms.
Evidence				
Productivity differential	Economy wide, U.S. firms have higher productivity ranging from 8 to 20 percent; no estimates given for productivity in auto sector.	On industry basis, Japanese are 20–25 percent more productive.	At the OEM level, Japanese are 41–50 percent more productive.	Depending on specific plant and process, Japanese are 35–200 percent more productive; in plants examined, average is 90 percent Japanese advantage.
Landed-cost difference	Japanese advantage of $1000–$1200.	Japanese advantage of $1400.	Japanese advantage of $1600.	Japanese advantage of $1500.

Definitions · Any attempt to define and evaluate the quality of a complex product such as the automobile must deal with the supposed distinction between perception and reality. It has been argued that the Japanese and European advantage in quality is not "real" in an objective sense but is only a perceived advantage. The implication is that through advertising and other forms of public persuasion the importers have created an image of quality that colors consumer perception. This argument misses the point. In the marketplace, perception *is* reality. The competitively important dimensions of the product are not those established by experts, nor are the key differences between manufacturers those determined by an objective evaluation. Competitive advantage accrues to those whose products are perceived by the buyers to be of higher quality.

Seen in these terms, quality is simply whatever the market defines it to be. A manufacturer can go to great lengths to offer a car with clearly superior rustproofing, but if corrosion protection is not an element of the market's definition of quality, little competitive advantage will be obtained. There appear to be three dimensions of quality that the market regards as significant. We propose to define each dimension and present some evidence on the relative U.S. position.

Assembly Quality · This category harks back to the notion of "workmanship" identified earlier. It has been described as the "fits and finishes" dimension and includes such things as body finish, squeaks and rattles, the alignment of doors and hoods, and paint quality. Within the industry, assembly quality is usually defined in terms of "building to spec," that is, making the vehicle as specified in the design. This definition focuses attention on the work performed on the assembly line and on the extent to which components and materials meet specifications. But it is clear that the design and thus the specifications themselves are also a significant factor in determining assembly quality. Not only does the design affect the ability of the manufacturing organization to achieve high-quality assembly, but the standards established in the specifications may not be as exacting as those of competitors.

Available information suggests that U.S. producers' assembly quality falls short of the implicit market standard set by the imports. Table 2 presents ratings of the condition of selected vehicles at

TABLE 2

RATING OF ASSEMBLY QUALITY: U.S. VERSUS THE IMPORTS, 1979

Vehicle category	Condition of car at delivery (scale of 1–10; 10 is excellent)		Condition of car after one month of service (number of defects per vehicle shipped)
Aggregates	*Domestic*	*Imports*	
Subcompact	6.4	7.9	
Compact	6.2	7.7	
Midsize	6.6	8.1	
Standard	6.8	—	
Specific Models			
Omni	7.4		4.10
Corolla	7.8		0.71[a]
Chevette	7.2		3.00
Pinto	6.5		3.70
Rabbit (U.S.)[b]	7.8		2.13
Fiesta	7.9		N/A
Civic	8.0		1.23[c]
Horizon	7.5		N/A
Colt	7.8		N/A

SOURCE: Aggregates: Rogers National Research, *Buyer Profiles,* 1979; Models: Industry Sources.

[a] Toyota average.

[b] European Rabbit averaged 1.42 defects per vehicle shipped.

[c] Honda average.

delivery and the number of defects after one month of service. Imports have a clear advantage in both measures, although the gap is largest in defects after one month. These data suggest that consumer perceptions are consistent with actual experience with purchased vehicles.

Reliability · The automobile is a collection of complex mechanical and electrical systems that are subjected to enormous stress—wide variance in temperatures, short bursts of heavy use followed by long periods of inaction, and so forth. To be even minimally competitive, cars must achieve a very high degree of reliability—that is, the ability to function as designed on demand. In these terms, reliability applies both to individual components and to entire vehicle systems. Failure to function as designed makes the vehicle less useful (at times unuseable), and repairing a malfunction is often a time-consuming hassle. Reliability is thus a critical dimension of overall quality.

To measure reliability we have used the repair incidence data published by Consumer's Union. These data were not drawn from a random sample of all owners but rather from the subscribers to *Consumer Reports*. They may not be representative of experience generally. The basic data cover repair frequency of mechanical systems and components and the body (structure, finish). Ratings are given in five categories: average, below average, far below average, above average, and far above average. Beginning with a score of 0 for far below average, we have assigned values of 5, 10, 15, and 20 to the other categories. A total score for each vehicle was obtained by summing the scores on individual body and mechanical systems. The results are reported in Table 3 for selected makes.

It is apparent that imported products have achieved repair records that exceed those of the domestic manufacturers, in some cases by substantial margins. While the imports have an advantage in both body and mechanical systems, the superiority of the foreign products is most pronounced in the body category. This is consistent with earlier evidence on assembly quality. In mechanical systems, reliability of some of the domestic and imported products is actually quite close. Given the nature of the data and size of the differences, strong conclusions about an overall import advantage in mechanical system reliability does not seem warranted.

Durability · There is little evidence about the long-term durability of Japanese products and thus little basis for comparison. It does appear that U.S. products have superior corrosion protection and that basic components and systems may be more durable.

Customer Loyalty · Perhaps the most significant test of quality production and customer satisfaction is loyalty, the willingness of buyers to purchase the same car again. The data presented in Table 4 generally confirm the evidence on assembly quality and reliability. The fraction of owners willing to buy the same make again is much higher in the import group. Since the Japanese dominate the import category, these results underscore their formidable competitive advantage. Not only are their costs significantly lower, but the quality of their products is higher.

TABLE 3

RATINGS OF BODY AND MECHANICAL REPAIR
FREQUENCY, 1979
(10 = average; 20 = best; 0 = worst)

Make	Body	Mechanical
Domestic		
Buick	10	10
Chevrolet	4	8
Dodge	8	8
Ford	9	7
Lincoln	10	10
Oldsmobile	11	9
Volkswagen	14	11
Imports		
Datsun	14	11
Honda	16	12
Mazda	18	13
Toyota	17	12
Volkswagen	N/A	N/A
Volvo	16	11

SOURCE: *Consumer Reports*, April 1979.

TABLE 4

CUSTOMER LOYALTY: WOULD BUY SAME MAKE/MODEL
AGAIN (percentage)

	Domestic	Imported	Total
Subcompact	77.2	91.6	81.2
Compact	74.2	91.4	72.4
Midsize	75.3	94.5	76.9
Standard	81.8	—	—
Luxury	86.6	94.6	87.2
Total	78.7	91.8	—

SOURCE: Rogers National Research, *Buyer Profiles*, 1979.

EXPLANATION AND PROGNOSIS

It has become almost commonplace to cite the superior quality of Japanese cars as a rationale for their competitive success. With the evidence on productivity and costs, it appears that the Japanese competitive position is buttressed by a significant cost advantage as well as by higher-quality production. On both counts the gap between the United States and Japan is significant. While there is little evidence of a serious attempt to exploit the cost differential through aggressive pricing it is clear that Japanese manufacturers can absorb very large increases in costs without raising prices and still obtain higher margins than their U.S. competitors. And it is equally clear that a sufficient margin exists for even more costly improvements in performance and quality. Japanese quality levels, however, are already perceived to be a cut above domestic production. With their emphasis on quality and performance the major Japanese firms have acquired a kind of "reputation capital" that enhances an already formidable competitive position.

Popular accounts of the emergence of Japanese producers as first-rate, worldwide competitors tend to emphasize the impact of new automation technology (e.g., robotics), strong support of the central government (i.e., "Japan, Inc."), and influence of Japanese culture (i.e., a dedicated work force). There is no doubt that these factors have played some role. Yet, it is our view that the sources of the Japanese advantage are not to be found in such factors. Rather, they are rooted in a commitment to manufacturing excellence and a strategy that uses manufacturing as a competitive weapon.

It may seem odd to think of manufacturing as anything other than a competitive weapon. After all, "manufacturing" refers to the production and distribution of the product—essential features of competition. Yet the history of the automobile market in the United States suggests that by the late 1950s manufacturing had become a competitively neutral factor. This is not to imply that it was not important; indeed, the Big Three expended great resources in improving technology and productivity. The point is that none of the major producers sought to achieve a competitive advantage through superior manufacturing performance. Except perhaps for economies of scale, which are affected by manufacturing decisions, the basis of competition was located outside manufacturing—in marketing, styling, and the dealerships.

But the Japanese advantage originates precisely in manufacturing operations. Productivity and quality are determined in the very heart of the operation, in the interaction of people, materials, and equipment. It is in the management of these elements that the

Japanese have excelled. And it is the dictates of strategy that have provided the impetus for that excellence.

The strategy of the Japanese producers was first and foremost an entry strategy. The fact that they started from the ground up in the U.S. market influenced their choices in all dimensions of competition. When the Japanese sought to penetrate the U.S. market it would have been foolish to try to compete with the domestic firms on their terms. Just as General Motors (GM) avoided head-on competition with Ford in the 1920s, so the Japanese approach avoided status quo competitive behavior in the 1960s. The domestic market was dominated by the large car, the annual model change, and the "boulevard ride." The new entrants had neither the experience, the production systems, nor the resources to compete on those terms. As with other imports, the Japanese sought out a niche in the small-car segment. Having learned from their early failures (the first attempt at penetration failed on the strength of a low-performance, low-quality product) and the success of VW, both Toyota and Nissan concentrated on establishing a dealer network and on producing a high-quality, solid-performance small car. It was essential that the level of quality and performance be noticeably superior. Otherwise the new product lines were destined to be lost in the competitive shuffle. Moreover, reputation for quality and performance was essential for success over the longer term when entry into higher-margin niches (sports cars, high-performance sedans) was envisioned.

Explaining the Performance Gap · If competitive strategy provides the broad driving force for excellence in manufacturing, what explains observed U.S.–Japanese differences in performance? What aspects of the production process should be singled out for particular notice?To cast some light on these issues, we have identified several characteristics of the production process that may be important in explaining differences in productivity.

The productivity of an operating system—in this case the number of employee hours required per vehicle produced—is determined by the state of technology (both product and process); by the amount and quality of inputs; and by the way in which the resources are combined, organized, and managed. At its most basic level the productivity of an existing operation and technology can be improved either by improving the quality of resource (e.g., hiring more highly skilled workers, using better materials, and so forth) or by more effectively utilizing the existing set. The latter may involve things like changes in supervision, changes in the procedures used to control materials, or a host of other management and organizational factors. Productivity can also be enhanced by introducing advanced technology—new equipment, new products, or new processes and technologies.

These basic determinants—technology, resources, and management systems—can be used to compare and contrast production operations. Our analysis of the U.S.–Japanese productivity gap in auto production is organized around seven factors that have been grouped into three categories: process systems (process yield, quality systems), technology (process automation, product design), and workforce management (absenteeism, job structure, work pace). Any attempt of this sort runs the risk of arbitrary categorization. While useful in clarifying determinants, it should be recognized that many of these are closely related.

Table 5 provides definitions of the factors affecting the productivity differential, along with a brief statement of comparative practice in the United States and Japan. The selection of the factors, their definition, and the comparisons are based on discussions with a panel of industry experts. We also asked the panel to rank the factors in order of their importance; some members of the panel provided a percentage allocation. The rankings are presented in Table 6.

Perhaps the most striking finding in the panel's assessment is the relative unimportance of the factors connected with technology. Neither automation nor product design is accorded a large measure of explanatory power. Despite the publicity devoted to robotics and advanced assembly plants, such as Nissan's Zama facility, U.S. firms appear to have maintained comparable levels of advanced process technique and equipment.

The panel's assessment is buttressed by evidence that suggests that the Japanese producers may use less capital per vehicle than their U.S. counterparts. While it is true that capital–labor ratios are higher in Japan, the large labor productivity gap cannot be explained by simple capital–labor substitution.

The comparison thus makes clear that an explanation of the productivity gap must be found in the quality of resources and management systems. The panel was unanimous in giving top billing to a

TABLE 5

Factors Affecting Productivity: A Comparison of Technology, Management, and Organization of U.S.–Japanese Auto Production

Factor	Definition	Comparative Practice in Japan Relative to the United States
Process Systems		
1. Process yield	Good parts per hour from a line, press, work group, or process line over an extended period of time; key determinants are machine cycle times, system uptime and reliability; affected by material control methods, maintenance practices, and operating patterns.	Production/materials control minimizes inventory, reduces scrap, exposes problems; line stops highlight problems, help eliminate defects; operators perform routine maintenance; two shifts instead of three leaves time for better maintenance.
2. Quality systems	The series of controls and inspection plans to assure that products are built to specifications.	Japanese use fewer inspectors; some authority and responsibility vested in production worker and supervisor relationship with supplier and very high standards lead to less incoming inspection.
Technology		
3. Process automation	The introduction and adaptation of advanced, state-of-the-art manufacturing equipment.	Overall, state of technology is comparable; Japanese use more robots; their stamping facilities appear to be somewhat more automated than average U.S. ones.
4. Product design	Differences in the way the car is designed for a given market segment; aspects affecting productivity: tolerances, number of parts, fastening methods, etc.	Japanese have more experience in small-car production and have emphasized design for manufacturability (i.e., productivity and quality); newer U.S. models (Escort, GM's J-car) are first models with design/manufacturing specifications comparable to Japanese.
Workforce Management		
5. Absenteeism	All employee time away from workplace, including excused, unexcused, medical, personal, contractual, and other.	Levels of contractual time off are comparable; unexcused absences are much higher in U.S. firms.
6. Job structure	The tasks and responsibilities included in job definitions.	Japanese practice is to create jobs with more breadth (more tasks/skill per job) and depth (more involvement in planning and control of operation); labor classifications are broader; regular production workers perform more skilled tasks; management layers are reduced.
7. Work pace	Speed at which operators perform tasks.	Evidence is not conclusive; some lines run faster, some appear to run more slowly.

TABLE 6

FACTORS EXPLAINING THE U.S.–JAPANESE PRODUCTIVITY GAP: RANKINGS AND RELATIVE WEIGHTS FROM EXPERT PANEL

| | Panel Members | | | | | | | | Average | |
| | A | | B | C | | D | E | | | |
Factor[b]	Rank	Weight[a] (percentage)	Rank	Rank	Weight[a] (percentage)	Rank	Rank	Weight[a] (percentage)	Rank	Weight[a] (percentage)
1. Process yield	1	30	1	1	30	1	1	40	1.0	30–40
2. Absenteeism	3	20	3	1	30	2	2	25	2.2	20–30
3. Job structure	2	25	2	5	5	5	4	10	3.6	10–25
4. Process automation	6	6	4	3	15	4	3	15	4.0	6–15
5. Quality systems	7	5.5	5	4	10	6	4	10	5.2	5.5–10
6. Product design	4	7	7	4	10	3	7	0	5.0	0–10
7. Work pace	5	6.5	6	7	0	7	7	0	6.4	0–6.5

[a] Fraction of the differential explained by the factor.
[b] For definitions, see Table 5.

factor we have labeled "process yield" but that is really an amalgam of several management practices and systems related to production planning and control. The "yield" category captures Japanese superiority in operating their processes at a high level of good output over extended periods of time. Although engineering (i.e., machine cycles, plant layouts) is of some importance, the key to Japan's lead in this category appears to be the interaction of the material control system, maintenance practices, and employee involvement.

Figure 1 graphically portrays the determinants of annual output of good parts (from a representative production process) and indicates some of the management practices and systems that lead to superior performance in Japan. The key to the material control system is the concept of "just in time" production. Often called "Kanban" (after the production cards or tickets used to trigger production), the system is designed so that materials, parts, and components used at a given step in production are produced or delivered just before they are needed. Thus, stages in the process (including suppliers) are tightly coupled, with very little work in-process inventory. Suppliers must therefore make frequent deliveries of parts, and lot sizes must be small to accommodate product variety. It is the Jap-

FIGURE 1

JAPANESE MANAGEMENT SYSTEMS AND THE DETERMINANTS OF PROCESS YIELD

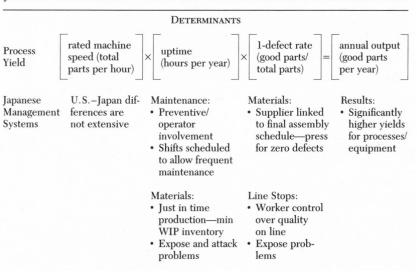

	DETERMINANTS				
Process Yield	rated machine speed (total parts per hour)	× uptime (hours per year)	× 1-defect rate (good parts/ total parts)	= annual output (good parts per year)	
Japanese Management Systems	U.S.–Japan differences are not extensive	Maintenance: • Preventive/ operator involvement • Shifts scheduled to allow frequent maintenance	Materials: • Supplier linked to final assembly schedule—press for zero defects	Results: • Significantly higher yields for processes/ equipment	
		Materials: • Just in time production—min WIP inventory • Expose and attack problems	Line Stops: • Worker control over quality on line • Expose problems		

anese view that reduction of decoupling inventory exposes "the real problems"—waste of time and materials, imbalance in operations, defective parts, equipment operating improperly, and so forth. (Table 7 provides comparative data on inventory levels. These data show that dramatically less inventory is used by Japanese firms in the production of automobiles. This is true whether one looks at the process as a whole or at specific plants.) With smaller buffer stocks the production system will simply not work if there are frequent or lengthy breakdowns. Thus, the just-in-time approach exposes opportunities for reducing waste and solving problems, while at the same time creating pressure for maximizing uptime and minimizing defects. Maintenance programs, preventive and scheduled, are therefore pursued vigorously. Plants operate with only two shifts,

TABLE 7

INVENTORY COMPARISONS—UNITED STATES AND JAPAN

Level/Process	*Japan*	*United States*
1. *Plant and Process Inventories*		
Assembly plant component inventories		
(equivalent units of production)		
heaters	1 hour	5 days
radiators	2 hours	5 days
brake drums	1.5 hours	3 days
bumpers	1 hour.	
Front-wheel-drive transfer case in process parts		
storage by operation (number of parts)		
mill	7	240
drill	11	200
ream and chamfer	13	196
drill	24	205
mill, washer, test	10	40
assemble	6	96
finish	7	87
Total	79	1064
2. *Company Inventories*		
Work in process inventories per vehicle		
1979	$80.2	$536.5
1980	$74.2	$584.3
Work in process turns[a]		
1979	40.0	12.1
1980	46.1	13.4

SOURCE: 1.—Industry sources (data provided by panel members); 2.—Annual reports for representative producers.
[a] Defined as cost of goods sold divided by work in process inventories.

and equipment is maintained during nonproduction time. The result is a much lower rate of machine failure and breakdown.

Pressure for defect elimination is reflected in relationships with suppliers and in-work practices on the line. "Just in time" production does not allow for extensive inspection of incoming parts. Suppliers must, therefore, achieve highly demanding quality levels, consistently and reliably. The major Japanese manufacturers work closely with outside vendors to make sure that responsibility for quality is felt and acted upon at the source of product. This same approach—quality control at the source—is used in production on the line, where workers have the authority to stop the operation if they spot defects or other production problems. Worker-initiated line stops are central to the concept of Jidoka: making problems visible to everyone's eye and stopping the line if trouble occurs; all thoughts, methods, and tools to avoid stops are Jidoka.

The basic thrust of the Kanban system and the concept of Jidoka are to eliminate waste, expose problems, and conserve resources. This is not simply a different technique of controlling production, but a very different way of managing the production process. It is clear that these systems interact with other factors in our list of productivity determinants. Separating their effects from the effects of quality systems and job structure, for example, is somewhat arbitrary. The Kanban-Jidoka system uses fewer inspectors, and its success requires broader and deeper jobs. Seen in this light, the panel's high ranking of "process yield" and the relatively lower importance attached to job structure and quality systems may reflect the difficulty of separating the three factors and a tendency to ascribe to "process yield" some of the impact of the other two.

Indeed, it appears that job structure plays an important role in explaining observed productivity differentials. We have already noted two features of the Japanese system (maintenance practices and Jidoka) in which jobs are designed to involve workers in a variety of tasks. The effects of structure, and the differences in management style and practices that go with it (fewer layers of management, more managing from the bottom up), extend to other aspects of production. Quality circles or "small group involvement activities" deal with such questions as layout, process methods, and automation. Such involvement appears to be an important factor in obtaining relatively high levels of commitment and motivation.

The nature of worker–management relations in Japan is further suggested by much lower levels of unexcused absence than that found in the United States. The panel accorded absenteeism second billing in its rankings, primarily due to the need to carry redundant workers in order to cover for unexpected absence. In general, absenteeism influences costs, not only through redundant labor but also through fringe costs of the absent group as well as indirect effects such as scrap, reduced learning, and so forth. It appears that absenteeism may actually account for as much as 10–12 percent of the cost gap.

Given the impact of absenteeism and the effects of job structure and the workforce influence in "process yield," it is clear that workforce management must be a significant factor in explaining the Japanese cost advantage. Likewise, an attempt to explain quality differences would certainly accord a major influence to the work force and its management. It seems evident, therefore, that in concert with different systems of production management and control, the work force plays a central role in the Japanese competitive advantage.

Much has been made recently of the enormous capital expenditure programs of the U.S. manufacturers. Indeed, the fact that we have identified the Japanese advantage as a "software" rather than a "hardware" problem in no way implies that new technology could not be effective in raising relative U.S. productivity. Yet it is unlikely that a substantially improved competitive position for U.S. production will be secured only through new bricks and mortar and new machines; comparable processes and machines are available around the world. At least as far as advances in productivity and quality are concerned, new "software" (new approaches to the management of people, materials, and processes) seems essential.

Industrial Robots in the United States and Japan

Organization for Economic Cooperation and Development

This is an excerpt from Industrial Robots: Their Role in Manufacturing Industry, *published by the Organization for Economic Cooperation and Development in 1983.*

UNITED STATES

Production of industrial robots in the United States has generally been based on independent, non-user, producing companies which have focused on marketing and development for customer requirements. The two largest producers of robots are Unimation and Cincinnati Milacron (CM). Unimation had a market share in the United States of about 44 percent in 1980–81, which declined to about 32 percent in 1982; in Europe, where it has also diversified, Unimation has about 25 percent of the market, while in Japan, Kawasaki Heavy Industries produce Unimation robots under licence. Unimation robots will also be produced in Finland for the Scandinavian and East European markets. Unimation's share of the world robot market is estimated at around 15 percent. CM's share of the U.S. market was approximately 32 percent for 1980–81, declining to 18 percent in 1982. The turnover of Unimation is derived 100 percent from

Note: All footnotes have been omitted from the original article.

sales of industrial robots, while about 5 percent of CM's turnover is attributed to robot sales.

The structure of production in the United States is rapidly changing. Many companies which are expecting to become large robot users are establishing themselves as producers for their own use as well as for general sale. These companies, notably General Motors, IBM, General Electric, Bendix and Westinghouse, should have a significant impact on the structure of production and the strategy of existing firms. A case in point is the recent acquisition by Westinghouse of a majority interest in Unimation and perhaps the eventual merger of the latter company as a wholly-owned subsidiary of Westinghouse. Many of the larger companies are entering into production by establishing divisions within their companies to develop expertise in robots and other forms of automation, and by entering into agreements with foreign (usually Japanese) producers. These agreements include technology exchanges, exclusive and non-exclusive marketing rights, often followed by licensing for manufacturing facilities in the United States. Many companies have also entered into agreements with several overseas producing companies providing them with a wide range of robots for sale and/or manufacture suitable for a variety of different industrial activities.

Examples of trends described in the previous paragraph include: (a) GM and Fanuc have established a joint venture under which Fanuc will share its robot design technology with GM and the two companies will jointly establish a plant in the United States; (b) General Electric will produce and market a robot developed by an Italian firm (DEA). GE has also agreed to exchange robot technology with Volkswagenwerke AG enabling GE to market and manufacture VW designed robots. GE has also a technology exchange, marketing and production agreement with Hitachi; (c) Westinghouse Electric Corporation has signed agreements with Mitsubishi Electric Corporation and Komatsu of Japan, and with Olivetti of Italy to market their robots in the United States; (d) IBM will market Sankyo Seiki robots in the United States until it produces its own robots domestically; (e) Yaskawa Electric Manufacturing and the Bendix COrporation have entered into an agreement for production and sales tie-ups. Bendix has also acquired a share of Comau of Italy. All of these agreements between United States, Japanese, and European producers and/or robot users are illustrative also of the fairly close cooperation in technology transfer among robot-producing companies.

The expected high growth in demand for industrial robots in the United States during the 1980s (from about \$200 million at present to \$2 billion in 1990) and the need to acquire technology and production experience for the future, have been obvious contributing factors to the fast evolution in the American producing industry. For many of the potentially larger using companies (GM, GE, Westinghouse, IBM) the need to have easy access to equipment which closely meets their requirements is an important factor. Another factor of interest is that many companies are supplying a fairly wide range of robots based on a strategy that a user prefers to buy from the same supplier to ensure compatibility and better servicing. While there has been a tendency in the United States for some major users and potential producing companies to purchase smaller companies specialised in automation or electronic engineering (General Electric is a particular example), this has not yet become a significant trend.

The structure of production in the United States is also being influenced by the considerable number of foreign industrial robot producers who are establishing footholds in the U.S. market either independently or through established American companies. Examples include the following: (*a*) The major Swedish producer, ASEA, is establishing a production facility in the United States; (*b*) KUKA of West Germany has acquired manufacturing capability in the States; (*c*) ACMA–Renault has set up a joint company with Ransburg of the United States for domestic production.

While it is difficult to predict the evolution of the producing industry in the United States, it seems clear that the present market leaders will lose their relative dominance in terms of market shares as the industry grows and becomes more diversified. The large number of new entrants into the industry from various sectors will tend to stimulate demand both because many of these companies are themselves large users but also as producers start pushing their products in the market. Given the diverse interests of many of the new entrants, the market base is likely to broaden to include a wider sectoral coverage, and a wider range of applications.

JAPAN

Japan's production of industrial robots has increased rapidly since the early 1970s so that it is now the foremost producer and user of robots, as well as the world's leading producer of computerized automation in general. From a production of 269 robots (narrowly-defined) in 1976 output has grown to 3,150 robots in 1980 averaging 85 percent growth per year in volume [Table 1]. Initially, Japanese production was concentrated on less sophisticated first generation robots. However, substantial developments in technology have taken place by producing companies so that the share of more sophisticated robots in total production has risen over the period 1976 to 1980 from 4 percent to 16 percent in volume terms. As a result Japanese companies are now in a position to provide technology to foreign countries.

The large internal Japanese market for industrial robots, in comparison to other industrialised countries, and the growth in this market during the late 1970s, played an important role in stimulating domestic production and thus in Japan's leading role as a robot producer. One consequence of this rapid growth is that a significant percentage of the world's stock of industrial robots is in use in Japan. Japan's robot industry is characterized by a wide dispersion of production and many firms. At present, about 100 firms are involved in the production of robots, about half of these medium and small-sized enterprises. Many of the enterprises involved in robot production are thus larger companies, mainly in the engineering industries, whose robot divisions are integrated into much larger manufacturing groups which are themselves frequent users of robots. Some of the new entrants are also companies which are not in the engineering or electrical sectors, but have entered the industry because they view it as a high growth sector and therefore as a potential profit centre in the future. Given the number of firms, and in spite of the fast growing market, domestic competition is fairly intense among producers in order to maintain and/or increase their market shares. At present, because of the small market relative to its potential size, the intense competition to gain market shares, and some "learning curve" pricing, robots add only a small proportion to total turnover of the larger integrated enterprises and do not yet, in many cases, represent a profit centre.

TABLE 1

Japan: Industrial Robot Production, By Type[1]

(a)

"Sophisticated" Robots	1976 Units	1976 Ymn	1977 Units	1977 Ymn	1978 Units	1978 Ymn	1979 Units	1979 Ymn	1980 Units	1980 Ymn
Playback Robot	183	1,999	357	3,761	506	4,373	662	6,653	2,027	15,785
N.C. Robot	6	52	11	85	25	273	89	1,745	992	21,795
Intelligent Robot	80	850	199	2,361	255	2,817	788	3,698	131	2,160
Total (2)	269	2,901	567	6,207	786	7,463	1,539	12,096	3,150	39,740
Annual Average Increase %	—	—	111%	114%	39%	20%	96%	62%	105%	228%
Total (based on a broad definition of robots)(3)	7,165	12,268	8,613	18,246	10,100	25,399	14,535	40,398	19,873	75,361
Share of sophisticated robots as % of total production broadly defined	4%	24%	7%	34%	8%	29%	11%	30%	16%	53%

(b)

Percent Distribution of Units

	1976	1977	1978	1979	1980
Playback Robots	68.0	63.0	64.4	43.0	64.3
N.C. Robots	2.2	1.9	3.2	5.8	31.5
Intelligent Robot	29.8	35.1	32.4	51.2	4.2
Total	100.0	100.0	100.0	100.0	100.0

SOURCE: JIRA

1. Japanese data may vary since they are often quoted on a fiscal year basis; the above data are for calendar years.

2. Variable sequence robots are not included in this total.

3. The broad definition includes manual manipulators and fixed sequence robots.

Present strategy by some of the large producing firms in Japan is to develop and utilise robots within their own plants in order to increase their own productivity. Examples of firms following such a strategy include Hitachi—one of Japan's largest general electric machinery producers—which is embarking on a R&D program for an "intelligent robot" to undertake sophisticated assembly tasks within its own plants.

Similarly, TODA Construction of Japan has launched a project in cooperation with a leading robot producer (Kawasaki Heavy Industries) to develop an "intelligent robot" for use in construction-engineering jobs. The project is aimed in particular for use of robots in nuclear power plants (building and dismantling) as well as in other construction jobs. Fanuc, a major numerical control tool manufacturer, is developing and using robots for use in its plants to produce parts of numerically controlled machine tools as well as robot parts.

Producers have primarily focused on supplying the fast growing internal market so that exports have represented only a small percentage of total robot production (approximately 2 percent). However, export considerations for the future have been taken into account in the many technical cooperation and commercial agreements which exist between Japanese companies and their Western European and United States counterparts. The number of such agreements taking place between Japanese and European and U.S. companies is in fact surprisingly high and perhaps indicative of the importance that companies are placing in the future impact of industrial robots and the need therefore for technological experience and expertise in the area. Although many of the agreements entered into between companies (U.S.–Japan, Europe–Japan) call for domestic manufacturing facilities, these will initially lead to a fairly rapid growth in exports since many agreements call for the marketing during the first few years of the licensors' products on an original equipment manufacturing basis.

In terms of size, Kawasaki is the largest builder of industrial robots in Japan. In 1981 it increased output by 30 percent over 1980 to 600 units. The next largest builder is Yaskawa Electric Manufacturing Company at around 600 units, followed by Hitachi, Mitsubishi, Kobe Steel and Fanuc. Foreign penetration of the Japanese market has been mainly by Unimation of the United States through its licensing agreement with Kawasaki. ASEA of Sweden has plans to directly set up production facilities in Japan.

Part Two

Decision Making, Costs,
and Production

SINCE managerial economics and operations research deal with decision making, we begin by considering the nature of the decision-making process as it presently exists in most industrial organizations. Herbert Simon discusses the various phases of the decision-making process, which he characterizes as: "finding occasions for making a decision; finding possible courses of action; and choosing among courses of action." In the next article, Eugene Grant points out that many managerial decisions are made improperly because the decision maker fails to reason clearly about the costs and benefits of alternative courses of action. The following paper describes Parkinson's law, which is based on the amusing proposition that "work expands so as to fill the time available for its completion." Although Parkinson is writing about the British bureaucracy, his observations also provide interesting insights into the decision-making process and the growth of bureaucracies in large industrial organizations.

Neil E. Harlan, Charles J. Christenson, and Richard F. Vancil, like Eugene Grant, are concerned with the proper measurement of the costs of alternative courses of action. Using a hypothetical case, they describe the different cost concepts used by accountants and economists, and conclude that the economist's notion of opportunity cost is more appropriate for decision-making than the accountant's notion of acquisition cost.

In the next paper, Leslie Cookenboo shows how the economist's concepts of production functions and cost functions can be estimated in the case of crude oil pipe lines. These concepts are central to managerial economics, and it is important that the student get some feel for how they can be applied in real-life cases. In the next paper, taken from a publication of the National Academy of Engineering, the production process for autos is described. Finally, the editor and Harold H. Wein describe in the last essay how the relationship between output and cost can be used to control cost and performance. This is a case study of the application of cost functions to the operating problems of the railroad industry.

The Decision-making Process

HERBERT A. SIMON

Herbert A. Simon, the 1979 Nobel Laureate in Economics, is Professor of Psychology and Industrial Administration at Carnegie-Mellon University. The following paper comes from his book, The New Science of Managerial Decision Making.

Decision making comprises three principal phases: finding occasions for making a decision; finding possible courses of action; and choosing among courses of action. These three activities account for quite different fractions of the time budgets of executives. The fractions vary greatly from one organization level to another and from one executive to another, but we can make some generalizations about them even from casual observation. Executives spend a large fraction of their time surveying the economic, technical, political, and social environment to identify new conditions that call for new actions. They probably spend an even larger fraction of their time, individually or with their associates, seeking to invent, design, and develop possible courses of action for handling situations where a decision is needed. They spend a small fraction of their time in choosing among alternative actions already developed to meet an identified problem and already analysed for their consequences. The three fractions, added together, account for most of what executives do.[1]

1. The way in which these activities take shape within an organization is described in some detail in James G. March and Herbert A. Simon, *Organizations* (New York: John Wiley & Sons, Inc., 1958), chapters 6 and 7.

The first phase of the decision-making process—searching the environment for conditions calling for decision—I shall call *intelligence* activity (borrowing the military meaning of intelligence). The second phase—inventing, developing, and analysing possible courses of action—I shall call *design* activity. The third phase—selecting a particular course of action from those available—I shall call *choice* activity.

Let me illustrate these three phases of decision. In the past five years, many companies have reorganized their accounting and other data processing activities in order to make use of large electronic computers. How has this come about? Computers first became available commercially in the early 1950s. Although, in some vague and general sense, company managements were aware that computers existed, few managements had investigated their possible applications with any thoroughness before about 1955. For most companies, the use of computers required no decision before that time because it hadn't been placed on the agenda.[2]

The intelligence activity preceding the introduction of computers tended to come about in one of two ways. Some companies—for example, in the aircraft and atomic energy industries—were burdened with enormously complex computations for engineering design. Because efficiency in computation was a constant problem, and because the design departments were staffed with engineers who could understand, at least in general, the technology of computers, awareness of computers and their potentialities came early to these companies. After computers were already in extensive use for design calculations, businesses with a large number-processing load—insurance companies, accounting departments in large firms, banks—discovered these new devices and began to consider seriously their introduction.

Once it was recognized that computers might have a place in modern business, a major design task had to be carried out in each company before they could be introduced. It is now a commonplace that payrolls can be prepared by computers. Programs in both the general and computer senses for doing this are relatively

2. Richard M. Cyert, Herbert A. Simon, and Donald B. Trow, "Observation of a Business Decision," *Journal of Business*, Vol. 29 (1956), pp. 237-248.

easy to design in any given situation.[3] To develop the first computer programs for preparing payroll, however, was a major research and development project. Few companies having carried their investigations of computers to the point where they had definite plans for their use, failed to install them. Commitment to the new course of action took place gradually as the intelligence and design phases of the decision were going on. The final choice was, in many instances, almost *pro forma*.

Generally speaking, intelligence activity precedes design, and design activity precedes choice. The cycle of phases is, however, far more complex than this sequence suggests. Each phase in making a particular decision is itself a complex decision-making process. The design phase, for example, may call for new intelligence activities; problems at any given level generate subproblems that, in turn, have their intelligence, design, and choice phases, and so on. There are wheels within wheels within wheels. Nevertheless, the three large phases are often clearly discernible as the organizational decision process unfolds. They are closely related to the stages in problem solving first described by John Dewey:

What is the problem?
What are the alternatives?
Which alternative is best?[4]

3. For a good discussion on the use of the computer for such purposes, see Robert H. Gregory and Richard L. Van Horn, *Automatic Data-Processing Systems* (San Francisco: Wadsworth Publishing Company, Inc., 1960).

4. John Dewey, *How We Think* (New York: D. C. Heath & Company, 1910), chapter 8.

The Comparison of
Alternatives

EUGENE L. GRANT AND
W. GRANT IRESON

*Eugene Grant is Professor of Economics of
Engineering at Stanford University. In 1960
he, together with W. Grant Ireson, wrote*Principles of Engineering Economy, *from which
this article is taken.*

The conduct of a business enterprise requires a successive series
of business decisions—decisions between possible alternatives
with reference to the future. These decisions are of all degrees of
importance, varying from trivial matters to matters of major policy. Some of them are made by intuitive judgments or "hunches"
without any conscious attempt to express the alternatives to be
compared in commensurable terms, or perhaps even to see clearly
what these alternatives really are. Others, however, involve
choices between definite alternatives which have been made
commensurable by reducing them to terms of money and time.
There is much evidence that many of these latter decisions, based
on conscious economy studies involving estimates of expected
costs (and possibly of revenues) are incorrectly made because of
the failure of the estimator to reason clearly about the *differences*
between alternatives which involve common elements.

WHAT IS THE "COST" OF AN AUTOMOBILE TRIP?

To illustrate the type of error that may occur if alternatives are not clearly defined, let us consider a familiar and relatively simple situation. Suppose it is desired to estimate the cost of a 600-mile automobile trip.

Bill Jones, who has agreed to "share the cost" of such a proposed trip to be taken in the car of his friend Tom Smith, may calculate merely the expected out-of-pocket expense for gasoline. If Smith's car makes 15 miles to the gallon, and gasoline costs 25 cents per gallon, this is 1⅔ cents per mile. He therefore concludes that the trip will cost $10.

Tom Smith, on the other hand, may estimate all of the costs associated with the ownership and operation of his automobile over its expected life in his service, in order to find an average cost per mile. His car has a first cost of $2,000; he expects to drive it 10,000 miles per year for four years; at the end of this time he hopes to realize $1,000 from its sale. His estimates of total cost might be as follows:

1. Gasoline (40,000 miles at 1⅔¢ per mile)	$ 667
2. Oil and grease	163
3. Tires	150
4. Repairs and maintenance	600
5. Insurance	400
6. Storage (48 months at $5 per month)	240
7. License fees and property taxes	120
8. Total depreciation in 4 years ($2,000-$1,000)	1,000
9. Interest on investment in car	260
(This is based on average interest at 4% per annum.)	
	$3,600

Divided among 40,000 miles of travel, this is an average cost of 9 cents per mile. At this rate a 600-mile trip appears to cost $54.

The Concept of Cost Must Be Related to Specific Alternatives if It Is to Be a Reliable Guide to Decisions · The second of these two figures for the cost of a given service is 540 percent of the first one. At first glance it would appear that one or the other of the two figures must be wide of its mark. However, a more critical consideration will disclose that the simple question "What is its cost?" with reference to a particular service does not define any mark for the estimator to shoot at.

To use a cost figure as a basis for a decision, it is necessary to have clearly in mind the alternatives between which it is desired to decide. Otherwise, certain costs which, after a clear definition of alternatives, would be recognized as common to both, may be given weight in influencing the choice. It is dangerous to base conclusions on average costs without regard to the specific alternatives which it is intended to compare. The fact that widely differing cost figures may be required for different decisions about a given service may be illustrated by examining some of the different pairs of alternatives which might arise relative to the service of a given automobile.

A Situation in Which It Is Necessary to Estimate Total Cost of Ownership and Operation · If Tom Smith did not own an automobile, and wanted to decide whether or not to purchase one, he might set up the following alternatives for comparison:

Alternative A. Buy a $2,000 car and operate it approximately 10,-000 miles per year for the next four years.

Alternative B. Do not buy a car. Use some others means of transportation as railway, street car, bus, taxicab, his friends' automobiles, and his own legs for part of the contemplated mileage and do without the rest.

If these are the alternatives, all of the items included in his estimate of $3,600 for four years' service are disbursements[1] which will take place if Alternative A is selected, and which will not take place if Alternative B is selected. Thus, the unit cost of 9 cents per mile is relevant to Smith's decision whether or not to own a car. The total cost (which in this case is more important than the average cost per unit of service) of $3,600 should be compared with the costs associated with Alternative B. The higher cost of A, if any, should then be judged in the light of differences which are not reducible to money terms, and in the light of Smith's prospective ability to pay this higher cost.

A Situation in Which It Is Necessary to Estimate the Increment Cost of an Added Service · On the other hand, if Smith has

1. That is, they are all disbursements with the possible exception of interest which might in some cases be a disbursement and in others an income given up—an opportunity foregone.

already purchased an automobile and intends to continue to own and operate it, but is undecided about the annual mileage he will drive, the kinds of alternatives to be compared are quite different. In order to determine the effect on cost of driving extra miles, he might set up two alternatives differing only in annual mileage:

Alternative A. Continue to own the car, driving it 12,500 miles per year for four years before disposing of it.

Alternative B. Continue to own the car, driving it 10,000 miles per year for four years before disposing of it.

In comparing these alternatives, it is necessary to consider the various elements of total cost of ownership which have already been listed, item by item, and estimate the effect on each of a total increase of 10,000 miles in the mileage driven over the life of the car.

Item 1, gasoline, and item 2, oil and grease, may be expected to increase at least in proportion to the increase in mileage. It is likely that the increase would be somewhat more than in direct proportion, because of the tendency of the rate of consumption of fuel and lubricants to increase after a car has been driven a good many miles. Perhaps if the car had averaged 15 miles per gallon in its first 40,000 miles, it might average only 14.3 miles per gallon in the following 10,000 miles. In general, item 3, tires, may be expected to increase in proportion to driving mileage; the actual effect of any proposed increase in mileage will depend on whether it requires the purchase of tires and tubes during the extended period of service. Item 4, repairs and maintenance, will doubtless tend to increase somewhat more than in direct proportion to mileage.

On the other hand item 5, insurance, item 6, storage, and item 7, license fees and property taxes, will be unchanged by an increase in mileage driven in any given time. Because the second-hand price of automobiles seems to depend almost entirely on age and not on miles driven, it is probable that the estimated realizable value after four years will be affected very little, if at all, by an increase of 25 percent in total mileage. If this is the case, neither item 8, total depreciation, nor item 9, interest, will be changed by the contemplated increase in mileage.

Smith might make his estimate of the extra costs associated

with increasing his total expected mileage from 40,000 to 50,000 somewhat as follows:

1.	Gasoline (10,000 miles at 1¾¢ per mile)	$175
2.	Oil and grease	50
3.	Tires	50
4.	Repairs and maintenance	225
		$500

If this estimate is correct, so that an increase of 10,000 miles would increase total costs by $500, then the average cost for each increased mile of travel is 5 cents. This unit increment cost might then be applied to the mileage of any proposed trip, in order to get an idea of how the proposed trip will affect automobile costs in the long run. If this is done for a proposed 600-mile trip, the conclusion will be that this trip ultimately will be responsible for $30 of extra expense.[2]

It will be noted that although this estimated unit increment cost of 5 cents per mile is much less than the estimated 9 cents per mile for ownership and operation over the life of the automobile, it is three times the 1¾ cents per mile estimate that Bill Jones made for the out-of-pocket expense of a short trip. The difference between the 5-cent and the 9-cent figures lies in those costs that are "fixed" by the decision to buy and to continue to own and operate the car, and which are, therefore, independent of its miles of operation. On the other hand, the difference between the 1¾-cent and the 5-cent figures is the difference between short-run and long-run viewpoints. It may well be true that the only out-of-pocket expenses of a 600-mile trip will be for gasoline; nevertheless, the long-run effect of increasing the number of miles' of

2. Incidentally, it may be noted that the question of what, in equity, Bill Jones ought to pay when he rides in Tom Smith's car "sharing the cost" of a trip is a question of social conduct which cannot be answered by an economy study. All an economy study can do is to disclose the expected differences between alternatives. Thus, if Tom is making the trip in any event, an economy study might indicate that the least he could afford to accept from Bill without loss would be nothing at all; this is the difference between the alternatives: (*a*) make the trip, taking Bill along, and (*b*) make the trip, leaving Bill behind. On the other hand, if he is making the trip entirely for Bill's convenience, his estimates would appear to indicate that the least he could afford to take for a 600-mile trip is $30; here the alternatives are: (*a*) make the trip with Bill and (*b*) do not make the trip at all.

operation of an automobile will be to increase the expenditures for lubricants, tires, and repairs.

A Situation in Which It is Necessary to Estimate the Costs of Continuing a Machine in Service · If Smith purchases an automobile, and then has misgivings as to whether or not he can afford to continue to own and operate it, the alternatives which present themselves to him are still different, and different cost figures from any we have yet discussed will be required as a basis for his decision. Suppose he sets up the following alternatives for comparison:

Alternative A. Continue to own the car, driving it 10,000 miles per year for four years.

Alternative B. Immediately dispose of the car for the best price obtainable, thereafter using other means of transportation.

In considering the difference between these two alternatives, it is necessary to recognize that the $2,000 purchase price of the car has already been spent, no matter which alternative is chosen. The important question here is not the past outlay for the car, but rather the "best price obtainable" for it if Alternative B is selected.

If Smith's decision had been made, say, in 1947, when it was possible to sell certain makes of new cars in a so-called used car market at several hundred dollars more than the purchase price, this best price obtainable might have been $2,500. If so, Smith's question would obviously have been whether or not he could afford to continue to own an automobile that he could sell for $2,500. On the other hand, if his decision is to be made under the more normal conditions where the resale price of a new automobile is substantially below its purchase price, even though the car may have been driven only a few miles, the best price obtainable might possibly be $1,700. Under these circumstances, Smith's question is whether or not he can afford to continue to own an automobile that he could sell for $1,700. The $300 difference between the $2,000 purchase price and the $1,700 resale price is gone whether he keeps the car or disposes of it at once.

The principles underlying financial calculations to determine whether or not to continue to own a given asset enter into a wide variety of engineering economy studies. . . . At this point it is sufficient to note that there is a substantial difference in principle between a decision whether or not to acquire an asset and a decision whether or not to continue to own and operate that asset once it is acquired. To guide the latter type of decision intelligently, attention must be focused on the net realizable value of the machine (that is, on the prospective net receipts from its sale if it should be disposed of). Once an asset has been purchased, its purchase price has been paid regardless of whether it is continued in service or disposed of at once. This past investment may be thought of as a "sunk cost" that, generally speaking, has no relevance in decisions for the future.

COMPARING ALTERNATIVES IN BUSINESS SITUATIONS

These examples from the familiar situation of automobile ownership have illustrated the necessity for recognizing definite alternatives to be compared before using cost as a basis for decisions. No doubt the different kinds of relevant "costs" which should be considered in automobile ownership and operation are recognized in their qualitative aspects by many automobile owners. However, even in these relatively simple situations which have been discussed, it will be noted that in order to express differences quantitatively we were obliged to make assumptions which, in order to be definite, were somewhat arbitrary. For instance, in order to estimate increment costs per mile of operation, we found it necessary to assume two definite total mileages, and to assume that the four-year period of ownership would be unchanged by a change in the total miles of operation.

In industry, the circumstances in which comparisons are made are likely to be more involved. The machines and structures which are the subjects of engineering economy studies are generally parts of a complex plant, and this complexity may create difficulties in differentiating the effects of alternatives. As has been stated, industrialists are often misled as to the costs which are relevant to particular decisions by failure to define alternatives clearly. In industrial situations, even more than in the automobile cost illustration, it is necessary to make definite assumptions in order to have a basis for decisions.

Irreducible Data in Comparing Alternatives · In the case of the alternatives involving Tom Smith's decision whether or not to purchase a car, we noted briefly that there would be certain advantages and certain hazards incident to the ownership of an automobile which could not be reduced to money terms, but which, nevertheless, would have considerable influence on Smith's choice.

This is characteristic of many economy studies. Although the reduction of units which would otherwise be incommensurable (for example, tons of coal, pounds of structural steel, barrels of cement, gallons of oil, kilowatt-hours of electric energy, hours of skilled machinists' labor, hours of common labor) to terms of money and time is essential to all business decisions which are not made entirely on "hunch," some differences between alternatives will generally remain which cannot be reduced to money terms. In an economy study, it is as much a part of the estimator's duty to note these irreducibles as it is to predict the money receipts and disbursements at various dates. The final decision must give weight to the irreducible differences, as well as to the money differences.

Differences Between Alternatives Are in the Future · If it is recognized that only those matters which are different as between two alternatives are relevant to their comparison, it should be obvious that everything that has happened in the past is irrelevant, except as it may help in the prediction of the future. Whatever has already happened is past and gone, regardless of which of two future alternatives is selected. This implies, among other things, that apportionments against future times of expenditures already past should not be included in economy studies. It also implies that economy studies are based on forecasts, and that their conclusions are dependent on predictions of future events, predictions which are either conscious forecasts or implied ones.

The Limitations of Accounting as a Basis for Estimates in Economy Studies · Generally speaking, the accounts of an enterprise constitute the source of information which has the greatest potential value in making estimates for economy studies. Nevertheless, the uncritical use of accounting figures is responsible for many errors in such estimates. There are a number of important differences between the point of view of accounting and that which should be taken in an economy study.

Accounting involves a recording of past receipts and expenditures. It deals only with what happened regarding policies actually followed and is not concerned with alternatives that might have been followed; it is concerned more with average costs than with differences in cost. It involves apportionment of past costs against future periods of time, and apportionment of joint costs between various services or products. It does not involve consideration of the time value of money.

Engineering economy, on the other hand, always involves alternatives; it deals with prospective differences between future alternatives. It is concerned with differences between costs rather than apportionments of costs. It does involve consideration of the time value of money.

Parkinson's Law

C. NORTHCOTE PARKINSON

C. Northcote Parkinson is Raffles Professor of History at the University of Singapore. This article first appeared in the Economist *in November 1955.*

It is a commonplace observation that work expands so as to fill the time available for its completion. Thus, an elderly lady of leisure can spend an entire day in writing and dispatching a postcard to her niece at Bognor Regis. An hour will be spent in finding the postcard, another in hunting for spectacles, half-an-hour in a search for the address, an hour and a quarter in composition, and twenty minutes in deciding whether or not to take an umbrella when going to the pillar-box in the next street. The total effort which would occupy a busy man for three minutes all told may in this fashion leave another person prostrate after a day of doubt, anxiety and toil.

Granted that work (and especially paper work) is thus elastic in its demands on time, it is manifest that there need be little or no relationship between the work to be done and the size of the staff to which it may be assigned. Before the discovery of a new scientific law—herewith presented to the public for the first time, and to be called Parkinson's Law[1]—there has, however, been insufficient recognition of the implication of this fact in the field of public administration. Politicians and taxpayers have assumed

1. Why? Why not?—Editor.

(with occasional phases of doubt) that a rising total in the number of civil servants must reflect a growing volume of work to be done. Cynics, in questioning this belief, have imagined that the multiplication of officials must have left some of them idle or all of them able to work for shorter hours. But this is a matter in which faith and doubt seem equally misplaced. The fact is that the number of the officials and the quantity of the work to be done are not related to each other at all. The rise in the total of those employed is governed by Parkinson's Law, and would be much the same whether the volume of the work were to increase, diminish or even disappear. The importance of Parkinson's Law lies in the fact that it is a law of growth based upon an analysis of the factors by which the growth is controlled.

The validity of this recently discovered law must rely mainly on statistical proofs, which will follow. Of more interest to the general reader is the explanation of the factors that underlie the general tendency to which this law gives definition. Omitting technicalities (which are numerous) we may distinguish, at the outset, two motive forces. They can be represented for the present purpose by two almost axiomatic statements, thus:

Factor I. An official wants to multiply subordinates, not rivals; and

Factor II. Officials make work for each other. We must now examine these motive forces in turn.

THE LAW OF MULTIPLICATION OF SUBORDINATES

To comprehend Factor I, we must picture a civil servant called *A* who finds himself overworked. Whether this overwork is real or imaginary is immaterial; but we should observe, in passing, that *A*'s sensation (or illusion) might easily result from his own decreasing energy—a normal symptom of middle-age. For this real or imagined overwork there are, broadly speaking, three possible remedies:

(1) He may resign.

(2) He may ask to halve the work with a colleague called *B*.

(3) He may demand the assistance of two subordinates to be called *C* and *D*.

There is probably no instance in civil service history of *A* choosing any but the third alternative. By resignation he would lose his pension rights. By having *B* appointed, on his own level in the hierarchy, he would merely bring in a rival for promotion to *W*'s vacancy when *W* (at long last) retires. So *A* would rather have *C* and *D*, junior men, below him. They will add to his consequence; and, by dividing the work into two categories, as between *C* and *D*, he will have the merit of being the only man who comprehends them both.

It is essential to realize, at this point, that *C* and *D* are, as it were, inseparable. To appoint *C* alone would have been impossible. Why? Because *C*, if by himself, would divide the work with *A* and so assume almost the equal status which has been refused in the first instance to *B*; a status the more emphasized if *C* is *A*'s only possible successor. Subordinates must thus number two or more, each being kept in order by fear of the other's promotion. When *C* complains in turn of being overworked (as he certainly will) *A* will, with the concurrence of *C*, advise the appointment of two assistants to help *C*. But he can then avert internal friction only by advising the appointment of two more assistants to help *D*, whose position is much the same. With this recruitment of *E*, *F*, *G* and *H*, the promotion of *A* is now practically certain.

THE LAW OF MULTIPLICATION OF WORK

Seven officials are now doing what one did before. This is where Factor II comes into operation. For these seven make so much work for each other that all are fully occupied and *A* is actually working harder than ever. An incoming document may well come before each of them in turn. Official *E* decides that it falls within the province of *F*, who places a draft reply before *C*, who amends it drastically before consulting *D*, who asks *G* to deal with it. But *G* goes on leave at this point, handing the file over to *H*, who drafts a minute, which is signed by *D* and returned to *C*, who revises his draft accordingly and lays the new version before *A*.

What does *A* do? He would have every excuse for signing the thing unread, for he has many other matters on his mind. Knowing now that he is to succeed *W* next year, he has to decide whether *C* or *D* should succeed to his own office. He had to agree to *G* going on leave, although not yet strictly entitled to it. He is worried whether *H* should not have gone instead, for reasons of health. He has looked pale recently—partly but not solely because of his domestic troubles. Then there is the business of *F*'s special increment of salary for the period of the conference, and *E*'s application for transfer to the Ministry of Pensions. *A* has heard that *D* is in love with a married typist and that *G* and *F* are no longer on speaking terms—no one seems to know why. So *A* might be tempted to sign *C*'s draft and have done with it.

But *A* is a conscientious man. Beset as he is with problems created by his colleagues for themselves and for him—created by the mere fact of these officials' existence—he is not the man to shirk his duty. He reads through the draft with care, deletes the fussy paragraphs added by *C* and *H* and restores the thing back to the form preferred in the first instance by the able (if quarrelsome) *F*. He corrects the English—none of these young men can write grammatically—and finally produces the same reply he would have written if officials *C* to *H* had never been born. Far more people have taken far longer to produce the same result. No one has been idle. All have done their best. And it is late in the evening before *A* finally quits his office and begins the return journey to Ealing. The last of the office lights are being turned off in the gathering dusk which marks the end of another day's administrative toil. Among the last to leave, *A* reflects, with bowed shoulders and a wry smile, that late hours, like grey hairs, are among the penalties of success.

THE SCIENTIFIC PROOFS

From this description of the factors at work the student of political science will recognize that administrators are more or less bound to multiply. Nothing has yet been said, however, about the period of time likely to elapse between the date of *A*'s appointment and the date from which we can calculate the pensionable service of *H*. Vast masses of statistical evidence have been collected and it is from a study of this data that Parkinson's Law has been deduced. Space will not allow of detailed analysis, but research began in the British Navy Estimates.

These were chosen because the Admiralty's responsibilities are more easily measurable than those of (say) the Board of Trade.

The accompanying table is derived from Admiralty statistics for 1914 and 1928. The criticism voiced at the time centered on the comparison between the sharp fall in numbers of those available for fighting and the sharp rise in those available only for administration, the creation, it was said, of "a magnificent Navy on land." But that comparison is not to the present purpose. What we have to note is that the 2,000 Admiralty officials of 1914 had become the 3,569 of 1928; and that this growth was unrelated to any possible increase in their work. The Navy during that period had diminished, in point of fact, by a third in men and two-thirds in ships. Nor, from 1922 onwards, was its strength even expected to increase, for its total of ships (unlike its total of officials) was limited by the Washington Naval Agreement of that year. Yet in these circumstances we had a 78.45 percent increase in Admiralty officials over a period of fourteen years; an average increase of 5.6 percent a year on the earlier total. In fact, as we shall see, the rate of increase was not as regular as that. All we have to consider, at this stage, is the percentage rise over a given period.

ADMIRALTY STATISTICS

	1914	*1928*	*Percentage increase or decrease*
Capital ships in commission	62	20	−67.74
Officers and men in Royal Navy	146,000	100,000	−31.50
Dockyard workers	57,000	62,439	+ 9.54
Dockyard officials and clerks	3,249	4,558	+40.28
Admiralty officials	2,000	3,569	+78.45

Can this rise in the total number of civil servants be accounted for except on the assumption that such a total must always rise by a law governing its growth? It might be urged, at this point, that the period under discussion was one of rapid development in naval technique. The use of the flying machine was no longer confined to the eccentric. Submarines were tolerated if not approved. Engineer officers were beginning to be regarded as almost human. In so revolutionary an age we might expect the storekeepers would have more elaborate inventories to compile. We might not wonder to see more draughtsmen on the payroll, more designers, more technicians and scientists. But these, the dockyard officials, increased only by 40 percent in number, while the men of Whitehall increased by nearly 80 percent. For every new foreman or electrical engineer at Portsmouth there had to be two or more clerks at Charing Cross. From this we might be tempted to conclude, provisionally, that the rate of increase in administrative staff is likely to be double that of the technical staff at a time when the actually useful strength (in this case, of seamen) is being reduced by 31.5 percent. It has been proved, however, statistically, that this last percentage is irrelevant. *The Officials would have multiplied at the same rate had there been no actual seamen at all.*

It would be interesting to follow the further progress by which the 8,118 Admiralty staff of 1935 came to number 33,788 by 1954. But the staff of the Colonial Office affords a better field of study during a period of Imperial decline. The relevant statistics are set down below. Before showing what the rate of increase is, we must observe that the extent of this department's responsibilities was far from constant during these twenty years. The colonial territories were not much altered in area or population between 1935 and 1939. They were considerably diminished by 1943, certain areas being in enemy hands. They were increased again in 1947, but have since then shrunk steadily from year to year as successive colonies achieve self-government.

COLONIAL OFFICE OFFICIALS

1935	1939	1943	1947	1954
372	450	817	1,139	1,661

It would be rational, prior to the discovery of Parkinson's Law, to suppose that these changes in the scope of Empire would be reflected in the size of its central administration. But a glance at the figures shows that the staff totals represent automatic stages in an inevitable increase. And this increase, while related to that observed in other departments, has nothing to do with the size— or even the existence—of the Empire. What are the percentages of increase? We must ignore, for this purpose, the rapid increase in staff which accompanied the diminution of responsibility during World War II. We should note rather the peacetime rates of increase over 5.24 percent between 1935 and 1939, and 6.55 percent between 1947 and 1954. This gives an average increase of 5.89 percent each year, a percentage markedly similar to that already found in the Admiralty staff increase between 1914 and 1928.

Further and detailed statistical analysis of departmental staffs would be inappropriate in such an article as this. It is hoped, however, to reach a tentative conclusion regarding the time likely to elapse between a given official's first appointment and the later appointment of his two or more assistants. Dealing with the problem of pure staff accumulation, all the researches so far completed point to an average increase of about 5¾ percent per year. This fact established, it now becomes possible to state Parkinson's Law in mathematical form, thus:

In any public administrative department not actually at war the staff increase may be expected to follow this formula:

$$x = \frac{2k^m + p}{n}$$

where k is the number of staff seeking promotion through the appointment of subordinates; p represents the difference between the ages of appointment and retirement; m is the number of man-hours devoted to answering minutes within the department; and n is the number of effective units being administered. Then x will be the number of new staff required each year.

Mathematicians will, of course, realize that to find the percentage increase they must multiply x by 100 and divide by the total of the previous year, thus:

$$\frac{100 \, (2k^m + p)}{yn} \%$$

where y represents the total original staff. And this figure will invariably prove to be between 5.17 percent and 6.56 percent, irrespective of any variation in the amount of work (if any) to be done.

The discovery of this formula and of the general principles upon which it is based has, of course, no emotive value. No attempt has been made to inquire whether departments ought to grow in size. Those who hold that this growth is essential to gain full employment are fully entitled to their opinion. Those who doubt the stability of an economy based upon reading each other's minutes are equally entitled to theirs. Parkinson's Law is a purely scientific discovery, inapplicable except in theory to the politics of the day. It is not the business of the botanist to eradicate the weeds. Enough for him if he can tell us just how fast they grow.

Cost Analysis

Neil E. Harlan,
Charles J. Christenson,
and Richard F. Vancil

Neil E. Harlan, Charles J. Christenson, and Richard F. Vancil are professors at the Harvard Business School. This is an excerpt from their book, Managerial Economics.

Why is cost analysis so important in making business decisions? The answer lies in the objectives of the business enterprise and in the way its accomplishments are measured in our economy.

In a narrow, simplified sense it might be said that business administration consists of the twin tasks of (1) allocating resources among alternative uses and (2) supervising the activities of people to insure that the resources are efficiently utilized toward achieving the assigned goals. While there is nothing wrong with this definition as a theoretical concept, it glosses over the uncertainties of the complex world of business. Business administration is an art. While there have been rapid advances in scientific, professional management during the last half-century, successful business administration still requires an intangible ability best described as *skill*.

The success of a commercial enterprise in allocating its resources effectively is usually measured by the profit it earns, and a primary goal of most firms is, therefore, to earn a profit, either the maximum possible profit or a satisfactory profit consistent with other goals of the firm. But what is profit? Both the accountant and the economist use this word to mean the difference between the revenues earned from the sale of goods and services and the costs incurred in earning these revenues. Yet, despite this agreement on the basic concept of profit, the accountant and the economist would generally disagree if each were asked to measure the profit of a particular business enterprise.

The disagreement would arise primarily because of a difference between the accounting concept and the economic concept of cost, Even here, however, there is an element of agreement: both the accountant and the economist consider cost as a measurement in monetary terms of the resources consumed by the firm in producing its revenue. The accountant usually measures the *acquisition cost* of these resources, in the sense of the money amount which the firm had to pay when it initially acquired the resources. The economist, in contrast, thinks in terms of the *opportunity cost* of the resources. The opportunity cost of devoting a resource to a particular use is the return that the resource could earn in its best alternative use. The economist's concept of cost, therefore, involves an explicit recognition of the problem of choice faced by the businessman in the utilization of resources.

Opportunity cost may be either greater or less than acquisition cost. Suppose, for example, that a firm is considering the production of an item which would require the use of material on hand for which $100 was originally paid; the acquisition cost, then, is $100. If the material could currently be sold on the market for $125, however, its opportunity cost must be $125, since the use of the material requires the firm to forego the opportunity of receiving $125. If, on the other hand, the material currently has no market value nor any alternative use, its opportunity cost is zero.

The businessman lives with both these concepts of cost. For decision-making purposes, the economist's concept of opportunity cost is the relevant one, since a rational decision must involve the comparison of alternative courses of action. The accountant's role as a "scorekeeper" for outside investors is also important to the businessman. Moreover, accounting records are often a primary source of information for decision-making purposes.

Types of Resources · The basic resource of business is money, or perhaps more precisely, the power that money has in our society to command the primary resources, the labor provided by men and the materials provided by nature. Money by itself is powerless, however, without a manager or entrepreneur to decide how to put it to work. Even then, capital does not become productive until it is exchanged for more tangible resources than imagination: labor, raw materials, and combinations of labor and materials in the form of products manufactured by other business. In the "raw" state, as money, the wise utilization of resources is difficult; it becomes even more difficult once the money resource has been exchanged for a wide variety of heterogeneous resources, each with a specialized productive capability.

An operating business possesses a variety of resources in addition to money: a building which is adaptable to a greater or lesser variety of uses, equipment which can be used to produce a range of products with varying degrees of efficiency, and employees whose productive skills may embrace a broad spectrum. At first glance, the problem of allocating physical resources might not seem vastly different from that of allocating money. All of these resources have been purchased with money, and their values can be measured in monetary terms. Why, then, did Henry J. Kaiser, a man with adequate capital resources and a reputation as an efficient shipbuilder during World War II, fail in his attempt to establish a new line of passenger cars in the late 1940's? It is not an easy task to convert raw capital into an efficient combination of productive resources. And the converse is also true: It is very difficult to measure the value of an existing set of productive resources in monetary terms.

In the "long run," money is the basic business resource. But business decisions are made in the short run, and money, the best available common denominator for all resources, is an imperfect yardstick. At the core of the broad problem of resource allocation, therefore, is the problem of measurement. Actually, the measurement problem can usefully be broken into two parts for purposes of analysis: (1) what types of resources will be required in order to carry out each course of action being considered? and (2) what is the value (or cost) of the combination of resources required for each alternative?

Classification of Problems · As a practical matter, businessmen rarely refer to their problems as problems in resource allocation. Rather, they say, "I've got a make-or-buy problem," or a "capital expenditure problem," or a "lease-or-buy problem," or a "pricing problem," and so forth. This "specific problem" orientation is not necessarily due to a failure to recognize the resource allocation characteristic of the problem, it is simply an attempt to find a practical way to begin the analysis that will eventually lead to a decision.

Dividing business decisions into problem categories has two advantages:

1. From his prior experience with similar problems in the past, the businessman may have observed the kinds of resources that typically are involved in the evaluation of alternatives, and may be familiar with some of the most common problems in measuring the cost of the resources required. Categorizing the problem facilitates making maximum use of this experience.

2. Some types of problems may be best resolved using analytical techniques that have been developed specifically for that class of problems. Identifying the type of problem thus serves also to identify the techniques which may aid in the solution.

There is a danger, too, in the classification of business problems: the danger of a closed mind that can only follow familiar decision patterns used in the past rather than searching imaginatively for new and better ways to grapple with the problems of today and tomorrow.

FORMULATING THE PROBLEM

In order to illustrate some of the most common problems of cost analysis, let us examine the decision process in a simple example. The Webber Company manufactures industrial equipment in a small plant with fifty employees. A recent increase in orders has taxed the one-shift capacity of the plant, and management can see that the company will fail to meet its delivery schedules unless some action is taken. What should be done?

The first step in analyzing this problem, and the most important step by far, is to determine the alternative courses of action that might solve the problem. The list is longer than one might first suppose. There are three main types of actions which might be taken: restricting the quantity sold to the present capacity of the plant; increasing the plant capacity on a permanent or semipermanent basis; or increasing capacity on a temporary basis. Under each of these broad headings, further actions can be identified, as the list below demonstrates.

1. Restricting the quantity sold by:
   (a) Refusing to accept orders in excess of present plant capacity.
   (b) Accepting all orders and apologizing to customers when deliveries are late.
   (c) Raising prices enough to reduce volume of orders down to present plant capacity.
2. Increasing plant capacity by:
   (a) Building an addition to the present plant.
   (b) Operating the present plant on two shifts.
3. Providing temporary capacity by:
   (a) Using overtime.
   (b) Buying some components from another manufacturer rather than making them.

This initial stage of formulating the problem is vital to wise decision making. It is a waste of time to do a careful analysis of three alternatives and to select the best of the three if a fourth course of action which is far better is completely overlooked. Analysis is no substitute for imagination. A few extra minutes devoted exclusively to the preparation of an exhaustive list of alternatives will nearly always be time well spent.

So that the exhaustive list does not become exhausting, the next (and sometimes simultaneous) step in problem formulation is to select those alternatives that merit further investigation. Several alternatives on Webber Company's list may be eliminated in this screening process. Items 1(a) and 1(c) would have the effect of reducing the demands placed on the factory. If the company had long-run growth in sales volume as one of its objectives, these two actions might be rejected as incompatible with the goal. Even if the company's only goal were "maximization of long-run profits" (as we will usually assume, in the absence of a specific statement of goals), alternative 1(a) is not acceptable if the additional product could be produced profitably. The profit effect of raising prices is more difficult to assess. Let us simply assume that we are interested in determining the best course of action at the present price in order to compare it with the results obtainable at a higher price.

Alternative 1(*b*) might appear attractive as a method of accepting the available orders without incurring additional production costs. Evaluation of this alternative should, however, recognize that it involves the consumption of an intangible business resource, customer "goodwill." Depending upon competition and normal trade practices in Webber's industry, it may be that stretching out of delivery schedules is the best solution to the problem. In most industries, however, this practice might be a costly one, and we will eliminate it from further consideration here.

The remaining four alternatives are ways to provide increased production in order to meet the increased demand. It is difficult to reject any of these solutions based only on a cursory analysis. It may be useful, however, to realize that there are major differences in type and magnitude of the resources required for each course of action. Expanding the plant or adding a second shift will cause significant changes in Webber's fixed costs as well as in its productive capacity. Even a second shift is a semipermanent action that involves hiring new supervisors as well as laborers, and may require a heavy expenditure of the vital *management* resource. Neither of these two actions would be wise unless Webber's management believed that the increase in demand was a relatively permanent one.

As a temporary solution to their problem, therefore, Webber's management might decide to narrow their analysis to a choice between alternatives 3(*a*) and 3(*b*), the use of overtime in the plant or the purchase of some components from outside vendors. The selection of either of these solutions can easily be changed in the future, and a few months from now management may be in a better position to assess the permanence of the current spurt in demand.

The final stage in formulating the problem is now at hand. How shall we evaluate the alternatives that we have decided to examine? What is the criterion on which we shall make our decision? A careful restatement of the problem at this point may help us to see the best way to point our subsequent analysis. It is little help at this point to say that we have a problem in resource allocation. It may be of more use to define the problem as "fulfilling our production requirements while minimizing the consumption of our resources." The businessman would say simply, "Which parts, if any, would it be cheaper to buy outside?"

In situations such as this where the decision has no revenue implications (we have already decided to accept all orders and deliver them on time), the best course of action is the one that costs the least. Realizing that we are equating "cost" with "resource consumption," therefore, we may say that our decision rule will be to choose the "least cost" alternative, and may then turn our attention to measuring the cost of pursuing each course of action.

RELEVANT COSTS

Before we can begin a detailed analysis, we need a more precise statement of the alternatives. For this purpose, we will assume that the anticipated capacity problem will arise only in the machining department of the Webber Company. Normally this department does the machining of all the component parts in the Webber product. Most of the parts are produced in small lots and require specialized skills not possessed by many outside vendors. Two parts, however, are produced in rather large quantities and the machining operations on them are routine. Clearly these parts are the best candidates for outside purchase. If they were purchased outside, the machining department would have no trouble making all the remaining components on schedule.

Having identified the alternatives, we must next determine the resources required to execute them. According to engineering estimates, the production of one unit of Part A requires raw materials costing $3.00 and a half hour of the time of a machine operator, while the production of one unit of Part B requires $8.00 of raw materials and one hour of operator time. The purchasing agent, after checking with several vendors, informs us that the Smithy Corporation, a reliable source, will deliver Part A for $4.50 each and Part B for $11.50 each.

The next step is to determine the cost of the resources required.

Earlier we referred to the different cost concepts used by accountants and economists and we argued that the economist's notion of opportunity cost is more appropriate for decision making than the accountant's notion of acquisition cost. Accounting records provide a useful source of cost data, however, and so we will begin by presenting the costs of the alternatives to the Webber Company as its accountants might prepare them; then we will indicate how these accounting costs must be analyzed and modified to reflect opportunity costs.

Accounting Costs · After being supplied with the list of resources required as given above, the accounting department of the Webber Company provides the following schedule of manufacturing costs:

	Cost per Unit	
	Part A	Part B
Prime Cost:		
Raw materials	$3.00	$ 8.00
Direct labor @ $2.00/hour	1.00	2.00
Total prime costs	$4.00	$10.00
Factory overhead @ 100% of labor	1.00	2.00
Normal manufacturing cost	$5.00	$12.00
Overtime premium @ 50% of labor	0.50	1.00
Overtime manufacturing cost	$5.50	$13.00

The accounting department explains its calculations as follows. The purchase of raw materials is, of course, a direct out-of-pocket cost. The machine operators are paid $2.00 per hour and this rate is applied to the time requirements to arrive at the direct labor cost. The total of raw materials and direct labor costs, representing the cost of resources directly consumed in the manufacture of the parts, is called *prime cost.*

Production of the parts would also require the use of certain common resources of the company: plant, equipment, supervision, and the like. The acquisition costs of these resources, called *overhead costs,* allocated to the machining department are given in Exhibit 1. Since total allocated overhead costs are equal to total direct labor costs, a charge of 100 percent of direct labor is made to cover these overhead costs. Finally, if work were done on overtime, an additional cost of 50 percent of direct labor would be incurred for overtime premium pay.

EXHIBIT 1

WEBBER COMPANY

MONTHLY BUDGET FOR MACHINING DEPARTMENT

Direct labor (2,000 hours @ $2.00)		$4,000
Overhead: Indirect labor—materials handling		$ 300
Department foreman		400
Payroll taxes, vacation and holiday pay, pension contributions, and other fringe benefits		900
Heat, light, and power		250
Shop supplies		150
Depreciation of machinery		800
Repairs and maintenance—machinery		600
Allocated share of plant-wide costs (superintendent, building depreciation and maintenance, property taxes and insurance, watchman, etc.)		600
Total overhead		$4,000

If we look at accounting costs, therefore, both parts are apparently cheaper to buy from Smithy than to produce in our own plant—even ignoring the premium paid for overtime work! But we must take a closer look at the behavior of manufacturing costs.

Another classification of manufacturing costs often used by accountants is into *direct costs* and *fixed costs*. This classification is a little closer to the economist's way of thinking about costs. Direct costs include those which vary at least approximately in proportion to the quantity of production. Prime costs are usually direct costs, but not all direct costs are prime costs: some overhead costs may also vary with production. Analysis of the overhead costs listed in Exhibit 1, for example, might reveal the following facts about the behavior of overhead costs under two circumstances: (*a*) at present volume if one man is laid off and parts are purchased outside; (*b*) at the anticipated increased volume, if overtime is used.

1. *Indirect Labor.* One man is employed as a materials handler in the department. If a machinist were laid off there would be no saving in the wages paid to this man; he would just be a little less busy. If the department worked overtime, however, the materials handling function would have to be performed by someone, either the machinist himself (thereby lowering his productive efficiency) or by the materials handler also working overtime.

2. *Department Foreman.* This cost probably would not vary with either a small decrease or small increase in production. The

machining work to be performed on overtime might not require the presence of a supervisor; if it did, the overtime paid to the supervisor would be relevant.

3. *Payroll Taxes, etc.* These costs amount to nearly 20 percent of Webber's expenses for labor and supervision. If a man were laid off, the entire 20 percent might be saved. There would be some increase in these costs on overtime, but the workers would not get more holidays or longer vacations. The variable portion, using overtime, might be 10 percent of the labor cost.

4. *Heat, Light, Power, and Shop Supplies.* These costs are difficult to analyze. There might be an insignificant saving in power if one machine were shut down. On overtime, additional power and light would be required.

5. *Depreciation.* This cost is not a cash expenditure but a pro rata portion of the original cost of the equipment. This cost, caused simply by the passage of time, will not be changed by management's decision to either lay off a man or use overtime.

6. *Repairs and Maintenance.* This expense is made up of two components: routine, preventive maintenance and the repair of breakdowns. The former is the larger expense, and might be reduced somewhat if one machine were shut down completely. The latter probably bears some relationship to the volume of work put through the equipment and would vary for either a decrease or increase in production.

7. *Allocated Plant Costs.* These overhead costs occur at the next higher level in the company, and would not change as a result of a minor change in production volume in the department.

We may now recapitulate the results of our analysis. Direct labor seems to be a useful measure of volume in this department because each man operates one machine and costs that vary in relation to machine utilization will also vary with labor costs. In Exhibit 2, therefore, we have computed the direct overhead cost for each of the two circumstances mentioned above (laying off one man or using overtime).

How variable are overhead costs? The preceding analysis illustrates how difficult it is to answer that question in a practical way. It seems safe to say that overhead is not completely variable, as might be inferred from the accountant's allocation mechanism. Saving $1.00 in labor cost will not save $1.00 in overhead in the machining department. But any further general statement about overhead variability is useless. For decision-making purposes, the most useful answer is one based on an analysis of the specific cost items in the specific situation in which a specific decision is

EXHIBIT 2

WEBBER COMPANY

Overhead Cost Analysis

Overhead Item	Monthly budget cost		Variable cost as a % of direct labor cost changes if	
	Amount	% of direct labor	one man laid off	overtime used
Indirect labor—materials handler	$ 300	7.5%	. . .	7.5%
Department foreman	400	10.0	. . .	. . .
Payroll taxes, etc.	900	22.5 *	19.1%	10.8
Heat, light, and power	250	6.2	1.0	2.0
Shop supplies	150	3.8	. . .	. . .
Depreciation of machinery	800	20.0		
Repairs and maintenance	600	15.0	12.0	5.0
Allocated plant costs	600	15.0	. . .	. . .
Total	$4,000	100.0%	32.1%	25.3%

* Stated as a percentage of total departmental payroll, this cost is $\dfrac{900}{4,700}$ = 19.1%. On overtime, it is estimated here that direct payroll taxes would be 10% of wage costs, but would also apply to the materials handler (10% of 7.5%).

to be made. Fortunately, it is possible to gain skill in this kind of analysis, with a concomitant reduction in the analytical time required. This is a skill worth developing, because reliance on rules of thumb or general cost variability classifications is a poor, and sometimes dangerous, substitute for such skill.

Opportunity Costs · The accountant measures the cost of resources consumed in terms of the outlay originally made to acquire them. The economist, in contrast, measures their cost in relation to alternative opportunities for their employment. Let us see how these two concepts differ in the Webber Company example.

On some costs, the accountant and the economist would agree. This would probably be true, for example, of the cost of buying the parts from the Smithy Corporation or the cost of the raw materials if the parts are manufactured. In these cases, the foregone opportunity is to refrain from buying the parts or the raw material, so that the opportunity cost and the acquisition cost would be identical.

It might seem, in fact, that opportunity cost is identical with the accounting concept of direct cost. While there is a close relationship between opportunity cost and direct cost and while they are often identical, there are important differences which must be borne in mind.

We can illustrate this point using the direct labor cost in the company example. The company employs eleven machinists in the machining department; approximately 2,000 hours of production labor are available each month. Before the company's anticipated sales volume increase, tnese men spent about 1,550 hours per month on machining the special, low-volume parts and used the balance of their time, as available, to turn out Parts A and B. Forgetting for the moment about the increase in volume, how would you decide whether or not to have Parts A and B made by Smithy? Are the labor costs true opportunity costs? The answer depends on what action Webber's management would take if the parts were purchased outside. A total of 450 labor hours could be saved. Would two and one-half machinists be laid off? Such action might mean reducing the range of skills now available in an eleven-man force, and might cause morale problems for the man working a short week. If, in fact, only one man would be laid off, then we should not say that the entire labor cost used in producing the parts is an opportunity cost of the parts. The relevant cost in this situation is the *total* amount of money that will be spent for labor under each course of action. If labor costs $2.00 per hour, the cost would be $4,000 if both parts are manufactured inside, and about $3,660 if one man is laid off and some parts were purchased. Although Webber's accountant would say that $900 is spent each month on machining labor for Parts A and B, the *opportunity cost* of that labor is only $340. The other $560 is spent primarily to maintain a balanced labor force with the necessary variety of skills—skills that may be a vital resource in Webber's overall success.

On the other hand, now that the demand for Webber's product is expected to increase, what is the relevant labor cost in deciding whetl er to use overtime to meet the requirements? With a 10 percent increase in demand, 1,705 hours per month are needed for low-volume parts and 495 hours of machining are needed for Parts A and B. Hiring a twelfth man might provide most of the 200 extra hours needed, but there is no room in the plant for another machine. If overtime is used, the additional labor will cost $3.00 per hour, or $600. This cost is relevant to the decision because its expenditure depends upon the course of action management selects.

Even in the relatively simple case of direct labor, therefore, opportunity cost is not necessarily identical with direct cost. In the example just considered, opportunity cost was less than direct cost, but the reverse could also be true, as we will demonstrate shortly. While the acquisition cost of fixed resources (i.e., accounting fixed overhead) is neither a direct cost nor an opportunity cost, there may be an opportunity cost associated with employing these facilities in one use rather than in an alternative. This opportunity cost is relevant in making decisions regarding the use of the fixed resources although it is not an acquisition cost.

Opportunity cost, then, depends upon the context of a particular decision whereas direct cost does not. The two concepts are similar enough to create both an advantage and a danger: an advantage in that direct cost can often be used to estimate opportunity cost, a danger in that this process can be carried farther than appropriate.

COMPARISON OF ALTERNATIVES

After the problem has been formulated and the relevant costs determined, the next step in the analysis of a decision problem is to recapitulate the results of our analysis to determine which alternative is least costly. If the problem has been formulated properly and the cost analysis done systematically, this ranking task is a simple one. Illustrative calculations for the Webber Company's make-or-buy decisions are shown in Exhibits 3 and 4.

Exhibit 3 is an evaluation of the alternatives that faced Webber under its "normal" demand conditions, i.e., before the anticipated increase in demand. As a result of our analysis, the most promising alternatives have now been more sharply defined. Only one man would be laid off if any parts were purchased outside, eliminating 170 labor hours per month. If this were done, Webber would then have to buy outside either 340 units of A or 170 units of B. In terms of total costs, the best alternative is to continue to manufacture all our requirements inside. The only difficult cost calculation is the overhead cost. If all parts were made inside, the labor and overhead budgets would be unchanged at $4,000 each per month. If one man were laid off, labor cost would decline by $340 and the overhead budget would fall by 32.1 percent of that amount (Exhibit 2).

An alternative analysis in Exhibit 3 arrives at the same conclusion in terms of opportunity costs. According to the cost accountant's statement on page 31, the "normal" cost of one unit of Part A was $5.00. We have seen that this figure is not useful

EXHIBIT 3

WEBBER COMPANY

MAKE-OR-BUY ANALYSIS

CONDITION NO. 1: NORMAL DEMAND

	Make 500 units of A and 200 of B	*Lay off one machinist and*	
		Buy 340 units of A	*Buy 170 units of B*
Raw material costs:			
Part A	$ 1,500	$ 480	$ 1,500
Part B	1,600	1,600	240
Purchased parts	. . .	1,530	1,955
Direct labor	4,000	3,660	3,660
Overhead costs	4,000	3,891	3,891
	$11,100	$11,161	$11,246

ALTERNATIVE ANALYSIS

	Opportunity cost of manufacturing	
	Part A	*Part B*
Raw material costs.....................	$ 3.00	$ 8.00
Direct labor—one man...................	1.00	2.00
Overhead at 32.1% of labor..............	0.32	0.64
Total opportunity cost................	$ 4.32	$ 10.64
Purchase price	4.50	11.50
Saving due to manufacturing.............	$ 0.18	$ 0.86
Number of units produced in 170 hours........	340	170
Total savings	$61.00	$146.00

for decision-making purposes; we are interested in the opportunity cost of manufacturing Part A. To measure opportunity cost, we must answer the question, "What costs (resources) will be saved if the parts are purchased outside?" For Part A, we will save $3.00 of raw material for each unit, the labor cost of one man divided by the units he could produce, and approximately 32 percent in overhead costs related to labor. What costs (resources) will be required to achieve those savings? Part A must be purchased at a price of $4.50 each. The savings are less than the additional cost, indicating that outside purchase is not the cheapest course of action. It is no coincidence that the total saving due to manufacturing is equal to the difference in the total costs of the alternatives as computed in the upper part of Exhibit 3.

Exhibit 4 is a similar set of calculations after a 10 percent increase in demand. The overhead cost increase of $138 was computed in two stages as follows: Variable overhead was estimated as 25.3 percent of labor in Exhibit 2, and this percentage was applied to the $400 straight time cost of the added labor. In addition, indirect labor and payroll taxes (18.3 percent of labor) would vary as a function of cost (not time), so that percentage was applied to the $200 of overtime premium pay. The best alternative is to buy 400 units per month of Part A rather than to use overtime.

We have said that most decision problems are basically problems in resource allocation. Cost analysis is used to solve these problems because money is the best common denominator for resources, and because money is the basic "scarce resource" which the business would like to utilize in an optimal fashion. In the Webber Company's overtime decision it is useful to conceive of the problem somewhat differently. The company has 2,000 hours of machining capacity available, and our analysis in Exhibit 3 has shown that this capacity should not be reduced. As demand increases, Webber's real question is, "How should the 2,000 hours be allocated among the available jobs?" The special, low-volume parts are of first priority, and require 1,705 of the available hours. The remaining 295 hours should be used in such a way as to maximize their value to Webber.

EXHIBIT 4

WEBBER COMPANY

MAKE-OR-BUY ANALYSIS

CONDITION NO. 2: INCREASED DEMAND

	Use 200 hours of overtime; make 550 units of A and 200 units of B	*Use no overtime and* buy 400 units of A	buy 200 units of B
Raw material costs:			
Part A	$ 1,650	$ 450	$ 1,650
Part B	1,760	1,760	160
Purchased parts	. . .	1,800	2,300
Direct labor—straight time.........	4,400	4,000	4,000
Overhead costs	4,000	4,000	4,000
Overtime premium	200	. . . .	. . . .
Overhead costs applied to premium pay	138	. . . .	. . . .
Total cost	$12,148	$12,010	$12,110

ALTERNATIVE ANALYSIS

	Opportunity cost of manufacturing	
	Part A	Part B
Raw material costs.........................	$ 3.00	$ 8.00
Direct labor—200 hours....................	1.00	2.00
Overhead at 25.3% of labor.................	0.25	0.51
Overtime premium	0.50	1.00
Overhead at 18.3% of premium..............	0.09	0.18
Total opportunity cost.....	$ 4.84	$11.69
Purchase price	4.50	11.50
Saving due to purchase...................	$ 0.34	$ 0.19
Number of units produced in 200 hours........	400	200
Total savings from purchase............	$138.00	$38.00

In Exhibit 5 we have computed the contribution per labor
hour that would be earned by using the available hours to manufacture Part A or Part B. Labor and its related overhead costs are
ignored in this calculation since these costs will not change as a
result of our decision. They are part of the fixed resources we
desire to allocate optimally. We will spend a total of $4,000 for
labor and $4,000 for overhead; our decision is to determine *how*
to use this capacity. Additional cash resources are required only

EXHIBIT 5

WEBBER COMPANY

Calculation of Contribution per Labor Hour

Hours available:

Total	2,000
Required for low-volume, special parts	1,705
Available for Parts A or B	295

	Part A	Part B
Purchase price per unit	$ 4.50	$11.50
Raw material cost per unit	3.00	8.00
Materials savings per unit	$ 1.50	$ 3.50
Number of units produced per labor hour	2	1
Contribution per labor hour	$ 3.00	$ 3.50

Cost of adding additional labor hours:

Labor per hour	$2.00		
Overhead at 25.3%	0.51		
Overtime premium per hour	1.00		
Overhead at 18.3% of premium	0.18		
Total cost	$3.69	3.69	3.69
Excess cost per hour of making rather than buying		$ 0.69	$ 0.19
Total excess cost for 200 hours		$138.00	$38.00

for materials. For every unit of Part A manufactured we will pay only $3.00 for materials rather than $4.50 for the completed part, a saving of $1.50 per unit or $3.00 per labor hour. Manufacturing Part B is even more attractive because we will save $3.50 per labor hour. In order to get maximum value from our scarce resource (capacity), we should manufacture all of our requirements of Part B before we use any of the capacity to manufacture Part A.

Next, we must decide whether it would be worthwhile to buy additional capacity by using overtime. The cost of adding capacity is $3.69 per hour (Exhibit 5). Since this cost exceeds the contribution earned by the labor hours, the use of overtime is not warranted. The last calculation on Exhibit 5 is proof that this method of analysis is consistent with the two methods shown in Exhibit 4.

Optimal allocation of scarce resources is a primary task of the businessman. The Webber Company example is a simple illustration of what is involved in this task.

Production Functions and Cost Functions: A Case Study

LESLIE COOKENBOO

Leslie Cookenboo is Senior Economics Adviser in the Corporate Planning Department of the Exxon Corporation. This piece comes from his book, Crude Oil Pipe Lines and Competition in the Oil Industry, *published by the Harvard University Press.*

This paper is concerned with a discussion of long-, short-, and intermediate-run costs of operating crude oil pipe lines. For the benefit of the reader not conversant with economic jargon, it might be well to begin with a description of the three cost categories. First, it is necessary to distinguish between the various types of costs that may be considered under any of these three categories. "Total" cost (be it long-, short-, or intermediate-run) is the total expenditure necessary for producing a given output. "Average" cost is the cost per unit of producing a given output; it is equal to total cost divided by output. For example, if the total expenditure for an output of 100 units is $1,000, then total cost is $1,000 and average cost (per-unit cost) is $10 per unit ($1,000 divided by 100 units). "Marginal" cost is the change in total cost associated with changes in output. If 100 units cost

$1,000 and 101 units cost $1,008, then "marginal" cost is $8 (the change in total cost divided by the change in output). "Fixed" and "variable" costs are simply parts of total (or average) cost. Fixed costs are those incurred even when no output is produced, for example, interest on the money borrowed to buy machinery, pay taxes, and so forth. Variable costs (out-of-pocket costs) are expenditures that would not be necessary were no output produced, for example, expenditures for labor and raw materials. Total cost is equal to the sum of total fixed cost and total variable cost. Average cost is equal to the sum of average fixed cost and average variable cost.

A "short-run" cost curve shows the cost of producing various outputs with a given amount of fixed capital equipment. In other words, it is the cost curve for a given size of plant, the output of which can be changed simply by using more or less labor and raw materials. Changes in short-run costs with changes in output represent changes in expenditures for items of variable cost *only;* no extra machinery or other capital equipment is needed to increase output.

A long-run cost curve (also called a "planning" curve) is an "envelope" of all possible short-run curves. It shows the least possible expenditure for producing any output. That is, it takes into account all individual plant cost curves in order to determine which plant can produce each output for the least amount possible (relative to all other plants). This is illustrated in Figure 1.

This diagram shows per-unit cost plotted against output (the short-run cost curves) for each of six possible plants (A–F) that might be used to produce some products. The long-run average cost curve is the envelope of these short-run curves (the heavy, wavy line). (If there were an infinite number of plants possible, then the long-run curve would be continuous, not wavy.) It shows the least possible expenditure for any given output in the range of outputs under consideration. Output Q_0 might be produced with either plant A, B, C, D, E, or F. However, D's short-run cost curve lies beneath all the others at Q_0; therefore its cost is the least possible for producing Q_0, and it may be said to be the "optimum" plant for producing that output. In the range of outputs where its cost curve lies beneath all others, its short-run cost is equal to long-run cost. A long-run cost

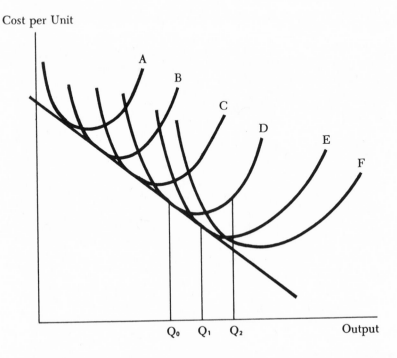

FIGURE 1

Long- and Short-run Average Cost Curves

curve such as that in Figure 1 is called a "planning" curve because it shows the least amount that could be spent to produce
various outputs if a firm had the option of choosing from several
sizes of plants. Such a long-run cost curve would be of value
when building a new plant or when contemplating entering an
industry. Once a plant is built, it is the short-run curve for this
plant which shows what the firm would spend in order to produce various outputs.

Note the paradox in Figure 1 that D is *not* the optimum plant
for the output at which it itself is most efficient (Q_1). Its most
efficient output is the output which it produces at the least possible cost per unit that *it* is capable of achieving. In Figure 1,

plant E could produce D's optimum output (Q_1) more cheaply than could D; hence E is the optimum plant at D's optimum output. It is a question of optimum *plant* relative to all *other* plants, versus optimum *output* for a *given* plant (without consideration of others) once that plant is built. Because of this paradox, any plant in Figure 1, say D, would be built originally to produce an output less than its own optimum output. Hence, it could subsequently increase its output, should it so desire, and thereby achieve a lower per-unit cost. Indeed, it could increase its output to Q_2 before average costs became higher than they were at the design output. It might be asked why a firm would ever consider producing Q_2 with D when E and F can produce it for less. If the need for Q_2 had been foreseen before any plant was built, then plant E would probably have been built. However, if the original output desired was Q_0, the correct choice would have been D. A subsequent expansion to Q_2 could then be made with plant D. This would be done instead of building a new plant if the cash costs of operating plant D at Q_2 were less than the total costs of operating plant F at Q_2.

One other "paradox" should be pointed out in Figure 1. Note that the short-run average costs decrease and then rise, even though the long-run cost curve falls throughout the range of outputs. Consequently a U-shaped short-run average cost curve may occur for each plant while long-run average costs decline continuously.

In the range of outputs where long-run average costs decrease (in this case throughout the range), there are said to be "economies of scale." That is, by producing larger amounts conglomerately in larger plants, it is possible to achieve lower per-unit costs, better known as "mass-production economies." If the long-run average cost curve declines throughout the range of outputs, then no plant can achieve the least possible (long-run) cost of producing the product, unless there is some size of plant, say F, which is the largest possible for one reason or another. However, something approaching the least possible long-run cost can be had with the large plants, for example, E and F in Figure 1, since the average cost curve declines more and more slowly as output rises. From the point of view of both society and the firm, plants in an industry having costs such as those shown in Figure 1 should be as large as possible in order to achieve as low average costs as possible—apart from any political or sociological disadvantages of large business.

In the case of pipe lines it is also necessary to utilize the concept of "intermediate-run" costs. If the curves labeled A–F in Figure 1 were the basis of a planning curve for pipe lines, they would be called not "short-run," but "intermediate-run" pipe-line cost curves, each representing a given line size carrying various "throughputs." (Pipe-line output is called "throughput"—the volume of liquid carried per unit of time.) In some industries the output of individual plants can be expanded above the original output simply by adding more labor or raw materials; these may be described with short-run cost curves. However, in the case of pipe lines, throughput can be increased above the designed capacity only by the addition of more capital equipment (pumping stations), along with extra labor and fuel. Short-run cost curves which allow for a fixed amount of capital equipment are "reversible." That is, when output is decreased (by laying off workers and buying smaller amounts of raw materials), the short-run curve shows the appropriate cost for the lower output. On the other hand, intermediate-run cost curves which include costs of varying amounts of capital equipment are not reversible. If pipe line D (again referring to Figure 1, this time as a series of intermediate-run curves) were built for throughput Q_0, then the costs of carrying throughput less than Q_0 in line D would *not* be shown by the curve labeled D; these costs would be higher for all throughputs less than Q_0. Why? The curve D would be based, for planning purposes, on the proper (minimum possible) number of pumping stations for each throughput. It takes more stations of a given size to push larger throughputs through a given size pipe. Consequently, the number of stations built on line D for throughput Q_0 would be larger than needed for lesser throughputs. If throughput is cut below Q_0, the number of stations cannot be cut (as could the number of workers in some other industry), since stations represent fixed capital investments—investments which incur costs even if the stations are not needed. In short, too many pumping stations would be present for any lower throughput; consequently there would be higher average costs than if the line had been designed for the lower throughput with the minimum number of stations required for that throughput. Hence, the necessity of the hybrid term "intermediate-run" in the pipe-line case. In this case the long-run curve is the envelope of the intermediate-run curves, not of the short-run curves.

With this digression into the principles of economics in mind, it is possible to proceed with the discussion of pipe-line costs. The costs computed for this study were determined primarily by the method of engineering estimation, not by the use of actual historical costs. Where engineering estimation is feasible for cost studies it should be used, since actual costs may be subject to any number of erratic variations arising from construction or operating conditions unique to particular cases. In the case of the majority of the cost items, the process of computation involved a physical determination of the amount of equipment or services required, followed by the pricing of this amount from current price quotations furnished by suppliers and/or pipe-line companies. In some cases where particular items did not readily lend themselves to a priori engineering estimation, it was necessary to use historical costs. One example of this is the construction materials cost of pumphouses, for which actual costs obtained from a pipe-line company were used as the basis of computation. This particular item also illustrates the dangers of using historical costs. The stations were built in a period of unusually bad weather; hence the labor costs were much higher than would be the case normally. The materials costs were usable, but the labor costs had to be estimated from other sources. The notable exceptions where actual costs were used as the principal basis for computation include costs of surveying the right-of-way, mainline valves, office operation, site improvement at stations, and the pipe-line communications system. Since the details of this cost study are reported elsewhere,[1] it will not be necessary to engage here in an extended discussion of such problems as optimum operating pressure, safety factor, wall thickness of pipe, centrifugal versus reciprocating pumps, diesel engines versus electric motors, and so forth. However, it is necessary to discuss in summary form certain points about pipe-line

1. See L. Cookenboo, Jr., "Costs of Operating Crude Oil Pipe Lines," *Rice Institute Pamphlet,* April 1954, pp. 35–113.

technology and the results of the cost study, since this information is all-important for the subsequent discussion.

In order to determine costs by engineering estimation, it is necessary to compute an "engineering production function" relating the factors of production (the goods and services used to produce a product) and output. Such a function shows the possible combinations of the factors of production which can be used to produce various levels of output.

A basic choice between two "factors of production" exists in the determination of the optimum line diameter for carrying any particular throughput. A given size of line may be used for several different throughputs by applying different amounts of power (hydraulic horsepower) to the oil carried—the more horsepower, the more throughput (but less than proportionately more). Conversely, any given throughput can be achieved by the use of several possible sizes of lines with the proper amount of horsepower applied. There are, in short, variable physical proportions of these two basic factors of production, line diameter and horsepower, which may be used to develop any given throughput. As a result, the management of a pipe-line company is forced to choose between several sizes of line when planning to develop a given throughput. Furthermore, the long-run cost of carrying crude oil might vary with throughput, as did the long-run costs in Figure 1. Larger throughputs might cost less or more per barrel. Managements, then, not only have the option of several sizes of line for each throughput, they also may have the option of choosing throughputs having different costs per barrel. Other things being equal, a pipe-line company planning to build a line should select the cheapest combination of line diameter and horsepower for the throughput which can be carried at the least cost per barrel.

A production function relating line diameter, horsepower, and throughput can be derived for crude oil pipe lines. Indeed, many such functions could be derived, depending of the density and viscosity of the oil carried, the wall thickness of pipe used, and so forth. However, for the purposes of this monograph one function will suffice. The only differences among the cost curves derived from different functions are in absolute dollars per barrel-mile for each throughput, not in the relative positions of the intermediate-run cost curves for each line. The latter is the important point for public policy considerations. A crude oil trunk pipe-line production function is shown in Chart 1. This

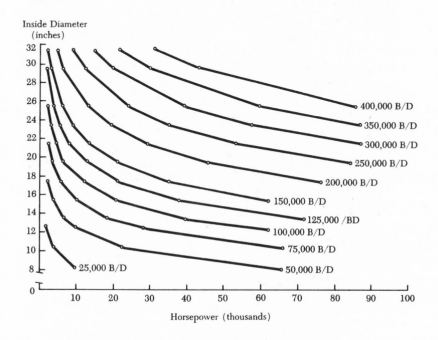

Inside Diameter
(inches)

Horsepower (thousands)

CHART 1

PRODUCTION FUNCTION FOR CRUDE OIL TRUNK PIPE LINES:
LINE DIAMETER VERSUS HORSEPOWER VERSUS
THROUGHPUT—1,000-MILE LINES *

* Assumptions: 60 SUS, 34° A.P.I. Crude; no influence of gravity on flow; 5 percent terrain variation (equalized up and down hill); ¼-in. pipe throughout.

chart assumes a more or less typical Mid-Continent (60 SUS viscosity, 34° A.P.I. gravity) crude, ¼-inch pipe throughout the lines, lines 1,000 miles in length with a 5 percent terrain variation (giving 1,050 miles of pipe), and no net gravity flow in the

line (there may be hills as long as there are offsetting valleys).
The production function covers throughputs of 25, 50, 75, 100,
125, 200, 250, 300, 350, and 400 thousand barrels per day; this encompasses the range of throughputs for crude oil trunk lines
which have yet been built. The curves in the chart show the
amounts of horsepower required for the several line sizes which
might be used for a given throughput; each curve applies to one
of the throughputs listed. The line sizes used are 8⅝, 10¾,
12¾, 14, 16, 18, 20, 22, 24, 26, 30, and 32 inches (outside
diameter) all having ¼-inch walls. This covers all line sizes used
for recent crude trunk lines. (Standard line pipe is only available
in these sizes in the 8–32-inch range.) It will be noted that this is
in reality a three-dimensional function, with line diameter and
horsepower on a plane and with the throughput axis rising per-
pendicularly to this plane. The production function was computed by the use of a hydraulic formula for computing required
horsepowers for various volumes of liquid flow in pipes of the
sizes just noted, with appropriate constants for oil of the type
used. This formula, simplified, is:

$$T^{2.735} = (H)\,(D^{4.735}) \div (0.01046),$$

where,

$T =$ Throughput,
$H =$ Horsepower, and
$D =$ Inside diameter of pipe.

Chart 2 shows vertical cross sections of the production function drawn perpendicular to the line-diameter axis. These are
intermediate-run physical productivity curves which show the
amount of horsepower that must be used with any given line size
for various throughputs. They are analogous to traditional physical productivity curves of economic theory. Such a physical productivity curve in the textbooks might show the amount of
wheat that can be produced from an acre of land by the use of
varying numbers of workers, where line diameter is equivalent to
the fixed factor (land) and horsepower is more or less equivalent
to the variable factor (labor). These curves are not, however, precisely equivalent to the traditional physical productivity curves,
since the horsepower factor includes some capital equipment.
When it is necessary to expand output over the designed capacity

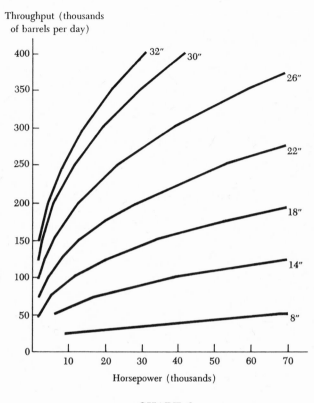

CHART 2

VERTICAL CROSS SECTION OF PRODUCTION FUNCTION:
HORSEPOWER VERSUS THROUGHPUT—LINE DIAMETER
HELD CONSTANT

of the line, it is necessary to add more capital equipment as well as more labor. When throughput is decreased below the designed capacity, unnecessary capital equipment exists—equipment on which fixed costs are incurred. Hence, as was noted above, the designation "intermediate-run" instead of short-run.

It will be observed that these productivity curves exhibit decreasing returns (marginal and average) throughout the range of throughputs. That is, there is a less than proportionate increase in throughput for a given increase in horsepower in a particular size of line. This is a physical phenomenon deriving from the characteristics of liquid flow in pipes. Other things being equal, this would mean that intermediate-run average costs attributable to horsepower should rise throughout the range of throughputs. (If the price of horsepower were constant and an addition to horsepower gave a less than proportionate increase in throughput, then the horsepower cost per barrel of throughput would rise.)

On the other hand, average costs attributable to line diameter will perforce fall throughout the range of throughputs for any given line size, since these costs are fixed in total. There are, then, offsetting forces at work, one tending to increasing average costs, the other to decreasing average costs. Whether aggregate average costs would rise, fall, or both, depends on the relative magnitudes of the horsepower and line diameter costs. In this case it will be seen that U-shaped intermediate-run average cost curves result. That is, average costs fall at first, but then level off and rise as more and more horsepower is added to a given line. (The initial fall is accentuated by the fact that the price of horsepower falls somewhat as total horsepower used on a given line increases, thereby offsetting to some extent the decreasing physical returns.)

Chart 3 shows vertical cross sections of the production function drawn perpendicular to the horsepower axis, as opposed to those in Chart 2 which are drawn perpendicular to the line-diameter axis. These cross sections indicate what happens when horsepower is held constant and additional throughput is obtained by the use of more line-diameter (a long-run movement over the production function surface that is possible only when planning the line, not after the line is built). It will be observed that these curves exhibit *increasing* physical returns (average and marginal) to scale. This means that the same amount of horsepower applied in a large-diameter line as in a small-diameter line will give a more than proportionate increase in throughput. In other words, there is more throughput per horsepower in a large line than in a small one. Since this relationship is the basic reason for the shape of the long-run cost curve, and is therefore the basis for the public policy conclusions which may be drawn from the long-run curve, it will be well to examine the physical reason for these increasing returns.

The increasing returns are attributable to the fact that there is less friction incurred per barrel of oil carried in a large-diam-

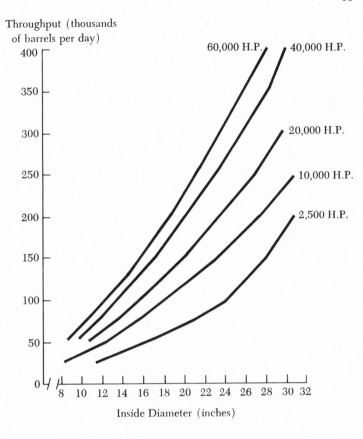

Throughput (thousands of barrels per day)

Inside Diameter (inches)

CHART 3

VERTICAL CROSS SECTION OF PRODUCTION FUNCTION:
LINE DIAMETER VERSUS THROUGHPUT FOR
SELECTED HORSEPOWERS

eter pipe than in a small-diameter pipe. Friction is created by only that part of the oil which touches the inside surface of the pipe. Hence it is the amount of surface area per barrel of oil carried that determines the amount of friction per barrel of oil carried. Solid geometry tells us that there is less surface area per unit of volume in a large-diameter cylinder (in this case the line pipe) of a given length than in a small-diameter cylinder of the same length. An open-ended cylinder of inside radius *r* and length L has a volume of $\pi r^2 L$ and an inside surface area of $2\pi rL$. A larger open-ended cylinder, say of inside radius $r + x$, and the same length, has a volume of $\pi(r + x)^2L$ and a surface area of $2\pi(r + x)L$. The volume increases more than the surface area. This may be shown as follows (where V_1 and A_1 are the volume and surface area of the smaller open-ended cylinder and V_2 and A_2 are the volume and area of the larger open-ended cylinder):

$$V_1 = \pi r^2 L$$
$$V_2 = \pi(r + x)^2 L = \pi(r^2 + 2xr + x^2)L =$$
$$\pi r^2 L + 2\pi xrL + \pi x^2 L$$
$$\Delta V = V_2 - V_1 = 2\pi xrL + x^2 \pi L$$
$$A_1 = 2\pi rL$$
$$A_2 = 2\pi(r + x)L = 2\pi rL + 2\pi xL$$
$$\Delta A = A_2 - A_1 = 2\pi xL.$$
$$\text{Since } 2\pi xrL + x^2 \pi L > 2\pi xL,$$
$$\Delta V > \Delta A.$$

The volume increased by $(2\pi xrL + x^2\pi L)$, while the surface area increased only by $2\pi xL$. It may be concluded that there is more volume per unit of surface area in a large than in a small pipe. This means that more oil can be transported per unit of surface area touched in a large than a small pipe. Since the amount of friction generated depends on the amount of surface area touched, it follows that more oil can be carried per given amount of friction developed in a large than in a small pipe. Therefore, the horsepower required to overcome a given amount of friction will propel more oil per day through a large pipe than through a small pipe. In short, because of the volume-area relationship it is possible to develop more throughput per horsepower applied in large pipes than in small ones. (It is interesting to note that the volume-area relationship is responsible for many other important technical economies of scale in industry, for example, economies of large tanks, heat containment, and so forth.) [2]

2. See H. B. Chenerey, *Engineering Bases of Economic Analysis* (unpublished doctoral thesis deposited in Widener Library, 1950), pp. 140–141, and E. A. Robinson, *Structure of Competitive Industry* (London, 1935), p. 29.

Chart 4 indicates the physical returns to scale characteristic of pipe-line operation. It will be remembered that there are decreasing physical returns as more horsepower is added to a given line, but that there are increasing physical returns from using larger lines with a given amount of horsepower. Which of these

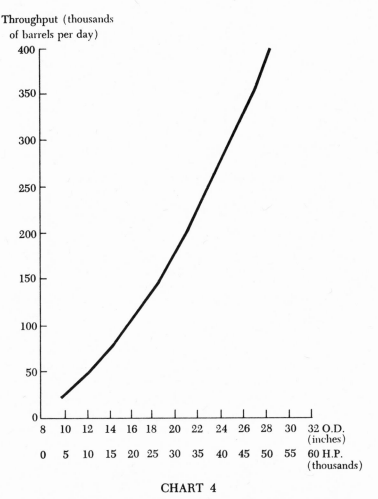

CHART 4

PHYSICAL RETURNS TO SCALE. VERTICAL CROSS SECTION OF
PRODUCTION FUNCTION THROUGH ORIGIN (45° ANGLE)

counteracting tendencies predominates in long-run movements where throughput is increased or decreased by varying the amounts of both factors used? In other words, are there increasing or decreasing returns to scale (to larger size) from carrying larger amounts of oil in the same facilities? This is shown physically by the shape of vertical cross sections of the production function drawn through the origin. Chart 4 shows such a cross section drawn at a 45° angle through the origin of the function. This section indicates the returns to scale when throughput is increased by increasing the use of horsepower and line diameter in equal proportions. (Note that this is only an approximation, since the production function is only realistic at certain points, not over its whole surface; consequently, the 45° line would only by chance intersect each throughput at a point where an available line size exists.) The curve exhibits increasing (average and marginal) returns to scale throughout the range of throughputs. In other words, if the amounts of horsepower and line diameter used are increased in equal proportions, then there would be a more than proportionate increase in throughput. This indicates that on an a priori basis it would be expected that long-run decreasing average costs would characterize pipe-line operation. Only if the price of one or both of the factors should increase sufficiently with the amount of the factor used to offset the increasing returns, would the long-run cost curve turn up. Actually, the price of horsepower decreases somewhat with the amount used, and the price of line diameter does not fluctuate sufficiently with the amount used to offset the physical relationship.

Lest the reader object to drawing these general conclusions only on the basis of an example where expansion is by increased utilization of the factors in equal proportions, it should be pointed out that this is a "homogeneous" production function. Homogeneous production functions exhibit the same type of returns to scale on all parts of the surface. The function used reduces to:

$$T^{2.735} = (H)(D^{4.735})(C), \text{ or}$$
$$T = (H^{\frac{1}{2.735}})(D^{\frac{4.735}{2.735}})(C) = (H^{.37})(D^{1.73})(C).$$

[C is a constant.] This is a function of the form,

$$T = H^m D^n C.$$

Such a function is homogeneous if $(m + n)$ is a constant, as it is in this case, where $(m + n) = 2.1$. This also indicates that there are marked increasing returns to scale, since the function is of order 2 (constant returns to scale are implied from a function having an order of one).

The discussion of the technological relationships peculiar to pipe-line transportation of oil may now be summarized. A basic physical relationship may be deduced for the purpose of computing pipe-line costs. This relationship shows that there will be markedly increasing long-run physical returns to scale if larger and larger throughputs are carried. In the intermediate run, physical returns decrease. It follows, assuming that factor prices are more or less constant with the amount of the factor used, that there will be long-run decreasing costs (economies of scale) for pipe-line operation. Intermediate-run costs might rise, fall, or both—since the increasing average costs attributable to horsepower are counteracted by fixed costs attributed to line diameter. Under such conditions, U-shaped curves are feasible. These cost conclusions are based solely on the physical relationships discussed and are independent of the cost determination to be considered next. The conclusions would be invalidated only if the price of one or both of the factors rose sufficiently with increases in the amount of the factor used to offset the increasing physical returns to scale. This is not the case. (This may also be predicted to a considerable extent apart from actual cost determination, since the amounts of the most important single cost items included in each factor are proportional to the amounts of the factors used.)

COSTS

Pipe-line costs may be divided into three basic categories: (1) those variant with line diameter; (2) those variant with horsepower; (3) those variant only with throughput or length of line (a relatively small part of total cost). Since there is a choice for any given throughput among several possible combinations of line diameter and horsepower (as is shown in the production function in Chart 1), in order to be able to compute a long-run cost curve it is necessary to determine which of several possible combinations is least expensive for any throughput. This is done for each throughput by determining the total cost of each possible combination, on, say, an annual basis. That combination whose total cost is least for a given throughput is the optimum combination for that throughput. Note that it is only the costs of line diameter and horsepower which must be so manipulated, since the other costs are irrelevant to the choice of the optimum combination of these two. The other costs are, of course, incurred and cannot be ignored; but they do not influence the choice of the proper size line for a given throughput.

Annual total intermediate-run costs are shown in Chart 5;

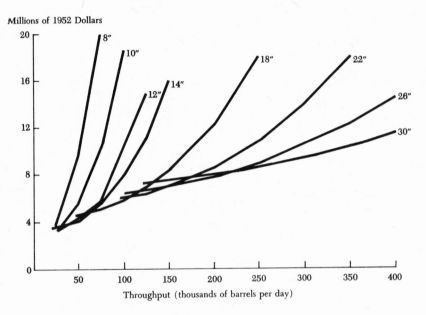

CHART 5

ANNUAL TOTAL COSTS OF OPERATING CRUDE OIL TRUNK PIPE LINES

Source: L. Cookenboo, Jr., "Costs of Operating Crude Oil Pipe Lines," *Rice Institute Pamphlet,* April 1954, pp. 106–107 (Table 19).

these are derived by plotting annual total cost against throughput for each line diameter covered in the study. The shaded envelope of the intermediate-run cost curves is the long-run total cost curve. Chart 6 shows intermediate-run costs per barrel per 1,000

Cents per Barrel per
Thousand Miles

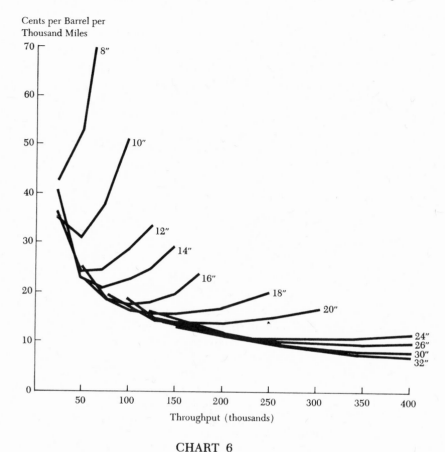

CHART 6

<small>C</small>OSTS PER <small>B</small>ARREL OF <small>O</small>PERATING <small>C</small>RUDE <small>O</small>IL
<small>T</small>RUNK <small>P</small>IPE <small>L</small>INES

Source: L. Cookenboo, Jr., "Costs of Operating Crude Oil Pipe Lines,"
Rice Institute Pamphlet, April 1954, pp. 106–107 (Table 19).

miles (that is, average costs). This is a chart analogous to
Figure 1 above. Its envelope is the long-run average cost curve.
In the range of throughputs where the average cost curve of a
given line size lies below all other average cost curves, that line
is the optimum line for the throughputs covered. For example,
the 30-inch line lies beneath all others between about 225,000

and 325,000 barrels per day; hence, it is the optimum line for throughputs between those limits.

The intermediate-run cost curves also show what it would cost to carry larger quantities of oil than the design throughput if stations were added subsequent to the building of the line. (Pipe lines cannot be operated at throughputs greater than the designed capacity without the additions of more stations, since the design capacity would require the highest operating pressures permitted by the safety factor.) Remember that the intermediate-run curve does *not* show the costs of throughputs less than the design throughput.

While, as was pointed out above, the details of the cost study lying behind the totals in Charts 5 and 6 are discussed at length elsewhere,[3] a word or two should be said about the assumptions involved in the engineering-type cost determination. The principal items involved in the cost of line diameter are all represented by initial outlays made during the construction of the line. The most important line costs are the service costs of laying the line, and the material costs of steel, pipe coating, line block valves, corrosion protection, and so forth. The assumptions of the characteristics of the lines, listed above, were 1,000 miles of ¼-inch pipe having 50 miles of terrain variation (with no net gravity flow). This means that the line costs include the material and service costs of laying 1,050 miles of pipe (coated in accord with the best coating practice and protected by magnesium anodes).

The principal items involved in the costs of horsepower are the annual expenditures for electric power and labor (and of less importance, maintenance) to operate the pumping stations. This category also includes the initial cost of the stations; this represents the most difficult, time-consuming part of a pipe-line cost computation (even though station costs are not too important in relation to total costs). The stations used on the pipe lines described in Charts 5 and 6 are semiautomatic, equipped with centrifugal pumps and electric motors. Stations pumping over 100,000 barrels per day are equipped with three full-size pumps and motors (one motor per pump) which together deliver the capacity throughput, and one half-size pump and motor. This provides flexibility of operation which would otherwise be

3. Cookenboo, "Costs of Operating Crude Oil Pipe Lines," pp. 35–113.

unattainable with constant speed electric motors. (With, as they say, 3½ pumps, seven stages of operation are possible: no pumps, ½ pump, 1½, 2, 2½, and 3 for capacity.) Stations pumping less than 100,000 barrels per day utilize two full-size pumps and one half-size pump. Each station utilizes in-an-out piping to permit the bypassing of any one pump without shutting down the whole station. The labor force required for such semi-automatic stations is two men per shift (regardless of the level of operation), unless the stations are very large; none used in this study was large enough to require extra operators. (In a semi-automatic pumping station the principal tasks of the operators are to watch the controls, shut off motor-operated valves when necessary, and maintain the equipment.)

The principal costs involved in the "other" category are the initial costs of (1) tankage (the lines in this study have 12.5 days' supply (of storage capacity along the line), (2) surveying the right-of-way, (3) damages to terrain crossed, and (4) a communications system (here assumed to be a 12-channel micro-wave system). It should be noted that while these costs vary either with throughput or with length of line, they are *proportional* to either throughput or length of line as the case may be. There are no significant per-barrel costs of a pipe line which change with length. The only such costs are those of a central office force; these are inconsequential in relation to total. Hence, it is possible to state that costs per barrel-mile for a 1,000-mile trunk line are representative of costs per barrel-mile of any trunk line (those, say, 75 or 100 miles in length and longer).

It will be observed in Chart 6 that there are economies of scale (decreasing long-run average costs) throughout the range of throughputs covered. The analysis was only carried through 32-inch lines and 400,000 barrels per day. However, if larger lines could be had at a constant price per ton of steel (the only price per unit of material likely to change with larger amounts than those used), then the long-run average cost curve would fall even farther. On the other hand, pipe much larger than 34 or 36 inches might well require the creation of special pipe-making facilities and, consequently, might command a higher price per ton than the pipe sizes used in this study. In this case, the long-run average cost curve might turn up near, say, 500,000 barrels per day.

In any event, the rate of decrease of the average cost curve has declined appreciably by the time a throughput of 400,000 barrels per day is reached. Consequently, the cost per barrel of carrying a throughput of 400,000 barrels per day is probably close to the minimum that can be achieved with present pipe-making facilities.

It may also be noted from Chart 6, especially in the case of the large-diameter lines, that throughput can be expanded appreciably over the design throughput before higher per-barrel costs than the original costs are incurred. (For a while, of course, there would actually be a decline in per-barrel costs.) For example, a 24-inch line built for 200,000 barrels per day could, if necessary, later be used for 300,000 barrels per day (after adding the required number of stations) without incurring increased costs per barrel.

Short-run cost curves could be computed for any of the possible combinations of line diameter and horsepower shown in Chart 1 —since each line would have a different short-run cost curve for each throughput it might carry. Building seven stations on an 18-inch line would yield one short-run curve. Building ten stations on an 18-inch line would yield another short-run curve. Building seven stations on a 20-inch line would yield yet another short-run curve—ad infinitum. To avoid the labor involved in computing short-run costs for every combination of line diameter and horsepower covered in the study (75 in all), two were computed: one for an 18-inch line carrying 100,000 barrels per day, another for a 30-inch line carrying 300,000 barrels per day. The relative positions of short- and intermediate-run curves would be the same for any other combinations of line diameter and horsepower. These short-run average cost curves are shown in Chart 7.

Observe that short-run average costs are always higher than intermediate-run average costs for throughputs less than the designed throughput (the short-run curve does not exist for higher throughputs, since pipe lines cannot be operated over the designed capacity without violating the safety factor). The significance of this is that a line built to carry 250,000 barrels per day will incur higher costs than necessary if it consistently carries 200,000 barrels per day. If it had been designed for 200,000

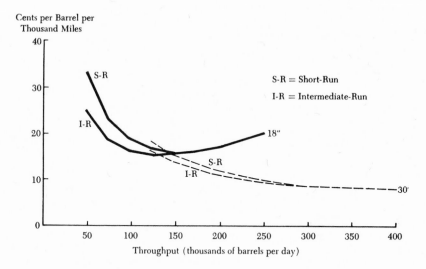

CHART 7

Note: Eighteen-in. line designed for 150,000 barrels per day. Thirty-in. line designed for 300,000 barrels per day.

barrels per day, then the intermediate-run cost for 200,000 barrels per day would be the cost incurred. This figure is less than the short-run cost of 200,000 barrels per day on a line with a capacity of 250,000 barrels per day.

This may be made clear by discussing briefly the process of computation of short-run costs. The only significant cost of a pipe line that is not fixed once the line is built is the cost of electric power. If the line is run below capacity, as many workers are still needed; and, of course, the same number of stations and the same amount of pipe exists. The only significant saving is in power costs. In order to compute short-run costs one simply subtracts the cost of the appropriate amount of electric power which is saved when throughput is cut to various levels from the intermediate-run cost at the designed output. This figure must be higher than intermediate-run costs of lesser throughputs because these costs are computed upon the basis of the proper (smaller) number of stations for the smaller throughputs. It should be noted that a given cut in throughput means a more than proportionate saving in power requirements, since electric power requirements vary with horsepower requirements. Remember that it takes a more than proportionate increase in horsepower to get a given increase in throughput; conversely, a decrease in throughput means a more than proportionate decrease in horsepower required—and hence a more than proportionate decrease in electric power required.

SUMMARY

Intermediate-, long-, and short-run costs for carrying crude oil were computed.

The long- and intermediate-run cost curves computed in a study of the engineering estimation type are of the same shape that would be predicted from the physical production functions for pipe-line transportation of crude (with no consideration of costs). The physical production function is homogeneous of order 2; under these conditions there will be marked economies of scale unless factor prices rise sharply with the amount of the factor used. This is not the case in the range of throughputs and line sizes covered.

The long-run average cost curve falls throughout the range of throughputs covered (see Chart 6), and it would continue to fall indefinitely if larger pipe could be obtained without paying a premium price. However, the rate of decline of long-run costs per barrel has slowed considerably by the time a throughput of 400,000 barrels per day is reached. Intermediate-run curves are U-shaped, but throughput can be increased appreciably over the designed level without increased per-barrel costs—especially ·in the case of large-diameter lines where the "U" is rather flat over wide ranges of throughputs.

Short-run costs are always greater than intermediate-run costs for a given line size. The only significant variable cost in pipe-line operation is the cost of power (or fuel).

It may be concluded from these cost curves that the economies of scale characteristic of the operation of pipe lines require that oil must be carried conglomerately in as large quantities as is possible in large-diameter line. This gives the least transportation costs obtainable—the optimum situation from the point of view of both the firm and society. Furthermore, pipe lines should not be run at throughputs appreciably below capacity; otherwise higher (short-run) costs per barrel will be incurred than need be. Finally, the capacity of a large line can be expanded appreciably without increasing average costs; indeed, *decreased* average costs can be obtained with moderate expansions.

How Cars Are Manufactured

National Research Council

This article comes from The Competitive Status of the U.S. Auto Industry, *published by the National Research Council in 1982.*

The automobile has become an integral part of everyday life for millions of people. What was once looked upon with wonder and awe has become commonplace, a durable consumption good taking its place alongside countless other gadgets and machines that inhabit modern garages and households. Thousands still flood to auto shows to see new and exotic hardware, but the technology in the basic run-of-the-mill automobile is taken for granted.

Yet the car is among the most sophisticated, complex consumer products ever devised. Early gas-powered vehicles were little more than a modified carriage with a crude (by modern standards) engine and chain drive; "horseless carriage" was a quite accurate description. Many years of refinement and development have resulted in an engineering- and technology-intensive product. Major technical systems include the engine with its advanced mechanics and materials, fuel delivery with sophisticated carburetion or fuel injection, automatic transmission and drive train, power-assisted steering and brakes, and complex electronic controls.

The technical complexity of the car is masked by the simplicity of its operation. From the standpoint of the driver, all that is required is a turn of the key, selection of forward or reverse, and pressure on

Note: All footnotes have been omitted from the original article.

the gas pedal. Beneath the sheet metal, behind the gear selector, however, the technical systems must function at high levels of performance, on demand, under extreme conditions, over and over again.

From the beginning of the industry, reliability under pressure and simplicity of operation were important parts of the motivation for increasing complexity and sophistication of the car's technical systems. Reliability, simplicity, and low cost were essential to the development of a true mass market oriented toward basic transportation. In this sense, design changes in the first 20 years of the industry were determined by market demands, and competitive success depended on significant advance in function and performance. At this stage, much of the new-car demand was "first time" purchase, with replacement demand playing a relatively small role.

The rapid and widespread acceptance of the automobile is evidence of the success of engineering and technical developments. As the product matured and basic technologies were refined, the design of basic systems and components was stabilized. The previously dominant need for basic transportation gave way to a more varied, more sophisticated set of demands and consequent segmentation of the market. Vehicles were developed to meet particular functions (e.g., station wagons, sports cars, family sedans). Moreover, within a given function, the use of optional equipment created wide divergence in the potential cost and performance characteristics of similar models.

Table 1 presents a four-segment characterization of the automobile market of the 1970s. The segments range from economy car to luxury/prestige car and are defined primarily in terms of consumer preferences and principal use. The table also contains an assessment of the priorities governing purchase decisions in each segment. Both the segments and the priorities reflect conditions in the mid-1970s before the oil crisis of 1979. Given changes in the relative price of fuel and in household types over the next several years, buyer priorities and segmentation are likely to change. Patterns of change expected for the future are somewhat evident in the shifting pattern of demands by size class over the last 10–12 years.

Although not a perfect measure of the diversity of demands in the postwar era, vehicle size has been an important competitive dimension. Larger cars have been associated with luxury, elegance, and prestige, and many important product innovations were first developed for larger cars and then diffused to the rest of the product line.

TABLE 1

MARKET SEGMENTS (BY MODEL) AND BUYER PRIORITIES IN THE 1970S

	Market Segments			
	Economy cars	*Sporting/ personal cars*	*Family cars*	*Prestige/ luxury cars*
	Chevette	BMW 320i	Fairmont	Audi 5000
	Civic	Camaro	Impala	Jaguar
	Corolla	Celica	LeBaron	Lincoln
	Omni	Cutlass Coupe	LTD	Mercedes-Benz
	Pinto	Grand Prix	Regal	Seville
	Rabbit	Mustang		
		Thunderbird		
Priorities				
Price	X	X	X	
Fuel economy	X			
Interior room			X	
Comfort			X	X
Reliability	X		X	X
Acceleration		X		
Handling		X		
Styling		X		X
Interior trim		X		X
Workmanship				X

SOURCE: Adapted from Arthur D. Little, Inc., *The Changing World Automotive Industry Through 2000*, 1980, pp. 24–25.

The dominance of the large car reached its zenith in the late 1960s. With the onset of higher operating costs the structure of demand in terms of vehicle size has shifted dramatically.

Table 2 presents data on new car sales by size class for selected years since 1967. The data document the sizeable shift in the structure of demand that occurred in the 1970s. In 1967 over 70 percent of new car sales were in the intermediate and standard categories, while the subcompact group, which includes imports, accounted for 9.3 percent. By early 1980 the subcompact group dominated the market, while standard models held fast at 12.5 percent of the market.

The shift to smaller cars has been well publicized, but the timing of the change and the patterns of adjustment within the large-car ranks (intermediate, standard, luxury) deserve emphasis. It is clear from Table 2 that the largest change in the share of standard models

TABLE 2

STRUCTURE OF NEW CAR SALES

Year			Size Class		
	Subcompact[a]	Compact	Intermediate	Standard	Luxury
1967	9.3	15.7	23.6	47.9	3.1
1972	22.7	15.4	21.7	36.1	3.4
1973	24.9	17.7	23.0	30.0	3.6
1974	28.4	20.0	24.2	22.6	3.7
1975	32.4	20.3	24.1	17.9	4.0
1976	26.1	23.5	27.3	19.4	3.7
1977	27.1	21.2	26.9	19.4	4.6
1978	26.4	21.6	26.8	18.4	5.5
1979	34.0	20.0	24.2	15.3	5.5
1980[b]	42.0	20.2	20.6	12.5	4.7

SOURCE: *Ward's Automotive Year Book*, Annual Reports, Detroit, Michigan.
[a] Includes imports.
[b] January and February.

occurred in 1974, but the downward trend was evident long before OPEC quadrupled the price of crude oil. From 1967 to 1972, for example, the large-car share fell from 71.5 to 57.8 percent, with most of the decline coming from the standard group. At the same time the share of subcompacts more than doubled to reach 22 percent. The shifts evident in the pre-1973 data set the pattern for the rest of the decade: a dramatic decline in the share of standard-size vehicles, a rise in subcompacts (including imports), and only modest changes in the share of other categories.

THE MANUFACTURING PROCESS

Changes in the structure of demand in the 1970s have had a profound impact on manufacturing facilities and processes. Transforming equipment, plants, and organization geared to the production of large road cruisers into a system for the design of much smaller and more efficient cars cannot be accomplished overnight. The expense and difficulty reflects the complexity, scale, and integration of the automobile production process. Indeed, the complexity and sophistication of the car itself pale in comparison to the organization and technology used to design, produce, and deliver the finished product to the market. Manufacturing involves the production or purchase of over 10,000 parts, combining parts into components and systems, and the coordination of all this activity so that the right systems and components can be assembled to produce an automobile. The basic structure of production in the industry is shown in Figure 1. The figure includes activities in the chain of supply from raw materials to final assembly.

Perhaps the dominant characteristic of the automobile production process is the importance of economies of scale. Over the last 70 years the production process has become increasingly mechanized, automated, and capital intensive. Indeed, the classic illustration of automation in U.S. industry is the modern automobile engine plant.

The modern engine plant can be seen as the outcome of an evolutionary progression from the general-purpose job-shop environment that characterized early engine manufacture. The highly specialized, capital-intensive process in today's plants reflects a strategic orientation toward low-cost production of a standardized product. Choices about equipment and process have created a setup in which high volumes are essential to low cost. Existing estimates of the minimum efficient scale in engine production range from 350,000 to 500,000 units per year, depending on the particular technology employed.

FIGURE 1

THE STRUCTURE OF PRODUCTION IN THE AUTOMOBILE INDUSTRY

PROCESS SEGMENT

Process Flow	Raw Materials[a]	→	Material Processing[b]	→	Components[b]	→	Systems and Subassembly[c]	→	Final Assembly[c]

| Basic Sectors | Iron and steel
Aluminum
Silicon
Plastics
Fibers
Alloys | Castings
Forging
Plastic
  forming
Glass
  forming
Stamping | Bearings
Batteries
Spark plugs
Shocks
Tires
Exhaust
Carburetor
Trim
Wheels
Brakes | Engine
Transmission
Axles
Suspension
Steering
Frame
Body | Completed automobile |

[a] Predominantly suppliers.   [c] Predominantly OEM.
[b] Mixed OEM/suppliers.

Engine plants are more automated than many of the processes in automobile manufacture, but the dependence of low cost on high volume is characteristic of all of them. In general, manufacturing policy has been oriented toward increased standardization and specialization in manufacturing operations and consequent reliance on high volume. At the same time, employment in jobs not directly related to production has increased substantially, possibly reflecting the growing complexity of coordination problems and changing regulatory requirements. In addition, the fixed component of engineering and research and development costs has grown under regulatory pressure and the need for new design initiatives. The net effect of these developments has been to enhance the importance of scale in the determination of profitability and competitive advantage.

The Plant Network: An Illustration · The basic structure of the overall manufacturing process, and in particular the plant network, can be illustrated by considering the impact of changes in the marketplace as demand has shifted to smaller, more efficient cars. The shift in demand has been met by "downsizing," by changes in basic components (e.g., shift from rear-wheel to front-wheel drive) and by material substitution. Though each change may have a direct impact on only part of the car, or a part of the manufacturing process, the various types of facilities are so tightly linked that even a small change can have major ramifications.

The key facilities in the manufacturing process and their linkages are illustrated in Figure 2. Though highly simplified, the diagram captures the basic relationships among the manufacture of materials (e.g., steel, aluminum, plastic), components (e.g., steering gears, brakes), systems (e.g., engines, transmission), and final assembly. The automobile companies [hereafter, OEMs (original equipment manufacturers)] do final assembly in their own facilities, and they generally produce major systems (engines, transmission) in-house; most materials and many components (e.g., brakes, steering assemblies, valves) are purchased from suppliers. The extent of integration varies significantly by company and even by model. It is not uncommon for OEMs to produce part of their need for a component in-house, while maintaining additional sources outside.

FIGURE 2

THE IMPACT OF DOWNSIZING ON PRODUCTION FACILITIES

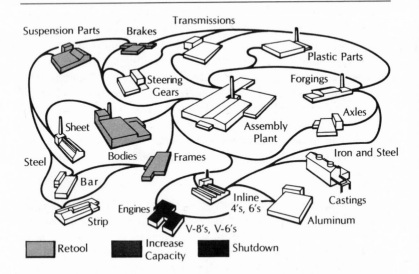

In Figure 2 the impact of "downsizing" is indicated by the cross hatches on various facilities. "Downsizing" involves all new body sheet metal (retool stamping plants), a shift to V-6 engines (change engine lines), smaller and lighter components (retooling at several plants—axles, suspension, brakes, and so forth), and new frames. The changes culminate in the final assembly plant, which requires some new fixtures and tooling. It is not hard to see why such changes require several hundred million dollars and take a few years to accomplish. Yet "downsizing" has a relatively modest impact on the manufacturing process in comparison to the redesign of basic components. The impact of moving from rear- to front-wheel drive and the introduction of unit body construction are illustrated in Figure 3. These changes in drive train and frame are accompanied by changes in several major components, as follows: (*a*) Elimination of the rear axle and addition of a new rear suspension; (*b*) Replacement of the standard V-8 engine with V-6 and IL-4 engines; (*c*) Elimination of the drive shaft and transmission and replacement with transaxle and twin front-wheel-drive shafts; (*d*) Addition of new suspension (McPherson struts) and steering (rack and pinion).

FIGURE 3

THE IMPACT OF BASIC COMPONENT REDESIGN ON PRODUCTION FACILITIES.

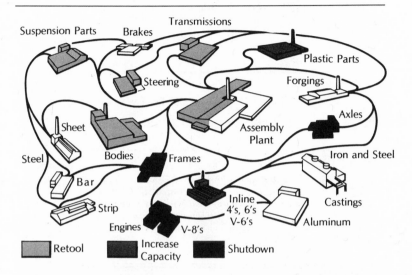

The impact on facilities is widespread: engine, frame, and axle plants are shut down, and major retooling occurs in the production of transmission bodies and other components. The significant capital adjustments, however, involve only modest use of new materials and do not require major changes in manufacturing processes. Future changes in design and in the use of new materials could have even more far-reaching effects. We have already seen the introduction of electronics, which adds another type of process and facility to the overall system. Increased use of plastics, composites, and lightweight metals could make older facilities and processes obsolete and require new manufacturing capabilities.

Cost Functions and Cost Control

Edwin Mansfield and Harold H. Wein

Edwin Mansfield is Professor of Economics at the University of Pennsylvania. Harold H. Wein is Professor of Management at Michigan State University. This paper is taken from their article in Applied Statistics.

There have been numerous studies where the relationship between cost and output has been estimated for manufacturing plants. These studies fall generally into two categories. In the first category, the chief purpose of the work has been to accumulate evidence concerning various cost curves that occupy an important place in economics. In the second category, the work has been done primarily with a view toward the direct usefulness of the relationship of cost and output to industrial managers. This paper falls into the second category.

We give an illustration here of how such a relationship may be used to formulate a simple control chart for costs, a topic which should be of interest to many applied statisticians and industrial managers. The problem of controlling performance and costs is important in almost every sector of industry and trade. Our data, and hence our specific results, pertain to the American railroad industry, but the statistical techniques that are used may be applicable to other industries as well.

Freight yards differ greatly in size, layout, and type, but they have certain physical characteristics and functions in common.

Physical Characteristics · All yards contain sets of tracts. In large yards they are generally of three types: receiving tracks where incoming freight cars are stored, classification tracks where cars are switched, and outbound tracks where cars that were situated on a classification track are stored until a locomotive hauls them away as a train.

Functions · Freight yards switch cars. That is, they sort incoming cars by putting them on the appropriate classification tracks, and in this way they break up incoming trains to form new trains. Most yards also deliver and pick up cars. Engines are assigned to deliver cars to industrial sidings and other yards and to pick them up there. Finally, many yards bill and inspect freight cars and perform such ancillary services as maintenance, repair, and storage.

The importance of freight yards to a railroad is illustrated by the fact that about one-third of its total operating costs may arise in these yards. In view of this, it is clearly important that proper control be maintained over the performance of the yards. However, this problem of maintaining adequate control is made difficult by their number and their distribution over a large area. (For example, in the railroad we studied, about 200 freight yards are scattered along approximately 12,000 miles of track.) It is virtually impossible for any team of managers to have each day a reasonably complete knowledge of what happened at each yard. They must examine selected data concerning the performance of the yards during the day, and from these data they must somehow evaluate a yard's performance. In evaluating performance, one piece of information that is used is the costs incurred in the yard during the day.

At present, the data and techniques used by most railroads do not seem well suited for their purpose. Judging by the opinions of the railroad management with which we worked, their purpose is to detect those days when the costs at a yard are unusually high for the output produced and those series of days when the costs are repeatedly higher than would be expected. Detection of either of these would result in an inquiry concerning the causes of the apparent deterioration of yard performance. In addition, the management is interested in detecting days when costs are unusually low or when they are repeatedly lower than would be expected. In this case there would also be an inquiry, but the intention would be to encourage the responsible factors rather than to remedy them.

In this paper we discuss a control chart based on the relationship between cost and output that may be useful for these purposes. Before discussing the chart, it seems worthwhile to describe the measures of freight-yard output and costs that are used. The two most important services performed at a yard are switching and delivery; and it seems reasonable to use the number of "cuts" switched and the number of cars delivered during a particular period as a measure of output. A "cut" is a group of cars that rolls as a unit on to the same classification track; it is often used as a measure of switching output. The number of cars delivered includes both the cars delivered to sidings and other yards and those that are picked up. This output measure is not ideal, one difficulty being that it conceals considerable heterogeneity. For example, two groups of cars may be delivered but one may be hauled a greater distance than the other. Some of this heterogeneity could be eliminated by further refinements in the output measure, but the extra complexity with regard to data collection and computation might result in a loss of feasibility.

The costs used here include all money costs incurred in the yard except fixed charges, repair costs, maintenance and storage costs, and vacation costs. Only money costs are included; the costs that may be imputed to car delay are not taken into account. Fixed charges are excluded, but some of the included costs are essentially fixed in the very short run.

THE CONTROL CHART

The control chart contains the deviation of actual cost from the cost that would be expected on the basis of the average relationship between cost and output. These deviations are used to detect days when costs are suspiciously high or low. The model that underlies the chart is as follows: for a particular yard, the expected cost on the i'th day (C_i) is assumed to be a linear function of the number of cuts switched on the i'th day (S_i) and the number of cars delivered on the i'th day (D_i).

When the railroad management refer to unusually high or low costs, it seems clear that they mean costs that are unusual if the cost-output relationship and the effects of numerous small disturbances remain at their previous, satisfactory levels. That is, they are interested in detecting those C_i that are unusually high or low if the average relationship between cost and output is unchanged. Similarly, when they refer to a sequence of days when costs are higher or lower than would be expected, it seems clear that they mean a run of the C_i that is unlikely if this relationship is unchanged.

If the model is adequate and if the average relationship between cost and output is known, it is a simple matter to set up a control chart that will aid the management. Each day, the deviation of actual cost from the cost that would be expected on the basis of this relationship can be plotted on a chart that has two sets of control limits. The outer control limits can be set so that, if this relationship remains the same, the probability that a point lies outside them is small. The inner control limits can be set so that, if this relationship remains the same, the probability that two consecutive points lie outside them (in one direction) is small. When a point lies outside the outer limits or a pair of points lies outside the inner limits, there is evidence that the relationship may have changed and that an inquiry should be made.

SETTING UP THE CHART

A control chart was set up at a freight yard located at Toledo, Ohio. This yard constitutes one of the largest and most important links in the railroad we studied. The chief types of freight that pass through the yard are livestock, perishables, coal, and automobiles. Table 1 shows the number of cars switched,

TABLE 1

OUTPUT, COST, AND EMPLOYMENT, FREIGHT
YARD, TOLEDO, 7 DAYS
(*Taken from records of cooperating railroad*)

Item	Fri.	Sat.	Sun.	Mon.	Tues.	Wed.	Thurs.
Number of cuts switched	869	792	762	586	669	732	659
Number of cars switched	2534	2303	2521	1849	2090	2114	1979
Number of cars delivered *	1015	1003	820	548	877	706	1038
Number of crews used	45	45	40	38	46	46	46
Number of engine hours	372	369	329	309	385	381	386
Money costs ($)	7523	7464	6932	6550	7606	7757	7701

* Includes number of cars picked up.

the number of cuts switched, the number of cars delivered, the number of crews employed, the number of engine hours used, and the costs at the yard, for a sample one-week period.

The first step in setting up the chart was to gather historical data concerning cost and output. Data similar to those in Table 1 were collected for sixty-one days, and the average relationship between cost and output was estimated. The resulting relationship was

$$(1) \qquad C_i = 4{,}914 + 0.42S_i + 2.44D_i$$

The second step was to test some of the assumptions underlying the chart. Some of these tests are quite similar to those used in quality control to determine if the process is "in control." Taken together, the results of these tests did not cast any great suspicion on the assumptions underlying the chart. Indeed, the results seemed to be quite compatible with these assumptions.

The third step was to draw the inner and outer control limits on the chart. The outer control limits were set at ± \$804, and the inner control limits were set at ± \$410. These limits (designated by ICL and OCL) are included in Figure 1. If there were no errors in the assumptions, the probability would be 0.05

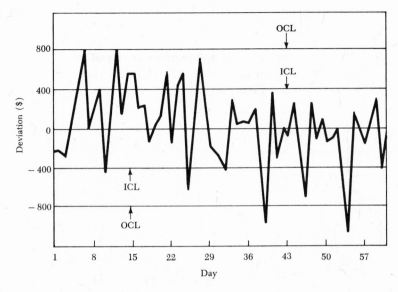

FIGURE 1

DEVIATION OF ACTUAL COST FROM EXPECTED COST BASED ON
AVERAGE RELATIONSHIP BETWEEN COST AND OUTPUT:
FREIGHT YARD, 61 DAYS
Source: records of cooperating railroad.

that a point would lie outside the outer limits if the relationship remained fixed. Similarly, the probability would be about 0.03 that two consecutive points would lie outside the same inner control limit.

After setting the control limits, an attempt was made to determine if any assignable cause could be found for the days that were "out of control." None could be found, and it was assumed that they were due to "chance." The number of such days was almost precisely what one would expect on a chance basis.

PERFORMANCE OF THE CHART

This section describes the performance of the chart during a six-week period that was several months subsequent to the time when the chart was set up. The results apply to the freight yard described above. On each day during the period data were collected concerning the money costs (C), the number of cuts switched (S), and the number of cars delivered (D) on the previous day. Then the deviation of actual cost from expected cost based on the average relationship in equation (1) was computed and plotted on the chart.[1] The deviations that were plotted are shown in Figure 2.

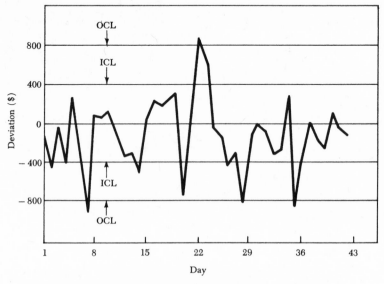

FIGURE 2

CONTROL CHART FOR COSTS: FREIGHT YARD, 42 DAYS
Source: records of cooperating railroad.

During the six-week period, four days seemed to be out of control, and in every case there seemed to be an assignable cause. One of these days was Labor Day. The exceptionally high costs on Labor Day can be attributed to the punitive wage-rates that were paid because it was a holiday. On the other days that were out of control (all of them Sundays) the exceptionally low costs can be attributed in part to the following circumstances: (1) Cars delivered to other yards constituted a large proportion of all cars delivered, and since such cars are rela-

1. Actually, the relationship was recomputed as more and more data became available.

tively easy to deliver, costs were depressed. (2) More efficient methods were used to handle incoming cars. (3) Some work ordinarily performed by the yard was done by another yard; hence costs were reduced somewhat.

The basic data were collected by railroad employees and the points on the chart were computed by officials of the railroad. From their evaluation of the performance of the yard it appeared that the chart provided a reasonably faithful picture of the level of performance. Moreover, the chart stimulated some inquiries that indicated where improvements in yard performance might be made.

To increase further the usefulness of the chart, it appeared that cars delivered to other yards might be separated in the output measure from cars delivered to industrial sidings. In this way an important factor (and in some ways an extraneous one) responsible in part for the low deviations on Sundays would be taken into account. No finality can be claimed for the results, but it appeared that the chart would be useful to the management in controlling yard costs.

Part Three

Demand, Pricing, and Corporate Strategy

FIRMS must constantly be concerned with demand, pricing, and strategy, the topics of Part Three. Thus, it behooves anyone interested in managerial economics to study these topics carefully. The opening article, taken from *Fortune*, describes the break-even chart, the diagram that projects a firm's revenues and costs at various levels of sales. To illustrate its use, two hypothetical cases are taken up. The next two papers are concerned with demand and pricing. One of the first things a firm must consider in pricing its product is the price elasticity of demand. The editor's paper discusses the nature and determinants of this elasticity and describes why it is of major importance. Next, A. D. H. Kaplan, Joel B. Dirlam, and Robert F. Lanzillotti show how a firm's pricing policy is influenced by the character of its product—the type of demand to which it caters, its physical attributes, production requirements, amenability to differentiation, and stage of maturity.

Michael E. Porter points out that "strategic interaction among firms is often guided by a strategy, or a coordinated plan consisting of a set of economic (and sometimes noneconomic) objectives and time-dimensioned policies in each functional area of the firm (e.g., marketing, production, distribution, and so on). . . ." His article discusses various important aspects of corporate strategy and interaction. In the following paper, published by the National Research Council, the nature of competition in the pharmaceutical industry is analyzed. Finally, in the last paper, the strategies of the Big Three of the auto industry—General Motors, Ford, and Chrysler—are discussed.

A Note on Break-Even Charts

Fortune MAGAZINE

This article appeared in Fortune, *one of America's leading business magazines.*

Essentially, the break-even chart is a graphic presentation of the relationship between revenue and expense, projected for all levels of sales. There is nothing complicated or novel about such a chart. Progressive managements have used this or similar visual aids for years. The break-even chart is no substitute for either detailed accountancy or management judgment.

The basic chart (Chart 1) was developed some forty years ago by Professor Walter Rautenstrauch of the Industrial Engineering Department of Columbia University. It is the great granddaddy of the many sales-profit charts in use today, and is, in some respects, superior to them. The 45-degree sales line makes it possible to plot the break-even points for any number of years or months on a single chart, and to compare charts for different companies, products, etc. A prerequisite to the construction of this or any other break-even chart, however, is a knowledge of which business expenses are constant and which are variable with changes in volume. Once that is known a total-expense line can be drawn for all levels of sales. Few firms customarily break down their costs in this manner, however. Take, for example, the remuneration paid a salesman. Normal accountancy would probably lump his commissions, salary, and bonus together as sales expense. Actually, however, his commission is a variable

CHART 1 FINDING XYZ COMPANY'S BREAK-EVEN POINT

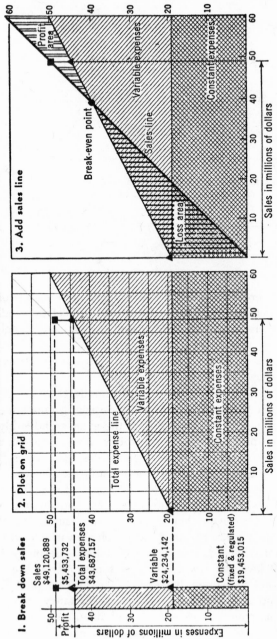

1. Break down sales

Sales $49,120,889
Profit $5,433,732
Total expenses $43,687,157
Variable $24,234,142
Constant (fixed & regulated) $19,453,015

Expenses in millions of dollars

2. Plot on grid

Total expense line
Variable expenses
Constant expenses
Sales in millions of dollars

3. Add sales line

Break-even point
Profit area
Sales line
Loss area
Variable expenses
Constant expenses
Sales in millions of dollars

The construction of a break-even chart involves three simple steps. Step 1: Expenses that vary directly with volume (materials, sales commissions, etc.) are segregated from constant expenses (real-estate taxes, depreciation, interest, etc.). Step 2: The total expense line is then plotted on a grid with identical horizontal and vertical dollar scales. Step 3: A sales line is superimposed on this grid forming a 45-degree angle with both scales. That this method of plotting the break-even point is accurate is attested by the fact that the computed break-even volume for the company above (an actual firm) was $38.4 million.

CHART 2

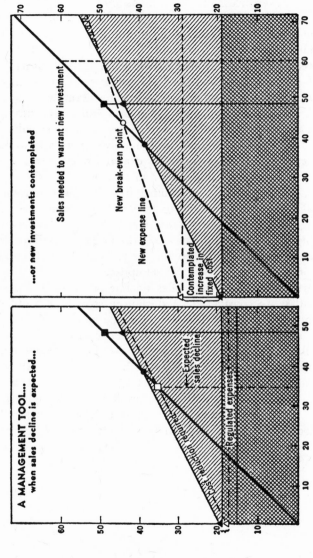

The hypothetical cases above illustrate two of the many ways a break-even chart can be used in management planning. If sales decline $15 million (left) a $4-million loss will result unless costs are cut. If, on the other hand, an investment is contemplated that will increase constant expense by $10 million (right) it can be seen that sales of $60 million are needed to justify the new expense structure.

expense, his salary a constant expense, and his bonus a regulated expense; i.e., although constant in that it is not directly related to sales, it is nevertheless subject to management discretion. The trick of constructing an accurate break-even chart, then, is largely dependent upon proper cost analysis, but that is equally true when the break-even point is computed.

The break-even chart is like a household tape measure. It has many practical uses and yet does not pretend to be microscopically accurate. The total-expense line, for example, is simply a straight line drawn from fixed costs at volume zero through total cost at current volume. No attempt is made at curvilinear refinement because cost figures are themselves mere approximations. Nor can valid deductions be drawn from a break-even chart at volumes widely different from that on which the chart is based. It is important to remember that the chart represents expense at a given moment and under given conditions and that any change in price, wages, *et al.*, will alter the sales-expense relationship. If these limitations are borne in mind, however, the break-even chart can be used to analyze and control costs and to estimate profits under a variety of assumptions.

In Chart 2, the effect of a sales decline or of an additional capital outlay are considered. A decline in sales of $15 million would obviously put the firm into the red unless regulatable expenses (research, promotion, the president's salary, etc.) were cut $4 million. In the other case it is assumed that a contemplated investment will increase constant cost by $10 million but will reduce variable expenses. The chart quickly shows at what volume the new investment becomes profitable. Although these charts are for an entire company, break-even charts can also be constructed for individual departments, plants, products, or even salesmen.

The Importance of the Price Elasticity of Demand

EDWIN MANSFIELD

Edwin Mansfield is Director of the Center for Economics and Technology at the University of Pennsylvania. This article was written for the present volume.

The price elasticity of demand is the percentage change in the quantity demanded that results from a 1 percent increase in price. A sharp distinction should be made between an industry's elasticity and a particular firm's elasticity. Whereas the former gauges the sensitivity of total industry demand to industry-wide changes in price, the latter shows the sensitivity of demand for a particular firm's product to changes in its price, the price set by other firms in the industry being held constant. A firm's elasticity depends heavily on the similarity of its product to that of competitors. For instance, a Gulf station is likely to lose a considerable share of its market to a neighboring Esso station whose price is half a cent a gallon less.

The price elasticity of demand is of great importance to the firm. When costs are increasing, it is tempting for the firm to pass on the increases by raising the price to the consumer. If demand for the product is relatively inelastic,[1] this action may succeed.

1. Demand at a particular price is said to be inelastic if the price elasticity is less than one in absolute value. In this case, total revenue decreases with decreases in price.

However, when there are many substitutes and demand is quite elastic,[2] increasing prices may lead to a reduction in total revenues rather than an increase. The result may be lower rather than higher profits. Similarly, businessmen are sometimes surprised by a lack of success of price reductions, this merely being a reflection of the fact that demand is relatively inelastic.

Most businessmen intuitively are aware of the elasticity of demand of the goods they make, although they may not have a detailed, precise estimate. Nonetheless, some firms tend to be conservative and underestimate the elasticity of demand. For example, classical phonograph records were high-priced luxury items for a long time. In 1938, Columbia cut the price per record from $2 to $1, and the response was overwhelming. To the surprise of much of the industry, total expenditure on classical records rose greatly, the price elasticity of demand being relatively large.

Using techniques like those described in "Estimating the Price Elasticity of Demand," it is possible to estimate the price elasticity of demand for a particular product. Some of the results are shown in Table 1. As would be expected, the price elasticity of demand for basic foodstuffs is relatively low. For sugar, potatoes, hay, and wheat, it is less than 0.5 percent in absolute value. That is, a 1 percent increase in the price of these products will result in less than a 0.5 percent decrease in the quantity consumed. On the other hand, the demand for millinery is quite elastic, a 1 percent increase in price leading to a 3 percent decrease in quantity consumed.

One of the most important factors influencing the price elasticity of demand is the availability of substitutes. If a product is faced with extremely close substitutes, its demand will be very elastic. For example, take the case of the Gulf and Esso dealers cited above. Their products, location, and services are so similar that a very small differential in price will result in a considerable shift in sales. On the other hand, in the case of basic foodstuffs such close substitutes do not exist, the result being that the price elasticity of demand is much lower.

2. Demand at a particular price is said to be elastic if the price elasticity is greater than one in absolute value, in which case total revenue increases with decreases in price.

TABLE 1

ESTIMATED PRICE ELASTICITIES OF DEMAND FOR SELECTED
COMMODITIES, UNITED STATES

Product	Price elasticity
beef	—0.92
millinery	—3.00
gasoline	—0.52
sugar	—0.31
corn	—0.49
cotton	—0.12
hay	—0.43
wheat	—0.08
potatoes	—0.31
oats	—0.56
barley	—0.39
buckwheat	—0.99

Source: H. Schultz, *Theory and Measurement of Demand* (Chicago: University of Chicago Press, 1938), and M. Spencer and L. Siegelman, *Managerial Economics* (Homewood, Ill.: Richard D. Irwin, 1959).

Finally, to illustrate very briefly the sorts of studies that have been made of the price elasticity of demand, consider a study of the fare structure of the New York subway and its effect on passenger travel. Table 2 gives forecasts of demand and revenues

TABLE 2

ALTERNATIVE ESTIMATES OF DEMAND CURVE FOR SUBWAY
SERVICE

(passengers and revenues in millions per year)

	Case A		Case B		Case C		Case D	
Fare (cents)	Passengers	Revenues	Passengers	Revenues	Passengers	Revenues	Passengers	Revenues
5	1945	$97.2	1945	$97.2	1945	$97.2	1945	$97.2
10	1683	168.3	1683	168.3	1683	168.3	1683	168.3
15	1421	213.2	1458	218.7	1530	229.5	1547	232.0
20	1159	231.8	1262	252.4	1421	284.2	1457	291.5
25	897	224.2	1092	273.0	1347	336.8	1390	348.2
30	635	190.5	945	283.5	1278	383.4	1340	402.0

Source: W. S. Vickrey, *The Revision of the Rapid Transit Fare Structure of the City of New York* (Technical Monograph No. 3, Finance Project, Mayor's Committee on Management Survey of the City of New York), p. 87.

based on various fare levels. In Case A, quantity demanded was
a linear function of price, i.e.,

$$q = a - bp$$

where q is quantity demanded and p is price. In Case B,

$$\log q = a - bp.$$

In Case C,

$$q = a - b \log p.$$

And in Case D,

$$\log q = a - b \log p.$$

The author concludes that Case B probably represents the most
reasonable case. We are not concerned here with the methods
used to derive such estimates or with the factors that prompted
him to choose Case B over the others. Methods of estimation
are discussed in the subsequent paper. For present purposes,
the important thing is the relevance of the information provided
in Table 2 to decisions that must be made by the firm. Table 2
shows that the demand for this product is inelastic—and the
extent to which it is inelastic. In determining its price policy,
the New York Transit Authority would do well to recognize this
fact. Although price reductions for some items, like Columbia's
records, may be profitable, in this case they will reduce both
revenues and profits.

Pricing and the Character of the Product

A. D. H. KAPLAN, JOEL B. DIRLAM, AND ROBERT F. LANZILLOTTI

A. D. H. Kaplan was a senior economist at the Brookings Institution. Together with Joel B. Dirlam and Robert F. Lanzillotti, he wrote Pricing in Big Business *from which the following paper is taken.*

The character of the product—the type of demand to which it caters, as well as its physical attributes, production requirements, amenability to differentiation, and stage of maturity—sets boundaries to the pricing discretion of the company, big or little. When interpreting the role of product characteristics, however, the possibility that reaction may run both ways must be kept in mind. These characteristics are not fixed or unadjustable. They themselves may be affected by price. But the basic concern at this point is with pricing policies that seem to be imposed by the nature of the product, rather than vice versa.

With a product like fresh meat, perishable and subject to unpredictable output and shipments of the primary commodity, even a firm of the importance of Swift & Company has a limited opportunity to bend wholesale prices to company policy. A durable product with controlled raw material output, and production based on orders, better lends itself to fairly stable price quotations, as in steel or crude oil. Copper, on the contrary, with its volatile price behavior points up the effect on the manageability of prices of a widely diffused raw material supply and a world market. Limitations on the transportability of the product (transportation cost in relation to product value) may give locational advantage in pricing even when there are business giants in the industry.

New products, with varying degrees of marketable uniqueness, provide opportunities for pricing discretion not generally available in standardized goods. Large companies whose resources are concentrated in established standard products are aware of the general unprofitability of price wars when confronted with similarly large and resourceful competitors; hence they keep in step with the competition on price and depend on such factors as favorable location, or availability of adequate supplies and satisfactory service to customers, for their competitive strength at the going price. In the use of these devices, however, product features (*e.g.*, vulnerability to substitution) may determine how successful a stable price policy can be, even for the large and resourceful company.

New Products and Matured Products · The natural frame of reference for pricing a new product is the price range of existing substitutes. For example, it was recognized that nylon was capable of penetrating the markets of a variety of textile fibers. The problem of effectively introducing this new fiber resolved itself through a compromise between pricing for the widest possible use and pricing for the more limited, but in the long run, more sustainable and profitable quality market. In cellophane, the same company reached more aggressively for more extensive market penetration without undermining the profit potential. Apparently, the cost elasticity of volume output and the price elasticity of growing demand were sufficiently high to permit a more rapid rate of expansion than was possible in nylon. The introduction of a major consumer appliance, for which demand is as yet an expectation rather than a reality, has entailed elaborate market research to select a price niche that will permit the inclusion of features required for optimum acceptance. In the pricing of a major piece of farm machinery such as the cotton picker, the decision settles on a middle ground between the estimated maximum economic value as a replacement for hand labor and a sufficiently low price to give assurance of widespread adoption. Prices determined in this manner may well limit the components that can be selected for incorporation in the assembled product; automobiles and other consumer durables considered earlier were cases in point. With the accumulation of know-how and the lowering of costs, subsequent pricing turns on whether the product can readily be imitated, whether the prestige acquired in its pioneering can be prolonged through improvement and product differentiation, or whether lower cost reflected in lower price will open up a highly profitable volume increase.

An established standard product, be it a metal, flour, or heavy chemical, does not entail such conscious balancing of alternative possibilities to fix its price levels. The price may start from a fairly well-recognized cost base, but the profit is a residual reflecting the current willingness or ability of the market to keep the capacity employed. Large firms with heavy investments in established areas of primary production have constantly feared that price changes will lead to hazards of unpredictable magnitude. This fear has often been justified in the past—witness the gyrations of price with accompanying demand fluctuations in copper, lead, or zinc; and even with price leadership, boom and depression fluctuations in steel prices have not been unknown. There is in consequence an undercurrent of antipathy in the firms interviewed to policies that would disturb the pattern of stable and infrequently changing prices. The instability of copper prices is certainy not due to lack of desire on the part of Kennecott and other primary producers to keep firm the price of their metal. The volatility issues rather from the fickleness of a world market, in which fluctuation is accentuated by extremes of overflow or scarcity in the supply of copper scrap.

At least until the Second World War, Alcoa supplied and priced aluminum in the United States with some regard to the fact that it had to penetrate the markets of copper and other metals as well as some non-metallic products. Its technical development in a capital-intensive form with integrated production and standardization of finished products now tends to assert itself; so that while product promotion remains vigorous, pricing in the basic aluminum lines is showing resemblances to steel's pattern of base prices and extras.

The type of use to which a product is put also has a bearing on the importance attached to price variations. The stable pricing of containers carried by American Can and Continental Can has met with little resistance by their customers, and this is not solely because of the duopoly leadership in can manufacture; it is largely due to the fact that what the final user is buying is not the container but the contents. Similarly, flexible packaging materials, aluminum fabrications, special electrical equipment items, and industrial gases permit the manufacturer a minimum of concern with price competition because these are products sold as part—an incidental part—of the larger end product in which the cost of the contributing item is not a prime consideration.

Cost Structure · Production and cost characteristics of the main product play a primary role in conditioning pricing policies. The overriding importance of certain materials in the total cost structure, as in the case of tin plate for can manufacture; the leanness of the ore, and the consequent magnitude of the mining operations of Kennecott Copper; the relatively small runs and large number of items, as in the case of Alcoa's fabricated operations; and of course the high proportion of indirect cost in basic steel production—all these distinctive features are transmuted into pricing policy. U. S. Steel seeks to avoid cutthroat price competition, and evolves a fair return philosophy. Alcoa finds a standard cost system unusable for many items. Kennecott, when prices drop, has to pile up inventory and await more settled prices; it looks with favor on stabilized prices. American Can, and perhaps even the oil companies, in the long run, become transmission belts for passing material and labor costs on to consumers with an inelastic demand. Thus a large part of price policy may be the response to the cost pattern inherent to the product.

Strategic Interaction
Among Firms

Michael E. Porter

Michael E. Porter is a professor at the Graduate School of Business Administration at Harvard University. This paper appeared in Strategy, Predation, and Antitrust Analysis *(edited by Steven Salop), published by the Federal Trade Commission in 1981.*

I. THE CONCEPT OF STRATEGY

Industry histories show that strategic interaction among firms is often guided by a strategy, or a coordinated plan consisting of a set of economic (and sometimes noneconomic) objectives and time-dimensioned policies in each functional area of the firm (e.g., marketing, production, distribution, and so on) to achieve these objectives. The objectives and policies are simultaneously determined and reflect the firm's assessment of its capabilities and limitations relative to competitors and its search for a distinctive competitive advantage. Since each firm is seen as a unique collection of tangible and intangible assets and skills built up through its past activities, the emphasis in strategy formulation is in staking out a position based on the firm's unique capabilities that can be defended (that is, which possesses mobility barriers—see below) against competitors. Strategic interaction among firms is the playing out of strategies over time through investment decisions and tactical moves and countermoves. Successful strategies are those that are internally consistent and accurately reflect the firm's strengths and weaknesses relative to its competitors and its competitors' expected behavior. . . .

II. STRATEGIC HETEROGENEITY

Industry histories and my discussion of strategy highlight the fact that firms compete with quite heterogeneous strategies, despite the fact that they are in the same industry. Heterogeneous strategies reflect firms' efforts to achieve a sustainable competitive advantage, given their differing and evolving bundles of tangible and intangible assets and skills, as well as the presence in many industries of market segments consisting of clusters of buyers who place differing weights on the market attributes under a firm's control (product characteristics, price, marketing practices, distribution channel, et cetera). A necessary corollary to these sources of strategic heterogeneity is that the pattern of strategies being followed in an industry will often shift over time and vary from industry to industry.

As I have argued elsewhere, heterogeneous strategies imply diverse bases for market power of different firms in the same industry. The notion of entry barriers protecting all incumbents in an industry must be supplanted by a broader concept of mobility barriers, or factors that deter other firms from replicating a particular strategic configuration. Strategic interaction, then, is the process by which firms seek to get behind or create sustainable mobility barriers. Within the same industry, firms with different strategies will possess differing types of mobility barriers as well as mobility barriers of varying overall height. . . .

III. DYNAMIC COST REDUCTION

The recent attention in corporate planning on strategies based on the "experience curve" has emphasized the importance of dynamic cost reduction in strategic interaction. Much of the recent discussion has centered around the so-called "experience curve." The term "experience curve," popularized by the Boston Consulting Group (BCG), mixes together two familiar but quite disparate phenomena—(static) economies of scale and (dynamic) product and process technological changes (learning) that lower cost. These together, holds BCG, propel real costs down in proportion to the firm's cumulative production volume.

For purposes of understanding strategic interaction, the BCG formulation is unsatisfying because it mixes static economies of scale, learning that depends on time, and learning that depends on cumulative production volume. Because the operation of static economies of scale is well known, I will concentrate here on the learning aspects.

Learning reduces costs over time as the firm discovers how to do things better in product design, process layout, job design for workers, machine operating rates, organizational coordination, and the like. Thus, firm learning can be very broadly based and involves managerial as well as technological dimensions. Some learning and the associated product and process changes can increase possibilities for static economies of scale, while other learning leads to absolute cost improvements.

There are three plausible ways to formulate the rate of learning, with very different implications for strategic interaction: (*a*) as a function of cumulative volume; (*b*) as a function of time in the industry; (*c*) as a function of exogenous technological change.

The one most often stressed in the corporate strategy field is that learning is a function of cumulative volume. In this formulation, the firm growing the fastest will be gaining cumulative volume (and lowering cost) the fastest. Thus the optimizing firm should price even below cost in the growth stages of an industry's development to gain market share and hence reduce cost relative to rivals. As the industry matures, this strategy can lead to a dominant firm with a large cost advantage over its competitors. All firms, including entrants, are compelled to seek market share—the firm with the greatest risk-taking ability and staying power will ultimately win out.

The formulation that learning is strictly a function of cumulative volume forces us to confront some familiar tradeoffs in economics, those between market power or monopoly (allocative efficiency) and cost (technical efficiency) on the one hand, and between market power and innovation on the other. A learning curve based on cumulative volume implies that the large-market-share firm, since it generally has the greatest "experience," will often be more efficient at any given time, even though it may have a great deal of market power. The learning curve also implies that the largest-market-share firm (that is accumulating volume the fastest) will likewise be the most innovative in improving product or process to lower cost. Thus, any policy that limits a firm's ability to strive for and later occupy a dominant market position will have negative consequences for long-run costs. This affects not only the appropriate policy towards what is an acceptable market share, but also complicates policy towards socalled "predatory" behavior. Pricing below variable costs in pursuit of market share may be justified by dynamic efficiency considerations, even though such behavior would violate even the lenient Areeda–Turner test recently proposed in the literature on predatory behavior.

While the strict cumulative volume formulation of the learning curve raises these problems, it is critical to recognize the conditions that underlie this strict formulation, because they often do not hold in practice. The strict formulation assumes that the process of learning based on accumulated volume goes on indefinitely, which is probably not true in all situations where much of the learning occurs early in the industry's development. The strict formulation also assumes that the leader's learning can be kept proprietary. If it can be copied, the leader may indeed be learning the fastest; but this does not imply greater efficiency for the leader, nor that the leader will pull away from the pack. Moreover, if we added the assumption that learning is costly and requires R&D spending, then the opportunity for low-cost copying can put the leader at a disadvantage, which will reduce incentives for learning.

Another qualification to the strict cumulative volume formulation of the learning curve is the possibility that innovations may change product or process technology enough to create a new learning curve that the leader is ill prepared to jump onto because of his past investments. Or, competitors may be able to chip away at a leader's market share by focusing on particular parts of the product line or customer segments, taking advantage of the leader's inflexibility due to high volume. The risks of these sorts of outcomes will rationally deter firms in many industries from even attempting learning-curve-driven strategies.

A second formulation of learning is that it is a function of time in the industry. Here costs decline for many of the same reasons, but the innovative process that discovers opportunities to lower costs is a function of how long the firm has been looking. If learning is a function of time, rather than cumulative volume, the implications for strategic interaction are much different. Here firms will strive for early entry or acquisitions of early entrants as a base for subsequent strategies. New entry and growth by followers do not threaten the learning advantages of leaders. Conversely, there is no mechanism for leaders to get further ahead. Rather, the cost differences are stable but shrinking as a proportion of total cost as the industry and firms grow older. The only way a firm can improve its relative position in such a world is to acquire an older firm (or its personnel). Unlike the cumulative volume formulation, however, the learning *rate* cannot be accelerated, and hence the ability of a firm to alter its position (and hence the incentive to do so) is much less pronounced.

Learning as a function of time raises few special problems for antitrust except in the premium it places on early entry. Since technical efficiency is maximized if there are many early entrants, policy that prevents one early entrant from erecting entry barriers towards others is indicated. While prevention of artificial entry barriers is a bread-and-butter concern of antitrust, however, what is novel here is the need to do so very early in an industry's development. Antitrust has, by and large, ignored this period of an industry's development, focusing rather on more mature industries, when remedies can have little or no impact on time-related learning.

A third formulation of learning is that it depends on exogenous technological changes, such as improvements in machinery purchased from equipment suppliers, improvements in raw materials, exogenous inventions such as computer controls, and so on. Here there is no link between learning and market position, except insofar as market position cuts against the ability of firms to assimilate exogenous developments. For example, exogenous learning may involve new scale-sensitive machinery, in which case small-scale firms then fall behind in cost position.

Exogenous learning also offers few novel concerns for antitrust. Where its employment in the industry is scale-related, exogenous learning can raise or exacerbate the static-efficiency/market-power dilemma. Where diffusion of exogenous learning is not scale-related, the primary antitrust concern is to insure that all firms in an industry get access to the learning and no firm is able to prevent diffusion to others through contractual arrangements or other practices. Policies to reach these ends should raise few dilemmas, because the fact that learning is exogenous to the industry should mean that there is little chance of blunting the incentives for innovation in the process controlling practices that impede wide diffusion.

This discussion suggests that the nature of the antitrust policy problem raised by dynamic cost reduction depends centrally on the precise nature of dynamic cost reduction present in the industry. Thus, policy towards monopolization can no longer aim for sweeping rules (like maximum market shares) or get lost in debates over intent, but must proceed on a market-by-market basis governed by the economic structure involved. Where conditions lead to a learning curve strictly related to cumulative volume, then the policy dilemma is perhaps most acute. Here a firm's desire to drive competitors out of a market to increase its market share can, in some industries, have a legitimate positive justification in efficiency. Policy must get over its preoccupation with sorting "good" monopolists from "bad" monopolists and confront directly the tradeoff between efficiency and market share that exists in such industries. Since appropriable learning curves based on cumulative volume clearly occur empirically, enhanced attention to dynamic cost reduction should add new respectability to the cost justification for firm behavior, which has had a tendency to be viewed as a smokescreen used by business to further its own ends. Some more specific policy options will be discussed below.

In practice, static scale economies and dynamic cost reductions of all three kinds often interact to cause a competitive process resulting in a dominant market leader with significant and stable cost advantages over existing and potential competitors. For example, Procter & Gamble (P&G) has dominated the huge disposable-diaper industry largely through the operation of scale economies and the learning curve. [One can construct] an estimated income statement for P&G in disposable diapers, compared to that of an entrant into the market aiming at a nationally branded position who begins an entry in 1974 and reaches equilibrium market share in 1980. The assumptions which yield the entrant's income statement are relatively optimistic, and P&G is assumed *not* to retaliate. P&G's estimated cost advantage of 15 percent once the entrant reaches equilibrium (with an even greater cost advantage while the entrant is reaching its target share) is due to a sharp proprietary learning curve in manufacturing and product development, significant static economies of scale in research, advertising, sales force, transportation, and (to a lesser extent) in manufacturing, product differentiation, and absolute cost advantages due to raw material access and favorable access to hospital sampling kits for new mothers. The bulk of these cost advantages are due to true economies due to scale and learning curve phenomena and not to bargaining power.

[This calculation] clearly illustrates the degree to which static and dynamic considerations cumulate and interact to produce a low-cost dominant leader, and the enormous risk an entrant would have to bear to enter the disposable-diaper market. It is also easy to see, using such a calculation, where P&G's costs of entry were lower than the hypothetical entrant's, largely because P&G avoided some of the fixed costs the entrant must bear once P&G is in the market. Remedies that would induce entry into disposable diapers or allow followers to gain significant market share from P&G must be extreme. Eliminating all P&G advertising, for example, would only lower P&G's cost advantage by perhaps 3 percentage points out of 15. Any effective remedy, further, would force a significant loss in efficiency. Breaking P&G into two equal pieces and forcing it to divest one might come close to restoring competitive balance, but would lead to higher costs as a percentage of sales in R & D, manufacturing, sales, and transportation.

IV. THE FIRM AS AN INTERRELATED PORTFOLIO OF BUSINESS

Industry histories reveal that in strategic interaction, firms must often be viewed as portfolios of activities rather than as entities competing independently in each industry in which they have operations. Widespread diversification in the U.S. since the 1960's has led to business units of multibusiness firms being the rule rather than the exception as competitors in most industries. Not only does logic argue that firms will simultaneously optimize over their entire range of business units, but modern strategic planning practice emphasizes that firms should view their businesses as a portfolio and should manage them accordingly. Modern portfolio management approaches place great stress on taking cash from less favorable or slow-growing business units and plowing it into gaining market share in promising business units, making the firm an internal capital market with a deep pocket. There is widespread belief among managers that the diversified firm gains resulting advantages in access to capital compared to single-business firms, implying imperfections in the external capital market.

Going hand in hand with the fact that many of today's large firms are managed as portfolios of businesses is the existence of pervasive interrelationships among the activities of many diversified firms. These interrelationships range from relatively intangible forms—like the fact that P&G has a high degree of accumulated knowledge in market research and consumer testing that can be applied to any of its consumer products—to actual sharing of brand names, distribution channels, purchases, logistical networks, service organization, sales forces, component fabrication, assembly plants and so on, among often disparate products.

Such interrelationships can have a major impact on costs, and mean that traditional product or industry boundaries are no longer sufficient to define relative cost positions among firms. For example, P&G employs the same retail channels, sales force, and logistical system in disposable diapers as it does in its other paper products (bathroom tissue, paper towels). It saves perhaps 2 to 4 percent of sales by using its Charmin Division sales force to sell both diapers and paper products during the same sales call, spreading the fixed costs of the call over more units. Before its diaper volume became large, P&G saved transportation costs (about 10 percent of sales) relative to a firm that only sold diapers, by shipping full carloads combining diapers and other paper products. P&G has probably taken advantage in diapers of expertise in paper products gained in its other paper products businesses and Buckeye Cellulose Division (and vice versa). Finally, P&G reportedly eliminates additional costs by not having to offer as many promotions to the retailers to secure favorable shelf positioning as other diaper brands, because of its presence in other grocery-store product lines as well as its diaper-market share. The competitor that is not optimally diversified, then, faces a significant cost disadvantage relative to P&G in disposable diapers, even before considering industry-specific economies of scale or other mobility barriers. Savings of this order of magnitude due to appropriate diversification are not atypical in my study of a wide range of industries, and they often involved cost savings in groups of products more disparate than those in the P&G example.

Where firms have interrelated portfolios of businesses that are managed as such, some important behavioral and normative implications are raised for examining strategic interaction in a particular industry. First, the objectives (and behavior) of a particular business unit can only be understood by studying the firm's entire portfolio. The firm will invest scarce capital, managerial time, and attention in pursuing learning curves or otherwise gaining market share in some businesses, while allowing market share in others to erode ("harvesting"). Further, a diversified firm's behavior in one business will be affected by how that behavior will impact interrelated businesses. The firm may rationally price below variable cost in one business in order to build market share and volume that will lead to cost reductions in shared distribution or logistics facilities that lower cost for the whole group of related businesses using these facilities. Conversely, a firm may defend a particular business against competitive attack to a degree that appears irrational (or "predatory") until one recognizes that if market share is lost in that business, the market position of other related businesses will be damaged. Thus, the complications raised by the learning curve for determining predation will be exacerbated by cost-related diversification. Any industry-specific test for market power or for the social appropriateness of a particular competitive practice becomes similarly suspect. Preventing an industry leader from defending its share in an industry may allow a related diversified firm to build even greater barriers through improving its position in that industry on top of superior volume in related industries.

Another consequence of the existence of interrelated businesses managed as portfolios is that there will be strong pressures in many industries for offensive or defensive related diversification or vertical integration. Firms will be motivated to search for related diversification in order to create strategic cost advantages that carry over to their other businesses. A firm making sophisticated castings which it assembles into one end product, for example, may look for other (otherwise unrelated) industries using similar castings, so that it can reap economies of scale that lower overall costs. Conversely, P&G's presence in disposable diapers in combination with facial tissue, bathroom tissue, and paper towels placed strong pressure on Scott Paper and Kimberly–Clark (Kleenex) to enter the disposable diaper field defensively. If they did not, both firms might face serious disadvantages in transportation costs, selling costs, relationships with retailers, and even raw material purchasing costs. Offensive and defensive motivations for related diversification can both be present in a given situation. Johnson & Johnson (J&J), for example, is the preeminent firm in many baby-care product lines. Disposable diapers represented the only rapidly growing new product area in the baby care field and offered obvious possibilities for transference of the J&J brand name and distribution system. Hand in hand with these as motivations for J&J's entry into disposable diapers was the threat that P&G and other diaper firms posed for entry into J&J's traditional baby care products, as these firms developed brand names associated with baby care and sales volumes that offered possibilities for economics of joint operation in several baby-care product lines.

The result of such offensive and defensive motivations for related diversification is that we should (and do) observe many situations in which firms are diversified in parallel or nearly parallel ways and compete with each other in multiple industries. For example, John Deere, Caterpillar Tractor, International Harvester, Ford, and J. I. Case, among other firms, all have come over time to operate in multiple and overlapping product areas in the farm equipment, construction equipment, and light- and heavy-truck sectors. Related diversification driven by the search for strategic interrelationships has become the dominant motivation for diversification in the 1970's and now the 1980's, supplanting the conglomerate diversification of the 1960's.

Such related diversification with important cost consequences raises some vexing questions for antitrust policy above and beyond confusing what is predatory behavior. On the one hand, cost-motivated offensive- and defensive-related diversification increases efficiency, and can and does have the procompetitive effect of encouraging entry when diversification involves green-field expansion or acquisition of a base that is subsequently developed. Often the synergies of related diversification allow entry into industries that might in their absence seem to offer insurmountable barriers. On the other hand, the process of offensive and defensive entry into related clusters of businesses may ultimately lead to a significant increase in overall entry barriers by forcing a newcomer to enter the whole cluster of businesses (be optimally diversified) or face a serious disadvantage. Further, related diversification can exacerbate the efficiency/market-power tradeoff posed by the learning curve when they occur together.

Another consequence of the existence of interrelated businesses managed as portfolios is that strategic interaction can and does involve multiple industries. Where businesses are interrelated, firms rationally formulate strategic plans in related groups of businesses simultaneously. A move by a competitor in one industry can be met by a response in that industry or in another related industry in which that competitor also operates. To preserve overall balance, for example, Scott Paper could counter a P&G move in facial tissue either through a response in facial tissue or one in bathroom tissue designed to preserve the total volume of product moving through the same sales force and distribution system (and thereby its relative cost position).

Where strategic interaction among firms occurs simultaneously in several industries, this in some ways complicates the achievement of tacit collusion by greatly increasing the number of variables in the implicit bargain. It also means that a firm's improvement in market share in one industry can have benefits elsewhere in the portfolio, raising the incentive for attempting to gain share. However, there are also some reasons which suggest that competition in multiple industries can facilitate tacit collusion. Competition in multiple industries offers possibilities for various forms of side payments. For example, one firm could yield share in an industry, allowing the leader to raise entry barriers to new firms, while the firm was allowed to gain share in another industry without retaliation. Furthermore, firms can maintain equal profits and market power despite unequal shares, as long as they divide up markets in such a way as to preserve balance in the volume of shared components, the volume of products moving under shared brand names, and volume through shared channels, sales force, or logistics facilities.

Competition in several industries may also allow otherwise unavailable forms of market signaling and competitor disciplining that enhance tacit collusion by lowering the risk of competitive outbreaks. For example, what I have called a cross-parry is a situation in which a firm responds to a competitive threat in one industry with a response in another industry in which it and the threatener compete. Compared to having to meet the threat directly, such a response can credibly signal displeasure, while being relatively easy to disengage from without triggering a series of moves and countermoves. This is because of the risk that a direct response might be interpreted mistakenly as an attack rather than as a signal of displeasure. Further, where firms compete in several industries, a punishing retaliation to a move in one industry can be much more severe, because it can involve simultaneous attacks in a number of businesses. Finally, a firm can punish another's transgressions in one market in another jointly contested market where the defender's share is small, or where the aggressor is the most vulnerable, thus forcing the aggressor to bear a high relative cost. Thus, simultaneous competition in multiple industries raises new issues for antitrust scrutiny of competitive practices.

V. GLOBAL COMPETITION

Some important issues for antitrust are raised by the increasing incidence of industries in which strategic interaction is global, an observation that becomes apparent when one examines industries such as automobiles, television sets, broadcast equipment, and many others. Global industries emerge when there are sources of strategic advantage to competing in a coordinated manner in a number of national markets, such as large scale economies in manufacturing or research or internationally cumulative learning. In some global industries the advantages stem from current scale economies or learning, while in others the global firm may be utilizing past investments in intangible assets.

In global industries, while some mobility barriers are market-specific (e.g., distribution channels), other potentially larger barriers stem from the firm's *global* position (e.g., manufacturing scale economies). In such industries, the firm's behavior and market power in any one national market are determined by its situation globally. It may price below cost in the U.S. market, for example, so that it can gain enough volume to lower production cost to successfully compete against global competitors in Europe or Latin America. If such economies are in fact attainable, such behavior is not predatory but motivated by real efficiencies, though it surely leads to barriers to entry. Barriers to entry/mobility in global industries clearly often exceed those that can exist in national industries.

Obviously, in global industries, antitrust analysis must be global. In an industry that is global, the tradeoff between domestic market and efficiency is eased because even the dominant domestic firm will face ample potential competition. Structural remedies that increase competitiveness from the sole point of view of the U.S.

market can seriously backfire in a global industry. Limiting a firm's market share in the United States can threaten its efficiency and hence competitive position elsewhere in the world, for example, and invite the entry of foreign firms into the U.S. market that might ultimately be able to erect even higher barriers.

Global competition and related diversification interact in many industries to produce situations in which a firm must be both global in scope and optimally diversified in order to be competitive. For example, a television-set manufacturer that is not global and not diversified into videotape recorders will have little chance of success in the next decade. This exacerbates the policy considerations that have been raised.

VI. SIGNALING AND TACIT COLLUSION

Industry histories can reveal much about the sources of the current competitive equilibrium by uncovering patterns of market signaling among existing competitors and potential entrants. There are myriad forms of market signals that communicate to competitors with varying degrees of credibility without the need for actual large-scale investments or moves in the marketplace. Some of the most common are shown in Table 1. Careful examination of competitive behavior and public and quasi-public statements by managements, with extreme attention placed on the sequencing of statements and events, can expose signaling behavior.

TABLE 1

FORMS OF MARKETING SIGNALING

Prior announcements

Public discussion of moves or industry events

Disclosure of data about costs, market position, or other company strengths

Publication of policies for pricing and determination of other competitive variables

Fighting brands

Form and timing of moves relative to industry convention

History of response to entry or competitor moves, in any of the industries in which the firm competes

Maintenance of retaliatory resources, such as excess cash

Actions against new competitors' products in test markets

Cross-parry in another jointly contested industry

Behavior divergent from apparent profit maximization

Binding (and communicated) commitments that raise exit barriers, such as long-term contracts, capital investments, and others

Since market signaling can clearly facilitate tacit collusion, elimi-nating market signaling practices enhances competition. However, while I am generally skeptical of market signals, they raise some vexing issues for antitrust. While signals surely can have socially undesirable effects in deterring entry or facilitating tacit collusion among existing firms, the problem is that nearly all market signals have some socially beneficial component. Announcements of capacity expansion can promote efficiency through reducing excess capacity due to bunching of capacity additions. Publication of actual prices or pricing policies can allow buyers to bargain more effectively. Public comment by executives on industry events, or company announce-ments which state the logic of firms' moves, can increase the degree to which the capital markets are well informed. The problem is that market signals contain information, and information is beneficial to market functioning.

Another problem with policy toward market signals is that there are so many forms of market signals that limits on particularly obvious ones for which the positive social benefits seem negligible may do little to control undesirable signaling behavior. Since so many aspects of company behavior can be signals, banning signals is a bit like trying to keep firms in a tight oligopoly from recognizing each oth-er's existence.

VII. ENTRY/MOBILITY DETERRENCE

Study of strategic interaction in industry histories reveals a wide array of behavior available to firms to deter entry, much of which has been little studied by industrial organization researchers. Since the same entry-deterring tactics can also be employed to deter or defend against attempts at increasing share by incumbents, the analysis of that case (mobility deterrence) is parallel.

Some behavioral and normative issues in entry-deterring tactics can be illustrated through pursuing my example of the disposable-diaper industry. Table 2 shows some of the feasible behavior avail-able to P&G to deter entry (or discourage market share gains by incumbents) in the disposable-diaper industry. The tactics in Table 2 are generalizable to many industries. Further, they reflect the fact that entry (and mobility) is not an instantaneous move but rather takes time and often occurs in a sequential fashion, involving the occupation of a series of strategic groups over time. Thus, if the

TABLE 2

Possible Entry/Mobility Deterring Tactics in Disposable Diapers

	Cost to Procter & Gamble (P&G)	*Cost to an entrant (competitor)*
Signaling		
1. Signal a commitment to defend position in diapers through public statements, comments to retailers, etc.	none	raises expected cost of entry by increasing probability and extent of retaliation
2. File a patent suit	legal fees	legal fees plus probability that P&G wins the suit with subsequent cost to the competitor
3. Announce planned capacity expansion	none	raises expected risk of price cutting and the probability of P&G's retaliation to entry
4. Announce a new generation of diapers to be introduced in the future	none	raises the expected cost of entry by forcing entrant to bear possible product development and changeover costs contingent on the ultimate configuration of the new generation
Capacity		
5. Build capacity[1] ahead of demand	present value of investment in excess capacity	raises the risk of price cutting and the probability of P&G's retaliation to entry
Price		
6. Cut price	across-the board reduction in sales revenue	equal proportional reduction in sales revenue but smaller total lost revenue; demand for entrant more likely to be price elastic if have lower product differentiation
7. Cut price in "new-born" diaper sizes	focuses price cut on first diaper a mother will buy	greatly raises the cost of inducing trial by the new mother, who is most susceptible to switching brands

(Continued)

TABLE 2 (continued)

	Cost to Procter & Gamble (P&G)	*Cost to an entrant (competitor)*
8. Increase cents-off couponing in test or rollout markets	focuses effective price cut on contested markets; most coupons will reduce revenues on sales P&G would have made anyway	most coupons redeemed will lead to incremental revenue from *new* buyers
9. Load buyer with inventory by discounting large economy size package in rollout markets	reduction in sales revenue part of sales; probably to price-sensitive customers most susceptible to competitor incursion	greatly raises the cost of inducing trial for the entrant
Advertising		
10. Raise advertising nationally	the cost of a given dollar increase in advertising will be spread over a large sales volume	must match P&G in absolute message volume to maintain relative position, but the cost of advertising is spread over much smaller base; may also suffer diseconomies by not having national media available
Price		
11. Spot advertising overlays in test or rollout markets	same, but focuses resources on contested markets	same, but no disadvantage due to national media access
Product		
12. Put a "blocking" brand[2] into test market	cost of product development and market testing	credible threat that second brand will be aggressively rolled out nationally if entry occurs; raise probability of closing off lowest-cost entry into the industry
13. Introduce a "blocking" brand[3]	cost of brand introduction	raise cost of entry by exposing entrant to more direct retaliation by the leader

TABLE 2 (continued)

	Cost to Procter & Gamble (P&G)	Cost to an entrant (competitor)
14. Introduce a new generation of the product[4]	fixed cost of new product development expenditures and manufacturing changeover spread over large volume	fixed cost of product development and manufacturing changeover must be spread over smaller volume; also elevates the risk of potential entrants that future product generations will make existing investment obsolete
Exit Barriers[5]		
15. Raise exit barriers through investment in specialized assets, long-term supply contracts with raw material sources, high labor severance or layoff benefits, etc.	increase cost of failure	credible threat that leader will defend his position

[1] This case was analyzed by A. M. Spence, "Entry Capacity Investment and Oligopolistic Pricing," 8 *Bell. J. Econ.* 534 (1978).

[2] A brand which occupies a natural market segment for entry. In the diaper industry, this is a premium brand. The second most natural segment would be a lower-cost, lower-quality brand positioned between the regular Pampers product and private labels. Given the product performance sensitivity of the customer, however, this is much less likely to succeed.

[3] This situation has been analyzed by R. Schmalensee, "Entry Deterrence in the Ready-to-Eat Cereal Market," 9 *Bell J. Econ.* (1978), pp. 313–14.

[4] Under some circumstances, it can be more effective to introduce the new generation after the entrant has begun a rollout, because this makes the entrant's investment in rollout of the old generation obsolete and damages its brand reputation, as well as forcing it to match the new generation. The entrant can be more likely to withdraw under these circumstances.

[5] For a discussion of exit barriers, see R. E. Caves and M. E. Porter, "From Entry Barriers to Mobility Barriers: Conjectural Decisions and Contrived Deterrence to New Competition," 91 *Q. J. Econ.* 241 (1977); M. E. Porter, *Competitive Strategy: Techniques for Analyzing Industries and Competitors* (1980).

entrant or competitor seeking to gain share can be punished early in the process, he may give up altogether. Much of the recent literature on entry deterrence makes a sharp distinction between the pre- and postentry game which is inappropriate. It may be rational for the incumbent to carry out a threat long after the entrant has first appeared in the market, for this reason and because the incumbent's reaction to this entrant (or uppity incumbent) can signal other entrants and incumbents.

The alternative entry-deterring behavior in Table 2 varies along a number of significant dimensions for the competitive outcome. The tactics vary in the certainty with which they inflict a penalty on the potential entrant (or competitor) and in the certainty with which the potential entrant (or competitor) will notice them. This means that they have differing entry-deterring values.

More importantly, though, the tactics also vary greatly in their *relative* cost to the dominant firm (P&G) compared to the potential entrants (or competitors). Some tactics, like public comment, or forms of signaling such as speculative patent suits, or introducing a blocking brand into test market, cost the leader relatively little but can significantly raise the expected costs (or risks) of the entrant. Other tactics, like increasing advertising in an entrant's rollout markets or introducing a new generation of the product, have a considerable cost to the leader but inflict a proportionally even higher cost on the entrant or smaller-share competitor, because advertising and product development are subject to economies of scale. Furthermore, such entry-deterring tactics may raise product differentiation or overall demand, which benefits the leader and offsets some of the cost to him. On the other extreme, competitive price-cutting inflicts a huge cost on the leader because of the leader's large overall volume and the fact that price cutting by the leader will induce few customers to switch to him because of his already large share. Offering cents-off coupons in the market where an entrant is introducing his product ("rolling out") can target the entry-deterring investment better than an across-the-board price cut, but still it is relatively more costly to the leader because of his larger share and the fact that unlike the entrant, most coupons will be redeemed by the leader's already existing customers.

Entry/mobility-deterring behavior also varies in its ability to be localized to a *particular* potential entrant or competitor. Advertising in test markets can localize the defense to the particular product features stressed by a particular entrant. Couponing, on the other hand, will affect (and thereby cause response from) all competitors in the market. The potential entrant or competitor is clearly placed in the best possible situation where the leader must make investments in entry/mobility deterrence across the board rather than being able to target its moves to the particular geographic market or part of the product line under siege.

This analysis of alternative entry-deterring behavior suggests that the form of competitive behavior often attacked in antitrust investigations of predatory aggressive price cutting may be the most benign in terms of the exercise of market power. Entry/mobility deterrence through predatory pricing is across the board and offers the dominant firm none of the scale economy benefits that some other forms of behavior do. The preoccupation of the predation literature (and antitrust scrutiny) with price is unfortunate, in this light, and might be better spent on finding ways of preventing tactics that deter entry or mobility which are effective and yet low-cost to a dominant firm.

Competition in the Pharmaceutical Industry

NATIONAL ACADEMY OF SCIENCES

This is an excerpt from The Competitive Status of the U.S. Pharmaceutical Industry, *published by the National Academy of Sciences in 1983.*

The importance of research and innovation for competition among major pharmaceutical firms places the ethical drug industry in a select grouping of high-technology industries. The most distinctive feature of pharmaceutical innovation lies in the spending strategies of the major firms—high rates of investment in R&D expenditures (as percentages of sales and profits), relatively high rates of spending for basic research, and little government financing of industrial R&D. These trends are illustrated in Table 1 and indicate that, while one or more of these features are present in other industries, rarely are all three. The pharmaceutical industry, along with the computer, photographic, and specialized machinery industries, all spend more than 50 percent of their recorded profits on research and development.

On the basis of this innovation, American firms were predominant in world markets during the period 1950 to 1960, accounting for a large majority of research expenditures and new products, over half of world pharmaceutical production, and one third of international trade in medicinals. American preeminence persisted, though in attenuated degree, through the 1960s. In the past decade, how-

Note: Some footnotes have been omitted from the original article.

TABLE 1

RESEARCH ATTRIBUTES OF VARIOUS U.S. BASED INDUSTRIES, 1977

Industry	Basic research as percentage of total R&D	R&D as percentage of sales	Government funding as percentage of R&D funds
Drugs and medicines	11.4	6.2	1.0
Industrial chemicals	9.7	3.6	19.0
Food and kindred products	5.2	0.4	na
Stone, clay, and glass products	14.0	1.2	na
"Other" chemicals	9.6	2.1	na
Petroleum refining and extraction	5.3	0.7	8.1
Communications equipment	5.2	7.6	43.1

SOURCE: *Research and Development in Industry, 1977*. Washington, D.C.: National Science Foundation, 1979.

ever, the competitive advantage of American firms has been not only reduced, but apparently eliminated. This study seeks to define and document these changes of competitive position within the multinational pharmaceutical industry, to determine why these changes have occurred, and to suggest an array of policy options to address the relative decline. This essay provides a primer on competition within the ethical drug industry.

EMERGENCE OF THE MODERN PHARMACEUTICAL INDUSTRY

The drug industry before 1930 was profoundly different from that of today. Innovation was infrequent and externally derived, and firms manufactured a limited number of unpatented products which were largely marketed without prescription directly to consumers. The mix of products available to consumers has been described by a pharmaceutical executive, Henry Gadsden of Merck, when he described the nature of the market in the 1930s:

> You could count the basic medicines on the fingers of your two hands. Morphine, quinine, digitalis, insulin, codeine, aspirin, arsenicals, nitroglycerin, mercurials, and a few biologicals. Our own Sharp and Dohme catalog did not carry a single exclusive prescription medicine. We had a broad range of fluids, ointments, and extracts, as did other firms, but we placed heavy emphasis on biological medicines as well. Most of our products were sold without a prescription. And 43 percent of the prescription medicines were compounded by the pharmacist, as compared with 1.2 percent today.[1]

1. Cited in Peter Temin, *Taking Your Medicine, Drug Regulation in the United States*, Harvard University Press, Cambridge, MA, 1980, p. 59.

None of these products mentioned by Gadsden had resulted from research efforts of the pharmaceutical industry. Only a handful of drug discoveries from any source had been made by 1930 (principally salversan in 1908 for treatment of syphillis and insulin in 1922 for treatment of diabetes) and these discoveries were infrequent, unrelated, and unanticipated, and resulted from prolonged and tedious research. Nothing about these discoveries suggested a method of research or a mechanism of disease prevention that could be economically exploited for development of new pharmacological agents.

This non-innovative technological environment changed rapidly just before and during World War II, in a "therapeutic revolution" that transformed the industry. First, during the period 1930 to 1950, a series of natural products, particularly the vitamins and hormones, were discovered, developed, and commercialized. These discoveries led to the conquest of scurvy, pernicious anemia, beri-beri, and pellagra as well as significant endocrine therapies. Second, the foundation was laid for modern research in anti-infectives. The discovery of the therapeutic properties of sulfanilamide by I. G. Farbenindustrie in 1935 and of penicillin by Oxford scientists in 1940 indicated the possibilities for *systematic* research in finding new sulfa drugs and new antibiotics. Neither sulfanilamide nor penicillin were patentable at the time, having been known discoveries with belated demonstration of therapeutic properties. Nonetheless, the tremendous demand for anti-infective agents by allied military forces during wartime made the manufacture of these scarce substances a national priority. The U.S. government spent almost $3 million to subsidize wartime penicillin research and encouraged private construction of penicillin manufacturing plants by allowing accelerated depreciation. The returns from sales of these and other drugs were subject to wartime "excess profits" taxes, but at the conclusion of World War II, federal penicillin plants were sold to private firms at half cost.

The simultaneous demonstration of new technological opportunities and of potential profits combined to dramatically change the pharmaceutical industry. The final step necessary for the emergence of the industry in its modern form was a legal mechanism to allow commercial exploitation of the new technological opportunities for biological products. This step occurred with the 1948 decision of the U.S. Patent Office to grant a patent for streptomyicin. A patent, of course, is a legal monopoly for 17 years over commercial exploitation of a new discovery. During the period before expiration of the patent, the innovative firm may charge prices above manufacturing costs and thus recoup earlier research expenditures that led to the innovation. Rapidly, a new form of competition emerged in the pharmaceutical industry—competition through product development.

At the outset of the 1950s, pharmaceutical competition remained largely national in scope, with the significant exception of the Swiss multinationals. Economic linkages among the various national pharmaceutical industries were largely confined to international trade, and even then were relatively unimportant. Imports amounted to less than 10 percent of domestic consumption in the major industrial nations, again with the exception of Switzerland. Firms engaged in new product development faced essentially three methods for foreign distribution of their innovations:

1. Exports—domestic production by the innovating firm for sale abroad through local distributors.
2. Licensing—production abroad by a foreign firm with profits shared between the innovating firm and the producer.
3. Multinational expansion—production abroad by a subsidiary of the innovating firm.

Starting in the 1950s, American firms began and Swiss firms continued substantial multinational expansion of operations (for data on U.S. firms, see Table 2). The presence of tariff and regulatory bar-

TABLE 2

Domestic and Foreign Sales of U.S. Owned Pharmaceutical Firms, Various Years (percentages)

Year	Domestic	Foreign
1956	88	12
1961	73	27
1966	71	29
1971	66	34
1976	60	40
1978	57	43

SOURCE: *Annual Survey Reports.* Washington, D.C.: Pharmaceutical Manufacturers' Association, various years.

NOTE: Table statistics are based on sales of human dosage. They exclude sales of bulk drugs and veterinary drugs.

riers imposed by foreign governments, greater physician and consumer acceptance of local production sources, and a general tendency toward vertical integration by pharmaceutical firms made reliance on exports a less viable and profitable strategy. In general, the choice between licensing and multinational investment depended on the breadth of a firm's product line. American and Swiss firms that enjoyed a surge in the number of new patented drugs during the 1950s and 1960s were able to spread the substantial overhead costs of direct foreign investment over the several drugs distributed abroad by their firms, making direct investment relatively less burdensome. Non-Swiss,European, and Japanese firms with narrower product lines that might have attempted direct investment abroad would have been forced to cover these overheads entirely from sales of just a few drugs—a potentially unprofitable endeavor. An additional factor that limited non-Swiss, European, and Japanese direct investment arose from the economic devastation of World War II and the financial burdens of reconstruction. The resulting pattern of multinational expansions can be seen in Table 3.

After 1960 the costs of developing commercially viable new drugs dramatically increased. One consequence of this important trend has been that larger earnings, available only from a larger market, were essential to cover the greater costs of R&D for each compound. This industrial need to cover rising research costs, along with the almost universal cross-cultural use of pharmaceuticals, and the dramatic expansion of third-party payments for health-care costs combined to insure the emergence of a world market in ethical drugs. While this world market is severely fragmented due to non-tariff barriers to trade and due to differing national regulations, it is nonetheless increasingly inescapable that the competitive vitality of the major pharmaceutical firms depends on distribution of new products on a worldwide scale.

NATURE OF PHARMACEUTICAL COMPETITION

Prior to the therapeutic revolution of the 1940s, the pharmaceutical industry exhibited three distinct divisions, each with its own form of competition. The first subindustry, *proprietary drugs,* or over-the-counter (OTC) medicines as they are also called, encompasses products sold directly to consumers without prescription in the context of extensive advertising. Competition in this segment of the pharmaceutical industry depends largely on market-

TABLE 3

MULTINATIONAL STRUCTURE OF MAJOR PHARMACEUTICAL MARKETS, 1973

Nationality (Ownership)	Nationality (location)									
	USA	Japan	Germany	France	Italy	Spain	UK	Brazil	Mexico	Canada
USA	*	12.2	12.6	17.4	15.8	14.4	38.4	35.4	49.6	63.4
Japan	–	*	–	–	–	–	–	–	0.1	–
West Germany	1.0	4.6	*	4.5	7.6	10.4	7.1	13.3	7.4	2.0
France	–	0.3	1.9	*	3.7	3.1	4.6	3.4	3.5	2.2
Italy	–	–	0.2	0.1	*	2.7	0.1	4.6	2.7	–
Switzerland	12.6	3.3	9.3	9.2	10.9	8.9	10.7	10.3	9.4	11.1
UK	2.2	2.3	1.8	3.5	5.1	1.2	*	1.9	3.5	4.9
Netherlands	0.1	0.4	1.8	1.2	0.3	0.8	1.7	1.1	1.3	–
Sweden	0.1	0.2	0.4	0.3	–	–	0.7	0.3	0.2	0.3
Other Foreign	–	0.1	1.7	1.6	1.1	2.1	0.4	–	–	0.8
Total Foreign	16.0	23.4	29.7	37.8	44.5	43.6	63.7	70.3	77.7	84.7
Local Ownership	84.0	76.6	70.3	62.2	55.5	65.4	36.3	29.7	22.3	15.3
Total	100.0%	100.0%	100.0%	100.0%	100.0%	100.0%	100.0%	100.0%	100.0%	100.0%

SOURCE: Barrie Jones, *The Future of the Multinational Pharmaceutical Industry to 1990.* New York: John Wiley, 1977.
NOTE: Asterisk takes place of local percentages in top half of table. Local percentages are given separately in the bottom half as Local Ownership.

ing of established brands with occasional new product development. New proprietary drugs rarely represent breakthroughs in treatment and often are simple reformulations of existing therapies that facilitate consumer convenience or are products switched from prescription to OTC status as a result of the U.S. FDA–OTC drug review. Proprietary drugs are thus characterized by high advertising intensity but a very low research intensity. Sales of proprietary drugs have grown at a markedly slower rate than other pharmaceutical sales and currently comprise less than 15 percent of total industry sales, as can be seen in Table 4. About 550 firms in the U.S. produce and distribute exclusively OTC medicines.

The second division of the industry, *generic products* or multisource drugs, exhibits the classical form of market competition. Generic drug products are off-patent, well-established compounds that are produced as standardized commodities by more than one firm. Generic products are generally unadvertised and usually subject to price competition among the various producers with the result of low profit margins for generic producers. Multisource drugs accounted for about 45 percent of ethical drug sales within the United States in 1979, though only 7 percent of these sales (or 3 percent of all drug sales) were achieved by the smaller, non-research-intensive firms. About 600 additional firms produce generic drugs in the United States. Almost all of these firms have exclusively domestic distribution, and many sell only to regional markets. Most generic drug houses have annual sales of less than $10 million.

This study focuses on the remaining segment of the pharmaceutical industry, *patented drugs*, distributed by prescription. Pat-

TABLE 4

Market Divisions of the Domestic U.S. Pharmaceutical Industry, Various Years (millions of dollars)

Year	Prescription drugs	All medicines	Prescription drugs as a percentage of all medicines
1929	190	600	32
1949	940	1,640	57
1969	5,395	6,480	83

SOURCE: Peter Temin, *Taking Your Medicine: Drug Regulation in the United States.* Cambridge: Harvard University Press, 1980.

ented drugs represent the driving force of the modern pharmaceutical industry and are responsible for the spectacular growth in sales since 1940. About 150 firms conduct research for and produce patented drugs in the United States. Only 20 of these firms have significant U.S.-based multinational operations, and about an equal number (20) are U.S.-located operations of foreign-owned multinational firms. The remaining firms have largely domestic sales, and some have very small research facilities. Industrial competition in this segment of the industry is quite distinctive and occurs through corporate development of new patented therapies.

Under patent protection, firms that introduce new products are able in principle to earn large returns on their innovations. There are, however, two constraints on the abilities of firms to generate earnings through innovation. The first is that it is generally technically possible for another firm to produce compounds of similar therapeutic action, though with different and hence also patentable molecular structure. The second constraint is, of course, that pharmaceutical innovation is a highly uncertain process that does not predictably yield therapeutically, let alone commercially, important products. Numerous firms have expended substantial funds for pharmaceutical R&D without development of a commercially successful product. Table 5 provides a tabulation of U.S. sales in 1972 of all new medicinal chemical compounds introduced into the U.S. market in the mid-1960s. While a very few products enjoyed substantial commercial success, the vast majority of products were relative commercial failures and did not contribute significantly to defraying R&D costs.

Given that the majority of contemporary pharmaceutical sales are comprised of generic products and patented drugs (both sold through prescription) and that profit margins in the generic products division of the industry are relatively low, it is clear that many industry profits are drawn from sales of patented drugs. Finally, given that most pharmaceutical innovations are commercially not very successful, it is clear that modern pharmaceutical firms depend crucially for positive cash flow on a small handful of successful innovations, as is demonstrated for the United States in Table 6. Failure to produce new products continuously to replace those that lose market share to imitation or on which patents expire would ultimately be devastating to the financial health of a pharmaceutical company. In short,

TABLE 5

NEW CHEMICAL ENTITIES (NCEs)
INTRODUCED IN U.S. 1962–1968 BY
1972 U.S. DOMESTIC SALES

Sales $000	Number of Drugs
0– 999	33
1,000– 1,999	14
2,000– 3,999	9
4,000– 5,999	5
6,000– 7,999	3
8,000– 9,999	1
10,000–14,999	4
15,000–19,000	2
20,000–29,999	2
30,000–39,999	2
40,000–49,999	2
50,000–59,999	0
60,000–99,999	1
100,000+	1
Total	70

SOURCE: David Schwartzman, *Innovation in the Pharmaceutical Industry.* Baltimore: Johns Hopkins University Press, 1976.

competitive advantage in sales of patented drugs, by far the most financially lucrative segment of the modern pharmaceutical industry, depends crucially on the ability of the firm to produce a slow but steady stream of commercially successful new products through industrial innovation.

BENEFITS AND RISKS OF TECHNICAL CHANGE

The rapid introduction of novel and complex products in any industry presents both social benefits and social costs. Because ethical drugs directly affect the health and lives of millions of consumers, the nonmarket implications of pharmaceutical innovation are especially pronounced.

As regards benefits, modern pharmaceutical products have substantially contributed to modern treatment of ill health. In this context, Victor Fuchs has observed:

Drugs are the key to modern medicine. Surgery, radiotherapy, and diagnostic tests are all important, but the ability of health care providers to alter

TABLE 6

Proportion of Total Domestic U.S. Pharmaceutical
Sales Provided by Three Best Selling Products,
Selected Pharmaceutical Corporations, Selected Years
(percentages)

	1970	1975	1979
Abbott	36	33	28
American Home Products			
Ayerst	64	74	84
Wyeth	37	44	43
Bristol-Meyers			
Bristol	69	46	28
Mead-Johnson	40	38	37
Burroughs Wellcome	na	56	51
Ciba	47	na	55
Lederle	48	31	32
Lilly	46	60	43
Merck	35	44	44
Pfizer	52	65	65
Robins	43	45	46
Roche	80	80	70
Schering	42	48	40
Searle	45	49	44
Smith Kline	44	42	66
Squibb	28	31	23
Upjohn	47	50	56
Warner-Lambert			
Warner	53	na	na
Parke-Davis	25	27	22

SOURCE: Merck & Co., Inc., MSD Strategic Planning and MSD Marketing and Sales Research, West Point, PA. Original data from Intercontinental Medical Statistics (IMS), Inc., Ambler, PA.

health outcomes—Dr. Walsh McDermott's "decisive technology"—depends primarily on drugs. Six dollars are spent on hospitals and physicians for every dollar spent on drugs, but without drugs the effectiveness of hospitals and physicians would be enormously diminished.

Until this century the physician could with confidence give a smallpox vaccination, administer quinine for malaria, prescribe opium and morphine for the relief of pain and not much more. A quarter-century later the situation was not much different. Some advances had been made in surgery, but the death rates from tuberculosis, influenza and pneumonia, and other infectious diseases were still extremely high. With the introduction and wide use of sulfonamide and penicillin, however, the death rate in the United States from influenza and pneumonia fell by more than 8 percent annually from 1935 to 1950. (The annual rate of decline from 1900 to 1935 had been only 2 percent.) In the case of tuberculosis, while some progress had been made since the turn of the century, the rate of decline in the death rate accelerated appreciably after the adoption of penicillin, streptomycin, and PAS (paraaminosalicylic acid) in the late 1940s and of isoniazid in the early 1950s. New drugs and vaccines developed since the 1920s have also been strikingly effective against typhoid, whooping cough, poliomyelitis, measles, diphtheria, and tetanus; more recently great advances have been made in hormonal drugs, antihypertension drugs, antihistamines, anticoagulants, antipsychotic drugs, and antidepressants.

Tables 7 and 8 illustrate the continuing influence of pharmaceutical products in lessened incidences of disease and death in the United States. These statistics provide documentation for the impact of ethical drugs on public health, but only few data are available to quantify the additional importance of pharmaceuticals for private health. These private health benefits are often of considerable importance: the effects of antiinflammatory agents on the functional capacity of arthritis patients, the implications of anti-anxiety and antidepressive drugs for patient quality of life, the cost savings of

TABLE 7

Reported Cases of Selected Diseases, 1951–1976

Diseases	1951	1960	1965	1976	Decline 1951–1976 (percent)
Measles (rubeola)	530,118	441,703	261,904	41,126	92
Meningococcal infections	4,164	2,259	3,040	1,605	61
Mumps	na[a]	na	152,109[b]	38,492	75 (from 1968)
Whooping Cough	68,687	14,809	6,799	1,010	99
Poliomyelitis	28,386	3,190	70	15	99
Rubella (German Measles)	na	na	45,975[d]	12,491	73 (from 1966)
Tuberculosis	85,607[c]	55,494	48,016	32,105	62
Typhoid Fever	2,128	816	454	419	80

SOURCE: U.S. Department of HEW, Public Health Service, Reported Morbidity and Mortality in the United States, 1976, *Morbidity and Mortality Weekly Report*, Vol. 25, No. 53. Atlanta: Center for Disease Control, August 1977, p. 2; and U.S. Department of HEW, Public Health Service, Annual Reported Incidence of Notifiable Diseases in the United States, 1960, *Morbidity and Mortality Weeky Report*, Vol. 9, No. 53. Atlanta: Communicable Disease Control, October 30, 1961, p. 4.

[a] na = not available.

[b] 1968 (not previously reportable).

[c] 1952 figure (1951 not available).

[d] 1966 figure.

cimetidine in treatment of peptic ulcers. Nonetheless, the ordinary measures of public health produced by government agencies fail to capture these benefits.

Offsetting these social benefits, there are clear social costs to pharmaceutical innovation. The complexity and diversity of patient reactions to ethical drugs restricts the abilities of consumers, their physicians, and often even pharmaceutical firms themselves to detect potential low incidence or long-term adverse side effects in the very potent drugs introduced since the therapeutic revolution of the 1940s. It is by now well-established that laissez-faire policies under these market circumstances will result in distribution of pharmaceuticals whose risk is not fully appreciated, with occasional disastrous results. As a result of such social cost, national government regulation of product safety and distribution for pharmaceuticals has emerged in all the developed nations.

Unfortunately, safety regulation of the pharmaceutical industry presents its own social benefits and costs as well. In addition to reducing the frequency of adverse reactions and inappropriate therapies, contemporary regulations reduce the availability of and increase the delay and cost for new pharmaceutical substances. Appropriate regulatory policy must strive to balance these social benefits and costs in order to insure the optimal use of medicinal products. In

TABLE 8

DEATH RATE PER 100,000 POPULATION, 1920–1978

Cause of death	1920	1940	1960	1978	Decline 1920–1978 (percent)
Tuberculosis, all forms	113.1	45.9	5.9	1.3	99
Dysentery	4.0	1.9	0.2	0.0[a]	100
Whooping Cough	12.5	2.2	0.1	0.0	100
Diphtheria	15.3	1.1	0.0[b]	–	100
Measles	8.8	0.5	0.2	0.0	100
Influenza and Pneumonia	207.3	70.3	36.6	26.7	87

SOURCE: Ernst B. Chain, *Academic and Industrial Contributions to Drug Research Nature*, November 2, 1963, p. 441; and U.S. Department of HEW, Public Health Service, Health Resources Administration Final Mortality Statistics, 1978, *Monthly Vital Statistics Report,* Vol. 29, no. 6, National Center for Health Statistics, Sept. 17, 1980.

[a] Bacillary dysentery and amebiasis.

[b] 1959 (figures for 1960 and 1978 not available).

determination of this balance, polls repeatedly suggest that the American people are unwilling to make sacrifices in the safety and quality of ethical drugs simply to promote jobs and economic growth, and this panel explicitly endorsed this view. On the other hand, numerous reforms of U.S. FDA regulation have been proposed on purely medical grounds, to improve therapy for American patients, and the panel endorses many of these reforms. It is most important for the reader to recognize that any advancement of the economic position of U.S. pharmaceutical firms caused by these reforms is an explicitly and appropriately secondary reason for their adoption.

One important point, however, should be made: any balanced and appropriate policies toward the pharmaceutical industry should seek to sustain a large and rapid flow of truly safe and significant new drugs from American firms. It is precisely such balanced and appropriate policies that in the long run will most effectively advance both the public health and the competitive position of the U.S. pharmaceutical industry.

Corporate Strategies in the Auto Industry

NATIONAL RESEARCH COUNCIL

This article comes from The Competitive Status of the U.S. Auto Industry, *published by the National Research Council in 1982.*

The scale and complexity of the auto production process and the emphasis on high volumes is not a recent event. Although the very early days of the industry were characterized by competition among small technological entrepreneurs, the emergence of the Model T in 1908 and the subsequent development of a mass market for automobiles gave strong impetus to the emergence of large-scale enterprise as the dominant form of organization. By 1923 Ford and General Motors (GM) held 71 percent of the market, with Ford's share amounting to 50.4 percent. Ford lost the leadership position to GM in the late 1920s, and GM has retained a dominant market share to the present time.

From 1925 to 1970, competition in the auto industry was essentially competition among a few giant domestic firms. While several so-called independents operated at the margin of the industry until the early 1950s, the bulk of sales was satisfied by the Big Three: GM, Ford, and Chrysler. The nature of competition in this period was strongly influenced by the strategy developed by GM in the 1920s and 1930s. In terms of pricing, product and process technology, and distribution, the Big Three developed broadly similar

Note: Some footnotes have been omitted from the original article.

approaches, although both Ford and Chrysler fashioned distinctive features.

Stated quite broadly, the history of competition in the auto industry up to the oil embargo of the 1970s was marked by two distinctive periods. Table 1 presents a brief characterization. In the first period,.

TABLE 1

Changing Mix of Competitive Factors

	Stage of development	
Competitive factor	*Early (1905–1948)*	*Late (1949–1973)*
Competitive pricing	*Secondary Factor* Product performance dominates price comparisons; initial buyers value performance over price.	*Primary Factor* Standardization leads to acceptable levels of performance; price becomes significant factor in purchase decision.
Model change (innovation in technology)	*Primary Factor* Significant improvement in product occurs rapidly; new models have major impact on market share.	*Secondary Factor* Technology is refined and standardized; new models offer styling changes.
Channels of distribution (dealerships)	*Primary Factor* Personal contact and dealer reputation are key to acceptance of new product.	*Primary Factor* Availability, cost, and quality of service are important to mature product.

SOURCE: Adapted from W. Abernathy, *The Productivity Dilemma*. Baltimore: Johns Hopkins, 1978, Table 2.5, p. 41.

from 1908 to 1948, major innovative changes in the product played a significant role in the jockeying for profits and share. The second period was marked by relative stability in product technology and increased emphasis on competitive pricing and styling. In the postwar era, competition occurred primarily on the basis of economies of scale, styling, and the dealer network. These broad evolutionary changes are reflected in the changing strategic orientation of the major firms.

STRATEGY AT FORD

The innovations in product and process that carried the Ford Motor Company to a dominant market position between 1908 and 1927 were motivated by a broad strategic plan. The essential outline of Henry Ford's strategy is suggested by an advertisement he placed more than two years before the Model T was introduced:

> [The] idea is to build a high grade, practical automobile that can be maintained as near $450 as it is possible to make it, thus raising the automobile out of the list of luxuries and bringing it to the point where the average American citizen may own and enjoy his own automobile—the question is not "how much can we get for the car?" but "how low can we sell it and make a small margin on each one?"[1]

The design of the Model T was followed by Ford's innovations in process methods and decentralized assembly plants, with mass production and distribution to provide control of the markets in an era of slow communications. The success of the strategy was evident in dramatic price reductions and in expansion of the market from 1908 to 1926; by 1923 Ford had 50.4 percent of a market that had grown to 3.6 million units.

By the early 1920s the Model T competed in a market far different from that of 1908. Its design had been improved upon, and the lack of variety had given GM an opportunity to differentiate and segment the market. Even though Ford added a starter and a closed steel body in the mid-1920s, there was no change in basic design. To retain market share, Ford dropped the price to $290, but GM still gained market share rapidly. Ford closed down completely in 1926 for nine months to design and change over to a new model.

Ford introduced a new product in 1927 (the Model A), but the strategy was unchanged. Although Ford briefly regained its prior market share, the old competitive approach of low price, standardized design, and mass production did not work for long. After three years, Ford's market share dropped below 25 percent. Product standardization was abandoned in 1932 with the introduction of the V-8 engine.

Alfred Sloan of GM criticized Ford's strategy as follows:

> Mr. Ford had unusual vision, imagination and foresight—[his] basic conception of one car in one utility model at an even lower price was what the market, especially the farm market, needed at the time. . . . [His] concept of the American market did not adequately fit the realities after 1923. Mr. Ford failed to realize that it was not necessary for new cars to meet the

1. Abernathy, *op. cit.*, p. 33.

need for basic transportation. . . . Used cars at much lower prices dropped down to fill the demand. . . . The old master has failed to master change.[2]

Ford's strategy was brilliant but rigid. A market need was identified; the product and the manufacturing, marketing, and distribution facilities to meet the need were developed and implemented. But Ford's strategy recognized neither the dynamics of market development nor the counteractions of competitors.

Under new management after World War II, Ford rapidly adopted a new strategy. Independent divisions, each having its own product lines and production facilities, were envisioned. Separate engine and assembly plants for Lincoln–Mercury and Ford divisions were introduced, but the market failure of the Edsel thwarted the planned development of three separate car divisions. After 1960 all North American production facilities were consolidated under a centralized functional organization; that is, many of the same production and engineering functions served all product lines.

In describing competitive policies, Lawrence J. White concludes that Ford has been a follower in styling but a leader in seeking out market niches. New models like the Mustang, Maverick, Pinto, and a combination car and truck called the Ranchero seem to confirm this characterization. Despite these successes, Ford has not been able to excel in head-on competition with GM across the full product line.

ALFRED SLOAN AND GM'S STRATEGY

GM's competitive policies evolved out of experience with both success and failure in the contest with Ford. The basic approach has been summarized by Alfred Sloan:

In 1921 . . . no conceivable amount of money, short of the United States Treasury could have sustained the losses required to take volume away from [Ford] at their own game. The strategy we devised was to take a bite from the top of his position—and in this way build up Chevrolet volume on a profitable base.

Nevertheless—the K Model Chevrolet—was still far from the Ford Model T in price for the gravitational pull we hoped to exert in Mr. Ford's area of the market. It was our intention to continue adding improvements and

2. A. Sloan, *My Years With General Motors*, New York: Doubleday, 1972, p. 4, 186–7.

over a period of time to move down in price on the Model K as our position justified it.

We first said that the corporation should produce a line of cars in each price area, from the lowest to one for the strictly high grade quality-production car. . . . We proposed in general that General Motors should place its cars at the top of each price range and make them of such quality that they would attract sales from below that price. . . . This amounted to quality competition against cars above a given price tag and price competition against cars about that price tag. . . . The policy we said was valid if our cars were at least equal in design to the best of our competitor's grade, so that it was not necessary to lead in design or run the risk of untried experiment.

The same idea held for production—it was not essential that for any particular car production be more efficient than that of its best competitor—coordinated operation of our plants would result in great efficiency—the same could be said for engineering and other functions.[3]

Thus, there were three essential elements in GM's strategy: 1. Product design was conceived as a dynamic process that would lead to an ultimate target through incremental change. Design was not a once-and-for-all optimization as it had been with Ford. This process later became the annual model-change policy of GM. 2. Market needs would be met through the product-line policy rather than independent designs. 3. Radical product innovations were to be avoided. As Sloan said, it was "not necessary to . . . run the risk of untried experiment."

The broad competitive strategy that GM hammered out in specific decisions was to prove unbeatable. The company gained a dominant position in the U.S. market in the 1920s and has held it to the present. Little change in the essentials of GM's strategy was apparent during the period 1923–1973. Increased centralization among operating divisions, less difference in technological characteristics of various cars in the product line, and greater sharing of common components tended to make the different car lines more like a single product. In general terms, however, the strategy seems to have remained intact.

CHRYSLER AND PRODUCT ENGINEERING

The Chrysler Corporation seized a foothold in the market when Ford faltered in the Model T program and shut down for nine months. By

3. *Ibid.*, pp. 71–73.

1929 Chrysler offered four basic car lines: Chrysler, DeSoto, Dodge, and Plymouth. Unlike GM, production for all product lines was centralized, and Chrysler apparently did not integrate vertically backward as extensively as either GM or Ford. Because Chrysler produced fewer of its own components, it was less constrained in adopting advanced innovative components. Thus, Chrysler could seek competitive advantages through flexibility in product engineering and in styling. Chrysler pioneered in high-compression engines in 1925; in frame designs permitting a low center of gravity in the 1930s; and in the experimental introduction of disc brakes in 1949, power steering in 1951, and the alternator in 1960.

This strategy of design flexibility and shallow vertical integration proved very successful in the prewar period, when the rate of technological change in the product was rapid. As product designs stabilized after the war, however, other factors like the strength of dealerships and economies of scale became more important. Chrysler's market share followed a downward trend after World War II. Chrysler did develop strength in some segments of the market (vans, compacts) but was generally a follower in product development after the war. Cost control was difficult during times of inflation, when cost increases could not be passed on to the consumer.

This aspect was particularly troublesome after 1970. Inflation, government price controls, and the consumer's loss of real purchasing power have squeezed margins and capital at the very time when resources have been needed to develop and introduce smaller, more efficient cars. Chrysler's product image has not been well defined, and it has suffered a loss of customer loyalty and sales potential. Its current financial difficulties raise serious questions about long-term viability as a full-line producer. A competitive strategy emphasizing flexibility in product design was well suited to prewar conditions. As with Ford's early policies, however, it would seem that the development of the industry changed the necessary conditions for success.

THE IMPORTS

Imports have played a major role in the compact and subcompact segments of the U.S. market since the late 1950s. Foreign producers, notably Mercedes, BMW, and Triumph, have been important in specialty and luxury cars. The distinguishing feature of import strategies has been their emphasis on uniqueness in selected market niches. Whether in terms of size, performance, or quality, foreign firms have sought an advantage by creating products that were different from the standard or traditional domestic products. Furthermore, the more successful firms have built strong sales and service networks.

The clearest example of the importance of the dealer network in entering the U.S. market is the case of Volkswagen (VW). Firmly established before sales were made, the VW system of dealers became a distinctive competitive factor, particularly in comparison with other European manufacturers. VW's strategy of "service first" allowed the company to maintain a strong market presence through the 1960s. When relative costs of production shifted in the late 1960s and early 1970s, VW established a production facility in Pennsylvania.

The lessons of the VW experience have not been lost on the Japanese or other Europeans. The major Japanese firms have payed close attention to the development of a dealer network. The Renault–American Motors Corporation (AMC) relationship is motivated in part by Renault's desire for an established dealer system. Furthermore, production of Renault designs in AMC facilities is likely within the next few years. Other foreign manufacturers, notably Honda and Nissan, plan to open car and light-truck production facilities in the United States.

FIRM PERFORMANCE IN THE 1970s: RESPONSE TO CRISIS

Historically, the auto industry as a whole has earned returns above the average for manufacturing, both in terms of returns on sales and stockholders' equity. At the same time, however, those returns have shown much greater than average cyclical variability. The decade of the 1970s witnessed a trend toward erosion of the profitability of the domestic producers and marked cyclical swings in the recessions of 1970, 1974–1975, and most recently in the 1979–1980 period. The downward trend in profitability may reflect declines in real income, rapid shifts in relative prices, an inappropriate product mix, and effects of increased price competition from imported products. The importance of price competition is evident in Table 2, which presents data on Ford's list prices expressed in constant 1958 dollars and cumulative units of production. The long decline in the real price of the Model T, from 1908 to 1926, is indicative of Ford's

TABLE 2

LIST PRICES AND CUMULATIVE VOLUME AT FORD MOTOR COMPANY,

1908–1972

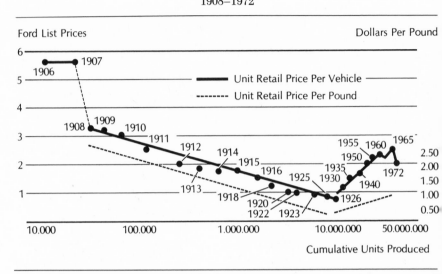

NOTE: Both axes are expressed in logarithms.

"experience curve" strategy. With the transformation of the market in the late 1920s and GM's leadership in building larger and more luxurious cars, the real price rose for over 30 years. Since 1960 two dips have occurred, both associated with import competition. It seems clear from these data that part of the weakening financial performance of the domestic producers can be traded to declining real prices, caused in part by intensive competition.

The oil price explosions in 1973 and again in 1979 played a key role in setting the economic context of industry performance. The oil crises affected the major firms very differently. Table 3 summarizes the basic competitive positions and market performance of the major domestic firms and indicates some of the actions taken in the aftermath of the twin oil shocks. Except for GM, which has gradually increased its share in the last few years, the domestic producers have lost significant market shares. The loss of markets is a reflection of rapid market shifts and lags in response. Ford, Chrys-

TABLE 3

COMPETITIVE STATUS AND FIRM PERFORMANCE IN THE U.S. AUTO INDUSTRY

Company	Dominant strategic orientation	Percentage of market share		Percentage of return on sales		Debt ratio[a]		Response to oil crisis
		1970–1978	1979	1970–1978	1979	1970–1978	1979	
General Motors	A car for "every purse and purpose"; full-line producer.	44.6	46.5	5.6	4.4	6.4	4.0	Downsize top of the line; diesehzation; new products (X body, J body); announced aggressive technology development.
Ford	Full-line producer; seek out specialty/unexploited niches.	23.8	20.3	3.4	2.2	15.5	11.0	Lag of 1–2 years in downsizing; product development (Escort).
Chrysler	Full-line producer; advanced product engineering; strength in vans/compacts.	12.9	9.0	0.5	–9.1	27.5	34.0	Lag in downsizing of large cars; product development (Omni, K cars).
AMC	Specialty small-car producer (jeeps, small cars).	2.8	1.5	0.5	2.7	20.4	11.0	Lag in product development and weight reduction; developed relationship with Renault.

SOURCE: Annual reports; *Moody's Industrial Manual* (cited in Arthur D. Little, Inc., *The Changing World Automotive Industry Through 2000*, 1980).

[a] Long-term debt as a percentage of total capitalization.

ler, and AMC have lagged behind GM in introducing strategic changes in vehicle size or new products. In general, GM has adopted a more aggressive posture, an approach consistent with traditional market leadership and greater financial resources.

Financial performance has deteriorated for all firms except AMC, for which 1979 was an exceptionally good year. All of the Big Three have experienced declining margins, with Chrysler suffering sizeable losses at the end of the decade. The addition of 1980 data would show negative returns from all producers, a situation that became evident in late 1979.

In retrospect, most of the 1970s was a time of transition for the U.S. auto industry. The once profitable, vigorous auto firms have experienced major financial and economic jolts; adjustments to the energy shocks and shifts in consumer tastes have not been smooth or easy.

Part Four

========

Capital Budgeting and Investment

========

To SOLVE most investment and capital budgeting problems, it is necessary to reduce funds received or spent at different points in time to comparable terms. Because a firm can realize a positive return from the investment of its funds, a dollar now is worth more than a dollar later. Pearson Hunt, Charles M. Williams, and Gordon Donaldson provide the solutions to various investment problems and show how to compute an investment's rate of return.

The next article, by David Hertz, describes risk analysis, a technique that is commonly employed in industry today. As Hertz emphasizes, "the discipline of thinking through the uncertainties of the problem will in itself help to ensure improvement in making investment choices. For to understand uncertainty and risk is to understand the key business problem—and the key business opportunity." This paper is a classic in the field.

To be competitive, firms must invest in new technology. In the next article, the editor discusses the returns from, and riskiness of, investments in research and development. Then Robert S. Kaplan indicates how discounted cash flow techniques can be, and should be, applied to determine whether firms should invest in computer-integrated manufacturing (CIM).

In the final article in this part of the book, Burton Malkiel describes and comments on various approaches to stock-market investing. He provides an informal and amusing account of modern portfolio theory and the capital-asset pricing model, both of which have had an enormous effect on the thinking of professional investors. In view of the attention devoted to the stock market, this article should be of widespread interest.

Time Adjustments of Flows of Funds

Pearson Hunt,
Charles M. Williams, and
Gordon Donaldson

*Pearson Hunt was Professor of Business Admin-
istration at Harvard University. Together with
Charles M. Williams and Gordon Donaldson, he
published* Basic Business Finance *from which this
paper is taken.*

Many decisions involve in some way a comparison of the usefulness of receiving or paying funds at one time rather than
another, and we need a means of evaluating the effect of the time
span involved. The procedure of *time adjustment* provides a
consistent and accurate means for the needed evaluation.

One basic assumption must be made before application of the
mathematical procedure, which involves nothing more than compound interest. We assume that a firm always can find some way
to invest funds to produce some net gain, or *rate of return*. The
rate may be very low, as when funds are temporarily placed in
short-term treasury bills, or it may be as high as the gain from
some new product greatly in demand. In fact, if a firm does not
act to obtain some return from the use of its funds, we speak of
the *opportunity cost,* which is the loss of revenue because an
opportunity was not taken. Therefore, since there can always be
earnings from the investment of funds, we can say as a general

rule that whenever a business has a choice of the time when it will obtain certain funds, the rule should be "the sooner, the better."

The first step to an understanding of time adjustment is to relate the amounts involved to one another along a scale of time. The time is divided into periods (e.g., days, months, years), and a particular point in time is selected as the starting point from which the effect of compound interest on the funds will be regarded. This time is named the *focal date*. Periods later than this date are designated by the plus sign, periods earlier by the minus sign, and the focal date is designated by zero. To the mathematician, it is unimportant what actual time is chosen as the focal date. The financial analyst can choose any date, past or present, most convenient for his purposes. In fact, for many problems of financial planning, it is convenient to have the focal date in the future, usually the date at which a specific sum will be received or paid, or at which a certain periodic flow of funds will terminate.

It is necessary to calculate the changing values of flows of funds as they occur both before and after the focal date. We first turn to *compounding*, that is, the subsequent growth in the value of funds initially invested at the focal date, because this process is one with which most readers will be familiar from such well-advertised operations as savings accounts on which interest is compounded. We shall then turn to *discounting*, which looks in the other direction from the focal date along the time scale.

COMPOUNDING

There are three quantities necessary for the calculation:

1. *The rate of return.* In the following exposition, to show the effects of different rates, we shall use two that are well within the range of business experience.

2. *The amount of funds in question.* It is convenient to use the sum of $1.00 to develop the formulas, since if one knows how the values of this sum are affected by time, one can compute the values of any other sum by simple multiplication.

3. *The length of time from the focal date.* This may be measured in days, weeks, etc., so that for the sake of generality,

one refers to the *period* rather than to some specific unit of time. One warning is necessary here. The rate of return used must be stated consistently with the actual length of the time period. Thus, 6 percent per year becomes 0.5 percent per month, and so on.

The growing amount that will be found at later times from an investment of $1.00 at the focal date is referred to as the *compound amount* (of a single sum). Interest is computed on the original sum and then added to the original sum at the end of the first period. The new and larger principal is then the base for the interest calculation in the second period, and so on. Jumping over the detailed mathematics, we can turn to any set of tables for business computations, among which we shall find values for the compound amount of a single sum invested at a given time. See Table 1 for a portion of such a table.

DISCOUNTING

The process of compounding discloses how the value of an investment made at the focal date grows in later time. We now turn to *discounting*, a process which looks at times preceding the focal date and answers the question: How much must be invested before the focal date to produce a desired sum at the time of the focal date?

The answers to such questions are determined by using the reciprocals of the values in the table of compound amounts, for the reasons exemplified in the following instance. Take four periods and 4 percent. Table 1 shows that if $1.00 is compounded

TABLE 1

COMPOUND AMOUNT OF $1.00

Periods	Rate 4%	Rate. 10%
0	1.000	1.000
+1	1.040	1.100
+2	1.082	1.210
+3	1.125	1.331
+4	1.170	1.464
+5	1.217	1.611

for this time and rate, it will increase to $1.17. To have only $1.00 at the end of four periods of compounding, we obviously need to invest less than $1.00. The calculation is:

$$x(1.170) = (1.000)(1.000)$$
$$x = \frac{(1.000)}{(1.170)} = 0.855$$

$$\frac{1.000}{1.170} = \frac{x}{1.000}$$
$$x = 0.855$$

The number so produced is known as the *present value* (at the selected time and rate) which will produce $1.00 at the focal date. The term *discounted value* is also used, although less frequently.

Since present values are often used in financial calculations, a table of present values is provided in most books on finance. For convenience, we reproduce a portion of such a table in Table 2.

Having shown how to evaluate a sum both before the focal date (by discounting) and after the focal date (by compounding), we are in a position to picture the changing value of the sum of $1.00 at the time of the focal date over a time scale. This is presented graphically in Chart 1, where the figures from Tables 1 and 2 are used.

The basic relationships to be observed are simple but very important:

1. The value of a sum invested at any time grows as time passes.
2. The necessary investment to produce a future sum decreases as the time to produce it is increased.
3. Both these effects are magnified as the rate of return increases.

TABLE 2

PRESENT VALUE OF $1.00

Periods	Rate 4%	Rate 10%
0	1.000	1.000
—1	0.962	0.909
—2	0.925	0.826
—3	0.889	0.751
—4	0.855	0.683
—5	0.822	0.621

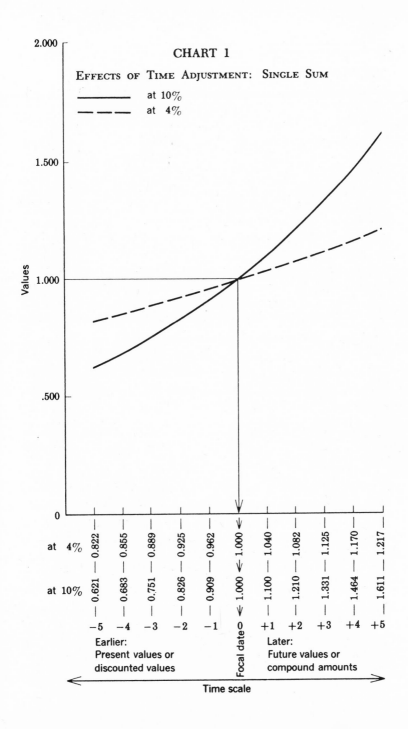

EXAMPLES OF COMPOUNDING AND DISCOUNTING

We shall now present two simple examples of how problems of compounding and discounting arise in business, and briefly indicate the nature of their solution.

Example 1. A firm with a major debt maturity at the end of two years sets aside $500,000 for investment in tax-exempt bonds at 4 percent to help meet the maturity. How much will be available from this source when the debt matures?

The problem is one of compounding. The focal date is the present, and the period is two years. From Table 1, we find 1.082 as the compound amount of $1.00 at 4 percent. Multiplying by $500,000 gives us $541,000, which is the sum that will be on hand.

Example 2. A factor often given importance when a firm is deciding whether to own or lease land and buildings is the residual value of the property that the firm would own if it bought rather than leased. Suppose that a certain property, now costing $1 million, is expected to be worth $2 million after allowance for taxes on the capital gain at the end of twenty-five years. How much importance should this terminal value have on a decision now?

The problem is one of discounting. The concept of opportunity cost also enters. Let us assume that the firm averages 10 percent return (after taxes) on assets invested in the business. One way to obtain $2 million at the end of twenty-five years is by holding the real estate. An alternative way would be to invest some funds now and use them at 10 percent to produce $2 million. What present investment at 10 percent will produce $2 million at a focal date twenty-five years hence? From Table 2 we find that the present value of $1.00 at 10 percent after twenty-five periods is 0.092. Multiplying by $2 million, we obtain $184,000. Thus, the desired value can be obtained either by using $184,000 in the business, allowing profits to compound, or by spending $1 million to buy the property. The possibility of error in overvaluing the expectation of remote capital gains is shown by this example. It is particularly serious when high rates of return are available from funds used otherwise in the business.

FINDING THE RATE OF RETURN

There is another use to which tables of present values are often put in financial work. Given values at two dates, one is sometimes required to find the rate of return that will produce a desired change in value. Using the figures from Example 2 above, the problem can be stated as follows: At what rate of return will $1 million grow to $2 million in twenty-five years?

The focal date is the end of the twenty-five-year period, when the present value table expects $1.00 to be paid. Converting the data from the actual case therefore requires division of the initial and terminal value by $2 million:

$$\frac{2,000,000}{2,000,000} = 1.000$$

and

$$\frac{1,000,000}{2,000,000} = 0.500.$$

The question has become: At what rate of discount will 0.50 become 1.00 at the end of twenty-five periods?

Looking at a table of present values for twenty-five periods, we find:

$$
\begin{aligned}
\text{Rate } 2\% &\dots\dots\dots\dots\dots\dots\dots 0.610 \\
\text{Rate } 4\% &\dots\dots\dots\dots\dots\dots\dots 0.375
\end{aligned}
$$

By the process of interpolation, we find the answer, which is 2.9 percent (much lower—and therefore less desirable—than the use of funds to produce 10 percent).

ANNUITIES

Our explanation of the effects of time on the value of funds has so far dealt only with single sums. That is, we have confined ourselves to watching the growth in value of a single in-

1. $2\% = 0.610$ $2\% = 0.610$
  $4\% = 0.375$ $x = 0.500$ $\dfrac{110}{235}$ $(2\%) = x = 0.9\%$
  $\overline{2\% = 0.235}$ $\overline{0.110}$

vestment, once it is made. We now turn to what is perhaps more frequently experienced in business, namely, the receipt or payment of a series of sums periodically over a stated number of time periods. Examples are rent and the flow of funds attached to a tax shield arising from depreciation.

There is much similarity between the mathematics already used and that which is necessary for *annuities,* as this type of periodic payment is termed by mathematicians. The focal date, however, takes on a new meaning, which the conventions of financial mathematics make even more complex. If one is looking into periods following the focal date, that date is the beginning of the first period of the annuity. In this case the applicable value at the focal date is zero, for the first payment of the annuity will take place only at the end of the first time period. If one is looking at times which are earlier than the focal date, however, the focal date is defined as the end of the last period, just after the moment of the final payment of the annuity. Again, the value is zero.

We shall introduce the annuity tables in the same order as before; that is, we first look ahead in time to consider the *compound amount* of an annuity, and then back to consider the *present value* of an annuity.

Compounding · Any annuity can be separated into a series of single payments and evaluated by the table of compound interest already described.

Suppose $1.00 is to be received at the end of each period, and that each $1.00 is to be invested at compound interest. How much will be the amount of the annuity a specified number of periods after the focal date? Let us take 4 percent and five years. The answer can be built up from Table 1, of compound amount, as follows:

$1.00 received at time $+1$ at 4% for 4 years becomes	$1.170
1.00 received at time $+2$ at 4% for 3 years becomes	1.125
1.00 received at time $+3$ at 4% for 2 years becomes	1.082
1.00 received at time $+4$ at 4% for 1 year becomes	1.040
1.00 received at time $+5$ at 4% for 0 year becomes	1.000
Total Value, Amount of Annuity	$5.417

From this example, we can see that a table of the desired values for annuities can be obtained by accumulating values from compound interest tables. See Table 3 for a brief portion of such a table.

TABLE 3

Amount of Annuity of $1.00 per Period

Periods	Rate 4%	Rate 10%
0	0	0
+1	1.000	1.000
+2	2.040	2.100
+3	3.122	3.310
+4	4.246	4.641
+5	5.416°	6.105

° The difference between this figure and 5.417, the amount of annuity given above, is due to rounding.

The question answered by such a table is: How much will the periodic receipt of $1.00 grow if all payments are held at compound interest at a specified rate and for a specified number of periods? In business terms, we are dealing with an annuity that is to be received.

Discounting · We now look at an annuity that is being paid out by the business, asking the question: How much must be invested in period $-n$ at the specified rate to permit the payment of an annuity of $1.00 per period, leaving nothing at the focal date? As before, this can be broken down into separate payments, which can be evaluated from the table of the present value of single sums. Let us take 4 percent and five years once more. Table 2 can be used.

> At the beginning of period -5:
>   it takes 0.822 to produce $1.00 in 5 years,
>   it takes 0.855 to produce $1.00 in 4 years,
>   it takes 0.889 to produce $1.00 in 3 years,
>   it takes 0.925 to produce $1.00 in 2 years,
>   it takes 0.962 to produce $1.00 in 1 year.
>
>   Total 4.453, Value of Annuity at Period -5

This example shows how the desired present values of annuities can be obtained by accumulating values from the table of the present values of a single sum. Such a table is included in most books on finance. For convenience, we reproduce a portion in Table 4.

TABLE 4

PRESENT VALUE OF $1.00 RECEIVED PERIODICALLY FOR *n* PERIODS

Periods	Rate 4%	Rate 10%
0	0	0
−1	0.962	0.909
−2	1.886	1.736
−3	2.775	2.487
−4	3.630	3.170
−5	4.452°	3.791

° The difference between this figure and 4.453, the value of the annuity given above, is due to rounding.

When we were dealing with the changing values of a single sum over time, we ended our explanation with a diagram. A similar one, Chart 2, can be presented for annuities, although the situation is more complex. The reader will note, in studying the charted annuities, that the values get larger as one proceeds in either direction from the focal date. This is because of the periodic payments of $1.00 that are involved. The reader will also note here, as in the more simple case, that changing the rate of return has considerable influence on the values, especially as time becomes more remote. In each instance the higher the rate, the greater the advantage to the user of the funds. That is, if 10 percent is applied, an annuity will cost less, or produce more, than if a lower rate were applied.

Before we leave the subject of the present values of annuities, we shall describe in another way the operation of the investment of $4.452 at 4 percent to permit paying $1.00 per year for five years. This will not add to the theoretical structure, but it will picture the process in a way that is more useful in financial thinking.

At the beginning of year −5, invest $4.452.
At the end of year −5, take interest of $0.178, and withdraw $0.822.
At the beginning of year −4, remainder invested becomes $3.630.

CHART 2

Effects of Time Adjustment: Annuity

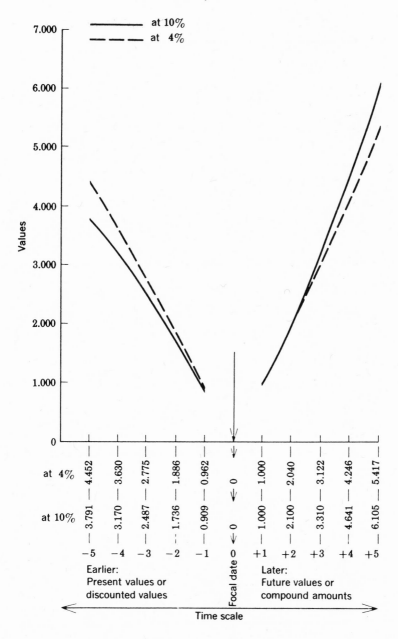

At the end of year − 4, take interest of $0.145, and withdraw $0.855.
At the beginning of year − 3, remainder invested becomes $2.775.
At the end of year − 3, take interest of $0.111, and withdraw $0.889.
At the beginning of year − 2, remainder invested becomes $1.886.
At the end of year − 2, take interest of $0.075, and withdraw $0.925.
At the beginning of year − 1, remainder invested becomes $0.961.
At the end of year − 1, take interest of $0.038, and withdraw $0.962.
There is a difference between $0.962 and $0.961, because of the use of
  abbreviated tables. Ignoring this, we can see that the annuity ends
  with the final payment of $1.00.

From this table, it can be seen that a company can receive $1.00
a year for five years with an initial investment of $4.452, if the
interest rate is 4 percent. It can also be seen, however, that the
initial investment of capital is consumed in the process. It is of
great importance to recognize that the table does *not* say that if
the rate of return is 4 percent, the annuity will go on without
reducing principal. If the principal is to be preserved, its with-
drawals must not be consumed, but invested elsewhere. Also,
if 4 percent is to continue to be obtained from the use of funds,
the new investment opportunities must yield this rate.

Examples Using Annuities · As before, we conclude our explanation of the derivation of tables of compound amount and
present value for annuities with examples taken from business
situations.

Example 1. A firm which is considering setting up a pension
fund determines that it can afford to set aside for this purpose
$100,000 a year for ten years. It is advised that a trustee can
earn 4 percent (tax exempt) with such moneys. How much will
have been accumulated after ten years?

The problem is to evaluate an annuity of $100,000 whose focal
date is the present, whose period is ten years, and whose rate is
4 percent. Tables of compound amount (not available in this
book) give a factor of 12.006 under these conditions. Multiplying
by $100,000 gives the desired answer, which is $1,200,600.

Example 2. Analysis of a certain investment project indicates
that it will produce $50,000 a year, before taxes, for ten years.
How much could the company justify investing in this project if
other investments are available at 4 percent? At 10 percent?

The problem is the evaluation as of now of an annuity whose

focal date is ten years from the present. We find the present value factor for ten periods to be 8.111 for 4 percent, and 6.145 for 10 percent. Multiplying by $50,000, we find $405,550 for 4 percent and $307,250 for 10 percent. These are the sums that could be invested at the specified rates to produce $50,000 a year for ten years.

Example 3. Taking the figures as developed in Example 2, assume that the firm finds that $350,000 is required as an investment to establish the project. Since this number is more than the present value at 10 percent, the firm should not undertake the project if it has other opportunities on which 10 percent can be earned. The firm should, however, consider the project an excellent one if the alternative opportunities are offering 4 percent return.

Finding the Rate of Return · One last step in the use of present value tables will be illustrated here. Given the periodic amount of an annuity and the original investment, what is the rate of return? Using the figures from Example 3, above, what rate of return will produce a ten-year annuity of $50,000 from the investment of $350,000?

The focal date is the end of the ten-year period, when the last payment will be received. The present value table is based on annuities of $1.00 per period, so the figures in the actual case must be converted by dividing through by $50,000:

$$\frac{50,000}{50,000} = 1.000$$

and

$$\frac{350,000}{50,000} = 7.000.$$

Looking at the table of present values of an annuity for ten periods, we find:

$$
\begin{array}{ll}
\text{Rate } 6\% & 7.360 \\
\text{Rate } 8\% & 6.710
\end{array}
$$

By interpolation, the answer can be computed. It is 7.1 percent.

RATE OF RETURN = NET PROFITS EARNED / TOTAL INVESTED CAPITAL

productivity of capital

Risk Analysis in Capital Investment

David B. Hertz

David B. Hertz is a Principal with McKinsey and Company. This paper appeared in the Harvard Business Review.

Of all the decisions that business executives must make, none is more challenging—and none has received more attention—than choosing among alternative capital investment opportunities. What makes this kind of decision so demanding, of course, is not the problem of projecting return on investment under any given set of assumptions. The difficulty is in the assumptions and in their impact. Each assumption involves its own degree—often a high degree—of uncertainty; and, taken together, these combined uncertainties can multipy into a total uncertainty of critical proportions. This is where the element of risk enters, and it is in the evaluation of risk that the executive has been able to get little help from currently available tools and techniques.

There is a way to help the executive sharpen his key capital investment decisions by providing him with a realistic measurement of the risks involved. Armed with this measurement, which evaluates for him the risk at each possible level of return, he is then in a position to measure more knowledgeably alternative courses of action against corporate objectives.

NEED FOR NEW CONCEPT

The evaluation of a capital investment project starts with the principle that the productivity of capital is measured by the rate of return we expect to receive over some future period. A dollar received next year is worth less to us than a dollar in hand today. Expenditures three years hence are less costly than expenditures of equal magnitude two years from now. For this reason we cannot calculate the rate of return realistically unless we take into account (a) when the sums involved in an investment are spent and (b) when the returns are received.

Comparing alternative investments is thus complicated by the fact that they usually differ not only in size but also in the length of time over which expenditures will have to be made and benefits returned.

It is these facts of investment life that long ago made apparent the shortcomings of approaches that simply averaged expenditures and benefits, or lumped them, as in the number-of-years-to-pay-out method. These shortcomings stimulated students of decision-making to explore more precise methods for determining whether one investment would leave a company better off in the long run than would another course of action.

It is not surprising, then, that much effort has been applied to the development of ways to improve our ability to discriminate among investment alternatives. The focus of all of these investigations has been to sharpen the definition of the value of capital investments to the company. The controversy and furor that once came out in the business press over the most appropriate way of calculating these values has largely been resolved in favor of the discounted cash flow method as a reasonable means of measuring the rate of return that can be expected in the future from an investment made today.

Thus we have methods which, in general, are more or less elaborate mathematical formulas for comparing the outcomes of various investments and the combinations of the variables that will affect the investments.[1] As these techniques have progressed,

1. See, for example, Joel Dean, *Capital Budgeting* (New York, Columbia University Press, 1951); "Return on Capital as a Guide to Managerial Decisions," *National Association of Accounts Research Report No. 35*, Decem-

the mathematics involved has become more and more precise, so that we can now calculate discounted returns to a fraction of a percent.

But the sophisticated businessman knows that behind these precise calculations are data which are not that precise. At best, the rate-of-return information he is provided with is based on an average of different opinions with varying reliabilities and different ranges of probability. When the expected returns on two investments are close, he is likely to be influenced by "intangibles"—a precarious pursuit at best. Even when the figures for two investments are quite far apart, and the choice seems clear, there lurks in the back of the businessman's mind memories of the Edsel and other ill-fated ventures.

In short, the decision-maker realizes that there is something more he ought to know, something in addition to the expected rate of return. He suspects that what is missing has to do with the nature of the data on which the expected rate of return is calculated, and with the way those data are processed. It has something to do with uncertainty, with possibilities and probabilities extending across a wide range of rewards and risks.

The Achilles Heel · The fatal weakness of past approaches thus has nothing to do with the mathematics of rate-of-return calculation. We have pushed along this path so far that the precision of our calculation is, if anything, somewhat illusory. The fact is that, no matter what mathematics is used, each of the variables entering into the calculation of rate of return is subject to a high level of uncertainty. For example:

> The useful life of a new piece of capital equipment is rarely known in advance with any degree of certainty. It may be affected by variations in obsolescence or deterioration, and relatively small changes in use life can lead to large changes in return. Yet an expected value for the life of the equipment—based on a great deal of data from which a single best possible forecast has been developed—is entered into the rate-of-return calculation. The same is done for the other factors that have a significant bearing on the decision at hand.

ber 1, 1959; and Bruce F. Young, "Overcoming Obstacles to Use of Discounted Cash Flow for Investment Shares," *NAA Bulletin,* March 1963, p. 15.

Let us look at how this works out in a simple case—one in which the odds appear to be all in favor of a particular decision:

The executives of a food company must decide whether to launch a new packaged cereal. They have come to the conclusion that five factors are the determining variables: *advertising and promotion expense, total cereal market, share of market for this product, operating costs, and new capital investment.* On the basis of the "most likely" estimate for each of these variables the picture looks very bright—a healthy 30 percent return. This future, however, depends on each of the "most likely" estimates coming true in the actual case. If each of these "educated guesses" has, for example, a 60 percent chance of being correct, there is only an 8 percent chance that *all five* will be correct (.60 × .60 × .60 × .60 × .60). So the "expected" return is actually dependent on a rather unlikely coincidence. The decision-maker needs to know a great deal more about the *other* values used to make each of the five estimates and about what he stands to gain or lose from various combinations of these values.

This simple example illustrates that the rate of return actually depends on a specific combination of values of a great many different variables. But only the expected levels of ranges (e.g., worst, average, best; or pessimistic, most likely, optimistic) of these variables are used in formal mathematical ways to provide the figures given to management. Thus, predicting a single most likely rate of return gives precise numbers that do not tell the whole story.

The "expected" rate of return represents only a few points on a continuous curve of possible combinations of future happenings. It is a bit like trying to predict the outcome in a dice game by saying that the most likely outcome is a "7." The description is incomplete because it does not tell us about all the other things that could happen. In Exhibit 1, for instance, we see the odds on throws of only two dice having six sides. Now suppose that each die has 100 sides and there are eight of them! This is a situation more comparable to business investment, where the company's market share might become any one of 100 different sizes and where there are eight different factors (pricing, promotion, and so on) that can affect the outcome.

Nor is this the only trouble. Our willingness to bet on a roll of the dice depends not only on the odds but also on the stakes.

EXHIBIT 1

DESCRIBING UNCERTAINTY—A THROW OF THE DICE

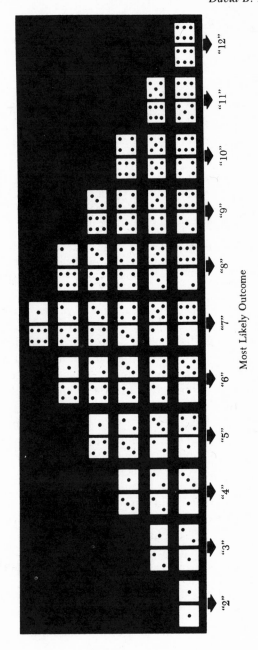

Most Likely Outcome

Since the probability of rolling a "7" is 1 in 6, we might be quite willing to risk a few dollars on that outcome at suitable odds. But would we be equally willing to wager $10,000 or $100,000 at those same odds, or even at better odds? In short, risk is influenced both by the odds on various events occurring and by the magnitude of the rewards or penalties which are involved when they do occur. To illustrate again:

Suppose that a company is considering an investment of $1 million. The "best estimate" of the probable return is $200,000 a year. It could well be that this estimate is the average of three possible returns —a 1-in-3 chance of getting no return at all, a 1-in-3 chance of getting $200,000 per year, a 1-in-3 chance of getting $400,000 per year. Suppose that getting no return at all would put the company out of business. Then, by accepting this proposal, management is taking a 1-in-3 chance of going bankrupt.

If only the "best estimate" analysis is used, management might go ahead, however, unaware that it is taking a big chance. If all of the available information were examined, management might prefer an alternative proposal with a smaller, but more certain (i.e., less variable), expectation.

Such considerations have led almost all advocates of the use of modern capital-investment-index calculations to plead for a recognition of the elements of uncertainty. Perhaps Ross G. Walker sums up current thinking when he speaks of "the almost impenetrable mists of any forecast." [2]

How can the executive penetrate the mists of uncertainty that surround the choices among alternatives?

Limited Improvements · A number of efforts to cope with uncertainty have been successful up to a point, but all seem to fall short of the mark in one way or another:

1. *More Accurate Forecasts.* Reducing the error in estimates is a worthy objective. But no matter how many estimates of the future go into a capital investment decision, when all is said and done, the future is still the future. Therefore, however well we forecast, we are still left with the certain knowledge that we cannot eliminate all uncertainty.

2. "The Judgment Factor in Investment Decisions," *Harvard Business Review,* March–April 1961, p. 99.

2. *Empirical Adjustments.* Adjusting the factors influencing the outcome of a decision is subject to serious difficulties. We would like to adjust them so as to cut down the likelihood that we will make a "bad" investment, but how can we do that without at the same time spoiling our chances to make a "good" one? And in any case, what is the basis for adjustment? We adjust, not for uncertainty, but for bias.

For example, construction estimates are often exceeded. If a company's history of construction costs is that 90 percent of its estimates have been exceeded by 15 percent, then in a capital estimate there is every justification for increasing the value of this factor by 15 percent. This is a matter of improving the accuracy of the estimate.

But suppose that new-product sales estimates have been exceeded by more than 75 percent in one-fourth of all historical cases, and have not reached 50 percent of the estimate in one-sixth of all such cases? Penalties for overestimating are very tangible, and so management is apt to reduce the sales estimate to "cover" the one case in six—thereby reducing the calculated rate of return. In doing so, it is possibly missing some of its best opportunities.

3. *Revising Cutoff Rates.* Selecting higher cutoff rates for protecting against uncertainty is attempting much the same thing. Management would like to have a possibility of return in proportion to the risk it takes. Where there is much uncertainty involved in the various estimates of sales, costs, prices, and so on, a high calculated return from the investment provides some incentive for taking the risk. This is, in fact, a perfectly sound position. The trouble is that the decision-maker still needs to know explicitly what risks he is taking—and what the odds are on achieving the expected return.

4. *Three-level Estimates.* A start at spelling out risks is sometimes made by taking the high, medium, and low values of the estimated factors and calculating rates of return based on various combinations of the pessimistic, average, and optimistic estimates. These calculations give a picture of the range of possible results, but do not tell the executive whether the pessimistic re-

sult is more likely than the optimistic one—or, in fact, whether the average result is much more likely to occur than either of the extremes. So, although this is a step in the right direction, it still does not give a clear enough picture for comparing alternatives.

5. *Selected Probabilities.* Various methods have been used to include the probabilities of specific factors in the return calculation. L. C. Grant discusses a program for forecasting discounted cash flow rates of return where the service life is subject to obsolescence and deterioration. He calculates the odds that the investment will terminate at any time after it is made depending on the probability distribution of the service-life factor. After calculating these factors for each year through maximum service life, he then determines an overall expected rate of return.[3]

Edward G. Bennion suggests the use of game theory to take into account alternative market growth rates as they would determine rate of return for various alternatives. He uses the estimated probabilities that specific growth rates will occur to develop optimum strategies. Bennion points out:

Forecasting can result in a negative contribution to capital budget decisions unless it goes further than merely providing a single most probable prediction. . . . [With] an estimated probability coefficient for the forecast, plus knowledge of the payoffs for the company's alternative investments and calculation of indifference probabilities . . . the margin of error may be substantially reduced, and the businessman can tell just how far off his forecast may be before it leads him to a wrong decision.[4]

Note that both of these methods yield an expected return, each based on only one uncertain input factor—service life in the first case, market growth in the second. Both are helpful, and both tend to improve the clarity with which the executive can view investment alternatives. But neither sharpens up the range of

3. "Monitoring Capital Investments," *Financial Executive,* April 1963, p. 19.
4. "Capital Budgeting and Game Theory," *Harvard Business Review,* November–December 1956, p. 123.

"risk taken" or "return hoped for" sufficiently to help very much in the complex decisions of capital planning.

SHARPENING THE PICTURE

Since every one of the many factors that enter into the evaluation of a specific decision is subject to some uncertainty, the executive needs a helpful portrayal of the effects that the uncertainty surrounding each of the significant factors has on the returns he is likely to achieve. Therefore, the method we have developed at McKinsey & Company, Inc., combines the variabilities inherent in all the relevant factors. Our objective is to give a clear picture of the relative risk and the probable odds of coming out ahead or behind in the light of uncertain foreknowledge.

A simulation of the way these factors may combine as the future unfolds is the key to extracting the maximum information from the available forecasts. In fact, the approach is very simple, using a computer to do the necessary arithmetic. (Recently, a computer program to do this was suggested by S. W. Hess and T. A. Quigley for chemical process investments.[5])

To carry out the analysis, a company must follow three steps:

1. Estimate the range of values for each of the factors (e.g., range of selling price, sales growth rate, and so on) and within that range the likelihood of occurrence of each value.

2. Select at random from the distribution of values for each factor one particular value. Then combine the values for all of the factors and compute the rate of return (or present value) from that combination. For instance, the lowest in the range of prices might be combined with the highest in the range of growth rate and other factors. (The fact that the factors are dependent should be taken into account, as we shall see later.)

3. Do this over and over again to define and evaluate the odds of the occurrence of each possible rate of return. Since there

5. "Analysis of Risk in Investments Using Monte Carlo Techniques," *Chemical Engineering Symposium Series 42: Statistics and Numerical Methods in Chemical Engineering* (New York, American Institute of Chemical Engineering, 1963), p. 55.

are literally millions of possible combinations of values, we need to test the likelihood that various specific returns on the investment will occur. This is like finding out by recording the results of a great many throws what percent of "7"s or other combinations we may expect in tossing dice. The result will be a listing of the rates of return we might achieve, ranging from a loss (if the factors go against us) to whatever maximum gain is possible with the estimates that have been made.

For each of these rates the chances that it may occur are determined. (Note that a specific return can usually be achieved through more than one combination of events. The more combinations for a given rate, the higher the chances of achieving it—as with "7"s in tossing dice.) The average expectation is the average of the values of all outcomes weighted by the chances of each occurring.

The variability of outcome values from the average is also determined. This is important since, all other factors being equal, management would presumably prefer lower variability for the same return if given the choice. This concept has already been applied to investment portfolios.[6]

When the expected return and variability of each of a series of investments have been determined, the same technique may be used to examine the effectiveness of various combinations of them in meeting management objectives.

PRACTICAL TEST

To see how this new approach works in practice, let us take the experience of a management that has already analyzed a specific investment proposal by conventional techniques. Taking the same investment schedule and the same expected values actually used, we can find what results the new method would produce and compare them with the results obtained when conventional methods were applied. As we shall see, the new picture of risks and returns is different from the old one. Yet the differences are

6. See Harry Markowitz, *Portfolio Selection, Efficient Diversification of Investments* (New York, John Wiley and Sons, 1959); Donald E. Farrar, *The Investment Decision Under Uncertainty* (Englewood Cliffs, New Jersey, Prentice-Hall, Inc., 1962); William F. Sharpe, "A Simplified Model for Portfolio Analysis," *Management Science*, January 1963, p. 277.

attributable in no way to changes in the basic data—*only to the increased sensitivity of the method to management's uncertainties about the key factors.*

Investment Proposal · In this case a medium-size industrial chemical producer is considering a $10-million extension to its processing plant. The estimated service life of the facility is ten years; the engineers expect to be able to utilize 250,000 tons of processed material worth $510 per ton at an average processing cost of $435 per ton. Is this investment a good bet? In fact, what is the return that the company may expect? What are the risks? We need to make the best and fullest use we can of all the market research and financial analyses that have been developed, so as to give management a clear picture of this project in an uncertain world.

The key input factors management has decided to use are:

1. Market size.
2. Selling prices.
3. Market growth rate.
4. Share of market (which results in physical sales volume).
5. Investment required.
6. Residual value of investment.
7. Operating costs.
8. Fixed costs.
9. Useful life of facilities.

These factors are typical of those in many company projects that must be analyzed and combined to obtain a measure of the attractiveness of a proposed capital facilities investment.

Obtaining Estimates · How do we make the recommended type of analysis of this proposal?

Our aim is to develop for each of the nine factors listed a frequency distribution or probability curve. The information we need includes the possible range of values for each factor, the average, and some ideas as to the likelihood that the various possible values will be reached. It has been our experience that for major capital proposals managements usually make a significant investment in time and funds to pinpoint information about each of the relevant factors. An objective analysis of the values to be assigned to each can, with little additional effort, yield a subjective probability distribution.

Specifically, it is necessary to probe and question each of the experts involved—to find out, for example, whether the estimated cost of production really can be said to be exactly a certain value or whether, as in more likely, it should be estimated to lie within a certain range of values. It is that range which is ignored in the analysis management usually makes. The range is relatively easy to determine; if a guess has to be made—as it often does—it is easier to guess with some accuracy a range rather than a specific single value. We have found from past experience at McKinsey & Company, Inc., that a series of meetings with management personnel to discuss such distributions is most helpful in getting at realistic answers to the a priori questions. (The term "realistic answers" implies all the information management does not have as well as all that it does have.)

The ranges are directly related to the degree of confidence that the estimator has in his estimate. Thus, certain estimates may be known to be quite accurate. They would be represented by probability distributions stating, for instance, that there is only 1 chance in 10 that the actual value will be different from the best estimate by more than 10%. Others may have as much as 100% ranges above and below the best estimate.

Thus, we treat the factor of selling price for the finished product by asking executives who are responsible for the original estimates these questions:

1. Given that $510 is the expected sales price, what is the probability that the price will exceed $550?
2. Is there any chance that the price will exceed $650?
3. How likely is it that the price will drop below $475?

Managements must ask similar questions for each of the other factors, until they can construct a curve for each. Experience shows that this is not as difficult as it might sound. Often information on the degree of variation in factors is readily available. For instance, historical information on variations in the price of a commodity is readily available. Similarly, management can estimate the variability of sales from industry sales records. Even for factors that have no history, such as operating costs for a new product, the person who makes the "average" estimate must have some idea of the degree of confidence he has in his prediction, and therefore he is usually only too glad to express his feelings. Likewise, the less confidence he has in his estimate, the greater will be the range of possible values that the variable will assume.

This last point is likely to trouble businessmen. Does it really make sense to seek estimates of variations? It cannot be emphasized too strongly that the less certainty there is in an "average" estimate, *the more important it is to consider the possible variation in that estimate.*

Further, an estimate of the variation possible in a factor, no matter how judgmental it may be, is always better than a simple "average" estimate, since it includes more information about what is known and what is not known. It is, in fact, this very *lack* of knowledge which may distinguish one investment possibility from another, so that for rational decision-making it *must* be taken into account.

This lack of knowledge is in itself important information about the proposed investment. To throw any information away simply because it is highly uncertain is a serious error in analysis which the new approach is designed to correct.

Computer Runs · The next step in the proposed approach is to determine the returns that will result from random combinations of the factors involved. This requires realistic restrictions, such as not allowing the total market to vary more than some reasonable amount from year to year. Of course, any method of rating the return which is suitable to the company may be used at this point; in the actual case management preferred discounted cash flow for the reasons cited earlier, so that method is followed here.

A computer can be used to carry out the trials for the simulation method in very little time and at very little expense. Thus, for one trial actually made in this case, 3,600 discounted cash flow calculations, each based on a selection of the nine input factors, were run in two minutes at a cost of $15 for computer time. The resulting rate-of-return probabilities were read out immediately and graphed. The process is shown schematically in Exhibit 2.

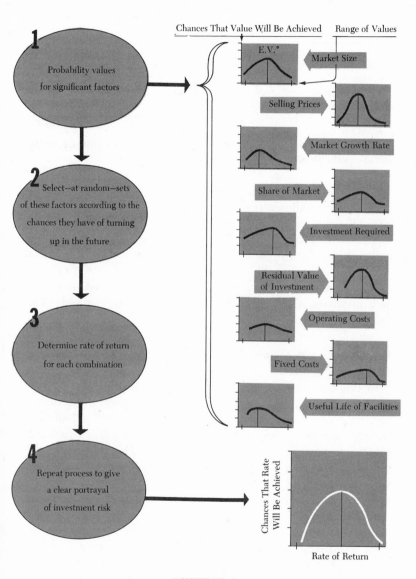

EXHIBIT 2

SIMULATION FOR INVESTMENT PLANNING

* Expected value = highest point of curve.

Data Comparisons · The nine input factors described earlier fall into three categories:

1. *Market analyses.* Included are market size, market growth rate, the firm's share of the market, and selling prices. For a given combination of these factors sales revenue may be determined.

2. *Investment cost analyses.* Being tied to the kinds of service-life and operating-cost characteristics expected, these are subject to various kinds of error and uncertainty; for instance, automation progress makes service life uncertain.

3. *Operating and fixed costs.* These also are subject to uncertainty, but are perhaps the easiest to estimate.

These categories are not independent, and for realistic results our approach allows the various factors to be tied together. Thus, if price determines the total market, we first select from a probability distribution the price for the specific computer run and then use for the total market a probability distribution that is logically related to the price selected.

We are now ready to compare the values obtained under the new approach with the values obtained under the old. This comparison is shown in Exhibit 3.

Valuable Results · How do the results under the new and old approaches compare?

In this case, management had been informed, on the basis of the "one best estimate" approach, that the expected return was 25.2 percent before taxes. When we ran the new set of data through the computer program, however, we got an expected return of only 14.6 percent before taxes. This surprising difference not only is due to the fact that under the new approach we use a range of values; it also reflects the fact that we have weighted each value in the range by the chances of its occurrence.

Our new analysis thus may help management to avoid an unwise investment. In fact, the general result of carefully weighing the information and lack of information in the manner I have suggested is to indicate the true nature of otherwise seemingly satisfactory investment proposals. If this practice were followed by managements, much regretted overcapacity might be avoided.

EXHIBIT 3

Comparison of Expected Values Under Old
and New Approaches

	Conventional "best estimate" approach	New approach
Market analyses		
1. *Market size*		
Expected value		
(in tons)	250,000	250,000
Range	—	100,000–340,000
2. *Selling prices*		
Expected value		
(in dollars/ton)	$510	$510
Range	—	$385–$575
3. *Market growth rate*		
Expected value	3%	3%
Range	—	0–6%
4. *Eventual share of market*		
Expected value	12%	12%
Range	—	3%–17%
Investment costs analyses		
5. *Total investment required*		
Expected value		
(in millions)	$9.5	$9.5
Range	—	$7.0–$10.5
6. *Useful life of facilities*		
Expected value		
(in years)	10	10
Range	—	5–15
7. *Residual value*		
(*at 10 years*)		
Expected value		
(in millions)	$4.5	$4.5
Range	—	$3.5–$5.0
Other costs		
8. *Operating costs*		
Expected value		
(in dollars/ton)	$435	$435
Range	—	$370–$545
9. *Fixed costs*		
Expected value		
(in thousands)	$300	$300
Range	—	250–$375

Note: Range figures in right-hand column represent approximately 1% to 99% probabilities. That is, there is only 1 in a 100 chance that the value actually achieved will be respectively greater or less than the range.

The computer program developed to carry out the simulation allows for easy insertion of new variables. In fact, some programs have previously been suggested that take variability into account.[7] But most programs do not allow for dependence relationships between the various input factors. Further, the program used here permits the choice of a value for price from one distribution, which value determines a particular probability distribution (from among several) that will be used to determine the value for sales volume. To show how this important technique works:

Suppose we have a wheel, as in roulette, with the numbers from 0 to 15 representing one price for the product or material, the numbers 16 to 30 representing a second price, the numbers 31 to 45 a third price, and so on. For each of these segments we would have a different range of expected market volumes; e.g., $150,000–$200,000 for the first, $100,000–$150,000 for the second, $75,000–$100,000 for the third, and so forth. Now suppose that we spin the wheel and the ball falls in 37. This would mean that we pick a sales volume in the $75,000–$100,000 range. If the ball goes in 11, we have a different price and we turn to the $150,000–$200,000 range for a price.

Most significant, perhaps, is the fact that the program allows management to ascertain the sensitivity of the results to each or all of the input factors. Simply by running the program with changes in the distribution of an input factor, it is possible to determine the effect of added or changed information (or of the lack of information). It may turn out that fairly large changes in some factors do not significantly affect the outcomes. In this case, as a matter of fact, management was particularly concerned about the difficulty in estimating market growth. Running the program with variations in this factor quickly demonstrated to us that for average annual growth from 3 percent and 5 percent there was no significant difference in the expected outcome.

In addition, let us see what the implications are of the detailed knowledge the simulation method gives us. Under the method using single expected values, management arrives only at a

7. See Frederick S. Hillier, "The Derivation of Probabilistic Information for the Evaluation of Risky Investments," *Management Science*, April 1963, p. 443.

hoped-for expectation of 25.2 percent after taxes (which, as we have seen, is wrong unless there is no variability in the various input factors—a highly unlikely event). On the other hand, with the method we propose, the uncertainties are clearly portrayed:

Percent return	Probability of achieving at least the return shown
0%	96.5%
5	80.6
10	75.2
15	53.8
20	43.0
25	12.6
30	0

This profile is shown in Exhibit 4. Note the contrast with the profile obtained under the conventional approach. This concept has been used also for evaluation of new product introductions, acquisitions of new businesses, and plant modernization.

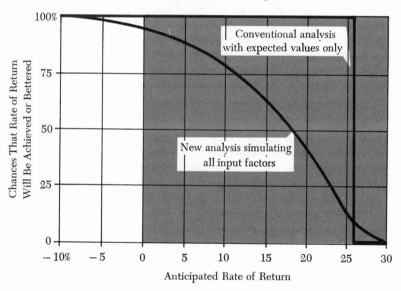

EXHIBIT 4

ANTICIPATED RATES OF RETURN UNDER
OLD AND NEW APPROACHES

COMPARING OPPORTUNITIES

From a decision-making point of view one of the most significant advantages of the new method of determining rate of return is that it allows management to discriminate between measures of (1) expected return based on weighted probabilities of all possible returns, (2) variability of return, and (3) risks.

To visualize this advantage, let us take an example which is based on another actual case but simplified for purposes of explanation. The example involves two investments under consideration, A and B.

When the investments are analyzed, the data tabulated and plotted in Exhibit 5 are obtained. We see that:

• Investment B has a higher expectant return than Investment A.

• Investment B also has substantially more variability than Investment A. There is a good chance that Investment B will earn a return which is quite different from the expected return of 6.8 percent, possibly as high as 15 percent or as low as a loss of 5 percent. Investment A is not likely to vary greatly from the expected 5 percent return. There is virtually no chance of incurring a loss on Investment A.

• Investment B involves far more risk than does Investment A. However, there is 1 chance in 10 of losing money on investment B. If such a loss occurs, its expected size is approximately $200,000.

Clearly, the new method of evaluating investments provides management with far more information on which to base a decision. Investment decisions made only on the basis of maximum expected return are not unequivocally the best decisions.

CONCLUSION

The question management faces in selecting capital investments is first and foremost: What information is needed to clarify the key differences among various alternatives? There is agreement as to the basic factors that should be considered— markets, prices, costs, and so on. And the way the future return on the investment should be calculated, if not agreed on, is at

EXHIBIT 5

COMPARISON OF TWO INVESTMENT OPPORTUNITIES

Selected Statistics

	Investment A	Investment B
Amount of investment	$10,000,000	$10,000,000
Life of investment (in years)	10	10
Expected annual net cash inflow	$ 1,300,000	$ 1,400,000
Variability of cash inflow		
1 chance in 50 of being *greater* than	$ 1,700,000	$ 3,400,000
1 chance in 50 of being *less* ° than	900,000	($600,000)
Expected return on investment	5.0%	6.8%
Variability of return on investment		
1 chance in 50 of being *greater* than	7.0%	15.5%
1 chance in 50 of being *less* ° than	3.0%	(4.0%)
Risk of investment		
Chance of a loss	Negligible	1 in 10
Expected size of loss		$ 200,000

° In the case of negative figures (indicated by parentheses), "less than" means "worse than."

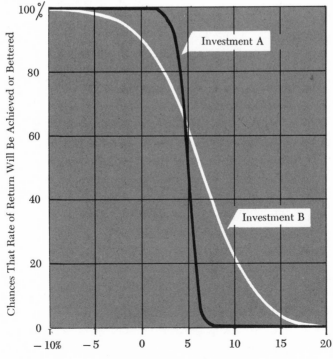

least limited to a few methods, any of which can be consistently used in a given company. If the input variables turn out as estimated, any of the methods customarily used to rate investments should provide satisfactory (if not necessarily maximum) returns.

In actual practice, however, the conventional methods do *not* work out satisfactorily. Why? The reason, as we have seen earlier in this article, and as every executive and economist knows, is that the estimates used in making the advance calculations are just that—estimates. More accurate estimates would be helpful, but at best the residual uncertainty can easily make a mockery of corporate hopes. Nevertheless, there is a solution. To collect realistic estimates for the key factors means to find out a great deal about them. Hence the kind of uncertainty that is involved in each estimate can be evaluated ahead of time. Using this knowledge of uncertainty, executives can maximize the value of the information for decision-making.

The value of computer programs in developing clear portrayals of the uncertainty and risk surrounding alternative investments has been proved. Such programs can produce valuable information about the sensitivity of the possible outcomes to the variability of input factors and to the likelihood of achieving various possible rates of return. This information can be extremely important as a backup to management judgment. To have calculations of the odds on all possible outcomes lends some assurance to the decision-makers that the available information has been used with maximum efficiency.

This simulation approach has the inherent advantage of simplicity. It requires only an extension of the input estimates (to the best of our ability) in terms of probabilities. No projection should be pinpointed unless we are *certain* of it.

The discipline of thinking through the uncertainties of the problem will in itself help to ensure improvement in making investment choices. For to understand uncertainty and risk is to understand the key business problem—and the key business opportunity. Since the new approach can be applied on a continuing basis to each capital alternative as it comes up for consideration and progresses toward fruition, gradual progress may be expected in improving the estimation of the probabilities of variation.

Lastly, the courage to act boldly in the face of apparent uncertainty can be greatly bolstered by the clarity of portrayal of the risks and possible rewards. To achieve these lasting results requires only a slight effort beyond what most companies already exert in studying capital investments.

Investing in R and D

EDWIN MANSFIELD

Edwin Mansfield is Director of the Center for Economics and Technology at the University of Pennsylvania. This paper was published in the Harvard Business Review *in 1981.*

American companies usually have been at the forefront of new technology. Their long-term profitability as well as their present success in the marketplace have often resulted from new products and processes. And these products and processes have come largely, if not exclusively, from an active commitment to R&D.

The past decade, however, has seen much soul-searching among business leaders, government officials, and academic experts about the apparent decline of innovation in several basic American industries. Given this threat to their technological leadership, the ability to manage innovation—once virtually taken for granted—is now high on many corporate agendas.

R&D, of course, is only part of the activity leading to technological success. Of the total cost of product innovation, 40 percent goes on average for tooling and for the design and construction of manufacturing facilities, 15 percent for manufacturing and marketing start-up. Moreover, in some industries only a small percentage of significant advance is a direct outgrowth of corporate R&D—17 percent in the railroad industry, for example, and 27 percent in housing.

But a company's ability to produce significant innovations *is* closely related to the amount it spends on R&D. Not only that, data from

Note: All footnotes have been omitted from the original article.

several industries show that a company's rate of productivity increase is also related, though with a time lag, to the amount it spends on R&D (as well as to the amount spent on R&D by its suppliers).

Findings like these suggest that professional economists have something of value to say to managers concerned with the development of technology. In fact, over two decades the "dismal science" has produced a sizable body of research that bears directly on the management of innovation in general and R&D in particular. Although these studies do not, for the most part, provide guidance for day-to-day decisions, they do help establish the context within which such decisions are made. At the least, they help define the major questions with which technology-oriented managers must be concerned: (1) What kinds of risks does R&D activity involve? (2) What factors appear to make that activity successful? (3) What is the best structure for a portfolio of technology-based projects? (4) What is the rate of return for investment in such projects?

WHAT ARE THE RISKS?

My research on the R&D programs of three companies (one in chemicals, two in proprietary drugs) revealed an average probability of only 12 percent that an R&D project would result in an economically successful product or process. In other words, roughly one out of every eight projects turned out well. The results of another study I directed, this one based on four years of data from 16 major companies in the chemical, drug, petroleum, and electronics industries, showed a slightly higher probability of success—about 20 percent.

To a great extent, the risks in industrial R&D are commercial, not technical. In fact, technical risk is often quite modest—outside, that is, military, space, and other areas in which major state-of-the-art innovations are sought. A survey of 19 laboratories in the petroleum, chemical, electronics, and drug industries, for example, found the likelihood of a project's reaching technical completion to be greater than 50-50. Most R&D projects, of course, aim at fairly modest advances and are thus reasonably well assured of success. And for those laboratories that devote a large percentage of their resources to development rather than research, the technical risk is smaller still.

By contrast, commercial risk—the possibility that a new product or process will not merit commercial introduction or application or that, if it does, it will not be an economic success—is often substantial. In the three companies cited earlier, 60 percent of the R&D projects reached technical completion, 30 percent were commercialized, but only 12 percent earned an economic profit. A project is, therefore, much more likely to achieve technical than commercial success.

WHAT MAKES FOR SUCCESS?

Of course, even companies in the same industry may differ markedly in their ability to make R&D pay off commercially. During a four-year period, for instance, three evenly matched chemical companies found the proportion of their R&D expenditures that earned a profit to be 69 percent, 54 percent, and 39 percent, respectively. These differences are too large to be attributed to errors of measurement or definition. What can explain them?

The Importance of Linkage · As already noted, an R&D project's likelihood of economic success is the product of three separate factors: (1) the probability of technical success, (2) the probability of commercialization (given technical success), and (3) the probability of economic success (given commercialization). One econometric study I helped conduct shows that all three of these probabilities are directly related to how quickly an R&D project is evaluated for its economic, as opposed to technical, potential.

In those companies whose R&D staff members do not work closely or responsively with marketing staff, the integration of R&D activity with market realities is haphazard, belated, or both. Yet commercially successful innovation depends on just this sort of integration. Numerous case studies of successful and unsuccessful innovation come to the same conclusion: the closer the link between marketing and R&D, the greater the probability of commercialization (given technical completion).

Consider, by way of illustration, the experience of three chemical companies of roughly the same size and level of R&D expenditure that underwent reorganization at roughly the same time. In two of them, the reorganization produced a closer integration of R&D with marketing by improving the channels of communication between them as well as by noticeably increasing marketing's input to R&D

decision making. In the third, however, integration decreased; R&D paid even less attention to marketing than it had before the reorganization.

Data on the probability of commercialization (given technical completion) of 330 R&D projects in these companies—projects carried out anywhere from three to seven years before reorganization to five to eight years after it—are highly suggestive. They show an increase of about 20 percentage points for the two companies that more closely linked R&D with marketing and a decrease of about 20 percentage points for the third.

More generally, a substantial portion of a company's R&D efforts may lie fallow because other parts of the company do not make proper use of them. One survey of executive opinion has noted the widely held belief that the economic success rate of R&D projects would increase by half if marketing and production people fully exploited them. If this figure is anywhere close to the truth, the faulty interface between R&D and the other functions has a very serious effect on the productivity of industrial R&D.

The Importance of Balance · A trade off exists between the probabilities of technical completion and of economic success (given commercialization). As more of a company's R&D effort goes into really ambitious projects, the probability of technical completion goes down, but the probability of economic success (given commercialization) usually goes up.

To a point that varies from company to company, projects of this sort are highly desirable. Any reduction they cause in the probability of technical completion is more than offset by the increase in the probability of economic success (given commercialization). Beyond this point, however, the logic runs the other way. Further reductions in the probability of completion are not offset by increases in the likelihood of economic success.

In recent years some companies, attracted by the higher odds of technical completion, have concentrated on too many unambitious projects with small potential for profit. The allure of technical safety notwithstanding, they might have done better to balance their low-risk R&D activity with technically more ambitious projects whose probability of economic success (given commercialization) was higher. In a well-managed R&D portfolio, both kinds of projects are needed—and in the right proportion.

WHAT IS THE RIGHT PORTFOLIO?

Companies in the same industry often devote markedly different proportions of their R&D expenditures to basic research and long-term, technically ambitious projects. To some extent these differences vary with size. In most industries, the larger the company, the larger the percentage of R&D devoted to basic research.

A portfolio's division into long- and short-term projects is important at the industry as well as the company level. Although the evidence is limited, there appears to be a significant relationship between an industry or company's expenditures on basic research and its rate of productivity increase. Technical questions make the calculations difficult, but statistical data from 1948–1966 strongly link an industry's rate of productivity increase with the extent to which its R&D was long term.

Recently, I conducted a study of the chemical and petroleum industries to determine whether the number of a company's major innovations has anything to do with the composition of its R&D expenditures. The answer is yes. Holding the total of those expenditures constant, the study shows that innovative output relates directly to the percentage of an R&D budget that goes for basic research. It is, however, still impossible to say whether basic research is itself the relevant variable or whether it is a proxy for something else.

Historical Changes · During the late 1960s and 1970s virtually all U.S. manufacturing industries reduced the proportion of R&D allocated to basic research, and many of them—including aerospace, chemicals, metals, and rubber—reduced proportional allocations to long-term projects generally. In a few, such as pharmaceuticals, the proportion increased, but largely in response to regulatory pressures.

According to many R&D executives, these changes resulted from (1) the increase in government regulations, which reduced the average profitability of risky projects; (2) the fact that certain kinds of technical breakthrough became more difficult to achieve because some fields had been thoroughly worked over; (3) the inflation of the 1970s, which discouraged long-term projects; and (4) the shift in management attention toward greater emphasis on detailed control, increased formality in R&D project selection, and heightened concern for the short-term effects of R&D on profits.

Project Selection · However well-founded the fears of excessively detailed control, some managerial oversight of R&D is essential. To make effective use of its R&D capacity, a company must first spell out its business objectives and then communicate them to its scientists and engineers. Research, after all, makes sense only when undertaken in areas relevant to economic goals.

Simply taking on a team of scientists and allowing them to do research in their favorite fields may produce novel results—but results that are unlikely to have much immediate commercial value. Most companies, therefore, have found it worthwhile to make economic evaluations of both project proposals and continuing projects, often adapting such capital budgeting techniques as rate of return or discounted cash flow to the task at hand.

Without question, these quantitative techniques have been useful, since they have forced managers to make their assumptions explicit. My research suggests that the sooner such evaluations are carried out, the greater a project's chances of ultimate commercial success.

The nature of these evaluations is different for a research as opposed to a development project. As a project moves from the laboratory toward the market, it receives more intensive scrutiny from both a

EVALUATING AN R&D PROJECT

Suppose that a company has a list of n possible R&D projects that it might carry out and that to undertake project i would cost C_i dollars. Moreover, suppose that project i has a probability of success of P_i and that, if successful, it will result in a profit (gross of R&D costs) of π_i. Then, if the company can spend no more than C dollars on R&D and if it wants to maximize the expected value of profit, its problem can be represented as follows:

Maximize

$$\sum_{i=1}^{n} X_i(P_i\pi_i - C_i)$$

where

$$\sum_{i=1}^{n} X_iC_i \leqslant C$$

and $X_i = 0, 1$

In other words, the company's problem is to choose the X_i—where $X_i = 1$ if project i is accepted and 0 if it is rejected—in such a way that it maximizes the expected value of profit, subject to the constraint that the total amount spent on R&D does not exceed C. This, of course, is an integer programming problem.

technical and an economic angle. In the early research phase, the screening of proposals will probably be quick and informal, since costs at this stage are still low and predicting outcomes is very difficult. But as projects enter the development phase, where costs and predictability are higher, they require a far more detailed process of economic evaluation.

Economists and operations researchers have developed a number of more or less sophisticated models to help solve these problems of evaluation. Some rely on the crudest of ranking procedures; some employ fairly straightforward adaptations of capital budgeting techniques; some use linear programming; others, dynamic programming; and still others, Bayesian decision theory. (See the ruled insert for a very simple example of such a model.) Among the best known are PROFILE (Programmed Functional Indices for Laboratory Evaluation) and QUEST (Quantitative Utility Estimates for Science and Technology)—both of which were developed for the U.S. Navy—and PATTERN (Planning Assistance Through Technical Evaluation of Relevance Numbers), developed by Honeywell.

The precise extent to which quantitative models of this sort are being used in the United States is unknown. Some surveys indicate that many of the laboratories—particularly the bigger laboratories—in the chemical, drug, and electronics industries have used them. But the surveys cannot tell how significant these techniques really are in the decision-making process. In some laboratories they are taken quite seriously indeed; in others, they are little more than window dressing for professional hunches and intracompany politics.

However, one fact is clear: the more sophisticated types of models have not been extensively used. Only 20 percent of the companies responding to one survey had tested or used linear programming models, and only about 10 percent had tested or used the more complicated techniques like PROFILE, QUEST, or PATTERN. The federal government, particularly the Department of Defense, has devoted considerable attention to such models, but it is not certain how much they have actually been applied in practice.

There are several reasons why the more complicated versions of these models have not found extensive use:

1. Many of the models fail to recognize that R&D is essentially a process of buying information, that unsuccessful projects can

provide valuable information, and that the real task is to facilitate sequential decision making under conditions of uncertainty.

2. Application of the more sophisticated versions is not cheap. One estimate puts the cost of setting up a PATTERN model at about $250,000 and the annual cost of maintaining it at about $50,000.

3. Perhaps most important, the models often rest on overly optimistic estimates that are not very reliable—estimates that reflect both the uncertainty of the undertaking and the desire to "sell" projects to top management.

Estimates and Projections · All project selection models require estimates of project cost and time, but these estimates are usually quite inaccurate. In the military, for example, large overruns in R&D costs and lesser overruns in R&D time are commonplace. In one sample of 12 airplane and missile development projects, the average ratio of actual to estimated cost was 3.2, and the average ratio of actual to estimated time was 1.4.

Estimates of this sort have proven almost as inaccurate for civilian as for military planning—especially when the projects attempt quite large technical advances. Even when commercial projects attempt minor advances, the estimates are often still considerably wide of the mark. In one proprietary drug firm, the average ratio of actual to estimated development cost was 2.1, and the average ratio of actual to estimated development time was 2.9. Moreover, the standard deviation of the cost ratio was 3.2; of the time ratio, 1.6. Estimates of the probability of technical success were not much better.

It is no wonder, then, that managers have been slow to adopt these project selection models. At the same time, however, they have found it worthwhile to make straightforward, often rough-and-ready evaluations of various project proposals and of continuing projects. But even these evaluations are a tricky business.

It is no simple matter to forecast the profitability of a new process or product. A recent study I conducted of all the major innovations developed during a five-year period by one of the nation's largest companies revealed that initial estimates of profitability were no more reliable than forecasts of development cost and time. The chances were about 50-50 that the estimated discounted profit from a new product or process would be more than double, or less than half, the actual discounted profit. So great was the uncertainty that the company took four or five years after developing a product or process innovation to estimate reasonably well its discounted profits.

This last point may seem surprising, since a company should presumably be able to estimate its savings from a new process far better than its sales of a new product. But the forecasting of input prices, royalty receipts, and the like is by no means an exact science.

Perhaps the study's most interesting finding was that the company consistently underestimated the profitability of very profitable innovations and overestimated the profitability of relatively unprofitable innovations. This pattern of inaccuracy may well have been the result of the forecasters' belief that the penalties for being too conservative in their estimates were less than those for being too far out on a limb. If uncorrected, such an understatement of the difference in anticipated discounted profits from "big winners" and the more run-of-the-mill innovations can result in a distorted allocation of resources. Because the extra profits from potential big winners are underestimated, management may pursue these ventures on a smaller scale or more hesitantly than it should.

WHAT IS THE RATE OF RETURN?

Some companies have for many years maintained careful audits of returns from past investments in technological innovation. Others are beginning to carry out such work. Retrospective studies of this sort can be very valuable in judging performance and in providing clues to instances of both overinvestment and underinvestment.

Historical Patterns · Every year since 1960, one of the nation's largest companies has put together an inventory of the technological innovations arising from its R&D-related activities. It has also made detailed estimates of the effect of each of these innovations on its profit stream. First, the company figures the expected difference in cash flows over time traceable to each one product, taking into account any loss of profits from displaced products. It then computes the expected difference in cash flows over time traceable to new processes. Finally, it updates past estimates each year, constantly refining them as time goes on.

Data are also kept on yearly expenditures for R&D-related activity. Using these cost data, as well as the figures on the total cash flow of benefits stemming from new products and processes, management can compute the rate of return represented by each year's

EXHIBIT 1

PRIVATE RATE OF RETURN FROM TOTAL INVESTMENT IN PROCESS
AND PRODUCT INNOVATIONS BY A MAJOR INDUSTRIAL COMPANY

Year	Both products and processes	Products	Processes
1	31%	21%	34%
2	9	0	15
3	7	17	negative[a]
4	26	13	30
5	15	9	18
6	16	27	−1
7	25	22	27
8	11	11	12
9	2	−1	5
10	3	13	−15
11	6	9	3
12	12	16	10
13	14	14	14
Total average	19%	14%	22%

[a] No major process innovations occurred in year three.

crop of innovations. The results covering one 13-year period are
shown in Exhibit 1.

Three points merit comment. First, the company's average rate
of return from investments in innovative activity was about 19 percent, a figure comfortably above its 15 percent hurdle rate. Second,
because innovation is a risky activity, the estimated rate of return
fell short of this 15 percent figure in about three years out of five,
although it averaged 19 percent overall. Third, year-to-year variations were greater for processes than for products.

The message to managers is clear: putting funds into R&D may
well prove an economically attractive use of resources over the long
run, but short-term fluctuations in returns do occur. Successful
management of innovation requires a generous time horizon.

The Social Good · Retrospective studies can also provide estimates
of the social rate of return from investments in R&D. The private
rate of return, discussed earlier, is the rate of return to the company
that makes the investment; the social rate measures the return to
society as a whole. In the past few years, economists have responded
to the needs of government agencies by publishing estimates of both

private and social rates of return from investments in more than 50 innovations in a variety of different industries.

Calculating private rates of return is, as already noted, a difficult operation, but the analytic problems in calculating social rates of return are greater still. Any innovation, particularly a major one, has subtle effects on the cash flows of many companies and industries, and any workable method must evaluate each of them and sum them all up properly. Nonetheless, economists have devised techniques that provide at least rough estimates of the social rates of return from particular innovations.

The estimates for 37 innovations are shown in Exhibit 2. Most of these innovations were of average or routine importance; few were breakthroughs. The figures are striking: although the median private rate of return was about 25 percent, the median social rate was about 70 percent.

It makes sense that the social rate often exceeds the private. Consider, for example, the new type of thread listed in Exhibit 2. This thread allowed higher sewing-machine speeds, which in turn reduced the costs to garment manufacturers. Since these savings were very large relative to the costs involved in developing the thread, the social rate of return was spectacularly high—more than 300 percent. But most of these benefits accrued to the garment manufacturers and the purchasers of finished garments. The innovator could not appropriate them because competitors could imitate the new thread easily, cheaply, and quickly—in fact, they did so within six months. Consequently, the private rate of return was only 27 percent.

To many economists, the relatively—and absolutely—high social rates of return are an indication that we as a nation are underinvesting in civilian technology, and this underinvestment has recently become an important factor in discussions of public policy.

A FINAL WORD

After many decades of neglecting technology, economists have devoted a great deal of attention to it during the past 20 years. Their studies should help managers in at least five ways:

1. They provide a much more accurate and detailed picture of the industrial innovation process than was previously available. Economists have identified the time intervals and costs associ-

EXHIBIT 2

Social and Private Rates of Return from Investment in 37 Innovations

Innovation	Rate of return in percent		Innovation	Rate of return in percent	
	Social	*Private*		*Social*	*Private*
Primary metals innovation	17%	18%	Industrial product A	62%	31%
Machine tool innovation	83	35	Industrial product B	negative	negative
Component for control system	29	7	Industrial product C	116	55
Construction material	96	9	Industrial product D	23	0
Drilling material	54	16	Industrial product E	37	9
Drafting innovation	92	47	Industrial product F	161	40
Paper innovation	82	42	Industrial product G	123	24
Thread innovation	307	27	Industrial product H	104	negative
Door-control innovation	27	37	Industrial product I	113	12
New electronic device	negative	negative	Industrial product J	95	40
Chemical product	71	9	Industrial product K	472	127
Chemical process A	32	25	Industrial product L	negative	13
Chemical process B	13	4	Consumer product M	28	23
Major chemical process	56	31	Consumer product N	62	41
Household cleaning device	209	214	Consumer product O	178	148
Stain remover	116	4	Consumer product P	144	29
Dishwashing liquid	45	46	Industrial process R	103	55
			Industrial process S	29	25
			Industrial process T	198	69
			Industrial process U	20	20

ated with various phases of this process as well as the company characteristics likely to help that process along.

2. They provide useful data on the nature of the risks involved in innovation and on the probabilities of success.
3. They provide new techniques of analysis, such as those for estimating social rates of return.
4. They provide guidance to managers on the various methods of project selection.
5. And, finally, they provide insight into basic linkages between the state of the economy and the rate of innovation.

The work of economists has by no means solved the riddle of technological change, but it has at last begun to offer practical, usable advice on the management of innovation.

Must CIM Be Justified by Faith Alone?

ROBERT S. KAPLAN

Robert S. Kaplan is a professor both at Harvard and Carnegie-Mellon Universities. This article was published in the Harvard Business Review *in 1986.*

When the Yamazaki Machinery Company in Japan installed an $18 million flexible manufacturing system, the results were truly startling: a reduction in machines from 68 to 18, in employees from 215 to 12, in the floor space needed for production from 103,000 square feet to 30,000, and in average processing time from 35 days to 1.5.[1] After two years, however, total savings came to only $6.9 million, $3.9 million of which had flowed from a one-time cut in inventory. Even if the system continued to produce annual labor savings of $1.5 million for 20 years, the project's return would be less than 10 percent per year. Since many U.S. companies use hurdle rates of 15 percent or higher and payback periods of five years or less, they would find it hard to justify this investment in new technology—despite its enormous savings in number of employees, floor space, inventory, and throughput times.

1. This example has appeared in several articles on strategic justification for flexible automation projects. Clifford Young of Arthur D. Little has traced the example to *American Market/Metalworking News*, October 26, 1981. Other examples of the labor, machinery, and throughput savings from flexible manufacturing system installations are presented in "Japan's Builders Embrace FMS," *American Machinist*, February 1985, p. 83.

The apparent inability of traditional modes of financial analysis like discounted cash flow to justify investments in computer-integrated manufacturing (CIM) has led a growing number of managers and observers to propose abandoning such criteria for CIM-related investments. "Let's be more practical," runs one such opinion. "DCF is not the only gospel. Many managers have become too absorbed with DCF to the extent that practical strategic directional considerations have been overlooked."[2]

Faced with outdated and inappropriate procedures of investment analysis, all that responsible executives can do is cast them aside in a bold leap of strategic faith. "Beyond all else," they have come to believe, "capital investment represents an act of faith, a belief that the future will be as promising as the present, together with a commitment to making the future happen."[3]

But must there be a fundamental conflict between the financial and the strategic justifications for CIM? It is unlikely that the theory of discounting future cash flow is either faulty or unimportant: receiving $1 in the future is worth less than receiving $1 today. If a company, even for good strategic reasons, consistently invests in projects whose financial returns are below its cost of capital, it will be on the road to insolvency. Whatever the special values of CIM technology, they cannot reverse the logic of the time value of money.

Surely, therefore, the trouble must not lie in some unbreachable gulf between the logic of DCF and the nature of CIM but in the poor application of DCF to these investment proposals. Managers need not—and should not—abandon the effort to justify CIM on financial grounds. Instead, they need ways to apply the DCF approach more appropriately and to be more sensitive to the realities and special attributes of CIM.

TECHNICAL ISSUES

The DCF approach most often goes wrong when companies set arbitrarily high hurdle rates for evaluating new investment projects. Perhaps they believe that high-return projects can be created by

2. John P. Van Blois, "Economic Models: The Future of Robotic Justification," Thirteenth ISIR/Robots 7 Conference, April 17–21, 1983 (available from Society of Manufacturing Engineers, Dearborn, Michigan).

3. Robert H. Hayes and David A. Garvin, "Managing As If Tomorrow Mattered," HBR May–June 1982, p. 70.

setting high rates rather than by making innovations in product and process technology or by cleverly building and exploiting a competitive advantage in the marketplace. In fact, the discounting function serves only to make cash flows received in the future equivalent to cash flows received now. For this narrow purpose—the only purpose, really, of discounting future cash flows—companies should use a discount rate based on the project's opportunity cost of capital (that is, the return available in the capital markets for investments of the same risk).

It may surprise managers to know that their real cost of capital can be in the neighborhood of 8 percent. (See Part I of the *Appendix* at the end of the article.) Double-digit hurdle rates that, in part, reflect assumptions of much higher capital costs are considerably wide of the mark. Their discouraging effect on CIM-type investments is not only unfortunate but also unfounded.

Companies also commonly underinvest in CIM and other new process technologies because they fail to evaluate properly all the relevant alternatives. Most of the capital expenditure requests I have seen measure new investments against a status quo alternative of making no new investments—an alternative that usually assumes a continuation of current market share, selling price, and costs. Experience shows, however, that the status quo rarely lasts. Business as usual does not continue undisturbed.

In fact, the correct alternative to new CIM investment should assume a situation of declining cash flows, market share, and profit margins. Once a valuable new process technology becomes available, even if one company decides not to invest in it, the likelihood is that some of its competitors will. As Henry Ford claimed, "If you need a new machine and don't buy it, you pay for it without getting it."[4] (For a more realistic approach to the evaluation of alternatives, see Part II of the *Appendix* at the end of the article.)

A related problem with current practice is its bias toward incremental rather than revolutionary projects. In many companies, the capital approval process specifies different levels of authorization depending on the size of the request. Small investments (under $100,000, say) may need only the approval of the plant manager;

---

4. Quoted in John Shewchuk, "Justifying Flexible Automation," *American Machinist*, October 1984, p. 93.

expenditures in excess of several million dollars may require the board of directors' approval. This apparently sensible procedure, however, creates an incentive for managers to propose small projects that fall just below the cut-off point where higher level approval would be needed. Over time, a host of little investments, each of which delivers savings in labor, material, or overhead cost, can add up to a less-than-optimal pattern of material flow and to obsolete process technology. (Part III of the *Appendix* shows the consequences of this incremental bias in more detail.)

Introducing CIM process technology is not, of course, without its costs. Out-of-pocket equipment expense is only the beginning. Less obvious are the associated software costs that are necessary for CIM equipment to operate effectively. Managers should not be misled by the expensing of these costs for tax and financial reporting purposes into thinking them operating expenses rather than investments. For internal management purposes, software development is as much a part of the investment in CIM equipment as the physical hardware itself. Indeed, in some installations, the programming, debugging, and prototype development may cost more than the hardware.

There are still other initial costs: site preparation, conveyors, transfer devices, feeders, parts orientation, and spare parts for the CIM equipment. Operating and maintenance personnel must be retrained and new operating procedures developed. Like software development, these tax-deductible training and education costs are part of the investment in CIM, not an expense of the periods in which they happen to be incurred.

Further, as some current research has shown, noteworthy declines in productivity often accompany the introduction of new process technology.[5] These productivity declines can last up to a year, even longer when a radical new technology like CIM is installed. Apparently, the new equipment introduces severe and unanticipated process disruptions, which lead to equipment breakdowns that are higher than expected; to operating, repair, and maintenance problems; to

5. See Robert H. Hayes and Kim B. Clark, "Exploring the Sources of Productivity Differences at the Factory Level," in *The Uneasy Alliance: Managing the Productivity, Technology Dilemma,* ed. Kim B. Clark, Robert H. Hayes, and Christopher Lorenz (Boston: Harvard Business School Press, 1985), and Bruce Chew, "Productivity and Change: Understanding Productivity at the Factory Level," Harvard Business School Working Paper (1985).

scheduling and coordination difficulties; to revised materials standards; and to old-fashioned confusion on the factory floor.

We do not yet know how much of the disruption is caused by inadequate planning. After investing considerable efforts and anguish in the equipment acquisition decision, some companies no doubt revert to business as usual while waiting for the new equipment to arrive.

Whatever the cause, the productivity decline is particularly ill timed since it occurs just when a company is likely to conduct a postaudit on whether it is realizing the anticipated savings from the new equipment. Far from achieving anticipated savings, the postaudit will undoubtedly reveal lower output and higher costs than predicted.

TANGIBLE BENEFITS

The usual difficulties in carrying out DCF analysis—choosing an appropriate discount rate and evaluating correctly all relevant investment alternatives—apply with special force to the consideration of investments in CIM process technology. The greater flexibility of CIM technology, which allows it to be used for successive generations of products, gives it a longer useful life than traditional process investments. Because its benefits are likely to persist longer, overestimating the relevant discount rate will penalize CIM investments disproportionately more than shorter-lived investments. The compounding effect of excessively high annual interest rates causes future cash flows to be discounted much too severely. Further, if executives arbitrarily specify short payback periods for new investments, the effect will be to curtail more CIM investments than traditional bottleneck-relief projects.

But beyond a longer useful life, CIM technology provides many additional benefits—better quality, greater flexibility, reduced inventory and floor space, lower throughput times, experience with new technology—that a typical capital justification process does not quantify. Financial analyses that focus too narrowly on easily quantified savings in labor, materials, or energy will miss important benefits from CIM technology.

Inventory Savings · Some of these omissions can be easily remedied. The process flexibility, more orderly product flow, higher quality, and better scheduling that are typical of properly used CIM equipment will drastically cut both work-in-process (WIP) and finished goods inventory levels. This reduction in average inventory levels represents a large cash inflow at the time the new process equipment becomes operational. This, of course, is a cash savings that DCF analysis can easily capture.

Consider a product line for which the anticipated monthly cost of sales is $500,000. Using existing equipment and technology, the producing division carries about three months of sales in inventory. After investing in flexible automation, the division heads find that reduced waste, scrap, and rework, greater predictability, and faster throughput permit a two-thirds reduction in average inventory levels. (This is not an unrealistic assumption: Murata Machinery has reported that its FMS installation permitted a two-thirds reduction in workers, a 450 percent increase in output, and a 75 percent cut in inventory levels.[6])

Pruning inventory from three months to one month of sales produces a cash inflow of $1 million in the first year the system becomes operational. If sales increase 10 percent per year, the company will enjoy increased cash flows from the inventory reductions in all future years too—that is, if the cost of sales rises to $550,000 in the next year, a two-month reduction in inventory saves an additional $100,000 that year, $110,000 the year after, and $121,000 the year after that.

Less Floor Space · CIM also cuts floor space requirements. It takes fewer computer-controlled machines to do the same job as a larger number of conventional machines. Also, the factory floor will no longer be used to store inventory. Recall the example of the Japanese plant that installed a flexible manufacturing system and reduced space requirements from 103,000 to 30,000 square feet. These space savings are real but conventional financial accounting systems do not measure their value well—especially if the building is almost fully depreciated or was purchased years before when price levels were lower. Do not, therefore, look to financial accounting systems for a good estimate of the cost or value of space. Instead, compute the estimate in terms of the opportunity cost of new space: either its square-foot rental value or the annualized cost of new construction.

6. "Japan's Builders Embrace FMS," *American Machinist*, February 1985, p. 83.

Many companies that have installed CIM technology have discovered a new factory inside their old one. This new "factory within a factory" occupies the space where excessive WIP inventory and infrequently used special-purpose machines used to sit. Eliminating WIP inventory and rationalizing machine layout can easily lead to savings of more than 50 percent in floor space. In practice, these savings have enabled some companies to curtail plant and office expansion programs and, on occasion, to fold the operations of a second factory (which could then be sold off at current market prices) into the reorganized original factory.

Higher Quality · Greatly improved quality, defined here as conformance to specifications, is a third tangible benefit from investment in CIM technology. Automated process equipment leads directly to more uniform production and, frequently, to an order-of-magnitude decline in defects. These benefits are easy to quantify and should be part of any cash flow analysis. Some managers have seen five- to tenfold reductions in waste, scrap, and rework when they replaced manual operations with automated equipment.

Further, as production uniformity increases, fewer inspection stations and fewer inspectors are required. If automatic gauging is included in the CIM installation, virtually all manual inspection of parts can be eliminated. Also, with 100 percent continuous automated inspection, out-of-tolerance parts are detected immediately. With manual systems, the entire lot of parts to be produced before a problem is detected would need to be reworked or scrapped.

These capabilities lead, in turn, to significant reductions in warranty expense. When General Electric automated its dishwasher operation, for example, its service call rate fell 50 percent. Designing manufacturability into products, making the production process more reliable and uniform, and improving automated inspection can all contribute to major cash flow savings. Although it may be hard to estimate these savings out to four or five significant digits, it would be grossly wrong to assume that the benefits are zero. We must overcome the preference of accountants for precision over accuracy, which causes them to ignore benefits they cannot quantify beyond one or two digits of accuracy.

We can estimate still other tangible benefits from CIM. John Shewchuk of General Electric claims that accounts receivable can be reduced by eliminating the incidence of customers who defer payment until quality problems are resolved.[7] Consider too that because improved materials flow can reduce the need for forklift trucks and operators, factories will enjoy a large cash flow saving from not having to acquire, maintain, repair, and operate so many trucks. All these calculations belong in a company's capital justification process.

INTANGIBLE BENEFITS

Other benefits of CIM include increased flexibility, faster response to market shifts, and greatly reduced throughput and lead times. These benefits are as important as those just discussed but much harder to quantify. We may not be sure how many zeros should be in our benefits estimate (are they to be measured in thousands or millions of dollars?) much less which digit should be first. The difficulty arises in large part because these benefits represent revenue enhancements rather than cost savings. It is fairly easy to get a ballpark estimate for percentage reductions in costs already being incurred. It is much harder to quantify the magnitude of revenue enhancement expected from features that are not already in place.

Greater Flexibility · The flexibility that CIM technology offers takes several forms. The benefits of economies of scope—that is, the potential for low-cost production of high-variety, low-volume goods—are just beginning to flow from FMS environments as early adopters of the technology start to service after-market sales for discontinued models on the same equipment used to produce current high-volume models. We are also beginning to see some customized production on the same lines used for standard products.

Beyond these economy-of-scope applications, CIM's reprogramming capabilities make it possible for machines to serve as backups for each other. Even if a machine is dedicated to a narrow product line, it can still replace lost production during a second or a third shift when a similar piece of equipment, producing quite a different product, breaks down.

Further, by easily accommodating engineering change orders and product redesigns, CIM technology allows for product changes over time. And, if the mix of products demanded by the market changes, a CIM-based process can respond with no increase in costs. The

7. John Shewchuk, "Justifying Flexible Automation."

body shop of one automobile assembly plant, for example, quickly adjusted its flexible, programmed spot-welding robots to a shift in consumer preference from the two-door to the four-door version of a certain car model. Had the line been equipped with nonprogrammable welding equipment, the adjustment would have been far more costly.

CIM's flexibility also gives it usefulness beyond the life cycle of the product for which it was purchased. True, in the short run, CIM may perform the same functions as less expensive, inflexible equipment. Many benefits of its flexibility will show up only over time. Therefore, it is difficult to estimate how much this flexibility will be worth. Nonetheless, as we shall see, even an order-of-magnitude estimate may be sufficient.

Shorter Throughput and Lead Time · Another seemingly intangible benefit of CIM is the great reductions it makes possible in throughput and lead time. At the Yamazaki factory described at the beginning of this article, average processing time per work piece fell from 35 to 1.5 days. Other installations, including Yamazaki's Mazak plant in Florence, Kentucky, have reported similar savings, ranging from a low of 50 percent reduction in processing time to a maximum of nearly 95 percent. To be sure, some of the benefits from greatly reduced throughput times have already been incorporated in our estimate of savings from inventory reductions. But there is also a notable marketing advantage in being able to meet customer demands with shorter lead times and to respond quickly to changes in market demand.

Increased Learning · Some investments in new process technology have important learning characteristics. Thus, even if calculations of the net present value of their cash flows turn up negative, the investments can still be quite valuable by permitting managers to gain experience with the technology, test the market for new products, and keep a close watch on major process advances.

These learning effects have characteristics similar to buying options in financial markets. Buying options may not at first seem like a favorable investment, but quite small initial outlays may yield huge benefits down the line. Similarly, were a company to invest in a risky CIM-related project, it could reap big gains should the technology provide unexpected competitive advantages in the future. Moreover, given the rapid pace of technological change and the advantages of being an early market participant, companies that defer process investments until the new technology is well established will find themselves far behind the market leaders. In this context, the decision to defer investment is often a decision not to be a principal player in the next round of product or process innovation.

The companies that in the mid-1970s invested in automatic and electronically controlled machine tools were well positioned to exploit the microprocessor-based revolution in capabilities—much higher performance at much lower cost—that hit during the early 1980s. Because operators, maintenance personnel, and process engineers were already comfortable with electronic technology, it was relatively simple to retrofit existing machines with powerful microelectronics. Companies that had earlier deferred investment in electronically controlled machine tools fell behind: they had acquired no option on these new process technologies.

THE BOTTOM LINE

Although intangible benefits may be difficult to quantify, there is no reason to value them at zero in a capital expenditure analysis. Zero is, after all, no less arbitrary than any other number. Conservative accountants who assign zero values to many intangible benefits prefer being precisely wrong to being vaguely right. Managers need not follow their example.

One way to combine difficult-to-measure benefits with those more easily quantified is, first, to estimate the annual cash flows about which there is the greatest confidence: the cost of the new process equipment and the benefits expected from labor, inventory, floor space, and cost-of-quality savings. If at this point a discounted cash flow analysis—done with a sensible discount rate and a consideration of all relevant alternatives—shows a CIM investment to have a positive net present value, well and good. Even without accounting for the value of intangible benefits, the analysis will have gotten the project over its financial hurdle. If the DCF is negative, however, then it becomes necessary to estimate how much the annual cash flows must increase before the investment does have a positive net present value.

To see how one manufacturer justified its investment in FMS, turn to the insert entitled "Example of an FMS Justification Analysis."

Suppose, for example, that an extra $100,000 per year over the life of the investment is sufficient to give the project the desired return. Then management can decide whether it expects heightened flexibility, reduced throughput and lead times, and faster market response to be worth at least $100,000 per year. Should the company be willing to pay $100,000 annually to enjoy these benefits? If so, it can accept the project with confidence. If, however, the additional cash flows needed to justify the investment turn out to be quite large—say $3 million per year—and management decides the intangible benefits of CIM are not worth that sum, then it is perfectly sensible to turn the investment down.

Rather than attempt to put a dollar tag on benefits that by their nature are difficult to quantify, managers should reverse the process and estimate first how large these benefits must be in order to justify the proposed investment. Senior executives can be expected to judge that improved flexibility, rapid customer service, market adaptability, and options on new process technology may be worth $300,000 to $500,000 per year but not, say, $1 million. This may not be exact mathematics, but it does help put a meaningful price on CIM's intangible benefits.

As manufacturers make critical decisions about whether to acquire CIM equipment, they must avoid claims that such investments have to be made on faith alone because financial analysis is too limiting. Successful process investments must yield returns in excess of the cost of capital invested. That is only common sense. Thus, the challenge for managers is to improve their ability to estimate the costs and benefits of CIM, not to take the easy way out and discard the necessary discipline of financial analysis.

EXAMPLE OF AN FMS JUSTIFICATION ANALYSIS

With the following analysis, one U.S. manufacturer of air-handling equipment justified its investment in an FMS installation for producing a key component:

1. Internal manufacture of the component is essential for the division's long-term strategy to maintain its capability to design and manufacture a proprietary product.

2. The component has been manufactured on mostly conventional equipment—some numerically controlled—with an average age of 23 years. To manufacture a product in conformance with current quality specifications, the company must replace this equipment with new conventional equipment or advanced technology.
3. The alternatives are conventional or numerically controlled standalone; transfer line; machining cells; FMS.
4. FMS compares with conventional technology as Table 1 shows.
5. Intangible benefits include virtually unlimited flexibility for FMS to modify mix of component models to the exact requirements of the assembly department.
6. The financial analysis for a project life of ten years compares the FMS with conventional technology (static sales assumptions, constant, or base-year, dollars) as Table 2 shows.
7. With dynamic sales assumptions showing expected increases in production volume, the annual operating savings will double in future years and the financial yield (still using constant, base-year, dollars) will increase to more than 17 percent per year.

On the basis of this analysis and recognizing the value of the intangible item (5), which had not been incorporated formally, the company selected the FMS option.

TABLE 1

	Conventional equipment	FMS
Utilization	30–40%	80–90%
Number of employees needed (including indirect workers, such as those who do materials handling, inspection, and rework)[a]	52	14
Reduced scrap and rework		$60,000 annually
Inventory	$2,000,000	$1,100,000[b]
Incremental investment		$9,200,000

[a] Each employee costs $36,000 a year in wages and fringe benefits.
[b] Inventory reductions because of shorter lead times and flexibility.

TABLE 2

Year	Investment	Operating savings	Tax savings ITC and ACRS depreciation	After-tax cash flow 50%
0	$9,200	$ 900[a]	$ 920	$ −7,380
1		1,428[b]	1,311	1,370[c]
2		1,428	1,923	1,675
3		1,428	1,835	1,632
4		1,428	1,835	1,632
5		1,428	1,835	1,632
6		1,428		714
7		1,428		714
8		1,428		714
9		1,428		714
10		1,428		714

NOTE: After-tax yield: 11.1%. Payback period: during year 5.

[a] $900—inventory reduction at start of project.

[b] $1,428—38 fewer employees at $36,000 year + $60,000 scrap and rework savings.

[c] $1,370 = (1,428)(1 − 0.50) + (1,311)(0.50).

APPENDIX: GETTING THE NUMBERS RIGHT

Part I: The Cost of Capital · A company always has the option of repurchasing its common shares or retiring its debt. Therefore, managers can estimate the cost of capital for a project by taking a weighted average of the current cost of equity and debt at the mix of capital financing typical in the industry. Extensive studies of the returns to investors in equity and fixed-income markets during the past 60 years show that from 1926 to 1984 the average total return (dividends plus price appreciation) from holding a diversified portfolio of common stocks was 11.7 percent per year. This return already includes the effects of rising price levels. Removing the effects of inflation puts the real (after-inflation) return from investments in common stocks at about 8.5% per year (see Table 3).

These historical estimates of 8.5 percent real (or about 12 percent nominal) are, however, overestimates of the total cost of capital. From 1926 to 1984, fixed-income securities averaged nominal before-tax returns of less than 5 percent per year. Taking out inflation reduces the real return (or cost) of high-grade corporate debt securities to about 1.5 percent per year. Even with recent increases in

TABLE 3

ANNUAL RETURN SERIES 1926–1984

Series	*Mean annual returns*		
	1926–1984	*1950–1984*	*1975–1984*
Common stocks	11.7%	12.8%	14.7%
Long-term corporate bonds	4.7	4.5	8.4
U.S. Treasury bills	3.4	5.1	9.0
Inflation (CPI)	3.2	4.4	7.4
Series	*Real annual returns net of inflation*		
	1926–1984	*1950–1984*	*1975–1984*
Common stocks	8.5%	8.4%	7.3%
Long-term corporate bonds	1.5	0.1	1.0
U.S. Treasury bills	0.2	0.6	1.6

the real interest rate, a mixture of debt and equity financing produces a total real cost of capital of less than 8 percent.

Many corporate executives will, no doubt, be highly skeptical that their real cost of capital could be 8 percent or less. Their disbelief probably comes from making one of two conceptual errors, perhaps both. First, executives often attempt to estimate their current cost of capital by looking at their accounting return on investment—that is, the net income divided by the net invested capital—of their divisions or corporations. For many companies this figure can be in the 15 percent to 25 percent range. There are several reasons, however, why an accounting ROI is a poor estimate of a company's real cost of capital. The accounting ROI figure is distorted by financial accounting conventions such as depreciation method and a variety of capitalization and expense decisions. The ROI figure is also distorted by management's failure to adjust both the net income and the invested capital figures for the effects of inflation, an omission that biases the accounting ROI well above the company's actual real return on investment.

The second conceptual error that makes an 8 percent real cost of capital sound too low is implicitly to compare it with today's market interest rates and returns on common stocks. These rates incorporate expectations of current and future inflation, but the 8.5 percent historical return on common stocks and the less than 2 percent return on fixed-income securities are *real* returns, after the effects of inflation have been netted out.

Now it is possible, of course, to do a DCF analysis by using nominal market returns as a way of estimating a company's cost of capital. In fact, this may even be desirable when you are doing an after-tax cash flow analysis since one of the important cash flows being discounted is the nominal tax depreciation shield from new investments. I have, however, seen many a company go seriously wrong by using a nominal discount rate (say in excess of 15 percent) while it was assuming level cash flows over the life of their investments.

Consider, for example, the data in Table 4, which is excerpted from an actual capital authorization request. Notice that all the cash flows during the ten years of the project's expected life are expressed in 1977 dollars, even though the company used a 20 percent discount rate on the cash flow of the several investment alternatives. This assumption of a 20 percent cost of capital most likely arose from

TABLE 4

EXAMPLE OF A CAPITAL AUTHORIZATION REQUEST

	Alternative 1: Rebuild present machines						
Year	*1977*	*1978*	*1979*	*1980*	*1981*	...	*1986*
Sales	$6,404	$6,404	$6,404	$6,404	$6,404	...	$6,404
Cost of sales:							
Labor	168	168	168	168	168	...	168
Material	312	312	312	312	312	...	312
Overhead	1,557	1,557	1,557	1,557	1,557	...	1,557
	Alternative 5: Purchase all new machines						
Year	*1977*	*1978*	*1979*	*1980*	*1981*	...	*1986*
Sales	$6,404	$6,724	$7,060	$7,413	$7,784	...	$7,784
Cost of sales:							
Labor	167	154	148	152	152	...	152
Material	312	328	344	361	380	...	380
Overhead	1,557	1,440	1,390	1,423	1,423	...	1,423

SOURCE: Adapted from Robert S. Kaplan and Glen Bingham, *Wilmington Tap and Die*. Case 185-124 (Boston: Harvard Business School, 1985).

a prior assumption of a real cost of capital of about 10 percent and an expected inflation rate of 10 percent per year. But if it believed that inflation would average 10 percent annually over the life of the project, the company should also have raised the assumed selling price and the unit costs of labor, material, and overhead by their expected price increases over the life of the project.

It is inconsistent to assume a high rate of inflation for the interest rate used in a DCF calculation but a zero rate of price change when you are estimating future net cash flows from an investment. Naturally, this inconsistency—using double-digit discount rates but level cash flows—biases the analysis toward the rejection of new investments, especially those yielding benefits five to ten years into the future. Compounding excessively high interest rates will place a low value on cash flows in these later years: a 20 percent interest rate, for example, discounts $1.00 to $.40 in five years and to $.16 in ten years. If companies use discount rates derived from current market rates of return, then they must also estimate rates of price and cost changes for all future cash flows.

Part II: Measuring Alternatives · Look again at the capital authorization request in Table 4. The cash flows from alternative 1 assume a constant level of sales during the next ten years; the cash flows from alternative 5 show a somewhat higher level of sales based on a small increase in market share. The difference in sales revenue as currently projected, however, is not all that great. Only if managers anticipate a steady decrease in market share and sales revenue for alternative 1, a decrease occasioned by domestic or international competitors adopting the new production technology, would alternative 5 show a major improvement over the status quo.

Obviously, not all investments in new process technology are investments that should be made. Even if competitors adopt new technology and profits erode over time, a company may still find that the benefits from investing would not compensate for its costs. But either way, the company should rest its decision on a correct reading of what is likely to happen to cash flows when it rejects a new technology investment.

Part III: Piecemeal Investment · Each year, a company or a division may undertake a series of small improvements in its production process—to alleviate bottlenecks, to add capacity where needed, or to introduce islands of automation based on immediate and easily quantified labor savings. Each of these projects, taken by itself, may have a positive net present value. By investing on a piecemeal basis, however, the company or division will never get the full benefit of completely redesigning and rebuilding its plant. Yet the pressures to go forward on a piecemeal basis are nearly irresistible. At any point in time, there are many annual, incremental projects scattered about from which the investment has yet to be recovered. Thus, were management to scrap the plant, its past incremental investments would be shown to be incorrect.

One alternative to this piecemeal approach is to forecast the remaining technological life of the plant and then to enforce a policy of accepting no process improvements that will not be repaid within this period. Managers can treat the money that otherwise would have been invested as if it accrued interest at the company's cost of capital. At the end of the specified period, they could abandon the old facility and build a new one with the latest relevant technology.

Although none of the usual incremental process investments may have been incorrect, the collection of incremental decisions could have a lower net present value than the alternative of deferring most investment during a terminal period, earning interest on the unexpended funds, and then replacing the plant. Again, the failure to evaluate such global investment is not a limitation of DCF analysis. It is a failure of not applying DCF analysis to all the feasible alternatives to annual, incremental investment proposals.

Investing in the Stock Market

Burton Malkiel

Burton Malkiel is Dean of the School of Organization and Management at Yale University. This is an excerpt from the fourth edition of his book, A Random Walk Down Wall Street, *published in 1985.*

REDUCING RISK: MODERN PORTFOLIO THEORY (MPT)

Portfolio theory begins with the premise that all investors are like my wife—they are risk-averse. They want high returns and guaranteed outcomes. The theory tells investors how to combine stocks in their portoflios to give them the least risk possible, consistent with the return they seek. It also gives a rigorous mathematical justification for the time-honored investment maxim that diversification is a sensible strategy for individuals who like to reduce their risks.

The theory was invented in the 1950s by Harry Markowitz. His book, *Portfolio Selection*, was an outgrowth of his Ph.D. dissertation at the University of Chicago. Markowitz is a scholarly academic "computenick" type with a most varied background. His experience has ranged from teaching at UCLA to designing a computer language at RAND Corporation and helping General Electric solve manufacturing problems by computer simulations. He has even practiced money management, serving as president of Arbitrage Management Company, which ran a "hedge fund."[1] What Markowitz discovered was that portfolios of risky (volatile) stocks might be put together in such a way that the portfolio as a whole would actually be less risky than any one of the individual stocks in it.

The mathematics of modern portfolio theory (also known as MPT) is recondite and forbidding; it fills the journals and incidentally, keeps a lot of academics busy. That in itself is no small accomplishment. Fortunately, there is no need to lead you through the labyrinth of quadratic programming to understand the core of the theory. A single illustration will make the whole game clear.

Let's suppose we have an island economy with only two businesses. The first is a large resort with beaches, tennis courts, a golf course, and the like. The second is a manufacturer of umbrellas. Weather affects the fortunes of both. During sunny seasons the resort does a booming business and umbrella sales plummet. During rainy seasons the resort owner does very poorly, while the umbrella manufacturer enjoys high sales and large profits. The following table shows some hypothetical returns for the two businesses during the different seasons:

	Umbrella Manufacturer	Resort Owner
Rainy Season	50%	−25%
Sunny Season	−25%	50%

Suppose that, on average, one-half the seasons are sunny and one-half are rainy (i.e., the probability of a sunny or rainy season is ½). An investor who bought stock in the umbrella manufacturer would find that half the time he earned a 50 percent return and half the time he lost 25 percent of his investment. On average, he would earn a return of 12½ percent. This is what we have called the investor's *expected return*. Similarly, investment in the resort would

1. Basically what Markowitz did was to search with the computer for situations where a convertible bond sold at a price that was "out of line" with the underlying common stock. He admitted, however, that it was "no great trick" and that competitors would be joining him in increasing numbers. "Then when we start tripping over each other, buying the same bonds almost simultaneously, the game will be over. Two, three years at most." I spoke to Harry three years later, and he admitted that convertible hedges were no longer attractive in the market. Consequently, he had moved on to do hedging operations on the Chicago Board Options Exchange.

produce the same results. Investing in either one of these businesses would be fairly risky, however, because the results are quite variable and there could be several sunny or rainy seasons in a row.

Suppose, however, that instead of buying only one security an investor with two dollars diversified and put half his money in the umbrella manufacturer's and half in the resort owner's business. In sunny seasons, a one-dollar investment in the resort would produce a fifty-cent return, while a one-dollar investment in the umbrella manufacturer would lose 25 cents. The investor's total return would be 25 cents (50 cents minus 25 cents), which is 12½ percent of his total investment of two dollars.

Note that during rainy seasons exactly the same thing happens—only the names are changed. Investment in the umbrella manufacturer produces a good 50 percent return while the investment in the resort loses 25 percent. Again, however, the diversified investor makes a 12½ percent return on his total investment.

This simple illustration points out the basic advantage of diversification. Whatever happens to the weather, and thus to the island economy, by diversifying investments over both of the firms an investor is sure of making a 12½ percent return each year. The trick that made the game work was that while both companies were risky (returns were variable from year to year), the companies were affected differently by weather conditions. (In statistical terms, the two companies had a negative covariance).[2] As long as there is some

---

2. Statisticians use the term *covariance* to measure what I have called the degree of parallelism between the returns of the two securities. If we let R stand for the actual return from the resort and $\bar{R}$ be the expected or average return, while U stands for the actual return from the umbrella manufacturer and $\bar{U}$ is the average return, we define the covariance between U and R (or COV_{UR}) as follows:

$$COV_{UR} = \text{Prob. rain } (U, \text{ if rain} - \bar{U}) (R, \text{ if rain} - \bar{R}) + \text{prob. sun}$$
$$(U, \text{ if sun} - \bar{U}) (R, \text{ if rain} - \bar{R}).$$

From the preceding table of returns and assumed probabilities we can fill in the relevant numbers:

$$COV_{UR} = \frac{1}{2}(.50 - .125)(-.25 - .125) + \frac{1}{2}(-.25 - .125)(.50 - .125) = -.141.$$

Whenever the returns from two securities move in tandem (when one goes up the other always goes up) the covariance number will be a large positive number. If the returns are completely out of phase, as in the present example, the two securities are said to have negative covariance.

lack of parallelism in the fortunes of the individual companies in the economy, diversification will always reduce risk. In the present case, where there is a perfect negative relationship between the companies' fortunes (one always does well when the other does poorly), diversification can totally eliminate risk.

Of course, there is always a rub, and the rub in this case is that the fortunes of most companies move pretty much in tandem. When there is a recession and people are unemployed, they may buy neither summer vacations nor umbrellas. Therefore, one should not expect in practice to get the neat kind of total risk elimination just shown. Nevertheless, since company fortunes don't always move completely in parallel, investment in a diversified portfolio of stocks is likely to be less risky than investment in one or two single securities.

It is easy to carry the lessons of this illustration to actual portfolio construction. Suppose you were considering combining General Motors and its major supplier of new tires in a stock portfolio. Would diversification be likely to give you much risk reduction? Probably not. It may not be true that "as General Motors goes, so goes the nation" but it surely does follow that if General Motors' sales slump, G.M. will be buying fewer new tires from the tire manufacturer. In general, diversification will not help much if there is a high covariance between the returns of the two companies.

On the other hand, if General Motors were combined with a government contractor in a depressed area, diversification might reduce risk substantially. It usually has been true that as the nation goes, so goes General Motors. If consumer spending is down (or if an oil crisis comes close to paralyzing the nation) General Motors' sales and earnings are likely to be down and the nation's level of unemployment up. Now, if the government makes a habit during times of high unemployment of giving out contracts to the depressed area (to alleviate some of the unemployment miseries there) it could well be that the returns of General Motors and those of the contractor do not move in phase. The two stocks might have very little or, better still, negative covariance.

The example may seem a bit strained, and most investors will realize that when the market gets clobbered just about all stocks go down. Still, at least at certain times, some stocks do move against the market. Gold stocks are often given as an example of securities that do not typically move in the same direction as the general market. The point to realize in setting up a portfolio is that while the variability (variance) of the returns from individual stocks is important, even more important in judging the risk of a portfolio is covariance, the extent to which the securities move in parallel. It is this covariance that plays the critical role in Markowitz's portfolio theory.

True diversification depends on having stocks in your portfolio that are not all dependent on the same economic variables (consumer spending, business investment, housing construction, etc.). Wise investors will diversify their portfolios not by names or industries but by the determinants that influence the fluctuations of various securities.

Figure 1 illustrates the theory quite nicely. Looking first at the

FIGURE 1

THE BENEFITS OF DIVERSIFICATION

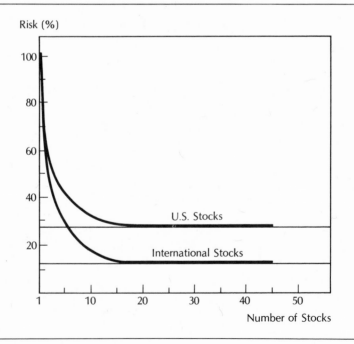

SOURCE: Solnik, "The International Pricing of Risk," *Journal of Finance*, May 1974.

top line of the figure, marked "U.S. Stocks," we see that as the number of securities in the portfolio increases, the total portfolio risk is reduced. By the time the portfolio contains about 20 equal-sized and well-diversified issues, the total risk (standard deviation of returns) of the portfolio is reduced by about 70 percent. Further increase in the number of holdings do not produce any significant further risk reduction. Of course, we are assuming that the stocks in the portfolio are widely diversified. Clearly, 20 oil stocks or 20 electric utilities would not produce an equivalent amount of risk reduction.

Having learned the twin lessons that diversification reduces risk and that diversification is most helpful if one can find securities that don't move in tandem with the general market, investors in the 1980s have sought to apply these principles on the international scene. Since the movement of foreign economies is not always synchronous with that of the U.S. economy, we should expect some additional benefits from including foreign companies in the portfolio. The potential benefits of international diversification are illustrated in the bottom line of the figure. Here, the stocks are drawn not simply from the U.S. stock market but also from the United Kingdom, France, Germany, Italy, Belgium, the Netherlands, and Switzerland. As expected, the international diversified portfolio tends to be less risky than the one of corresponding size drawn purely from stocks directly traded on the NYSE.

MODELING RISK: THE CAPITAL-ASSET PRICING MODEL (CAPM)

Portfolio theory has important implications for how stocks are actually valued. If investors seek to reduce risk in anything like the manner Harry Markowitz described, the stock market will tend to reflect these risk-reducing activities. This brings us to what is called the "capital-asset pricing model," a creation devised by Stanford professor William Sharpe, the late Harvard professor John Lintner, and others.

I've mentioned that the reason diversification cannot usually produce the miracle of risk elimination, as it did in my mythical island economy, is that usually stocks tend to move up and down together. Still, diversification is worthwhile—it can eliminate some risks. What Sharpe and Lintner did was to focus directly on what part of a security's risk can be eliminated by diversification and what part can't.

Can you imagine any stockbroker saying, "We can reasonably describe the total risk in any security (or portfolio) as the total variability (variance or standard deviation) of the returns from the security"? He'd probably scare away the few individual customers who are left. But we who teach are under no such constraints, and we say such things often. We go on to say that part of total risk or variability may be called the security's *systematic risk* and that this arises from the basic variability of stock prices in general and the tendency for all stocks to go along with the general market, at least to some extent. The remaining variability in a stock's returns is called *unsystematic risk* and results from factors peculiar to that particular company; for example, a strike, the discovery of a new product, and so on.

Systematic risk, also called market risk, captures the reaction of individual stocks (or portfolios) to general market swings. Some stocks and portfolios tend to be very sensitive to market movements. Others are more stable. This relative volatility or sensitivity to market moves can be estimated on the basis of the past record, and is popularly known by the Greek letter beta.

You are now about to learn all you ever wanted to know about beta but were afraid to ask. Basically, beta is the numerical description of systematic risk. Despite the mathematical manipulations involved, the basic idea behind the beta measurement is one of putting some precise numbers on the subjective feelings money managers have had for years. The beta calculation is essentially a comparison between the movements of an individual stock (or portfolio) and the movements of the market as a whole.

The calculation begins by assigning a beta of 1 to a broad market index, such as the NYSE index or the S&P 500. If a stock has a beta of 2, then on average it swings twice as far as the market. If the market goes up 10 percent, the stock rises 20 percent. If a stock has a beta of 0.5, it tends to be more stable than the market (it will go up or down 5 percent when the market rises or declines 10 percent). Professionals often call high-beta stocks aggressive investments and label low-beta stocks as defensive.

Now the important thing to realize is that *systematic risk cannot be eliminated by diversification.* It is precisely because all stocks move more or less in tandem (a large share of their variability is systematic) that even diversified stock portfolios are risky. Indeed, if you diversified perfectly by buying a share in the S&P index (which by definition has a beta of 1) you would still have quite variable (risky) returns because the market as a whole fluctuates widely.

Unsystematic risk is the variability in stock prices (and therefore, in returns from stocks) that results from factors peculiar to an individual company. Receipt of a large new contract, the finding of mineral resources on the company's property, labor difficulties, the discovery that the corporation's treasurer has had his hand in the company till—all can make a stock's price move independently of the market. The risk associated with such variability is precisely the kind that diversification can reduce. The whole point of portfolio theory was that, to the extent stocks don't move in tandem all the time, variations in the returns from any one security will tend to be washed away or smoothed out by complementary variation in the returns from other securities.

Figure 2, similar to Figure 1, illustrates the important relation-

FIGURE 2

How Diversification Reduces Risk

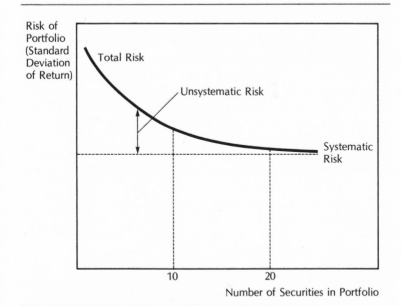

SOURCE: Modigliani and Pogue, "An Introduction to Risk and Return, I," *Financial Analysts Journal*, March–April 1974.

ship between diversification and total risk. Suppose we randomly select securities for our portfolio that tend on average to be just as volatile as the market (the average betas for the securities in our portfolio will always be equal to 1). The chart shows that as we add more and more securities the total risk of our portfolio declines, especially at the start.

When ten securities are selected from our portfolio, a good deal of the unsystematic risk is eliminated, and additional diversification yields little further risk reduction. By the time 20 well-diversified securities are in the portfolio, the unsystematic risk is substantially eliminated and our portfolio (with a beta of 1) will tend to move up and down essentially in tandem with the market. Of course, we could perform the same experiment with stocks whose average beta is 1½. Again, we would find that diversification quickly reduced unsystematic risk, but the remaining systematic risk would be larger. A portfolio of 20 or more stocks with an average beta of 1½ would tend to be 50 percent more volatile than the market.

Now comes the key step in the argument. Both financial theorists and practitioners agree that investors should be compensated for taking on more risk by a higher expected return. Stock prices must therefore adjust to offer higher returns where more risk is perceived, to insure that all securities are held by someone. Obviously, risk-averse investors wouldn't buy securities with extra risk without the expectation of extra reward. But not all of the risk of individual securities is relevant in determining the premium for bearing risk. The unsystematic part of the total risk is easily eliminated by adequate diversification. So there is no reason to think that investors will be compensated with a risk premium for bearing unsystematic risk. The only part of total risk that investors will get paid for bearing is systematic risk, the risk that diversification cannot help. Thus, the capital-asset pricing model says that returns (and, therefore, risk premiums) for any stock (or portfolio) will be related to beta, the systematic risk that cannot be diversified away.

The proposition that risk and reward are related is not new. Finance specialists have agreed for years that investors do need to be compensated for taking on more risk. What is different about the new investment technology is the definition and measurement of risk. Before the advent of the capital-asset pricing model, it was believed that the return on each security was related to the total risk inherent in that security. It was believed that the return from a security varied with the instability of that security's particular performance, that is, with the variability or standard deviation of the returns it produced. The new theory says that the *total* risk of each individual security is irrelevant. It is only the systematic component of that total instability that is relevant for valuation.

While the mathematical proof of this proposition would stun even a Yoda, the logic behind it is fairly simple. Consider a case where there are two groups of securities—Group I and Group II—with 20 securities in each. Suppose that the systematic risk (beta) for each security is 1; that is, each of the securities in the two groups tend to move up and down in tandem with the general market. Now suppose that, because of factors peculiar to the individual securities in Group I, the total risk for each of them is substantially higher than the total risk for each security in Group II. Imagine, for example, that in addition to general market factors the securities in Group I are also particularly susceptible to climatic variations, to changes in exchange rates, and to natural disasters. The specific risk for each of the securities in Group I will therefore be very high. The specific risk for each of the securities in Group II, however, is assumed to be very low, and hence the total risk for each of them will be very low. Schematically, this situation appears as follows:

Group I (20 Securities)	Group II (20 Securities)
Systematic risk (beta) = 1 for each security	Systematic risk (beta) = 1 for each security
Specific risk is high for each security	Specific risk is low for each security
Total risk high for each security	Total risk low for each security

Now, according to the old theory, commonly accepted before the advent of the capital-asset pricing model, returns should be higher for a portfolio made up of Group I securities than for a portfolio made up of Group II securities, because each security in Group I has a higher total risk, and risk, as we know, has its reward. The advent of the new investment technology changed that sort of thinking. Under the capital-asset pricing model, returns from both portfolios should be equal. Why?

First, remember Figure 1. (The forgetful can turn the pages back to take another look.) There we saw that as the number of securities in the portfolio approached 20, the total risk of the portfolio was reduced to its systematic level. All of the unsystematic risk had been eliminated. The conscientious readers will now note that in our schematic illustration, the number of securities in each portfolio is 20. That means that the unsystematic risk has essentially been washed away: an unexpected weather calamity is balanced by a favorable exchange rate, and so forth. What remains is only the systematic risk of each stock in the portfolio, which is given by its beta. But in these two groups each of the stocks has a beta of 1. Hence, a portfolio of Group I securities and a portfolio of Group II securities will perform exactly the same with respect to risk (standard deviation) even though the stocks in Group I display higher total risk than the stocks in Group II.

The old and the new views now meet head on. Under the old system of valuation, Group I securities were regarded as offering a higher return because of their greater risk. The capital-asset pricing model says there is no greater risk in holding Group I securities if they are in a diversified portfolio. Indeed, if the securities of Group I did offer higher returns, then all rational investors would prefer them over Group II securities and would attempt to rearrange their holdings to capture the higher returns from Group I. But by this very process they would bid up the prices of Group I securities and push down the prices of Group II securities until, with the attainment of equilibrium (when investors no longer want to switch from security to security), the portfolio for each group had identical returns, related to the systematic component of their risk (beta) rather than to their total risk (including the unsystematic or specific portions). Because stocks can be combined in portfolios to eliminate specific risk, only the undiversifiable or systematic risk will command a risk premium. Investors will not get paid for bearing risks that can be diversified away. This is the basic logic behind the capital-asset pricing model.

In a big fat nutshell, the proof of the capital-asset pricing model (henceforth to be known as CAPM because we economists love to use letter abbreviations) can be stated as follows:

If investors did get an extra return (a risk premium) for bearing unsystematic risk, it would turn out that diversified portfolios made up of stocks with large amounts of unsystematic risk would give larger returns than equally risky portfolios of stocks with less unsystematic risk. Investors would snap at the chance to have these higher returns, bidding up the prices of stocks with large unsystematic risk and selling stocks with equivalent betas but lower unsystematic risk. This process would continue until the prospective returns of stocks with the same betas were equalized and no risk premium could be obtained for bearing unsystematic risk. Any other result would be inconsistent with the existence of an efficient market.

The key relationship of the theory is shown in Figure 3. As the systematic risk (beta) of an individual stock (or portfolio) increases, so does the return an investor can expect. If an investor's portfolio has a beta of zero, as might be the case if all his funds were invested in a bank savings certificate (beta would be zero since the returns from the certificate would not vary at all with swings in the stock market), the investor would receive some modest rate of return, which is generally called the risk-free rate of interest. As the individual takes on more risk, however, the return should increase. If the investor holds a portfolio with a beta of 1 (as, for example, holding a share in one of the broad stock market averages) his return will

FIGURE 3

RISK AND RETURN ACCORDING TO THE CAPITAL-ASSET PRICING
MODEL[a]

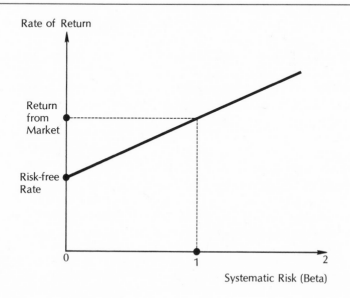

Systematic Risk (Beta)

equal the general return from common stocks. This return has over long periods of time exceeded the risk-free rate of interest, but the investment is a risky one. In certain periods the return is much less than the risk-free rate and involves taking substantial losses. This, as we have said, is precisely what is meant by risk.

The diagram shows that a number of different expected returns are possible simply by adjusting the beta of the portfolio. For example, suppose the investor put half of his money in a savings certificate and half in a share of the market averages. In this case he would receive a return midway between the risk-free return and the return from the market and his portfolio would have an average beta of 0.5.[3] The CAPM then asserts very simply that to get a higher average long-run rate of return you should just increase the beta of your portfolio. An investor can get a portfolio with a beta larger than 1 either by buying high-beta stocks or by purchasing a portfolio with average volatility on margin. (See Table 1.) There was an actual fund proposed by a West Coast bank that would have allowed an investor to buy the S & P average on margin, thus increasing both his risk and potential reward. Of course, in times of rapidly declining stock prices, such a fund would have enabled an investor to lose his shirt in a hurry. This may explain why the fund found few customers in the 1970s.

Just as stocks had their fads, so beta came into high fashion by the early 1970s. The *Institutional Investor*, the glossy prestige magazine that spent most of its pages chronicling the accomplishments of professional money managers, put its imprimatur on the movement in 1971 by featuring on its cover the letters BETA on top of a temple and including as its lead story "The Beta Cult! The New Way to Measure Risk." The magazine noted that money men whose mathematics hardly went beyond long division were now "tossing betas around with the abandon of Ph.D.s in statistical theory." Even the Securities and Exchange Commission gave beta its approval as a risk measure in its Institutional Investors Study Report.

In Wall Street the early beta fans boasted that they could earn higher long-run rates of return simply by buying a few high-beta stocks. Those who thought they were able to time the market thought they had an even better idea. They would buy high-beta stocks

---

3. In general, the beta of a portfolio is simply the weighted average of the betas of its component parts.

TABLE 1

Illustration of Portfolio Building[a]

Desired beta	Composition of portfolio	Expected return from portfolio
0	$1 in risk-free asset	10%
½	$.50 in risk-free asset	$\frac{1}{2}(.10) + \frac{1}{2}(.15) = .125$,
	$.50 in market portfolio	or 12½%[b]
1	$1 in market portfolio	15%
1½	$1.50 in market portfolio borrowing $.50 at an assumed rate of 10 percent	$1\frac{1}{2}(.15) - \frac{1}{2}(.10) = .175$, or 17½%

[a] Assuming expected market return is 15 percent and risk-free rate is 10 percent.

[b] We can derive the figure for expected return using directly the formula that accompanies the preceding chart:

$$\text{Rate of Return} = .10 + \frac{1}{2}(.15 - .10) = .125, \text{ or } 12\frac{1}{2}\%.$$

when they thought the market was going up, switching to low-beta ones when they feared the market might decline. To accommodate the enthusiasm for this new investment idea, beta measurement services proliferated among brokers, and it was a symbol of progressiveness for an investment house to provide its own beta estimates. The beta boosters in the Street oversold their product with an abandon that would have shocked even the most enthusiastic academic scribblers intent on spreading the beta gospel.

Part Five

Business and Economic Forecasting

PRACTICALLY all problems in managerial economics involve forecasting. The decision of whether or not to build a new plant may depend crucially on forecasts of demand. Whether or not to cut price may depend crucially on forecasts of the price of materials. The opening article, by Wharton Econometric Forecasting Associates, describes the Wharton Model, a 250-equation econometric model. The emphasis is on the general features and structure of the model, not the technical details. Next, Stephen K. McNees evaluates the accuracy of various economic forecasters. In view of the important role of large econometric models in business forecasting, these papers should be of considerable interest.

Econometric models are not the only available forecasting devices. The following article, published by the Federal Reserve Bank of New York, describes how firms' production plans can be used to help forecast auto output. Then William Dunkelberg discusses the uses of survey data in forecasting. Among other things, he takes up the Survey Research Center's surveys of expected inflation and the National Federation of Independent Business's surveys of planned price increases.

Besides econometric models and survey data, leading indicators are often used for forecasting purposes. Ronald A. Ratti, in the next paper, describes and evaluates the U.S. Department of Commerce's Index of Leading Economic Indicators. He concludes that "the usefulness of the index of leading economic indicators for forecasting would seem to be seriously circumscribed by the problem of the highly variable lags by which economic activity follows the index, and by the large revisions by which initial estimates of the index are adjusted."

The Wharton Econometric Model

WHARTON ECONOMETRIC FORECASTING ASSOCIATES

The Wharton Econometric Model is one of the leading macroeconomic forecasting models. This is a relatively non-technical description of its structure.

The PC-Mark7 model depicts the economic decision processes of households, businesses, governments, and financial institutions, and shows how they interact to produce emerging economic history. The model is designed primarily for short-term forecasting of the U.S. economy, for policy analysis, and for driving an endless variety of industry- or company-specific models.

PC-Mark7 is in the neo-Keynesian tradition, with important supply-side and financial influences. It is a structural model of the U.S. economy that is basically demand-driven but incorporates a fully articulated supply side and makes extensive use of expectations. For example:

• Consumption is primarily determined by the permanent income hypothesis originally developed by Milton Friedman.
• Housing is largely determined by demographic and financial variables.
• Business fixed investment is determined by the neoclassical flexible accelerator theory originally put forth by Dale Jorgenson. This means that the important driving variables include the user cost of capital.
• Inventory investment results from the disequilibrium between expected sales and the desired stock of inventories.

• Federal government spending on goods and services is the result of an exogenous policy decision.

• State and local spending on goods and services is the endogenous result of an implicit utility maximization problem subject to a budgetary constraint.

• Exports are fundamentally determined by world activity levels, as forecast by the Wharton World Economics Group.

• Imports are primarily determined by U.S. incomes, foreign prices, and exchange rates. The exchange rate assumptions are derived from the Wharton Foreign Exchange Service.

At the heart of the supply side is an endogenous determination of full-employment GNP, which is determined by full-employment factor endowments of labor and capital. Full-employment GNP plays several important roles in the model:

• Full-employment GNP is the major determinant of productivity.

• Productivity and wages interact to determine unit labor costs.

• Unit labor costs are the major building block in the stage-of-processing price sector.

The stage-of-processing price sector starts with unit labor costs to determine wholesale prices. Wholesale prices are then a major determinant of the conventional deflators. The CPI is finally determined as an appropriate weighted average of these conventional deflators.

PC-Mark7 features important interactions between the financial and real sectors of the economy. The major channels of influence are from interest rates to the user cost of capital, which is important in both the housing and business fixed investment sectors. There is also a strong linkage from financial variables to the consumer sentiment index, which is an important determinant of consumption.

PC-Mark7 is a 250-equation condensed version of the full Mark VII Wharton Quarterly Model, and was developed concurrently. The major design goal for the condensed model was to retain the same structure and simulation properties of the larger model, while reducing coverage in several sectors so that the model could be simulated effectively on the present generation of microcomputers. PC-Mark7 incorporates useful coverage of all sectors of the economy, it solves quickly on an IBM PC/XT or equivalent microcomputer, and its dynamic simulation properties approximate those embedded in the larger Mark VII model. This overview is designed to discuss the various sectors of PC-Mark7 in general terms.

LINKAGES AMONG SECTORS IN THE PC-MARK7 MODEL

One way of approaching the structure of a macroeconometric model is to consider the relationships among the sectors. An archetype model may be divided into five sectors for ease of exposition: demand, supply, wage-price, incomes, and financial.

• The demand sector consists of the major components of aggregate demand—consumption, investment, government, exports, and imports.
• The supply sector determines the levels of the factors of production. The major output from the supply sector is a measure of full-employment GNP, a measure of what the economy could produce if all factors of production were used at a level consistent with full employment of the labor force.
• The wage-price sector determines wage rates and price levels.
• The division of output among the factors of production is determined by the income sector.
• The major output from the financial sector is a spectrum of interest rates, which serve as signals reflecting the optimal capital intensity of production.

A stylized economic model consisting of these five sectors could be described by the following simple algebraic equations:

$$QS = f(K, L) \tag{0.1}$$
$$QD = f(Y, P, R, K) \tag{0.2}$$
$$Y = f(W, L, R) \tag{0.3}$$
$$W = f(L, K, P) \tag{0.4}$$
$$P_i = f(W, L, K, P_j) \tag{0.5}$$
$$R = f(M, QD, P, \text{Fed}) \tag{0.6}$$

where:

QS = aggregate supply
K = capital stock
L = labor force
QD = aggregate demand
Y = income
P = price level
R = interest rate
W = wage rate
M = money supply
Fed = Federal Reserve System policy.

The first equation suggests that aggregate supply is determined by the level of the factors of production. The second equation suggests that aggregate demand is determined by income, (relative) prices, interest rates, and stocks. The third equation indicates that incomes are related to the wage rate, employment, and interest rates. The fourth equation suggests that the wage rate is determined by the (expected) price level and by labor supply (generally, the unemployment rate). The fifth equation indicates that prices (P_i) are determined by wages, input prices (P_j), and the factors of production. The last equation indicates that interest rates are determined by the money supply, aggregate demand, the (expected) price level, and policy actions by the Federal Reserve. Keeping this simple stylized model in mind will make it easier to discuss intersectoral linkages.

In the final analysis, the intersection of aggregate demand and aggregate supply determine output as well as inflation, incomes, the unemployment rate, and interest rates. If aggregate demand exceeds aggregate supply, the economy adjusts via higher prices and higher interest rates. If aggregate demand falls short of aggregate supply, the economy adjusts via lower prices and lower interest rates.

The stylized model appears to suggest that the economy is capable of sustained equilibrium, which is in substantial disagreement with history. The stylized model should be interpreted as showing the direction the economy will move in while adjusting toward the generally unachievable equilibrium.

We turn now to the linkages of PC-Mark7, first of all in the context of the stylized model. If aggregate demand exceeds aggregate supply, there will be upward pressure on wages as the unemployment rate falls. Wages are the first step in the stage-of-processing price sector. Hence, the increase in wages will directly affect prices. As the economy tries to expand output beyond sustainable levels, capacity bottlenecks will develop and delivery times will lengthen. Both of these factors will exert additional pressures on prices. With output above sustainable levels, the productivity of factor inputs decreases, adding to the upward pressure on prices. Thus the first step in the economy's adjustment back toward equilibrium depends on the important linkages between the supply and the wage-price sector.

Interest rates will be adjusting as well. If aggregate demand exceeds aggregate supply, there will be upward pressure on interest rates. The excess demand puts direct upward pressure on interest rates. The increase in inflation also puts upward pressure on interest rates. Finally, if we assume a reaction function for the Federal Reserve, it is likely that the Fed, in an attempt to cool the economy, would take actions to put still further upward pressure on interest rates. This illustrates the close linkage between aggregate supply, inflation, the Fed, and interest rates.

The movements in prices and interest rates cause aggregate demand to adjust toward aggregate supply, because of the linkages between relative prices and aggregate demand as well as the linkages between interest rates, credit, and the credit-sensitive components of aggregate demand.

As aggregate demand adjusts toward aggregate supply, incomes will adjust in generally the same direction as aggregate demand. The main linkage in this adjustment is that reductions in demand cut employment, which reduces the wage bill.

These linkages may be made more concrete in terms of PC-Mark7 by looking through the equations in more detail, sector by sector. The important linkages in the adjustment process from aggregate demand to aggregate supply are:

• The linkages from the supply sector to the wage sector, which cause wage rates to rise or fall, depending on the relationship between aggregate demand and aggregate supply.
• The linkages from the supply sector and wages to prices via the stage-of-processing price sector, which cause prices to rise or fall, depending on the relationship between aggregate demand and aggregate supply.
• The linkages from the supply and wage-price sectors to the financial sector, which cause interest rates and credit flows to increase or decrease, depending on the relationship between aggregate demand and aggregate supply.
• The linkages from the wage-price sector to aggregate demand, which cause aggregate demand to rise or fall, depending on movements in prices and relative prices.
• The linkages from the financial sector to the credit-sensitive components of aggregate demand, which serve to adjust aggregate demand toward equilibrium.
• The linkages from the wage-price sector to the income sector, which cause the constant-dollar value of incomes to rise or fall, depending on the price level.

The linkages emphasized so far are those that operate strongly to move aggregate demand toward a sustainable level. There are, of course, a variety of other linkages that affect the speed of adjustment. The major elements of these include:

• Employment from the aggregate supply sector and wages from the wage-price sector, which combine to determine the wage bill, an important variable in the income sector.

• The linkages between the financial and income sectors, where movements in interest rates play an important role in the net interest component of income.

Having discussed the major linkages between the sectors, we turn now to a more detailed discussion of the equation specifications in PC-Mark7.

CONSUMPTION

The discussion of most models starts with the consumption sector, on the grounds that consumption is the predominant share of GNP and is not particularly difficult to model. Most theories of the consumption function start with the well-known microeconomic theory of consumer behavior, where spending decisions are formulated from household preferences, income—which determines the budget constraint—and relative prices. Macroeconomic theory has gone on to suggest refinements such as the distinction between permanent and transitory income, the use of demographics, and the use of consumer sentiment.

The consumption sector is generally specified as:

$$\log(C \; / \; N) = AO + A1 \; \log(YP \; / \; N) + A2 \; \log(YT \; / \; N) \qquad (1.1)$$
$$+ A3 \; \log(CSI) - A4 \; \log(RELPRICE)$$

where

C = consumption

N = population

YP = permanent income, defined as exponentially smoothed personal disposable income, mean adjustment lag 4.7 quarters

YT = transitory income, defined as observed income less permanent income

CSI = consumer sentiment

RELPRICE = relative price (price of the ith consumption good relative to the total).

The major driving variables in the consumer sentiment index are the unemployment rate, the inflation rate, and financial variables.

PC-Mark7 explains four categories of consumption—automobiles and parts, other durables (furniture plus other), nondurables, and services.

HOUSING

Housing starts are specified as a function of demographics, consumer sentiment, capacity utilization, financial variables, and the occupancy rate, as follows:

$$
\begin{aligned}
\text{HSPR} / \text{NCH} = A0 + &A1\ CSI - A2\ CU \\
&- A3\ (\ RM\ /\ P - RM(-1)\ /\ P(-1)\ ) \\
&+ A4(\ OCC - OCC(-1)\ ) \\
&+ A5\ (((M - M(-1))\ /\ P)\ /\ \text{NCH})
\end{aligned} \tag{2.1}
$$

where:

HSPR = housing starts
NCH = number of households
CSI = consumer sentiment index
CU = capacity utilization
RM = mortgage rate (the effective mortgage rate, all lenders)
P = implicit consumption deflator
OCC = occupancy rate
M = proxy for deposit inflows into savings intermediaries.

The occupancy rate is next determined by income—thus income affects housing starts only indirectly via the occupancy rate. Residential investment is finally determined as a distributed lag on starts. The key housing equation in PC-Mark7 is akin to (2.1), which explains total starts.

BUSINESS FIXED INVESTMENT

Most modern treatments of business fixed investment start with the flexible accelerator model developed by Dale Jorgenson and his associates in the 1970s. PC-Mark7 is no exception to this tradition—investment is related to output, the lagged stock, capacity utilization, and relative prices. The function can be written in general terms as:

$$I = A0 + A1\ Q + A2\ (P\ /\ C) + A3\ K(-1) + A4\ CU \tag{3.1}$$

where:

I = investment
Q = output
P = price of output
C = rental cost of capital (a Jorgensonian concept)
K = capital stock
CU = capacity utilization.

Capacity utilization—a more recent addition to the Jorgensonian theory—is included on the grounds that businesses are more likely to spend money on additions to capital if there is pressure on existing capital.

PC-Mark7 contains separate equations for investment in producers' durable equipment and for investment in nonresidential structures.

INVENTORIES

Inventory investment is formulated by the relationship between expected sales and the desired stock of inventories—that is, it is formulated by the familiar adaptive expectations hypothesis. The speed of adjustment is influenced by interest rates and several cyclical variables. We can formally write:

$$SEXP = S(-1) + A1\ (S(-1) - S(-2)) \tag{4.1}$$
$$K^* = A2\ SEXP \tag{4.2}$$
$$I = A3\ (K^* - K(-1)) + A4\ (SEXP - S) \tag{4.3}$$

where:

$SEXP$ = expected sales
S = observed sales
K^* = desired inventory stock
K = observed inventory stock
I = inventory investment
     $0 < A1 < 1$
$A2$ = "normal" inventory-to-sales ratio
     $0 < A3 < 1$
     $0 < A4 < 1$.

These equations can then be combined to produce the following relationship between observables:

$$I = B0 + B1 \; SEXP + B2 \; K(-1) - B3 \; S \qquad (4.4)$$

PC-Mark7 explains aggregate business inventory investment.

GOVERNMENT

Federal government fiscal policy is assumed to be exogenous, but total government (including state and local) revenues and expenditures are not set exactly. Instead, such parameters as tax rates or levels of exemptions are set. The economy then interacts with these parameters to produce tax bases and effective rates—and thus revenues. In other words, fiscal policy sets the fundamental parameters, and the economy then determines both the cyclical and trend components of revenues and—to a lesser extent—expenditures. One of the functions of a macroeconomic simulation model is to permit analysis of different government fiscal policy scenarios.

Spending on goods and services by state and local governments is endogenously determined. This is formulated as a constrained utility maximization problem. The community's utility function—as viewed by government decision makers—is hypothesized to be the following:

$$U = A0 + A1 \; G - A2 \; T + A3 \; DEF \qquad (5.1)$$

where:

$U =$ "utility"
$G =$ spending on goods and services
$T =$ taxes
$DEF =$ deficit.

The above is assumed to be maximized subject to the long-run constraint that the operating deficit must be near zero. This eventually leads to the following estimating function:

$$G/N = A0 + A1\ (GVGIA)/N) + A2\ (Q/N) + A3\ DEF \qquad (5.2)$$

where:

$$N = \text{population}$$
$$GVGIA = \text{grants-in-aid from the federal government}$$
$$Q = \text{output.}$$

State and local receipts are modeled as the product of average rate (determined exogenously) and relevant base.

TRADE

Trade flows have become increasingly important as the U.S. economy continues to grow more open. The behavior of the exchange rate has a significant impact on the U.S. price level, and there have been episodes when monetary policy has been influenced by movements in the exchange rate.

The major problem in formulating trade equations is the asymmetry between exports and imports. Export equations have to be fundamentally driven by exogenous world variables, whereas imports can be successfully modeled like consumption functions. Similarly, export deflators can be modeled like other domestic prices, whereas import prices are fundamentally driven by exogenous world variables.

The export functions are specified as:

$$\log(X) = A0 + A1\ \log(QF) - A2\ \log(RELPRICE) \qquad (6.1)$$

where:

$$X = \text{exports}$$
$$QF = \text{foreign activity}$$
$$RELPRICE = \text{relative price} = (PX/EXRATE)/PF$$
$$PX = \text{export price}$$
$$EXRATE = \text{exchange rate (denominated as the price of a market basket of foreign currencies)}$$
$$PF = \text{foreign price.}$$

The import functions are specified as:

$$\log(M/N) = A0 + A1 \log(Y/N) - A2 \log(PM/PD) \qquad (6.2)$$

where:

$M =$ imports
$N =$ population
$Y =$ income
$PM =$ price of imports
$PD =$ domestic price.

PC-Mark7 explains overall exports of goods and services. Imports are broken down into petroleum imports and the remainder, on the grounds that petroleum imports—and their associated price—have been subject to influences different from other import categories, at least since the first OPEC disruption.

Import prices are determined in the following manner:[1]

$$\log(PM) = A0 + A1 \log(\text{EXRATE} * PF) \qquad (6.3)$$

where:

$PM =$ price of imports
$\text{EXRATE} =$ exchange rate (denominated as the price of a market basket of foreign currencies)
$PF =$ foreign price.

Baseline values for foreign activity, foreign prices, and exchange rate variables come from the Wharton World Economics Group and the Wharton Foreign Exchange Service.

The treatment of export deflators is covered in the following section on wages and prices.

WAGES AND PRICES

The wage-price sector of PC-Mark7 is based on three propositions:

---

1. Here and in subsequent equations, an asterisk is used as a multiplication sign.

• The major wage equation has a long-run elasticity with respect to inflation of approximately unity, but this is separated into a short-run and a long-run response.

• Prices are developed by a stage-of-processing framework, in which, for example, PPIs determine deflators and deflators determine the CPI.

• Demand measures—such as capacity utilization or vendor performance—are used nonlinearly in the price sector.

The key wage equation is cast in the form:

$$\log(W) = A0 + A1 \ \log(PL) + A2 \ \log(PS) \qquad (7.1)$$
$$+ A3 \ \log(MW) + A4 \ (1/NRUT) + A5 \ \log \ (PDY)$$

where:

W = wage rate
PL = long-run inflation, mean adjustment lag 7.5 quarters
PS = short-run inflation, mean adjustment lag 1 quarter
MW = minimum wage
NRUT = civilian unemployment rate
PDY = productivity.

The key wage variable is the Bureau of Labor statistics index of nonfarm wages, and the most important explanatory forces are the long-run inflation measures and the unemployment rate. That is, the model does have an imbedded Phillips curve-type tradeoff.

Components of the wholesale price index are determined in the following general way:

$$\log(PPIi) = A0 + A1 \ \log(LETPPIi) + A2 \ (1 / CU) \qquad (7.2)$$

where:

PPIi = ith component of the all-commodity PPI
LETPPIi = input price term for PPIi
$(1 / CU) = 1.0 / (1.0 - .01 * CU)$
CU = capacity utilization

The nonlinear form of the capacity utilization term used means that high levels of capacity utilization will exert more impact on prices than low levels.

The input price term can be thought of as a representation of underlying cost, which is then modified by demand pressure—as represented by the *CU* term. It is defined as follows:

$$\text{LETPPIi} = Aj\ \text{PPIj} + \ldots + Ak\ \text{PPIk} + Am\ \text{ULC} + An\ \text{PM} \quad (7.3)$$
$$+ Aq\ (TX\ /\ Q)$$

where:

> PPIj = jth component of the all-commodity PPI
> PPIk = kth component of the all-commodity PPI
> ULC = normal unit labor cost
> *PM* = price of imports
> (*TX/Q*) = indirect taxes relative to output.

and where:

> ULC = *W* / PDYAVG8
> PDYAVG8 = eight-period moving average of nonfarm productivity

The weights in (7.3) sum to unity and were derived from the 1972 input/output table.

Of the all-commodity PPI, PC-Mark7 explains the following categories: PW010 (raw farm), PW020 (processed food), PW050 (energy), and PWI-50 (industrial commodities less energy). The aggregate variables PWI (all industrial commodities) and PW (all-commodity PPI) are then determined by the relevant identities.

The conventional deflators are then determined in a stage-of-processing approach as follows:

$$\log(P) = A0 + Ai\ \text{PPIi} + \ldots + Aj\ \text{PPIj} + Ak\ PM + Am\ \text{ULC} \quad (7.4)$$
$$+ An\ (1\ /\ CU)$$

where:

> *P* = conventional final demand deflator
> PPIi = ith component of the all-commodity PPI
> *PM* = import price
> ULC = normal unit labor cost
> *CU* = capacity utilization.

Ideally, the sum $(A_i + \ldots + A_m)$ is near unity. Deflators for consumption, investment, government spending, and exports are all based on (7.4).

Finally, the all-urban CPI is related to a weighted average of the relevant final demand deflators.

SUPPLY

The supply side of PC-Mark7 starts with an aggregate production function that determines the full-employment level of GNP. This starts with a simple Cobb-Douglas production function of the form:

$$Q = A * K \exp(B) * L \exp(C) * exp(f(T)) \tag{8.1}$$

where:

Q = output (here GNP)
K = capital stock utilized = CU * KTOT
CU = capacity utilization
KTOT = total capital stock
L = labor (hours)
T = time trend
A, B, and C are parameters and where $B + C = 1.0$

and where hours are measured as:

$$L = AVHH * NEHT \tag{8.2}$$

where:

AVHH = average hours per week
NEHT = employment, household survey.

Note that NEHT is also equal to:

$$NEHT = (1.0 - .01 * NRUT) * NLC \tag{8.3}$$

where:

NRUT = unemployment rate
NLC = civilian labor force.

This means that (8.2) can be rewritten as:

$$L = \text{AVHH} * (1.0 - .01 * \text{NRUT}) * \text{NLC}. \tag{8.4}$$

Equation (8.1) can be estimated by taking the familiar double-log transformation:

$$\log(Q \,/\, L) = A + B \log(K \,/\, L) + f(T) \tag{8.5}$$

Full-employment output is then determined by assuming full-employment factor endowments:

$$\text{LFE} = \text{AVHHFE} * (1.0 - .01 * \text{NRUTFE}) * \text{NLC} \tag{8.6}$$

and:

$$\text{KFE} = \text{CUFE} * \text{KTOT} \tag{8.7}$$

where:

> LFE = full-employment labor input (hours)
> AVHHFE = average hours per week at full employment
> NRUTFE = full-employment unemployment rate, Council of Economic Advisers concept
> KFE = full-employment capital input
> CUFE = full-employment capacity utilization.

Full-employment GNP then determines full-employment productivity, which is defined as full-employment GNP divided by full-employment hours. This represents an index of the level of output per hour of labor input that the economy could produce if it were at full employment. The growth rate in full-employment output is then determined by growth in the full-employment levels of both labor and capital, which interact to determine the growth rate of full-employment GNP.

The main use of full-employment productivity is to explain the trend values of observed productivity. The cyclic elements of observed productivity are then accounted for by cyclic factors. The equation that relates observed productivity to full-employment productivity is of the form:

$$\log(\text{PRDY} / \text{PRDYFE}) = A0 + A1\ CU \qquad (8.8)$$

where:

> PRDY = observed productivity
> PRDYFE = full-employment productivity
> CU = capacity utilization.

The level of capacity utilization thus determines the cyclic movements of observed productivity around their trend—which is basically explained by movements in full-employment output and full-employment labor input. Observed productivity—not trend productivity—is then an important element in the determination of normal unit labor costs, which are a major determinant of prices.

The GNP gap—defined as GNP divided by full-employment GNP—is the major determinant of capacity utilization, which feeds back into much of the model. Therefore, full-employment GNP is perhaps the single most important variable in the model. It determines full-employment productivity, which is the major determinant of observed productivity—which is crucial to the wage-price sector. Full-employment GNP is also a major determinant of capacity utilization, which has widespread impacts throughout the model.

The major employment equation determines the private portion of the establishment survey. This is formulated as an inverted Cobb–Douglas production function similar to (8.1) except that it uses the private portion of the establishment survey (NEETTPV) as the measure of L.

The civilian labor force is formulated as a macro participation rate equation. The macro participation rate is related to demographics, the lagged unemployment rate (which is a measure of the discouraged/encouraged worker effect), the real after-tax wage rate, and a time trend. The civilian unemployment rate is then the usual residual between the civilian labor force and employment as measured by the household survey.

INCOMES

Income sectors of most models are generally straightforward, and the income sector of PC-Mark7 follows this pattern. Generally, the individual pieces are modeled along the lines of the way the data are collected. For example, the wage bill is functionally related to employment and hours. The less rigorous theory and less interesting modeling of income sectors are justified, at least in part. Macro decisions are rarely made about income or income shares. Instead, these result from the interactions of the economy as the various economic actors make their decisions.

Basic economic theory suggests that profits are properly the residual on the income side, determined as the excess of revenues over costs. Carrying this over to the macro level suggests that adjusted profits (CPABT$) are properly the residual, and this is the standard way of simulating PC-Mark7. However, it will always be difficult to control the residual on the income side in simulation.

FINANCIAL

PC-Mark7 starts with a reserves block that determines the money supply. There are several demand equations for monetary aggregates. The interaction of supply and demand forces leads to the determination of several interest rates. There are structural equations for one key short rate and two key long rates. All other interest rates run off one or more of these key rates via term-structure relationships.

The key reserves equation is for borrowed reserves. It is formulated as:

$$BR = A0 + A1\,(\text{FRMFF} - \text{FRMDNY}) + A2\,(NR - NR(-1)) \quad (10.1)$$

where:

$$BR = \text{borrowed reserves}$$
$$\text{FRMFF} = \text{interest rate on federal funds}$$
$$\text{FRMDNY} = \text{discount rate}$$
$$NR = \text{nonborrowed reserves.}$$

Excess reserves, free reserves, required reserves, and total reserves are then determined by identities. The exogenous policy variable is normally taken to be nonborrowed reserves, although M1 or the federal funds rate can also be chosen.

The key short-term interest rate equation is for federal funds, formulated as:

$$FRMFF = A0 + A1 \ CU - A2 \ (FR \ / \ FT) + P^* \qquad (10.2)$$

where:

$FRMFF$ = interest rate on federal funds
CU = capacity utilization
FR = free reserves
FT = total reserves
P^* = "expected" short-run inflation, defined with mean lag
to adjustment of 3.25 quarters.

The structural equations for long rates are of the form:

$$RL = A0 + A1 \ P^* + A2 \ CU + A3 \ (CU - CU(-1)) \qquad (10.3)$$
$$- A4 \ (NR - NR(-1)) + A5 \ SD(RTB)$$

where:

RL = long rate
P^* = "expected" long-run inflation, mean lag 7.5 quarters
CU = capacity utilization
NR = nonborrowed reserves
$SD(RTB)$ = four-period moving standard deviation of the three-
month Treasury bill rate.

The coefficient on P* was constrained to unity, to make this term represent a pure inflation premium.

The structural long-term equations explain the rate on Moody's Aaa bonds and the 20-year Treasury bond rate.

The demand-for-money equations are standard and are formulated as:

$$\log(Mi \ / \ P) = A0 + A1 \ \log(Q) - A2 \ \log(R) + A3 \ \log(Mi(-1) \ / \ P) \quad (10.4)$$

where:

Mi = ith component of the money supply
P = GNP deflator
Q = GNP (constant dollars)
R = short-term interest rate.

This equation says that the short-run elasticity of Mi with respect to P is $(1-A3)$ and with respect to Q is $A1$. The long-run elasticity of Mi with respect to P is 1.0 and with respect to Q is $A1 / (1.0-A3)$.

PC-Mark7 explains $M1$, $M2$, $M3$, and L.

ENERGY

PC-Mark7 has a condensed version of the energy sector contained in the Mark VII model. There is a behavioral equation for the demand for oil. Domestic supply is exogenous. Imports of petroleum then cover the gap between demand and supply.

On the price side, the OPEC price is exogenous. This price drives both the deflator for oil imports and part of the energy component of the all-commodity PPI.

How Accurate Are
Economic Forecasts?

Stephen K. McNees

Stephen K. McNees is Assistant Vice President and Economist at the Federal Reserve Bank of Boston. This is part of an article that appeared in the New England Economic Review *in 1974.*

Most economic decisions hinge ultimately on an economic forecast, whether it is explicit or implicit. It is important therefore to have some idea of how accurate forecasts have been. The primary purpose of this article is to present a recent record of the predictive performance of major forecasters. The article documents the well-known fact that recent forecasts have been highly inaccurate and places these "abnormally" large errors in historical perspective by contrasting them with previous norms.

The study is based on the "track record" of seven of the better-known forecasters over the last four years, the longest period for which comparable data are available. Since the seven forecasters utilize a wide variety of approaches, the record suggests several hypotheses about the relative merits of alternative forecasting techniques, even though no firm conclusions can be drawn without further information and standardization.

This study is descriptive not prescriptive. In a strict sense, it furnishes no information about the future forecasting ability of the forecasters considered because there is no assurance that their forecasting techniques (i.e., their models and judgment) will remain unchanged, uninfluenced by the past. The errors described below are the net result of the compounding and off-setting of model errors, errors in projections of "input" variables, errors introduced by statistical estimation techniques, errors in the sample and in the "actual" data, errors resulting from external "noneconomic events," and errors in the subjective adjustments by the forecasters themselves.[1] Standardization for any of the various sources of incomparability could alter the results. In no case should the results be interpreted as errors made by econometric *models* as opposed to errors made by *forecasters,* some of whom place heavy reliance on econometric results.

The search for the "best" forecaster quickly bogs down into the narrower issues of what is meant by "best" (e.g., best for which variable? which time horizon?) and how to measure forecast quality. The general impression emerging from this study is the broad similarity in the forecasts and the forecasting record—similarity among forecasters and over varying time horizons. The source of the variability lies instead in the time period being forecasted. The chaotic environment of the first half of the 1970s has provided a severe test of economic forecasting. While the recent record is certainly no cause for complacency, the best forecasters have been able to anticipate the growth of GNP and real GNP one year ahead with an average absolute error of 1 percent and the unemployment rate a year ahead by .3 percent.

FORECASTERS INCLUDED IN THE STUDY

The seven forecasters included in this study can best be classified by the blend of econometrics and judgment which is used in constructing an economic forecast. At the most econometric extreme are the forecasts of the Fair model.[2] The forecasts are generated by a small econometric model which is reestimated each quarter. The values of the "input" variables for the model

1. For a more complete discussion of the methodology underlying this forecast evaluation, see Stephen K. McNees, "The Predictive Accuracy of Econometric Forecasts," *New England Economic Review,* Federal Reserve Bank of Boston, Sept./Oct., 1973, pp. 4–9.

2. Ray C. Fair, *A Short-Run Forecasting Model of the United States Economy* (Lexington, Mass.: D. C. Heath and Co., 1971).

forecast are either taken from outside sources (e.g., the budget, the Commerce Department's survey of investment plans, the Michigan survey of consumer sentiment) or from straightforward extrapolations. No adjustments are made to make the model's forecast look "reasonable" in the forecaster's eye. Major economic events outside the structure of the model (strikes, controls, embargoes, and shortages) are ignored since incorporating information on them inevitably involves a good deal of subjective judgment.

At the other end of the spectrum, the median forecast from the American Statistical Association and the National Bureau of Economic Research (ASA/NBER) Survey of regular forecasters is included. Since the survey is primarily of non-econometrically oriented forecasters and since it is the median forecast which is used, this forecast set is the most heavily judgmental in this study and need not even give consistent predictions. The survey does not report forecasts for 4 of the 10 variables discussed below.

Somewhere in between the Fair model forecast and the ASA survey forecast, are a group of forecasters who utilize large, simultaneous econometric models of the U.S. economy; the models were developed by Chase Econometrics, Inc. (Chase), Data Resources, Inc. (DRI), the Bureau of Economic Analysis (BEA) at the U.S. Department of Commerce, and by the Wharton School's Economic Forecasting Unit (Wharton).[3] Like the Fair model, each of these forecasting groups can create an economic forecast or simulation merely by supplying values of the "input" variables. Unlike forecasts from the Fair model, however, each of these forecasters predicts more than a hundred economic variables and, more importantly, each relies on subjective judgment to adjust the "pure model" forecasts for past

3. Albert A. Hirsch, Maurice Liebenberg, and George R. Green, "The BEA Quarterly Model," Bureau of Economic Analysis Staff Paper No. 22, July, 1973. Otto Eckstein, Edward W. Green, and Allen Sinai, "The Data Resources Model: Uses, Structure, and the Analysis of the U.S. Economy." *International Economic Review,* October 1974. Michael D. McCarthy, *The Wharton Quarterly Econometric Model Mark III* (Philadelphia: University of Pennsylvania, 1972). No published account of the Chase model is available, but much of its content derives from the published work of Michael K. Evans.

errors, external events, and the unreasonable results which occasionally accompany large model solutions. There is probably no way to separate the mixture of "science" and pure hunch used in generating the actual (ex ante) forecasts and, therefore, to rank them on an econometric-judgmental continuum.[4]

While the General Electric Company (GE) forecasts also evolve from an interplay of econometrics and economic judgment, unlike the model forecasts, they do not derive from a formal, simultaneous model which could, in theory, mechanically grind out a projection from a set of "input" variables.[5] Instead, the GE forecasts are the outcome of an iterative process in which the initial values are obtained from individual economic relationships but the final results are strongly influenced by the experience, "feel," and intuition of business economists. This procedure has the advantage of "taking everything into account" along with the disadvantage of being time consuming. The GE group, like the large model forecasters, forecasts more than a hundred economic variables, including items of special interest to the company such as total appliance sales and electrical power generation. Without a large, consistent model, this task is impossible to do rapidly. As a result, the GE forecasts used in this study were not available until late in the quarter. As explained below, this poses problems for comparing the GE forecasts with others.

In order to achieve maximum comparability among forecasters, the attempt was made to utilize the first forecast made after the preliminary GNP data for the preceding quarter had been released but before those data had been revised. Most forecasts, in other words, were made either in the first month of a quarter (when no monthly and little weekly actual data for that quarter had been released) or early in the following month. This procedure was followed by Chase, DRI, Fair, and Wharton. Although the GE forecasts are not dated, all appear to have been released after the revised GNP data which become available in the middle of the quarter. Similarly, 9 of the 16 BEA forecasts and 4 of the 16 ASA forecasts were issued after the revised

4. After the fact forecasts could be made by solving the models with the historical values of the "input" variables.

5. Prior to 1971, GE relied more heavily on econometric models.

GNP figures, and consequently a considerable body of monthly and weekly data, were available. These forecasts had the advantage of one or two months of additional data and are, therefore, not strictly comparable to those issued earlier by the other forecasters.

GNP

The mean absolute errors (MAEs) of the GNP growth forecasts of the seven economic forecasters are presented in Table 1. The table is based on each forecaster's 58 forecasts in the period 1970:III to 1974:II. Overall, the average error of all forecasters of the quarterly growth in GNP (as simple annual rates) is about 2 percentage points for forecasts made from one to four quarters in advance. The range among forecasters goes from 1.7 to 2.4 percentage points. The overall average error of forecasts of GNP growth over time spans one to four quarters in length ranged from 1.2 to 1.8 percentage point with a median of 1.3 percentage points. The Chase and GE forecasts are the most accurate and the Fair model forecasts distinctly the least accurate.

The figures in Table 1 are not good indicators of the variability of forecast accuracy over different time horizons since each time span includes a different number of quarters. Considering only the period 1971:II through 1974:II where 13 one- to four-quarter-ahead forecasts are available there is very little error variation as the forecast horizon changes between two and four quarters ahead. The two-quarter-ahead MAEs are about 13 percent larger than the one-quarter ahead. Due to error offsetting, multiperiod forecasts generally increase in accuracy as the forecast horizon increases from one to four quarters. While the average error of all forecasters for the next quarter is 1.6 percentage points, the average error for the cumulative growth over a one-year interval is only 1.2 percentage points.

Whereas the period from mid-1973 to mid-1974 was the most difficult for inflation forecasts, and the first half of 1974 for output forecasts, the first quarter of 1973, when nominal GNP grew at a 14.7 percent simple annual rate, stands out as the most difficult single quarter to predict GNP. The first quarter of 1971, the quarter of the post-auto strike rebound, came also as a surprise.

TABLE 1

MEAN ABSOLUTE ERRORS, FORECASTS OF NOMINAL GNP
(PERCENT, ANNUAL RATE)

Period of Forecast (Quarters)

	1	2	3	4	Average
Forecaster	A. Spans: 1970:III–1974:II				
ASA/NBER	1.4	1.5	1.4	1.3	1.4
BEA	1.5	1.1	1.3	1.2	1.3
Chase	1.3	1.4	1.0	1.0	1.2
DRI	1.7	1.2	1.1	1.3	1.3
Fair	2.2	1.9	1.6	1.5	1.8
GE	1.4	1.3	1.0	1.0	1.2
Wharton	2.0	1.3	1.3	1.3	1.5
	B. Quarterly Changes: 1970:III–1974:II				
ASA/NBER	1.4	2.0	2.2	1.8	1.8
BEA	1.5	1.6	2.9	2.2	2.0
Chase	1.3	1.8	2.1	1.8	1.7
DRI	1.7	1.9	2.3	2.0	2.0
Fair	2.2	2.9	2.5	2.1	2.4
GE	1.4	2.1	2.2	1.7	1.8
Wharton	2.0	2.2	2.1	2.2	2.1

Other major errors occurred in 1972:IV and 1973:IV. In each of these cases, with only a trivial exception, the rate of GNP growth was underestimated by all forecasters in all of their forecasts. For multiperiod forecasts, the four quarters of 1973 were the four most difficult of the entire period. Here again, with only minor exceptions, all forecasters generally underestimated the rate of growth of GNP. The only quarters in which above-average errors were overestimated were the three quarters in which real output declined—1970:IV, 1974:I, and 1974:II. It would not be surprising, in light of this performance, to find a downward bias in GNP forecasts.

Although the evidence is somewhat mixed, statistical tests do generally confirm the presence of downward bias in GNP forecasts. This bias, of course, further reflects the previously noted downward bias in the inflation forecasts combined with the lack of evidence of a strong, general bias in output forecasts. The evidence of bias is most conclusive in the case of span forecasts for all forecasters except Wharton where bias is not suggested by the binomial test but is marginally significant by the t test.[6] For the quarterly growth rates, bias is suggested for all forecasters using the t test but for only two forecasters using the binomial test.

HOW GOOD ARE ECONOMIC FORECASTS?

The traditional standard of comparison in forecast evaluations is often a naive "no-change" or "same-change" extrapolation. The "no-change" standard is a particularly feeble strawman for GNP in this forecast period. While the "same-change" standard is more plausible, and the very sophisticated moving-average extrapolative techniques can be very powerful, there is something unsettling about using a statistical "black box," completely independent of economic theory or information, for decision-making. Even if such techniques were in fact most accurate, there would inevitably be efforts to improve on them.

This study has included forecasts of the Fair model which are reasonable to select as a standard of comparison. The model is small enough to be understandable, based on economic theory and data, and can produce plausible forecasts with only a minimum of human judgment. It stands as close to an approximation as we are likely to have of a "computer forecast."

There is another reasonable standard of comparison for GNP forecasts which is simple, understandable, based on economic theory, and capable of producing a plausible tracking of the historical record. This is the money-GNP relationship which has recently been described by Professor Milton Friedman.[7] Friedman points out that the velocity of money (broadly defined to include time deposits in commercial banks other than large negotiable certificates of deposit) "has displayed no appreciable trend in either direction since" 1962. This implies that GNP and money will grow at the same rate or, to be more precise and ac-

6. The t value of the 58 Wharton GNP span forecasts is −1.85, which is significantly different from zero at a 10 percent level of confidence but not at a 5 percent level (using a 2-tailed test).

7. Milton Friedman, *The Morgan Guaranty Survey*, February 1973, pp. 5–10.

count "for the well-established lag between monetary change and income change," GNP will be proportionate "to the average level of money two quarters *earlier*." [8] Strictly speaking, this relationship can only be used to forecast GNP two quarters ahead. However, a one-year-ahead forecast seems to be a more relevant test since it largely overcomes any possible problems associated with seasonal adjustment of the data, as well as for the reasons mentioned above. The Friedman money-GNP forecasting relationship can be adapted to one-year forecasts by adding the assumption that the stock of money two quarters ahead can be controlled fairly precisely. [9]

Table 2 contrasts the one-year GNP forecasts of the seven forecasters with two reasonable standards of comparison— (1) Friedman's constant velocity rule, and (2) the naive forecasting rule that the growth of GNP will be equal to the latest observed growth rate. Clearly, the naive same-change rule is far inferior to the monetarist forecasting procedure. All of the economic forecasters, on the other hand, were more successful than the monetarist rule. The margin of superiority varies widely: the Fair model's forecasting errors were, on average, about 10 percent smaller than the monetarist technique while the most successful GNP forecasters' errors are only a little more than half as large as the monetarist formula.

The Fair "pure model" forecasts can be taken as another relevant standard of comparison, illustrating the performance of an economic (i.e., non-naive) forecasting technique used in a mechanical (i.e., non-judgmental) manner. The conclusion, with regard to the other six forecasters, is about the same, although the margin of superiority of the judgmentally adjusted forecasts

---

8. *Ibid*, p. 7.

9. To be precise, Friedman hypothesized $Y_t = M2_{t-2}V$, the forecasts below are based on

$$(1) \quad \frac{Y_t - Y_{t-4}}{Y_t} = \frac{M2_{t-2} - M2_{t-6}}{M2_{t-6}}$$

so that, in order to forecast Y_t at time t-4 one would need to forecast or control the level of money two quarters ahead, $M2_{t-2}$, relative to the level a half year ago, $M2_{t-6}$. Adding a constant term to equation (1) proves statistically significant over the sample period but does not produce smaller errors in the forecast period.

TABLE 2

FORECAST ERRORS
ONE-YEAR GNP GROWTH [1]
1971:II TO 1974:II

Forecaster	Mean Absolute Error	Root Mean Squared Error
ASA/NBER	1.3	1.6
BEA	1.2	1.5
Chase	1.0	1.2
DRI	1.3	1.5
Fair	1.5	1.9
GE	1.0	1.1
Wharton	1.3	1.6
M2 Rule [2]	1.7	2.1
Same Growth [3]	2.5	2.7

[1] Simple percent change over four-quarter period.
[2] See footnote 10 for explanation of method used.
[3] The growth rate of the previous four-quarter period was projected to continue for the next four-quarter span.

is somewhat smaller, the errors of the judgmentally adjusted forecasts range from about 60 to 90 percent of the Fair "pure model" errors.

CONCLUSION

This article has presented the forecasting errors of seven major economic forecasters over the last four years. It has shown that the errors of the last year or so have been far outside the range of previous experience. Despite the larger errors in recent forecasts judgmental economic forecasts continue to outperform mechanical approaches.

Forecasting Automobile Output

FEDERAL RESERVE BANK OF NEW YORK

This article, authored by Ethan S. Harris, was published by the Federal Reserve Bank of New York in 1985.

As a share of GNP, the auto sector has been on the decline since the early 1970s. Auto output accounted for only about 2½ percent of GNP from 1980 to 1985, down from almost 3 percent in the 1970s. Judged in terms of its contribution to GNP *fluctuations,* however, the auto industry remains a key sector of the economy. In the last six years changes in auto output accounted for 29 percent of the quarter-to-quarter change in GNP, slightly more than its 27 percent contribution in the 1970s.[1] In addition to its strong direct effect on the economy, the auto sector continues to have substantial spillover effects. Purchases of raw materials by the auto industry account for more than half of the rubber and lead consumed in the United States, as well as a major portion of the steel, aluminum, platinum, copper, and zinc. On the consumer end, spending associated with buying and using automobiles has been running above 10 percent of GNP in recent years.[2]

1. In absolute value, the average change in real auto output was $4.5 billion from 1980 to 1985, compared with $15.8 billion for total real GNP.
2. Motor Vehicle Manufacturers Association, *Motor Vehicle Facts and Figures* (1984), pages 60 and 72.

Estimates of the Econometric and Combination Models

Our econometric model is based on a simple supply and demand model. Demand for autos increases when real disposable income rises, the price of new autos falls, or the price of other durable goods increases. The supply of autos expands when inventories are low relative to sales or when the cost of borrowing declines. Low interest rates also increase the demand for autos.

Estimates for both the econometric model and the combination model are presented at right. Each variable is lagged one quarter, since the actual value of each variable would not be known at the time of each forecast. All the variables are significant and have the correct sign in the econometric model.[a] Adding the *Ward's* projection to the econometric model significantly improves the overall fit, reducing the standard error of the model by 100,000 autos.[b] The *Ward's* projection is the most significant variable in this "combination" model, although all the other variables, except "other price," remain significant.

The forecast comparisons reported in the text are not the within-sample predictions of these models. Instead, each model is estimated recursively over the sample, using data from 1967-II to

[a]The coefficient on the own-price variable is positive, which suggests that it is capturing supply-side effects.

[b]A formal F-test shows that the *Ward's* projections add significantly (at the 1 percent level) to the explanatory power of the econometric model. The opposite test, of whether the econometric model improves the *Ward's* projections, was also supported by the data (at the 5 percent level). Together these tests confirm the results reported in the table in the text: the best forecast combines the *Ward's* projections with an econometric model.

Because of its far-ranging importance, the auto sector is central to any assessment of prospects for the economy as a whole. The auto production plans published in *Ward's Automotive Reports* provide a timely two-quarter projection of this important sector, and, as a result, have become a popular tool in forecasting. In this paper we examine the usefulness of the *Ward's* projections for forecasting auto output over the near term. Adjusted for systematic over-prediction, the projections compare favorably with those from some alter-the quarter of the forecast. The prediction errors from these one-quarter-ahead projections are then used to compare the out-of-sample forecasting power of the models.

Variable	Econometric	Combination
Constant	−22301.8	−7931.4
	(−4.5)	(−1.7)
Income	12.9	5.4
	(6.6)	(2.6)
Prime rate	−97.8	−90.0
	(−3.2)	(−3.7)
IS ratio	−19.9	−8.7
	(−6.1)	(−2.7)
Own price	230.4	93.8
	(5.0)	(2.1)
Other price	6.0	1.9
	(2.1)	(0.8)
Ward's projection	[a]	0.55
		(5.3)
$\bar{R}^2$	0.862	0.914
SEE	532	420
Durbin Watson	2.26	1.82

The sample period is 1973-I to 1985-III. The t-values are in parentheses. All independent variables, except the *Ward's* projections, are lagged one period. The dependent variable is units production (in thousands at an annual rate) and the other variables are defined:

Income	= real disposable income in 1972 dollars.
IS ratio	= ratio of retail auto inventories to sales.
Own price	= the CPI for new autos divided by the overall CPI.
other price	= the implicit deflator for non-auto durable goods sales, divided by the overall CPI.

[a] Not applicable.

native methods, but they do not provide the best overall predictions.In particular, combining the *Ward's* projections with a simple econometric model significantly improves the accuracy of the forecast.

ANALYSIS OF THE WARD'S PROJECTIONS

Each month *Ward's* asks eight U.S. auto makers to state their domestic production plans for the next three to six months. Chart 1 plots domestic auto production and the *Ward's* projections made

CHART 1

WARD'S PROJECTIONS AND ACTUAL AUTOMOBILE PRODUCTION

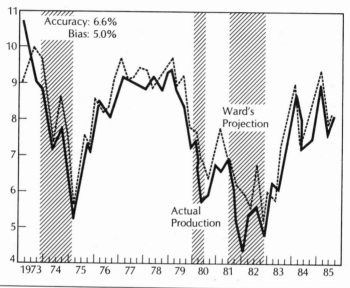

Seasonally Adjusted Annual Rates

Millions of Units

Accuracy: 6.6%
Bias: 5.0%

Ward's Projection

Actual Production

1973 74   75   76   77   78   79   80   81   82   83   84   85

SOURCE: Various issues of *Ward's Automotive Reports* (1973–85) and unpublished data from the Bureau of Economic Analysis.

Shaded areas represent periods of recession, as defined by the National Bureau of Economic Research.

"Accuracy" is the mean absolute error and "bias" is the mean error, each as a percent of actual production.

at the beginning of each quarter.[3] Although the *Ward's* projections generally track the up and down movement of production they have two shortcomings. First, they are not very accurate, with an average error of about one-half of a million cars at an annual rate. Second, they systematically over-predict auto output, by an average of 0.42 million cars at an annual rate, or 5.5 percent of actual produc-

3. The raw data are monthly, but the analysis has been simplified by aggregating the three months of each quarter. In addition, the data is adjusted using seasonal factors from the Bureau of Economic Analysis.

tion. The *Ward's* projections, therefore, may be best viewed as production "targets" rather than forecasts.[4]

We can analyze the *Ward's* projections more rigorously by estimating the relationship between actual production and the *Ward's* projections:

$$\text{Auto output} = 0.275 + 0.909 \; Ward's + 0.277 \; \text{error} \; (-1).$$
$$\quad\quad\quad (0.59) \quad (15.67) \quad\quad\quad (2.54)$$

Sample period = 1973-I to 1985-III, SEE = 0.431, R^2 = 0.838
(The t-values are in parentheses.)

The statistical results from this regression suggest three problems with the *Ward's* projections. First, they provide statistical confirmation that *Ward's* systematically over-predicts.[5] Second, the errors are serially correlated; that is, they tend to persist from one period to the next. This means the errors, as well as the projections them-selves, can be used to forecast production. It also implies that better forecasts could be achieved by adding economic variables to the equation. Third, the large standard error means that even adjusted for systematic over-prediction the projections are not very accurate.

WARD'S IN COMPARISON WITH OTHER FORECASTS

Despite these limitations, the *Ward's* projections are useful for forecasting auto output. Table 1 compares *Ward's* with three alternative models: an extrapolative forecast in which next period's pro-

4. The projections are supposed to be "actual production schedules," as reported by production planners, taking into account both production capacity and market outlook. There are at least three possible reasons for systematic over-prediction. First, the normal amalgam of strikes and bottlenecks may thwart plans. Second, the market may be weaker than the (generally optimistic) outlook embodied in the production plans. Third, as part of its marketing strategy each firm has an incentive to exaggerate its plans. An optimistic outlook may help promote sales and increase the stock market value of the firm. Furthermore, by reporting strong production plans each firm may hope to dissuade production by its competitors and thereby capture greater market share

5. If the projections were unbiased, with no tendency to predict too high or too low, then the constant term would be close to zero and the slope coefficient would be close to one. A formal F-test of this joint hypothesis shows that *Ward's* does significantly over-predict. The $F_{(2,49)}$ value is 12.51, which is more than double the 1 percent critical value.

TABLE 1

Comparison of *Wards* to Alternative Models

Model	Bias[a] (percent)[b]	Accuracy[a] (percent)[b]	Predictive power[c]
Wards	0.381	0.498	0.859
	(5.0)	(6.6)	
Extrapolative	0.028	0.686	0.690
	(0.4)	(9.0)	
Econometric model	0.283	0.524	0.838
	(3.7)	(6.9)	
Combination model	0.209	0.368	0.886
	(2.8)	(4.9)	

[a] "Bias" is the mean error and "Accuracy" is the mean absolute error.

[b] Millions of units at an annual rate. The numbers in parentheses are the bias and accuracy as a percent of actual production.

[c] "Predictive power" is the coefficient of determination (*i.e.*, the $\bar{R}^2$). It measures the percent of variation in actual production explained by each model.

duction is assumed to equal current production; an econometric model of the auto sector including income, price, and cost variables; and a combination of the *Ward's* projections and the econometric model. (Details of the econometric and combination models are given in the box.) Since there is no single criterion for a "good" forecast, we present three standard measures: a good forecast should have little bias (small average over- or under-prediction), high accuracy (small average absolute errors), and high predictive power (explain a large portion of the variation in production). Overall, the *Ward's* projections perform about as well as the econometric model and are clearly superior to the extrapolative model; among the three basic forecasts they rank the worst on bias but the best on the other measures.

A BETTER FORECAST

To take advantage of the relative merits of the *Ward's* and econometric models, we tried to improve the forecast by combining them. The last row of Table 1 shows the results for a "combination forecast," constructed by adding the *Ward's* projections as a variable to the econometric model. The combination model is better than its components by all three criteria: it has the least bias, the greatest accuracy, and the most predictive power. This suggests that both the *Ward's* projections and the econometric model contain information valuable in forecasting.

Chart 2 plots forecast errors for the combination model and compares them with the *Ward's* projections. The combination forecast shows small errors and no tendency to over- or under-predict.[6] Of course, more complicated models might provide better forecasts. It seems clear, however, that the *Ward's* projections will remain useful for assessing the outlook for the auto sector and the economy as a whole.

CHART 2

FORECAST ERRORS OF THE *WARD'S* PROJECTION AND THE COMBINATION MODEL

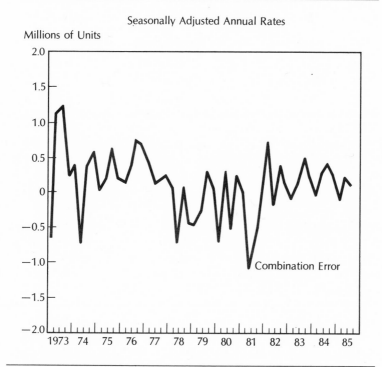

Seasonally Adjusted Annual Rates

Millions of Units

SOURCE: Federal Reserve Bank of New York staff estimates.

6. The *Ward's* projections appear to have performed better in the last two years. This is more a reflection of the unexpected strength of demand than a fundamental change in forecast accuracy. In fact, if we compare the period 1973–79 with 1980–85, the track record of *Ward's* actually deteriorates over time while the combination model improves.

The Use of Survey Data in Forecasting

WILLIAM C. DUNKELBERG

William C. Dunkelberg is chief economist of the National Federation of Independent Business. This paper appeared in Business Economics *in 1986.*

For most economists, the term "economic forecasting" conjures up images of large computers cranking out solutions to large models consisting of hundreds of complex equations and submodels. The results of these models are, of course, subject to the definitional rigor imposed by the GNP identity. For practitioners of this lofty art (a group in which I claim membership), a keen awareness also exists of the "judgemental" aspects of such forecasting and a growing sensitivity to the limitations of forecasting with large-scale models.

Many of the difficulties we have with these models arise from the "oversimplifications" of the environments that they represent. Risking the perils of such oversimplifications, "macro" models can be characterized as complex "averaging" devices that simply multiply our "assumptions" by a set of complex constants estimated from historical data. Thus, it should come as no surprise that models produce forecasts that reflect the forecaster's "priors" about the economy; if one "assumes" a recession, the model will indeed verify that it will occur.

It also should come as no surprise that our models do very well when nothing interesting is going on, but let us down when "inter-

Note: All footnotes have been omitted from the original article.

esting" things happen. A corollary to this proposition is that models typically will reflect turning points after they have occurred, especially those models heavily dependent upon "lagged" variables (either lagged dependent variables, where this point is obvious, or lagged independent variables that are highly correlated with the dependent variable).

Thus, it is not surprising that, during the turbulent 1980s, the large-scale models did not forecast well. Those that were right usually were right only once. And, as might typify such uncertain times, economists' forecasts reflected the variance in assumptions both about important exogenous variables and about the structure of the economy that pervaded the profession.

Forgotten also by our large models is the importance of "discretion" to short-run economic activity. George Katona argued for years that the increasing affluence of our economy introduced the potential for wide fluctuations in spending that would, in the short-run, be inconsistent with the predictions of the consumption function and other relationships in our macro models. The availability of consumer credit and its increasing use enlarged the potential magnitude of deviations from the predictions of our models. Thus, parameters estimated for twenty years of data become relatively useless as predictors of *short-run* behavior.

Some interesting distributional issues are present as well. The estimation of a parameter such as the marginal propensity to consume (MPC) reflects joint distributions of characteristics, such as income and age in the population. The MPC for the economy in the consumption function is fundamentally a weighted average reflecting the income receipts, the debt use, and the spending propensities of population subgroups. If the distribution of these groups changes substantially, the reliability of the parameters will be diminished. Today, the thirty-five to forty-four age group is seven percentage points larger in the population than was the case ten years ago. Their spending and home-buying behavior is quite different from other age groups in the population, and such a bulge cannot help but compromise the quality of our model parameters.

In the "longer-run," our models should serve us better, as economic activity becomes subject to the discipline of important economic relationships that are the core of our economic models. But, tracking the short-run course of the economy with these models in a period of uncertainty and altered economic structures can be perilous. Survey data augment this particular weakness of models most successfully.

THE USE OF SURVEYS IN THE FORECASTING PROCESS

Traditional forecasting requires the explicit formulation of a model, including precise specification of "causal" variables and the nature of their relationship to the dependent variable of interest. Once estimated, the parameters of the relationship are taken as immutable behavioral constants. Because theory is an abstraction, a simplification of reality, our model necessarily excludes all but the most important variables. It assumes further that the relationship between the included predictors and the dependent variable does not change. And, finally, it assumes that excluded variables never become important enough to be included.

Survey data short-cut much of this process. If a consumer is asked to predict the inflation rate, it is not necessary to specify the causal model that drives prices in our economy nor is it necessary to specify the model used by the agent. It therefore becomes unnecessary to decide which factors are important and to measure their quantitative importance. It also is not necessary to be concerned about changes in the importance of variables over time. The agent uses whatever "model" seems appropriate and incorporates whatever information is available at the time in constructing a forecast. Right or wrong, this forecast influences the behavior of the agent, and it is the aggregation of this behavior we seek to predict.

This factor is perhaps the major strength of survey data for producing a short-term forecast. Survey data reflect whatever is happening at the moment of importance to economic agents, events that are impossible to anticipate and include in a formal model, and the importance of which cannot be estimated from past data (because of too few occurrences). Survey data quickly reflect the market response to changes in economic news and information, anticipating changes in spending or other behavior that this new information will produce.

It is also the "current" character of the survey measures that make them generally useless (depending upon the nature of the data collected) for long-term forecasting. Many of the survey variables available for predicting consumer and business spending will carry their own weight in expanded structural equations describing spending behavior. But, as a result of the importance of the "current component" of the survey measures, the lags between spending and the survey measures are typically short, i.e., one to two quarters. Thus, any model incorporating these variables cannot be "pushed" out very far into the future without the need to make assumptions about the future values of these survey measures. We are more comfortable predicting future government spending than we are at choosing a level of consumer optimism four quarters out. Thus, forecasters, after examining the usefulness of survey data, have discarded these measures.

APPLICATIONS OF SURVEY DATA

The usefulness of survey measures does not depend solely upon how well they can be integrated into our large-scale econometric models. Other widely used forecast methodologies easily embrace the nature of survey data.

The first potential application is that of a "leading indicator." Many data series are available, some already combined into an "index," such as the well-known Index of Consumer Sentiment produced monthly by the Survey Research Center at the University of Michigan. In this application, we are most concerned with the regularity of the relationship between the survey measure and the dependent variable of interest. Figure 1 illustrates a simple plot of the annualized percentage change in real GNP and the Small Business Optimism Index produced from the National Federation of Independent Business (NFIB) Quarterly Economic Surveys.

The next logical step is to formalize this relationship with a simple bivariate regression, as was done in the models used by the National Federation of Independent Business [1985] in their forecasts of the economy based on surveys of small firms. An example is shown in Figure 2, which utilizes an index of ten questions to predict the percentage change in real GNP. Their survey clearly does not cover all economic agents in the economy, omitting consumers and large businesses. However, over time this bias is systematic and does not compromise the correlation between economic aggregates and the survey measures. The regression simply "scales" the parameters to reflect the systematic bias.

A third use is for anticipating the response of agents to expected changes in economic policy or economic conditions. Economic agents

FIGURE 1

SMALL BUSINESS OPTIMISM INDEX AND REAL GNP CHANGE
(ten questions, 1978 = 100)

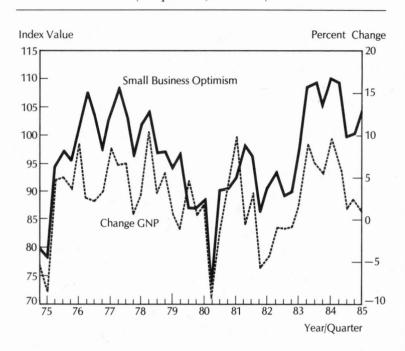

anticipate events based on currently available information, e.g., make forecasts and alter their behavior accordingly. Thus, it was possible to show that as consumers became more certain of tax cuts and increases, they adjusted their spending behavior in a consistent manner prior to the actual passage of the tax change. While "traditional" models failed to detect the spending adjustments, survey measures reflected the changes prior to actual passage of the tax law.

Most forecasting is done on a conditional basis. If Assumption Set A turns out to be correct, then GNP will grow X percent. If Assumption Set B is correct, then GNP will grow Y percent.

Survey data, collected on a monthly basis, provide early infor-

FIGURE 2

PREDICTED CHANGE IN REAL GNP
(small business optimism index)

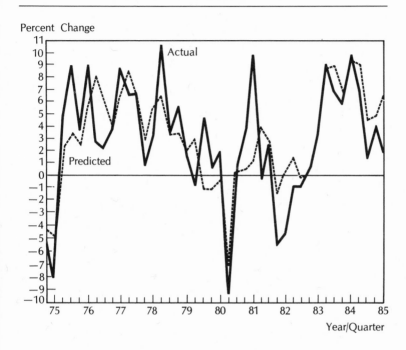

Percent Change

Year/Quarter

mation as to which scenario seems to be unfolding, A or B. The survey results are not subject to revision. Thus, they provide a more reliable indicator of developments than most of the aggregate statistical data released each month. Consequently, survey findings can provide some of the earliest indications of whether or not a "most likely" forecast and its underlying assumptions (scenario) are on track.

TYPES OF SURVEY DATA AVAILABLE

A survey can provide several types of variables. First, a survey can provide us with a direct forecast of a dependent macro variable, such as each agent's forecast of the inflation rate for the economy.

These then can be averaged (possibly applying some type of weighting process, e.g., by size of income or firm sales) to provide a forecast of the inflation rate. The estimate of inflation derived from the University of Michigan surveys is an example of such an application. (Table 1.)

TABLE 1

EXPECTED INFLATION—NEXT TWELVE MONTHS

Year/Quarter	Mean expected increase	Variance
1982:1	5.7	68
2	5.4	61
3	5.9	59
4	5.6	64
1983:1	4.3	53
2	4.6	49
3	4.9	47
4	5.1	45
1984:1	4.9	49
2	5.3	44
3	4.4	38
4	5.1	48
1985:1	4.4	40

SOURCE: Survey Research Center, University of Michigan.
Question: During the next twelve months, do you think that prices in general will go up, or go down, or stay where they are now? By what percent do you expect prices to go up, on average, during the next twelve months?

Second, surveys can provide us with a "forecast" of each individual agent's behavior, such as the firm's intention to raise prices. These data might be averaged to provide a forecast of inflation for the group represented by the survey. One additional step, based on correlation analysis, is all that is needed to link this forecast to the desired macro inflation measure, say the CPI inflation rate.

The data collected in the National Federation of Independent Business surveys on expected price increases typifies this approach. Each firm is asked about planned price increases for the firm. These plans are then aggregated for the sample, producing an index of planned price increases. (Table 2.) The index produced ultimately is used to predict inflation as measured by the non-food CPI.

Buying intentions are closely related variables. Although buying

TABLE 2

Index of Planned Price Increases

Year/Quarter	IPPI Index of planned price increases[1]	Actual inflation[2]	Predicted inflation[3]
1980:1	3.05	17.4	13.8
2	2.67	8.7	12.0
3	2.04	9.5	8.9
4	2.26	10.7	10.0
1981:1	2.69	10.2	12.1
2	2.00	12.8	8.7
3	1.89	9.2	8.2
4	1.90	3.4	8.3
1982:1	1.90	2.1	8.3
2	1.05 [.97]	12.2	4.2 [3.8]
3	1.07 [.83]	3.4	4.3 [3.1]
4	1.16 [.78]	−1.9	4.7 [2.9]
1983:1	1.29 [.95]	2.9	5.3 [3.7]
2	1.02 [.60]	6.2	4.0 [2.0]
3	1.05 [.84]	5.2	4.2 [3.2]
4	1.17 [.91]	2.1	4.7 [3.5]
1984:1	1.31 [1.13]	5.0	5.4 [4.4]
2	1.20 [1.03]	4.4	4.9 [4.1]
3	1.17 [.93]	5.3	4.7 [3.6]
4	1.12 [.88]	—	4.5 [3.4]
1985:1	1.51 [1.29]	—	6.4 [5.3]

SOURCE: National Federation of Independent Business.
Question: In the next three months, do you plan to change the average selling prices of your goods and/or services? _____Yes, raise prices _____Yes, lower prices _____No change _____Don't know. If raise or lower, by what percent, on average? ____Less than 1% ____1.0–1.9% ____2.0–2.9% ____3.0–3.9% ____4.0–4.9% ____5.0–7.9% ____8.0–9.9% ____10% or more ____D.K.

[1] Prior to the second quarter, 1982, firms were asked only about price increases. The IPPI is calculated by multiplying the mid-point of each category by the percent of firms planning price increases in each category. The "don't know how much of an increase" [DK] category is assigned at the mean increase. Those planning no increase are assigned 0 in the weighted average.

[2] Based on the CPI less food, calculated over the three month period following the survey month.

[3] Forecast in [ ] includes planned price *reductions,* not available prior to 1982, second quarter. The formula used for the forecasts is: Inflation = −.87 + 4.80* IPPI.

intentions data have not proven to be highly reliable predictors of spending at the individual level, they have proven to be good predictors at the macro level. The National Federation of Independent Business successfully uses its inventory intentions variables to predict constant dollar non-farm inventory investment in the quarter following the survey. (Figure 3.)

General expectations about the economy or the agent's personal outlook represent a fourth class of variables generally available. These relate to no particular dependent variable (such as plans to increase inventories, or raise prices), but can be used to anticipate changes in specific variables nevertheless. Examples include expected changes in the personal financial condition, expected changes in the economy and the expected course of business conditions. These variables can be effectively used to predict both general spending measures and specific outlays.

Some survey variables are measures of current status, such as financial well-being compared to a year earlier, current satisfaction

FIGURE 3

PREDICTED AND ACTUAL INVENTORY INVESTMENT
(non-farm inventory, 1972 dollars)

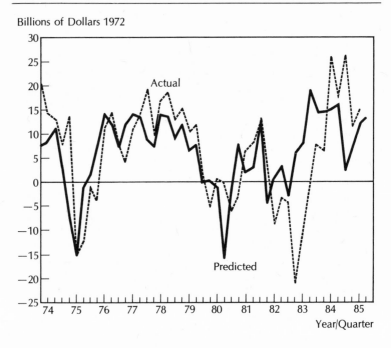

with inventories, or profits now compared to a quarter of a year earlier. This type of variable may reflect past changes in important macro variables and also embody forecasts that account for numerous but unspecified factors. For example, current inventory satisfaction must implicitly embody not only current levels of inventories (affected by last period sales), but also expected inventory requirements in the near future, which implies a forecast of real sales.

One widely used methodology combines several survey variables into a single index. Perhaps the best known example is the University of Michigan's Index of Consumer Sentiment, a combination of questions about buying conditions, past and expected personal financial developments, and past and expected business conditions (ten questions). The National Federation of Independent Business combines questions about profits, expected real sales, planned capital, labor, and inventory outlays, and general expectations about the economy to form the Small Business Optimism Index used to predict changes in real GNP. (Figure 2.) These well-known indices are simple linear combinations of their base variables. No "optimal" procedure is established for constructing such indices, and many complex methodologies are available. For the most part, after scaling the component variables where required, simple additive indexes (usually normalized to a base period) have proven to be quite robust.

Survey data are becoming more widely available. Many forecasters have begun collecting their own "survey" results for forecasting purposes. We have well-known surveys of consumers (The University of Michigan, the Conference Board, Sindlinger), of purchasing agents, and small business (National Federation of Independent Business, Dun and Bradstreet). McGraw–Hill surveys of business investment have been widely used, and the Department of Labor relies on surveys for estimates of employment and unemployment. Hundreds of specialized surveys have been initiated in recent years, covering states (usually conducted by a bureau of business research at a university), individual communities, trade associations, etc. Most of them have too short a history to permit empirical verification of their validity. While there is no ideal number of observations, forty quarters (ten years) of data are needed to permit reliable evaluations of survey data in both boom and bust years.

The quality of a survey data base depends on the character of the frame (in the case of NFIB, its membership of over half a million firms) from which samples will be drawn, the sampling procedure (random is best), the response rate (how many and which firms answer the question), the consistency of the questions over time (minor changes in a question can destroy the empirical meaning of a variable), and how well the questions are drafted and how meaningful, in an economic sense, the questions are.

The process of analyzing the NFIB data is fairly typical of the procedures followed to convert cross-section survey data into corresponding macro data observations. Once the NFIB data are collected, selected cross-tabulations are run on each quarterly survey. Each survey contains about 2,200 firms, produced by a response rate of about 33 percent. The percentages produced by the cross-tabulations become one set of quarterly time series observations. For example, each quarter, the percent of firms planning capital outlays is recorded. Since the surveys were started in the last quarter of 1973, we now have forty-four observations on this variable (and most other variables in the survey).

These variables provide the raw material for estimating the simple bivariate regression models used to predict economic activity. Here, the choice of functional form becomes important, because most of the variables to be predicted have very strong time trends, while the survey variables are all percentages, conceptually bound by 0 and 100 and in fact displaying a much smaller variance *with no time trend*.

In some instances, the question clearly dictates the appropriate form of the dependent variable. For example, the percent of firms planning to add to inventory holdings makes the National Income Accounts definition of inventory investment (defined as the change in inventories) the logical choice. However, the percent of firms expecting business conditions to be better implies no specific dependent variable or form for whatever variable is selected (level, change, percentage change, etc.). The percentage of firms planning to make capital outlays (weighted by the number of firms in the population to handle the time trend in the dependent variable) might be used to predict the *level* of plant and equipment spending. The change (raw or percentage) in the percent of firms planning such outlays might be used to predict the *percentage change* in plant and equipment outlays. In general, percentage changes appear to be the appropriate form for dependent variables to be predicted by these survey measures, but considerable leeway exists for experimentation when logic dictates no clear structure.

The quality of available surveys varies dramatically, and users should devote some time to evaluating the methodology used to collect the data. Even well-known surveys have deficiencies about which the user should be aware. Although systematic overtime bias can be "scaled" out of the results, a large number of observations is needed to perform the necessary adjustments. Variable bias produced by poor methodologies, particularly for surveys with short histories, can produce very misleading results.

Having both built and used large-scale macroeconomic models, I am inclined to think that the greatest value of the models comes from the understanding of the structure of our economy that one gains by trying actually to build one. In part, this experience explains the personal success of our premier model-builders. Then, the testing of "scenarios" involves complexities too numerous to handle without the benefit of such models. This testing includes the "conditional" forecasts we typically produce, all premised on an initial (but usually undisclosed) set of assumptions beyond those implicit in the model. It is asking too much that these models predict, with consistency and accuracy, short term fluctuations in the economy. Successful tracking of economic activity in the short-term requires techniques that reflect the ever-changing factors that influence spending decisions beyond those important fundamentals identified in our macro models. The use of survey data is one approach that holds great promise.

A Descriptive Analysis of Economic Indicators

RONALD A. RATTI

Ronald A. Ratti is a professor of economics at the University of Missouri. This article was published by the Federal Reserve Bank of St. Louis in 1985.

Each month the U.S. Department of Commerce publishes a series of economic indicators, the most widely followed of which are the composite indexes of leading, coincident and lagging indicators. The significance attached to these series is attested to by the promptness with which their month-to-month movements are reported and analyzed by the news media. Economic agents monitor the behavior of these indexes because, historically, they have been thought to provide useful information on current and future changes in the economy.

The objective of this paper is to describe how these indexes are constructed and revised, to provide a descriptive explanation for why they might provide information on future economic conditions, and to examine critically their usefulness. In the final section of the paper, the difficulties inherent in using the index of leading indicators as a forecaster of future economic conditions are discussed. Emphasis is placed on the leading indicator index since it is the most widely reported and well known of the indexes considered.

Note: All footnotes have been omitted from the original article.

A DESCRIPTION OF COMPOSITE INDEXES

Individual and composite indicators are used to predict downturns and upturns in the economy and to monitor the degree of strength or weakness in a recession or recovery. Analysts generally acknowledge that in order for individual indicators to provide useful information they should have the following characteristics: (1) they should represent and accurately measure important economic variables or processes; (2) they should bear a consistent relationship over time with business cycle movements and turns; (3) they should not be dominated by irregular and non-cyclical movements; and (4) they should be promptly and frequently reported. These requirements ensure that the best indicators regularly provide timely economic information on the stages of the business cycle.

On the basis of these criteria, the Bureau of Economic Analysis has evaluated, and continues to evaluate, hundreds of economic time series. Only those series with a good overall performance that are available monthly with a short time lag and are not subject to large revisions are candidates for inclusion in the three major composite indexes.

The composite indexes of leading, coincident and lagging cyclical indicators each measure the average behavior of series showing similar leading, coincident and lagging timing at business cycle turns. Components of the indexes are also chosen so as to represent as broad an array of diverse activities and sectors as possible. This requirement is meant to ensure that the composite indicators continue to monitor and closely shadow economic activity, even if the causes and nature of cyclical change vary over time and the performance of some individual indicators deteriorate. Since each business cycle has unique characteristics, individual series can be expected to perform better during some cycles than others. Without prior information on the causes of current economic change, it seems best to rely for information on groupings of series rather than individual series.

The Index of Leading Indicators · Table 1 lists the components of the three composite indexes. The leading index consists of individual components that might lead measures of economic activity. For example, housing starts, new incorporations, contracts for construction and new orders for machinery and equipment are leading indi-

TABLE 1

STANDARDIZATION FACTORS AND WEIGHTS FOR COMPOSITE INDEX COMPONENTS

BEA series number and title	Standardization factor[1]	Weight[2]
Leading index components		
1. Average weekly hours of production of nonsupervisory workers, manufacturing	0.467	1.014
5. Average weekly initial claims for unemployment insurance, State programs[3]	5.374	1.041
8. Manufacturers' new orders in 1972 dollars, consumer goods and materials industries	2.818	0.973
32. [a]Vendor performance, percent of companies receiving slower deliveries	3.840	1.081
12. Index of net business formation	0.996	0.973
20. Contracts and orders for plant and equipment in 1972 dollars	6.194	0.946
29. Index of new private housing units authorized by local building permits	5.064	1.054
36. [a]Change in manufacturing and trade inventories on hand and on order in 1972 dollars, smoothed[4]	2.530	0.986
99. [a]Change in sensitive materials prices, smoothed[4]	0.324	0.892
19. Index of stock prices, 500 common stocks	2.633	1.149
106. Money supply M2 in 1972 dollars	0.417	0.932
111. [a]Change in business and consumer credit outstanding	2.627	0.959
Coincident index components		
41. Employees on nonagricultural payrolls	0.321	1.064
51. Personal income less transfer payments in 1972 dollars	0.502	1.003
47. Index of industrial production	0.924	1.028
57. Manufacturing and trade sales in 1972 dollars	1.021	0.905
Lagging index components		
91. Average duration of unemployment in weeks[3]	3.587	1.098
77. [a]Ratio, manufacturing and trade inventories to sales in 1972 dollars	0.016	0.894
62. [a]Index of labor cost per unit of output, manufacturing—actual data as a percent of trend	0.557	0.868
109. [a]Average prime rate charged by banks	0.376[5]	1.123
101. Commercial and industrial loans outstanding in 1972 dollars	0.901	1.009
95. [a]Ratio, consumer installment credit outstanding to personal income	0.062	1.009

SOURCE: U.S. Department of Commerce, *Handbook of Cyclical Indicators,* 1984.

[a]First differences rather than symmetrical percent changes are computed for this series.

[1]Standardization factors are computed over the period 1948–81.

[2]The weight for a given series is the ratio of its performance score to the average score of all series in that index.

[3]Changes for this series are inverted; i.e., they are multiplied by -1.

[4]This series is a four-term moving average (weighted 1,2,2,1) placed on the terminal month of the span.

[5]This standardization factor is computed over the period 1966–81.

cators, since they represent early commitments to future economic activity.

The inclusion of some other components in the leading index is less obvious and more involved. This is partly because there is no single well-developed theory linking each of the indicators to the business cycle. The economic series that make up the composite indicators are included primarily because they perform well statistically in relation to the cycle, not because they are the operational counterparts of variables in an economic theory of business cycles.

There is usually some economic rationale, however, for including each series in the index. An increase in average weekly hours worked, for instance, presumably leads the business cycle since it is easier for employers to move to higher output levels in the initial stages of an expansion by increasing the utilization of labor than by increasing the number of employees.

The remaining components of the index of leading indicators and the rationale for including them in the index are the following: Initial claims for unemployment insurance represent first claims filed by workers newly unemployed or claims for subsequent periods of unemployment. Slower deliveries, which inversely reflect the volume of business of firms supplying purchasing agents in the Greater Chicago area, has been found to precede changes in the actual volume of business. The sum of changes in inventories on hand and on order are assumed to reflect changes in the desired stock of inventories. The desired stock of inventories is assumed to rise if the anticipated level of sales increases.

"Change in sensitive materials prices, smoothed" is based on indexes of crude and intermediate materials prices and spot market prices of raw industrial materials. Movements in these prices are assumed to reflect variations in demand relative to supply in the process of building up or drawing down raw material inventories. A rise in prices is taken to indicate increased demand for the output of the manufacturing and construction sectors. Stock price movements affect and measure the general state of business expectations about future profits. When prospects for profits deteriorate, investment plans are shelved and expansionary business operations are contracted.

The inclusion of money and credit indicators capture the impact of changes in real balances and the availability of credit on future activity. During the late stages of a boom, bank deposit creation is limited by the availability of reserves, and the rate of increase in consumer prices begins to accelerate. The opposite is true during a downturn. These effects cause the turning points in the rate of change in real M2 to lead the turning points in the business cycle. The change in business and consumer credit also is a leading indicator, since many economic actions require financial arrangements before their inception.

The Index of Coincident Indicators · The components of the Index of Coincident Indicators are measures of aggregate economic activity in the areas of employment, real income, production and real sales. The Index of Coincident Indicators, together with other coincident indicators, show how well the economy is faring and is used to identify and date the peaks and troughs in the business cycle. This indentification and dating, however, can only be done after the turning points have occurred.

The Index of Lagging Indicators · The Index of Lagging Indicators is designed to confirm both downturns and upturns in business activity. Lagging indicators can also be useful for forecasting purposes, because their turns sometimes lead the opposite turns of the leading indicators. Lagging indicators, such as bank interest rates, unit labor costs, inventory holdings and outstanding debt are associated with the costs of doing business. Reductions in these items during a recession lay the basis for the subsequent upturn, as well as having an enhancing effect on such leading indicators as commitments to invest, inventory accumulation and new credit outstanding.

CONSTRUCTION OF COMPOSITE INDEXES

Construction of the composite indexes involves several statistical operations on both the individual data series that make up the indexes and on the indexes themselves. These steps are described in this section. The accompanying insert provides an illustration of how the indexes are constructed.

The first step in constructing the composite indexes involves standardizing the individual series. Standardization prevents the relatively volatile series from dominating movements in the composite index. If, for example, a series typically exhibits large percentage changes, a failure to standardize would cause this series to swamp the effects of series that typically change by more modest amounts.

For each individual series, the month-to-month percentage change is calculated. (For series already in percentage form or in ratio form the month-to-month difference is taken.) The percentage changes in a component series are then standardized by dividing them by the long-run average percentage change in that series without regard to sign (the standardization factor). These standardization factors are shown in Table 1.

A composite index is constructed by weighting the standardized changes of its components. The weight assigned each component is determined by the overall score each series receives on the basis of a number of economic and statistical criteria. The application of these criteria involves both objective and subjective evaluations of such factors as economic significance, timely recognition of business cycle turning points, degree of conformity to the stages of the business cycle, quality and availability of current data, and the importance of non-cyclical movements in the series. The largest weights are attached to those components with the best overall performance on the basis of these criteria. The weights attached to the components of the composite indexes are shown in Table 1. As can be seen, these weights do not vary between components by as much as the standardization factors do.

The raw percentage changes in the leading and lagging indexes, given by the sum of the weighted standardized percentage changes of their components, are then adjusted so as to facilitate comparison with the coincident index. This is done by equating the cumulative sum over time of the absolute values of changes in the leading and lagging index with the sum of the absolute values of changes in the coincident index. The index standardization factors based on data over 1948–81 appear in Table 2.

In addition, a trend adjustment procedure is used to make the trends in the three major composite indexes equal to the average of the trends in the components of the coincident index. This is done by subtracting the trends in the leading, coincident and lagging indexes (0.132, 0.446 and 0.253, respectively) and adding in the average of the monthly trends in the components of the coincident indexes (0.271). The trend adjustment facilitates the use of the three indexes as indicators of levels of activity. The trend adjustment factors are listed in Table 2.

TABLE 2

INDEX STANDARDIZATION AND TREND ADJUSTMENT FACTORS: 1948–81

Composite index	Average absolute change[1]	Index standardization factor[2]	Trend in raw index	Trend adjustment factor[3]
Leading index	0.496	0.582	0.132%	+0.139%
Coincident index	0.852	1.000	0.446	−0.175
Lagging index	0.602	0.707	0.253	+0.018

SOURCE: U.S. Department of Commerce, *Handbook of Cyclical Indicators*, 1984.

[1] The average absolute change for each index is obtained as follows: *(a)* for each month, a weighted average of the standardized changes of all components in that index is computed; *(b)* a long-term (1948–81) average without regard to sign is calculated from these monthly averages.

[2] This measure is the ratio of the average absolute change in each index to the average absolute change in the coincident index.

[3] The trend adjustment factor is 0.271 minus the trend in the raw index.

THE IMPORTANCE OF REVISIONS

A preliminary estimate of the performance of the composite indexes for a given month appears toward the end of the following month. The July issue of *Business Conditions Digest*, for example, carries a preliminary estimate of the composite indexes in June. The August issue of *Business Conditions Digest* will then carry a revised estimate of the June indexes. The second estimate typically differs from the first because data on some series were not originally available and because data that were originally available have been updated.

The net effect of these revisions is often a significant change in the estimate of the performance of the composite indicators. Table 3 illustrates that the absolute size of the first revision in the indexes of leading, coincident and lagging indicators averaged about 0.5, 0.3 and 0.3 percentage points, respectively, for the first nine months of 1984. These revisions appear to be substantial, given that the preliminary estimates of the monthly changes in these indexes have average absolute values of only about 0.7, 0.7 and 1.0 percentage points.

The sources of revisions in the three indexes vary from one month to the next. It appears, however, that for the monthly estimates during 1984 the subsequent availability of data on series *not available initially* accounts, on the average, for over two-thirds of the

TABLE 3

FIRST AND SECOND ESTIMATES OF COMPOSITE INDEXES: 1984
(percent changes)

	Leading		Coincident		Lagging	
	First[1]	Second[2]	First	Second	First	Second
January	1.1%	1.0%	1.0%	1.4%	−0.9%	−0.9%
February	0.7	1.3	0.9	0.8	0.9	1.6
March	−1.1	−0.1	0.3	0.0	1.1	1.3
April	0.5	0.5	0.8	0.9	1.7	1.8
May	−0.1	0.4	0.5	0.9	1.0	1.7
June	−0.9	−1.3	0.7	0.9	0.6	0.9
July	−0.8	−1.8	0.8	0.1	0.9	1.2
August	0.5	−0.1	0.2	0.0	1.1	1.0
September	0.4	0.6	0.1	0.0	0.6	0.8
Average absolute revision	0.5		0.3		0.3	

SOURCE: U.S. Department of Commerce, *Business Conditions Digest,* various issues.

[1] First estimate for a month is obtained from the issue of *Business Conditions Digest* for the following month.

[2] Second estimate for a month is obtained from the issue of *Business Conditions Digest* dated two months later.

first revision in leading and lagging indexes and about one-half of the revision in the coincident index. The balance of the revisions are due to updated estimates of data *that were available* for the initial estimates.

Estimates of the composite indexes are subject to revision for a period of 12 months. The first and last available estimates of the leading indicator from 1979 to 1983 appear in Chart 1. As we can see, these estimates sometimes diverge by substantial amounts. In Table 4, the average absolute values of successive revisions in estimates of changes in each composite indicator from 1979 to 1983 are presented. For purposes of comparison, the table also includes the average absolute value of selected estimates of the percentage change in each index. The average absolute value of the first revision (the difference between the first and second estimates) in the leading indicator is calculated to be 0.4, and the average absolute value of revisions subsequent to the first revision (the difference between the final and second estimates) in the leading indicator is found to be 0.5 Since the average absolute value of the total revision (the difference between the final and first estimates) in the leading indi-

Construction of Composite Indexes: An Example

The procedures for constructing composite indexes from the basic monthly data series are illustrated in the example below. In the example, the preliminary estimates of the leading coincident and lagging indicators are calculated for June 1984. The data, taken from the July 1984 issue of *Business Conditions Digest*, are presented in the table on the opposite page.

Note that data on several components—change in inventories, business and consumer credit, manufacturing and trade sales, the ratio of manufacturing and trade inventories to sales, and the ratio of consumer installment credit outstanding to personal income—were not available. These omissions and subsequent revisions in the original data will be sources of change in successive estimates of the three indexes.

The column headed "weighted and standardized percentage change" is obtained by dividing the percentage change in each component by its standardization factor, then multiplying by its weight, both of which are presented in Table 1 and explained in the text.[1] The sum of the number in this column provide estimates of the movements during June in each of the indexes that have not yet been standardized for compatibility across the three indexes or detrended. For the leading, coincident and lagging indicators, these figures are -0.577, 0.888 and 0.398 percent, respectively. Dividing each of those numbers by the index standardization factors and then adding the trend factors, both of which are given in Table 2, yields the following preliminary estimates of the changes in the three indexes for June:

Percentage change in

Leading Index $= -(0.577/0.582) + 0.139 = -0.9$;
Coincident Index $= (0.888/1.000) - 0.175 = 0.7$;
Lagging Index $= (0.398/0.707) + 0.018 = 0.6$.

[1] The numbers are also divided by the sum of the weights on the components included in an index. These sums are 10.005, 3.095 and 4.098 for the available components of the leading, coincident and lagging indexes, respectively.

CONSTRUCTION OF COMPOSITE INDEXES: AN ILLUSTRATION

Index and BEA series number	Basic data		Percentage change	Weighted and standardized percentage change[1]
	May 1984	*June 1984*	*May to June 1984*	*May to June 1984*
Leading Index Components				
1.	40.6	40.6	0	0.000
5.	348	350	−0.6	−0.012
8.	34.46	36.18	−5.9	−0.203
32.	70	66	−4	−0.112
12.	116.2	115.8	−0.3	−0.029
20.	17.11	15.59	−8.9	−0.135
29.	141	142.8	1.3	0.027
36.	34.26	NA	NA	NA
99.	0.27	−0.12	−0.39	−0.107
19.	156.55	153.12	−2.2	−0.095
106.	914	917.8	0.4	0.089
111.	26.2	NA	NA	NA
				−0.577
				−0.577/0.582
				+0.139
				Leading index = −0.9
Coincident Index Components				
41.	93.72	94.02	0.3	0.321
51.	1170.5	1177.3	0.6	0.387
47.	162.8	163.6	0.5	0.180
57.	177.35	NA	NA	NA
				0.888
				0.888
				−0.175
				Coincident Index =0.7
Lagging Index Components				
91.	18.4	18.6	−1.1	−0.068
77.	1.52	NA	NA	NA
62.	86.6	86.2	−0.4	−0.152
109.	12.39	12.60	0.21	0.153
101.	114.20	116.19	1.7	0.465
95.	14.17	NA	NA	NA
				0.398
				0.398/0.707
				+0.018
				Lagging Index =0.6

SOURCE: U.S. Department of Commerce, *Business Conditions Digest,* July 1984.
[1] Percentage change in component series is divided by the relevant standardization factors and multiplied by the relevant weight given in tables 1 and 2.
NA = not available

CHART 1

First and Final Estimates of Leading Index

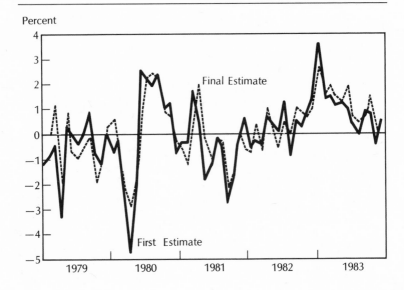

Percent

TABLE 4

Average Absolute Values of Estimates and Revisions of Composite Indicators: 1979–83

	Leading	Coincident	Lagging
First estimate	1.1	0.7	2.5
Second estimate	1.1	0.7	1.8
Final estimate	1.0	0.7	0.9
First revision	0.4	0.4	0.8
Revisions subsequent to first revision	0.5	0.2	1.2
Revision from first to final estimates	0.6	0.4	1.9

SOURCE: U.S. Department of Commerce, *Business Conditions Digest*, various issues.

cator (0.6) is less than the sum of the individual revisions (0.9), it is apparent that successive revisions sometimes overshoot the final estimate. Given that the final estimates of the leading, coincident, and lagging indicators have average absolute values of only 1.0, 0.7 and 0.9, respectively, errors in early estimates would seem to be substantial.

The difficulty created by error in early estimates can be illustrated by considering recent months during 1984. From Table 3, it can be seen that the first estimate of the percentage change in the leading indicator in May was negative. The second and subsequent (not shown) estimates for May are positive. The first and subsequent estimates for June and July (as of the middle of December) are negative. This makes the behavior of the index during August of some interest. For August, the first estimate was positive (+0.5), the second negative (−0.1), and the third (available in November) positive (+0.1). A further illustration of the difficulties created for forecasting is taken up in the next section.

THE USEFULNESS OF THE INDEX OF LEADING INDICATORS IN FORECASTING

One way of evaluating the index of leading indicators is to examine its ability to predict the onset of a recovery or a recession. This is usually done by observing the number of consecutive monthly declines or increases in the index. If the index has been rising steadily and the economy has been expanding, a fall in the index for several months heralds a recession. Likewise, if the index has been falling for several months and the economy has been depressed, a rise in the index over several months heralds a recovery.

This approach to forecasting the business cycle begins by specifying the number of successive months of reversal in the index's behavior necessary to predict a turning point in the cycle. In general, the method is more reliable the greater the number of consecutive months of decline or increase required to forecast a turning point. When the lead time in the forecast is increased, however, it reduces the number of consecutive months of reversal required to make a forecast.

Using both two and three months of consecutive movement in the index as a criteria for prediction, Wood (1984) has reported the reliability and lead time of using the leading index to forecast turning points in the economy's rate of growth. His observations are reported in Table 5.

These data reveal that the index of leading indicators has forecasted every recession and growth recession (which occurs when the rate of growth in the economy slows down) since 1948. A negative number indicates the number of months by which either a two- or three-month rule leads a peak or trough in the rate of growth. A positive number indicates the number of months by which the use of the rule lagged behind a turning point. For example, since the leading indicator declined for several months starting in August 1948, two- and three-month declines in the indicator lead the growth cycle peak in November 1948 by one and zero months, respectively.

Use of a two-month rule for forecasting a growth cycle peak gives a longer lead time than the three-month rule by more than one month for the recessions starting in both December 1969 and January 1980. This means that there were isolated consecutive monthly declines in the index in February and March 1969 and in November and December 1978, that is, declines that were not immediately followed by recession.

TABLE 5

Ex Ante Timing of the Leading Indicators During Growth
Cycle Turning Points: 1948–82

Growth cycle peaks	Two consecutive monthly decreases	Three consecutive monthly decreases	Growth cycle trough	Two consecutive monthly increases	Three consecutive monthly increases
Nov. 1948	−1	0	Oct. 1949	−3	−2
Mar. 1951*	−4	−3	July 1952	−5	−4
July 1953	−1	0	May 1954	−5	−4
Aug. 1957	−19	−18	Apr. 1958	+1	+2
Apr. 1960	−9	−8	Feb. 1961	−8	−7
May 1962*	+1	+2	Oct. 1964	missed	missed
June 1966*	0	+1	Oct. 1967	−6	−5
Dec. 1969	−9	−5	Nov. 1970	+1	+2
Nov. 1973	−4	−3	Mar. 1975	+1	+2
Jan. 1980	−13	−5	July 1980	0	+1
July 1981	−6	−5	Dec. 1982	−7	−1
Average	−6	−4	Average	−3	−2

NOTE: *indicates that a growth recession followed. Negative numbers indicate a positive lead time.

The lead times in Table 5 refer to the forecasting performance of the final estimates of the leading indicator. In general, the final estimates are not the same as the initial estimates. These differences between early and final estimates of the indexes can sometimes create serious problems in forecasting turning points in the growth cycle. For example, Table 5 indicates that three consecutive monthly declines in the leading indicator forecasted the onset of the 1980 recession by five months. These declines in the final estimate of the leading indicator, which occurred during June, July and August 1979, are shown in Table 6. The problem with this analysis from a forecasting viewpoint is that the first and second estimates of the leading indicator did not register declines for August. The second estimate for August 1979, which became available at the end of October 1979, showed a positive rise in the leading indicator of 0.1 percent. As this example illustrates, the likely magnitude of revisions in preliminary estimates of change in the composite indexes complicates the interpretation of signals in the short run.

TABLE 6

ESTIMATES OF THE LEADING INDICATOR: 1979 (percent changes)

	Final estimate	First estimate	Second estimate
May 1979	0.8%	0.4%	0.3%
June	−0.7	−0.1	−0.3
July	−0.9	−0.4	−0.2
August	−0.5	0.0	0.1
September	0.0	0.8	0.2
October	−1.9	−0.9	−1.4
November	−1.1	−1.3	−1.2
December	0.3	0.0	−0.2

SOURCE: U.S. Department of Commerce, *Business Conditions Digest*, various issues.

Additional qualifications also need to be made concerning the forecasting ability of the index of leading indicators:

1. The leading index has falsely forecasted the onset of recession on at least three occasions. The index declined for three consecutive months in late 1960 and a recession didn't start until 17 months later. The index fell for two consecutive months in mid-1963 and mid-1971 and recessions did not begin until two or three years later.

2. There is no clear a priori criteria as to whether declines in the index forecast a full-blown recession or merely a significant slowing in the economy. Consecutive monthly declines in the index preceded slowdowns, but not recessions, in economic growth in 1951, 1962 and 1966.

3. The lead times by which the leading indicator predicts a turning point are highly variable. Indeed, the three monthly declines in the index in December 1955, January and February 1956 were so far ahead of the business cycle peak that occurred in August 1957 that they can almost be regarded as a false signal. Given the historical tendency of the U.S. economy to exhibit cyclical fluctuations, a recession eventually will follow a decline (or any other movement for that matter) in the indicator. In order for the indicator to be a really useful forecaster, it also would need to forecast the timing of a recession within narrower bounds than it has since 1948.

4. By using the most up-to-date version of the index, a favorable bias is introduced into this evaluation of the predictive performance of the leading indicator. The components of the index and the standardization, weighting and trend factors have been altered continually through the years. Currently, they are based on data from 1948–81. The current index has been designed so as to obtain as favorable an ex post record as possible. While this is the appropriate means for constructing an index that will lead future economic activity as reliably as possible, the application of the current index to historical business cycle data does not measure the forecasting performance of the leading indicator actually in use when the forecasts were made.

In summary, the usefulness of the index of leading economic indicators for forecasting would seem to be seriously circumscribed by the problem of the highly variable lags by which economic activity follows the index, and by the large revisions by which initial estimates of the index are adjusted.

Part Six

Linear Programming, Decision Theory, and Scheduling Techniques

THE ESSAYS in Part Six provide an introduction to the nature, purpose, and usefulness of linear programming, decision theory, and scheduling techniques, all of which are extremely important to managerial economics. They do not go far into technical details, but concentrate on those aspects which a general manager would find useful. Case studies of real-world applications are emphasized.

In the opening article, George Dantzig discusses the basic concepts involved in linear programming and describes the sort of problems that this technique can handle. "To be a linear programming model," Dantzig explains, "the system must satisfy certain assumptions of proportionality, nonnegativity, and additivity." In a classic expository paper, Robert Dorfman uses simple graphical techniques to describe the nature and application of mathematical programming.

The next article, by Garvin and his associates, describes in more detail how linear programming has been used to help solve specific problems in the oil industry. This article is somewhat more difficult than the others in this book and is for readers with some familiarity with algebra.

In recent years, firms have come to use various types of decision-theoretic techniques to help them arrive at better decisions. The next paper, by Jacob Ulvila and Rex Brown, describes how decision analysis has been employed and with what success. Then John Pratt, Howard Raiffa, and Robert Schlaifer present elements of modern statistical decision theory, including a description of decision trees, after which Martin Shubik discusses some alternative theories of decision making under uncertainty. A. A. Walters then presents a detailed application of decision theory to a specific example, the problem being to determine whether or not a tax should be imposed on a particular commodity and whether a survey should be carried out to obtain relevant information.

In the final article, Jerome D. Wiest discusses the nature and significance of heuristic programming. A heuristic is "a rule of thumb used to solve a particular problem . . . [and] a heuristic program is a collection or combination of heuristics." Wiest describes how heuristic programming can be used to help solve scheduling problems as well as a variety of other types of problems.

Linear Programming:
Examples and Concepts

George Dantzig

*George Dantzig was head of the Operations
Research Center at the University of California,
Berkeley. This article comes from his book,* Linear Programming and Extensions.

THE PROGRAMMING PROBLEM

Industrial production, the flow of resources in the economy, the exertion of military effort in a war theater—all are complexes of numerous interrelated activities. Differences may exist in the goals to be achieved, the particular processes involved, and the magnitude of effort. Nevertheless, it is possible to abstract the underlying essential similarities in the management of these seemingly disparate systems. To do this entails a look at the structure and state of the system, and at the objective to be fulfilled, in order to *construct a statement of the actions to be performed, their timing, and their quantity (called a "program" or "schedule"), which will permit the system to move from a given status toward the defined objective.*

If the system exhibits a structure which can be represented by a mathematical equivalent, called a mathematical model, and if the objective can also be so quantified, then some computational method may be evolved for choosing the best schedule of actions among alternatives. Such use of mathematical models is termed mathematical programming. The observation that a number of military, economic, and industrial problems can be expressed (or reasonably approximated) by mathematical systems of linear inequalities and equations[1] has helped give rise to the development of linear programming.

The following three examples are typical programming problems which can be formulated linearly; they are analogous to the ones which originated research in this area. It is well to have them in mind before we discuss the general characteristics of linear programming problems.

The objective of the system in each of the three examples to be considered happens to be the minimization of total costs measured in monetary units. In other applications, however, it could be to minimize direct labor costs or to maximize the number of assembled parts or to maximize the number of trained students with a specified percentage distribution of skills, etc.

1. *A cannery example.* Suppose that the three canneries of a distributor are located in Portland (Maine), Seattle, and San Diego. The canneries can fill 250, 500, and 750 cases of tins per day, respectively. The distributor operates five warehouses around the country, in New York, Chicago, Kansas City, Dallas, and San Francisco. Each of the warehouses can sell 300 cases per day. The distributor wishes to determine the number of cases to be shipped from the three canneries to the five warehouses so that each warehouse should obtain as many cases as it can sell daily at the minimum total transportation cost.

The problem is characterized by the fifteen possible *activities* of shipping cases from each of the canneries to each of the warehouses (Fig. 1). There are fifteen *unknown activity levels* (to be determined) which are the *amounts* to be shipped along the fifteen routes. This *shipping schedule* is generally referred to as the *program.* There are a number of constraints that a shipping schedule must satisfy to be feasible: namely, the schedule must

1. The reader should especially note we have used the word *inequalities.* Systems of linear inequalities are quite general; linear inequality relations such as $x \geqq 0$, $x + y \leqq 7$ can be used to express a variety of common restrictions, such as quantities purchased, x, must not be negative or the total amount of purchases, $x + y$, must not exceed 7, etc.

FIGURE 1

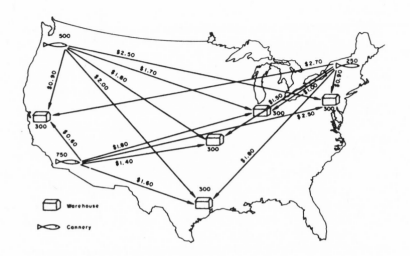

The problem: find a least cost plan of shipping from canneries to warehouses (the costs per case, availabilities and requirements are as indicated).

show that each warehouse will receive the required number of cases and that no cannery will ship more cases than it can produce daily. (Note there is one constraint for each warehouse and one for each cannery.) Several *feasible shipping schedules* may exist which would satisfy these constraints, but some will involve larger shipping costs than others. The problem then is to determine an *optimal shipping schedule*—one that has least costs.

2. *The housewife's problem.* A family of five lives on the modest salary of the head of the household. A constant problem is to determine the weekly menu after due consideration of the needs and tastes of the family and the prices of foods. The husband must have 3,000 calories per day, the wife is on a 1,500-calorie reducing diet, and the children require 3,000, 2,700, and 2,500 calories per day, respectively. According to the prescription of the family doctor, these calories must be obtained for each member by eating not more than a certain amount of fats and carbohydrates and not less than a certain amount of proteins. The diet, in fact, places emphasis on proteins. In addition, each member of

the household must satisfy his or her daily vitamin needs. The problem is to assemble menus, one for each week, that will minimize costs according to Thursday food prices.

This is a typical linear programming problem: the possible activities are the purchasing of foods of different types; the program is the amounts of different foods to be purchased; the constraints on the problem are the calorie and vitamin requirements of the household, and the upper or lower limits set by the physician on the amounts of carbohydrates, proteins, and fats to be consumed by each person. The number of food combinations which satisfy these constraints is very large. However, some of these feasible programs have higher costs than others. The problem is to find a combination that minimizes the total expense.

3. *On-the-job training*. A manufacturing plant is contracting to make some commodity. Its present work force is considerably smaller than the one needed to produce the commodity within a specified schedule of different amounts to be delivered each week for several weeks hence. Additional workers must, therefore, be hired, trained, and put to work. The present force can either work and produce at some rate of output, or it can train some fixed number of new workers, or it can do both at the same time according to some fixed rate of exchange between output and the number of new workers trained. Even were the crew to spend one entire week training new workers, it would be unable to train the required number. The next week, the old crew *and* the newly trained workers may either work or train new workers, or may both work and train, and so on. The commodity is semi-perishable so that amounts produced before they are needed will have to be stored at a specified cost. The problem is to determine the hiring, production, and storage program that will minimize total costs.

This, too, is a linear programming problem, although with the special property, not shared with the previous two examples, of *scheduling activities through time*. The activities in this problem are the assignment of old workers to either of two jobs, production or training, and the hiring of new workers each week. The quantities of these activities are restricted by the number of workers available at the beginning of each week and by the instructor-student ratio. The cumulative output produced by all workers through the number of weeks in the contractual period has to equal or exceed the required output. A possible production-training program is shown in Fig. 2. The problem can now be stated

FIGURE 2

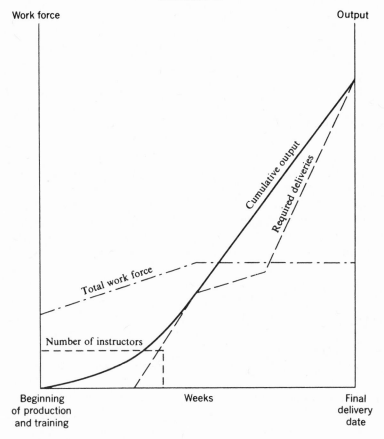

The problem: determine a least-cost hiring, production and storage program to meet required deliveries.

more precisely: determine the proper balance between hiring and training of workers, between teaching and production, and between over- and under-production in order to minimize total costs.

LINEAR PROGRAMMING DEFINED

We shall use the term *model building* to express the process of putting together of symbols representing objects according to certain rules, to form a structure, *the model*, which corresponds to a system under study in the real world. The symbols may be small-scale replicas of bricks and girders or they may be, as in our application, algebraic symbols.

Linear programming has a certain philosophy or approach to building a model that has application to a broad class of decision problems encountered in government, industry, economics, and engineering. It probably possesses the simplest mathematical structure which can be used to solve the practical scheduling problems associated with these areas. Because it is a method for studying the behavior of systems, it exemplifies the distinguishing feature of management science, or operations research, to wit: "Operations are considered as an entity. The subject matter studied is not the equipment used, nor the morale of the participants, nor the physical properties of the output, it is the combination of these in total as an economic process." (Cyril Herrmann and John Magee, 1953).

Linear programming[2] is concerned with describing the interrelations of the components of a system. As we shall see, the first step consists in regarding a system under design as composed of a number of elementary functions that are called "activities."[3] As a consequence, T. C. Koopmans introduced the term *activity analysis* to describe this approach. The different activities in which a system can engage constitute its technology. These are the representative building blocks of different types that might be recombined in varying amounts to rear a structure that is self-supporting, satisfies certain restrictions, and attains as well as possible a stated objective. Representing this structure in mathematical terms often results in a system of linear inequalities and equations; when this is so, it is called a linear programming model. Like

2. The term "linear programming" was suggested to the author by T. C. Koopmans in 1951 as an alternative to the earlier form, "programming in a linear structure."

3. The term "activity" in this connection is military in origin. It has been adopted in preference to the term "process," used by von Neumann in "A Model of General Economic Equilibrium."

architects, people who use linear programming models manipulate "on paper" the symbolic representations of the building blocks (activities) until a satisfactory design is obtained. The theory of linear programming is concerned with scientific procedures for arriving at the best design, given the technology, the required specifications, and the stated objective.

To be a linear programming model, the system must satisfy certain assumptions of proportionality, nonnegativity, and additivity. How this comes about will be discussed below. It is important to realize in trying to construct models of real-life situations, that life seldom, if ever, presents a clearly defined linear programming problem, and that simplification and neglect of certain characteristics of reality are as necessary in the application of linear programming as they are in the use of any scientific tool in problem solving.

The rule is to *neglect the negligible.* In the cannery example, for instance, the number of cases shipped and the number received may well differ because of accidental shipping losses. This difference is not known in advance and may be unimportant. In the optimum diet example the true nutritional value of each type of food differs from unit to unit, from season to season, from one source of food to another. Likewise, production rates and teaching quality will vary from one worker to another and from one hour to another. In some applications it may be necessary to give considerable thought to the differences between reality and its representation as a mathematical model to be sure that the differences are reasonably small and to assure ourselves that the computational results will be operationally useful.

What constitutes the proper simplification, however, is subject to individual judgment and experience. People often disagree on the adequacy of a certain model to describe the situation.

BASIC CONCEPTS

Suppose that the system under study (which may be one actually in existence, or one which we wish to design) is a complex of machines, people, facilities, and supplies. It has certain over-all reasons for its existence. For the military it may be to provide a striking force, or for industry it may be to produce certain types of products.

The linear programming approach is to consider a system as decomposable into a number of elementary functions, the *activities*. An activity is thought of as a kind of "black box"[4] into which flow tangible inputs, such as men, material, and equipment, and out of which may flow the products of manufacture, or the trained crews of the military. What happens to the inputs inside the "box" is the concern of the engineer or of the educator; to the programmer, only the rates of flow into and out of the activity are of interest. The various kinds of flow are called *items*.

The quantity of each activity is called the *activity level*. To change the activity level it is necessary to change the flows into and out of the activity.

Assumption 1: Proportionality · In the linear programming model the quantities of flow of various items into and out of the activity are always proportional to the activity level. If we wish to double the activity level, we simply double all the corresponding flows for the unit activity level. For instance, in Example 3, if we wish to double the number of workers trained in a period, we would have to double the number of instructors for that period and the number of workers hired. This characteristic of the linear programming model is known as the proportionality assumption.

Assumption 2: Nonnegativity · While any positive multiple of an activity is possible, negative quantities of activities are not possible. For instance, in Example 1, a negative number of cases cannot be shipped. Another example occurs in a well-known classic: the Mad Hatter, you may recall, in *Alice's Adventures in Wonderland*, was urging Alice to have some more tea, and Alice was objecting that she couldn't see how she could take more when she hadn't had any. "You mean, you don't see how you can take *less* tea," said the Hatter, "it is very easy to take more than nothing." Lewis Carroll's point was probably lost on his pre-linear-programming audience, for why should one emphasize the obvious fact that the activity of "taking tea" cannot be done in negative quantity? Perhaps it was Carroll's way of saying that mathemati-

4. Black box: Any system whose detailed internal nature one willfully ignores.

cians had been so busy for centuries extending the number system from integers, to fractions, to negative, to imaginary numbers, that they had given little thought on how to keep the variables of their problems in their original nonnegative range. This characteristic of the variables of the linear programming model is known as the nonnegativity assumption.

Assumption 3: Additivity · The next step in building a model is to specify that the system of activities be complete in the sense that a complete accounting by activity can be made of each item. To be precise, for each item it is required that the total amount specified by the system as a whole equals the sum of the amounts flowing into the various activities minus the sum of the amounts flowing out. Thus, each item, in our abstract system, is characterized by a *material balance equation,* the various terms of which represent the flows into or out of the various activities. In the cannery example, the number of cases sent into a warehouse must be completely accounted for by the amounts flowing out of the shipping activities from various canneries including possible storage or disposal of any excess. This characteristic of the linear programming model is known as the additivity assumption.

Assumption 4: Linear Objective Function · One of the items in our system is regarded as "precious" in the sense that the total quantity of it produced by the system measures the payoff. The precious item could be skilled labor, completed assemblies, an input resource that is in scarce supply like a limited monetary budget. The contribution of each activity to the total payoff is the amount of the precious item that flows into or out of each activity. Thus, if the objective is to maximize profits, activities that require money contribute negatively and those that produce money contribute positively to total profits. The housewife's expenditures for each type of food, in Example 2, is a negative contribution to total "profits" of the household; there are no activities in this example that contribute positively. This characteristic of the linear programming model is known as the linear objective assumption.

The Standard Linear Programming Problem · The determination of values for the *levels* of activities, which are positive or zero, such that flows of each item (for these activity levels) satisfy the material balance equations and such that the value of the payoff is a maximum is called the standard linear programming problem. The representation of a real system, as in any one of the three examples above, as a mathematical system which exhibits the above characteristics, is called a linear programming model. The problem of programming the activities of the real system is thus transformed into the problem of finding the solution of the linear programming model.

Mathematical, or "Linear," Programming: A Non-mathematical Exposition

ROBERT DORFMAN

Robert Dorfman is Professor of Economics at Harvard University. This well-known expository article appeared in the American Economic Review.

This paper is intended to set forth the leading ideas of mathematical programming [1] purged of the algebraic apparatus which has impeded their general acceptance and appreciation. This will be done by concentrating on the graphical representation of the method. While it is not possible, in general, to portray mathematical programming problems in two dimensional graphs, the conclusions which we shall draw from the graphs will be of general validity and, of course, the graphic representation of

1. The terminology of the techniques which we are discussing is in an unsatisfactory state. Most frequently they are called "linear programming" although the relationships involved are not always linear. Sometimes they are called "activities analysis," but this is not a very suggestive name. The distinguishing feature of the techniques is that they are concerned with programming rather than with analysis, and, at any rate, "activities analysis" has not caught on. We now try out "mathematical programming"; perhaps it will suit.

multidimensional problems has a time-honored place in economics.

The central formal problem of economics is the problem of allocating scarce resources so as to maximize the attainment of some predetermined objective. The standard formulation of this problem—the so-called marginal analysis—has led to conclusions of great importance for the understanding of many questions of social and economic policy. But it is a fact of common knowledge that this mode of analysis has not recommended itself to men of affairs for the practical solution of their economic and business problems. Mathematical programming is based on a restatement of this same formal problem in a form which is designed to be useful in making practical decisions in business and economic affairs. That mathematical programming is nothing but a reformulation of the standard economic problem and its solution is the main thesis of this exposition.

The motivating idea of mathematical programming is the idea of a "process" or "activity." A process is a specific method for performing an economic task. For example, the manufacture of soap by a specified formula is a process. So also is the weaving of a specific quality of cotton gray goods on a specific type of loom. The conventional production function can be thought of as the formula relating the inputs and outputs of all the processes by which a given task can be accomplished.

For some tasks, e.g., soap production, there are an infinite number of processes available. For others, e.g., weaving, only a finite number of processes exist. In some cases, a plant or industry may have only a single process available.

In terms of processes, choice in the productive sphere are simply decisions as to which processes are to be used and the extent to which each is to be employed. Economists are accustomed to thinking in terms of decisions as to the quantities of various productive factors to be employed. But an industry or firm cannot substitute factor A for factor B unless it does some of its work in a different way, that is, unless its substitutes a process which uses A in relatively high proportions for one which uses B. Inputs, therefore, cannot be changed without a change in the way of doing things, and often a fundamental change. Mathematical programming focuses on this aspect of economic choice.

The objective of mathematical programming is to determine the optimal levels of productive processes in given circumstances. This requires a restatement of productive relationships in terms of processes and a reconsideration of the effect of factor scarcities on production choices. As a prelude to this theoretical discussion, however, it will be helpful to consider a simplified production problem from a commonsense point of view.

I. AN EXAMPLE OF MATHEMATICAL PROGRAMMING

Let us consider a hypothetical automobile company equipped for the production of both automobiles and trucks. This company, then, can perform two economic tasks, and we assume that it has a single process for accomplishing each. These two tasks, the manufacture of automobiles and that of trucks, compete for the use of the firm's facilities. Let us assume that the company's plant is organized into four departments: (1) sheet metal stamping, (2) engine assembly, (3) automobile final assembly, and (4) truck final assembly—raw materials, labor, and all other components being available in virtually unlimited amounts at constant prices in the open market.

The capacity of each department of the plant is, of course, limited. We assume that the metal stamping department can turn out sufficient stampings for 25,000 automobiles or 35,000 trucks per month. We can then calculate the combinations of automobile and truck stampings which this department can produce. Since the department can accommodate 25,000 automobiles per month, each automobile requires 1/25,000 or 0.004 percent of monthly capacity. Similarly each truck requires 0.00286 percent of monthly capacity. If, for example, 15,000 automobiles were manufactured, they would require 60 percent of metal stamping capacity and the remaining 40 percent would be sufficient to produce stampings for 14,000 trucks. Then 15,000 automobiles and 14,000 trucks could be produced by this department at full operation. This is, of course, not the only combination of automobiles and trucks which could be produced by the stamping department at full operation. In Figure 1, the line labeled "Metal Stamping" represents all such combinations.

Similarly we assume that the engine assembly department has monthly capacity for 33,333 automobile engines or 16,667 truck engines or, again, some combination of fewer automobile and truck engines. The combinations which would absorb the full capacity of the engine assembly department are shown by the "Engine Assembly" line in Figure 1. We assume also that the automobile assembly department can accommodate 22,500 automobiles per month and the truck assembly department 15,000 trucks. These limitations are also represented in Figure 1.

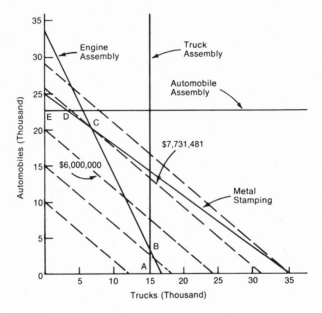

FIGURE 1

CHOICES OPEN TO AN AUTOMOBILE FIRM

We regard this set of assumptions as defining two processes: the production of automobiles and the production of trucks. The process of producing an automobile yields, as an output, one automobile and absorbs, as inputs, 0.004 percent of metal stamping capacity, 0.003 percent of engine assembly capacity, and 0.00444 percent of automobile assembly capacity. Similarly the process of producing a truck yields, as an output, one truck and absorbs, as inputs, 0.00286 percent of metal stamping capacity, 0.006 percent of engine assembly capacity, and 0.00667 percent of truck assembly capacity.

The economic choice facing this firm is the selection of the numbers of automobiles and trucks to be produced each month, subject to the restriction that no more than 100 percent of the capacity of any department can be used. Or, in more technical phraseology, the choice consists in deciding at what level to employ each of the two available processes. Clearly, if automobiles alone are produced, at most 22,500 units per month can be made, automobile assembly being the effective limitation. If only trucks are produced, a maximum of 15,000 units per month can be made because of the limitation on truck assembly. Which of these alternatives should be adopted, or whether some combination of trucks and automobiles should be produced, depends on the relative profitability of manufacturing trucks and automobiles. Let us assume, to be concrete, that the sales value of an automobile is $300 greater than the total cost of purchased materials, labor, and other direct costs attributable to its manufacture. And, similarly, that the sale value of a truck is $250 more than the direct cost of manufacturing it. Then the net revenue of the plant for any month is 300 times the number of automobiles produced plus 250 times the number of trucks. For example, 15,000 automobiles and 6,000 trucks would yield a net revenue of $5,000,000. There are many combinations of automobiles and trucks which would yield this same net revenue; 10,000 automobiles and 12,000 trucks is another one. In terms of Figure 1, all combinations with a net revenue of $6,000,000 lie on a straight line, to be specific, the line labeled $6,000,000 in the figure.

A line analogous to the one which we have just described corresponds to each possible net revenue. All these lines are parallel, since their slope depends only on the relative profitability of the two activities. The greater the net revenue, of course, the higher the line. A few of the net revenue lines are shown in the figure by the dashed parallel lines.

Each conceivable number of automobiles and trucks produced corresponds to a point on the diagram, and through each point there passes one member of the family of net revenue lines. Net revenue is maximized when the point corresponding to the number of automobiles and trucks produced lies on the highest possible net revenue line. Now the effect of the capacity restrictions is to limit the range of choice to outputs which correspond to points lying inside the area bounded by the axes and by the broken line *ABCDE*. Since net revenue increases as points move out from the origin, only points which lie on the broken line need be considered. Beginning with point *A* and moving along the broken line we see that the boundary of the accessible region intersects higher and higher net revenue lines until point *C* is reached. From there on, the boundary slides down the scale of net revenue lines. Point *C* therefore corresponds to the highest attainable net revenue. At point *C* the output is 20,370 automobiles and 6,481 trucks, yielding a net revenue of $7,731,481 per month.

The reader has very likely noticed that this diagram is by no means novel. The broken line *ABCDE* tells that maximum number of automobiles which can be produced in conjunction with any given number of trucks. It is therefore, apart from its angularity, a production opportunity curve or transformation curve of the sort made familiar by Irving Fisher, and the slope of the curve at any point where it has a slope is the ratio of substitution in production between automobiles and trucks. The novel feature is that the production opportunity curve shown here has no defined slope at five points and that one of these five is the critical point. The dashed lines in the diagram are equivalent to conventional price lines.

The standard theory of production teaches that profits are maximixed at a point where a price line is tangent to the production opportunity curve. But, as we have just noted, there are five points where our production opportunity curve has no tangent. The tangency criterion therefore fails. Instead we find that profits are maximized at a corner where the slope of the price line is neither less than the slope of the opportunity curve to the left of the corner nor greater than the slope of the opportunity curve to the right.

Diagrammatically, then, mathematical programming uses angles where standard economics uses curves. In economic terms, where does the novelty lie? In standard economic analysis we visualize production relationships in which, if there are two products, one may be substituted for the other with gradually increasing difficulty. In mathematical programming we visualize a regime of production in which, for any output, certain factors will be effectively limiting but other factors will be in ample supply. Thus, in Figure 1, the factors which effectively limit production at each point can be identified by noticing on which limitation lines the point lies. The rate of substitution between products is determined by the limiting factors alone and changes only when the designation of the limiting factors changes. In the diagram a change in the designation of the limiting factors is represented by turning a corner on the production opportunity curve.

We shall come back to this example later, for we have not exhausted its significance. But now we are in a position to develop with more generality some of the concepts used in mathematical programming.

II. THE MODEL OF PRODUCTION IN
MATHEMATICAL PROGRAMMING

A classical problem in economics is the optimal utilization of two factors of production, conveniently called capital and labor. In the usual analysis, the problem is formulated by conceiving of the two factors as cooperating with each other in accordance with a production function which states the maximum quantity of a product which can be obtained by the use of stated quantities of the two factors. One convenient means of representing such a production function is an "isoquant diagram," as in Figure 2. In this familiar figure, quantities of labor are plotted along the horizontal axis and quantities of capital along the vertical. Each of the arcs in the body of the diagram corresponds to a definite quantity of output, higher arcs corresponding to greater quantities.

If the prices per unit of capital and labor are known, the combinations of labor and capital which can be purchased for a fixed total expenditure can be shown by a sloping straight line like CC' in the figure, the slope depending only on the relative prices. Two interpretations follow immediately. First, the minimum unit cost of producing the output represented by any isoquant can be achieved by using the combination of labor and capital which corresponds to the point where that isoquant is tangent to a price line. Second, the greatest output attainable

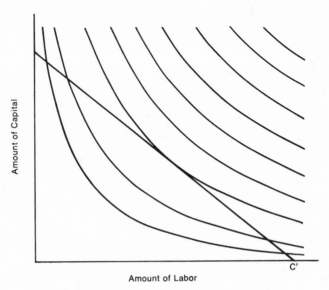

FIGURE 2

AN ISOQUANT DIAGRAM

with any given expenditure is represented by the isoquant which is tangent to the price line corresponding to that expenditure.

This diagram and its analysis rest upon the assumption that the two factors are continuously substitutable for each other in such wise that if the amount of labor employed be reduced by a small amount it will be possible to maintain the quantity of output by a *small* increase in the amount of capital employed. Moreover, this analysis assumes that each successive unit decrement in the amount of labor will require a slightly larger increment in the amount of capital if output is to remain constant. Otherwise the isoquants will not have the necessary shape.

All this is familiar. We call it to mind only because we are about to develop an analogous diagram which is fundamental to mathematical programming. First, however, let us see why a new diagram and a new approach are felt to be necessary.

The model of production which we have just briefly sketched very likely is valid for some kinds of production. But for most manufacturing industries, and indeed all production where elaborate machinery is used, it is open to serious objection. It is characteristic of most modern machinery that each kind of machine operates efficiently only over a narrow range of speeds and that the quantities of labor, power, materials, and other factors which cooperate with the machine are dictated rather inflexibly by the machine's built-in characteristics. Furthermore, at any time there is available only a small number of different kinds of machinery for accomplishing a given task. A few examples may make these considerations more concrete. Earth may be moved by hand shovels, by steam or diesel shovels, or by bulldozers. Power shovels and bulldozers are built in only a small variety of models, each with inherent characteristics as to fuel consumption per hour, number of operators and assistants required, cubic feet of earth moved per hour, etc. Printing type may be set by using hand-fonts, linotype machines, or monotype machines. Again, each machine is available in only a few models and each has its own pace of operation, power and space requirements, and other essentially unalterable characteristics. A moment's reflection will bring to mind dozens of other illustrations: printing presses, power looms, railroad and highway haulage, statistical and accounting calculation, metallic ore reduction, metal fabrication, etc. For many economic tasks the number of processes available is finite, and each process can be regarded as inflexible with regard to the ratios among factor inputs and process outputs. Factors cannot be substituted for each other except by changing the levels at which entire technical processes are used, because each process uses factors in fixed characteristic ratios. In mathematical programming, accordingly, process substitution plays a role analogous to that of factor substitution in conventional analysis.

We now develop an apparatus for the analysis of process substitution. For convenience we shall limit our discussion to processes which consume two factors, to be called capital and labor, and produce a single output. Figure 3 represents such a process. As in Figure 2, the horizontal axis is scaled in units of labor and the vertical axis in units of capital. The process is represented by the ray, *OA*, which is scaled in units of output. To each output there corresponds a labor requirement found by locating the appropriate mark on the process ray and reading

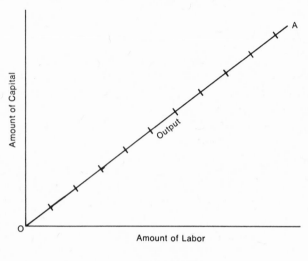

FIGURE 3

A PROCESS

straight down. The capital requirement is found in the same manner by reading straight across from the mark on the process line. Similarly, to each amount of labor there corresponds a quantity of output, found by reading straight up, and a quantity of capital, found by reading straight across from the output mark.

It should be noted that the quantity of capital in this diagram is the quantity used in a process rather than the quantity owned by an economic unit; it is capital-service rather than capital itself. Thus, though more or less labor may be combined with a given machine—by using it more or fewer hours—the ratio of capital to labor inputs, that is, the ratio of machine hours to labor hours—is regarded as technologically fixed.

Figure 3 incorporates two important assumptions. The fact that the line *OA* is straight implies that the ratio between the capital input and the labor input is the same for all levels of output and is given, indeed, by the slope of the line. The fact that the marks on the output line are evenly spaced indicates that there are neither economies or diseconomies of scale in the use of the process, i.e., that there will be strict proportionality between the quantity of output and the quantity of either input. These assumptions are justified rather simply on the basis of the notion of a process. If a process can be used once, it can be used twice or as many times as the supplies of factors permit. Two linotype machines with equally skilled operators can turn out just twice as much type per hour as one. Two identical mills can turn out just twice as many yards of cotton per month as one. So long as factors are available, a process can be duplicated. Whether it will be economical to do so is, of course, another matter.

If there is only one process available for a given task there is not much scope for economic choice. Frequently, however, there will be several processes. Figure 4 represents a situation in

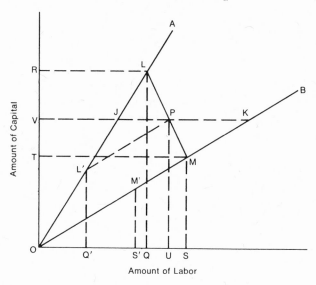

FIGURE 4

Two Processes

which two procedures are available, Process A indicated by the line *OA* and Process B indicated by *OB*. We have already seen how to interpret points on the lines *OA* and *OB*. The scales by which output is measured on the two rays are not necessarily the same. The scale on each ray reflects the productivity of the factors when used in the process represented by that ray and has no connection with the output scale on any other process ray. Now suppose that points L and M represent production of the same output by the two processes. Then LM, the straight line between them, will represent an isoquant and each point on this line will correspond to a combination of processes A and B which produces the same output as OL units of Process A or OM units of Process B.

To see this, consider any point P on the line LM and draw a line through P parallel to OB. Let L' be the point where this line intersects OA. Finally mark the point M' on OB such that $OM' = L'P$. Now consider the production plan which consists of using Process A at level OL' and Process B at level OM'.[2] It is easy to show that this production plan uses OU units of labor, where U is the labor coordinate of point P, and OV units of capital, where V is the capital coordinate of point P.[3]

Since the coordinates of point P correspond to the quantities of factors consumed by OL' units of Process A and OM' units of Process B, we interpret P as representing the combined production plan made up of the specified levels of the two processes. This interpretation implies an important economic assumption, namely, that if the two processes are used simultaneously they will neither interfere with nor enhance each other, so that the inputs and outputs resulting from simultaneous use of two processes at any levels can be found by adding the inputs and outputs of the individual processes.

In order to show that P lies on the isoquant through points L and M it remains only to show that the sum of the outputs corresponding to points L' and M' is the same as the output corresponding to point L or point M. This follows at once from

2. An alternative construction would be to draw a line through point P parallel to OA. It would intersect OB at M'. Then we could lay off OL' equal to $M'P$ on OA. This would lead to exactly the same results as the construction used in the text. The situation is analogous to the "parallelogram of fôrces" in physics.

3. Proof: Process A at level OL' uses OQ' units of labor, Process B at level OM' uses OS' units of labor; together they use $OQ' + OS'$ units of labor. But, by construction, $L'P$ is equal and parallel to OM'. So $Q'U = OS'$. Therefore, $OQ' + OS' = OQ' + Q'U = OU$ units of labor. The argument with respect to capital is similar.

the facts that the output corresponding to any point on a process ray is directly proportional to the length of the ray up to that point and that the triangles *LL'P* and *LOM* in Figure 4 are similar.[4] Thus if we have two process lines like *OA* and *OB* and find points *L* and *M* on them which represent producing the same output by means of the two processes, then the line segment connecting the two equal-output points will be an isoquant.

We can now draw the mathematical programming analog of the familiar isoquant diagram. Figure 5 is such a diagram with four process lines shown. Point *M* represents a particular output by use of Process A and points *L, K, J* represent that same output by means of Processes B, C, D, respectively. The succession of line segments connecting these four points is the isoquant for that same output. It is easy to see that any other succession of line segments respectively parallel to those of *MLKJ* is also an isoquant. Three such are shown in the figure. It is instructive to compare Figure 5 with Figure 2 and note the strong resemblance in appearance as well as in interpretation.

We may draw price lines on Figure 5, just as on the conventional kind of isoquant diagram. The dashed lines *XX'* and *YY'* represent two possible price lines. Consider *XX'* first. As that line is drawn, the maximum output for a given expenditure can be obtained by use of Process C alone, and, conversely, the minimum cost for a given output is also obtained by using Process C alone. Thus, for the relative price regime represented by *XX'*, Process C is optimal. The price line *YY'* is drawn parallel to the isoquant segment *JK*. In this case Process C is still optimal, but Process D is also optimal and so is any combination of the two.

It is evident from considering these two price lines, and as many others as the reader wishes to visualize, that an optimal production program can always be achieved by means of a single process, which process depending, of course, on the slope of the

4. Proof: Let Output (X) denote the output corresponding to any point, X, on the diagram. Then Output (M')/Output $(M) = OM'/OM$ and Output (L')/Output $(L) = OL'/OL$. By assumption: Output $(L) =$ Output (M). So Output (M')/Output $(L) = OM'/OM$. Adding, we have:

$$\frac{\text{Output } (M') + \text{Output } (L')}{\text{Output } (L)} = \frac{OM'}{OM} + \frac{OL'}{OL} = \frac{L'P}{OM} + \frac{OL'}{OL} = \frac{L'L}{OL} + \frac{OL'}{OL} = 1.$$

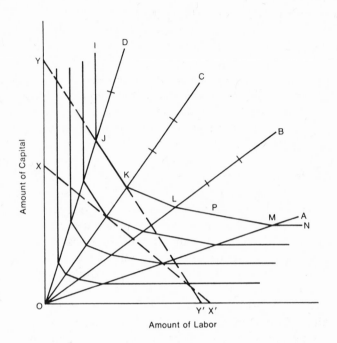

FIGURE 5

Four Processes

price line. It should be noted, however, that the conventional tangency criterion is no longer applicable.

We found in Figure 5 that an optimal economic plan need never use more than a single process for each of its outputs.[5] That conclusion is valid for the situation depicted, which assumed that the services of the two factors could be procured in any amounts desired at constant relative prices. This assumption is not applicable to many economic problems, nor is it used much in mathematic programming. We must now, therefore, take factor supply conditions into account.

III. FACTOR SUPPLIES AND COSTS

In mathematical programming it is usual to divide all factors of production into two classes: unlimited factors, which are

5. Recall, however, that we have not taken joint production into account nor have we considered the effects of consideration from the demand side.

available in any amount desired at constant unit cost, and limited or scarce factors, which are obtainable at constant unit cost up to a fixed maximum quantity and thereafter not at all. The automobile example illustrates this classification. There the four types of capacity were treated as fixed factors available at zero variable cost; all other factors were grouped under direct costs which were considered as constant per unit of output.

The automobile example showed that this classification of factors is adequate for expressing the maximization problem of a firm dealing in competitive markets. In the last section we saw that when all factors are unlimited, this formulation can be used to find a minimum average cost point.

Both of these applications invoked restrictive assumptions, and, furthermore, assumptions which conflict with those conventionally made in studying resource allocation. In conventional analysis we conceive that as the level of production of a firm, industry, or economy rises, average unit costs rise also after some point. The increase in average costs is attributable in part to the working of the law of variable proportions,[6] which operates when the inputs of some but not all factors of production are increased. As far as the consequences of increasing some but not all inputs are concerned, the contrast between mathematical programming and the marginal analysis is more verbal than substantive. A reference to Figure 4 will show how such changes are handled in mathematical programming. Point *J* in Figure 4 represents the production of a certain output by the use of process A alone. If it is desired to increase output without increasing the use of capital, this can be done by moving to the right along the dotted line *JK*, since this line cuts successively higher isoquants. Such a movement would correspond to using increasingly more of Process B and increasingly less of Process A and thus, indirectly, to substituting labor for capital. If, further, we assume that unit cost of production is lower for Process A than for Process B this movement would also correspond to increasing average cost of production. Thus both marginal analysis and mathematical programming lead to the same conclusion when factor proportions are changed: if the change starts from a mini-

6. Cf. J. M. Cassels, "On the Law of Variable Proportions," in W. Fellner and B. F. Haley, eds., *Readings in the Theory of Income Distribution* (Philadelphia, 1946), pp. 103–18.

mum cost point the substitution will lead to gradually increasing unit costs.

But changing input proportions is only one part of the story according to the conventional type of analysis. If output is to be increased, any of three things may happen. First, it may be possible to increase the consumption of all inputs without incurring a change in their unit prices. In this case both mathematical programming and marginal analysis agree that output will be expanded without changing the ratios among the input quantities, and average cost of production will not increase.[7] Second, it may not be possible to increase the use of some of the inputs. This is the case we have just analyzed. According to both modes of analysis the input ratios will change in this case and average unit costs will increase. The only difference between the two approaches is that if average cost is to be plotted against output, the marginal analyst will show a picture with a smoothly rising curve while the mathematical programmer will show a broken line made up of increasingly steep line segments. Third, it may be possible to increase the quantities of all inputs but only at the penalty of increasing unit prices or some kind of diseconomies of scale. This third case occurs in the marginal analysis, indeed it is the case which gives long-run cost curves their familiar shape, but mathematical programming has no counterpart for it.

The essential substantive difference we have arrived at is that the marginal analysis conceives of pecuniary and technical diseconomies associated with changes in scale while mathematical programming does not.[8] There are many important economic problems in which factor prices and productivities do not change in response to changes in scale or in which such variations can be disregarded. Most investigations of industrial capacity, for example, are of this nature. In such studies we seek the maximum output of an industry, regarding its inventory of physical

---

7. Cf. F. H. Knight, *Risk, Uncertainty and Profit* (Boston, 1921), p. 98.

8. Even within the framework of the marginal analysis the concept of diseconomies of scale has been challenged on both theoretical and empirical grounds. For examples of empirical criticism see Committee on Price Determination, Conference on Price Research, *Cost Behavior and Price Policy* (New York, 1943). The most searching theoretical criticism is in Piero Sraffa, "The Laws of Returns under Competitive Conditions," *Econ. Jour.*, Dec. 1926, pp. 535–50.

equipment as given and assuming that the auxiliary factors needed to cooperate with the equipment can be obtained in the quantities dictated by the characteristics of the equipment. Manpower requirement studies are of the same nature. In such studies we take both output and equipment as given and calculate the manpower needed to operate the equipment at the level which will yield the desired output. Studies of full employment output fall into the same format. In such studies we determine in advance the quantity of each factor which is to be regarded as full employment of that factor. Then we calculate the optimum output obtainable by the use of the factors in those quantities.

These illustrations should suffice to show that the assumption made in mathematical programming can comprehend a wide variety of important economic problems. The most useful applications of mathematical programming are probably to problems of the types just described, that is, to problems concerned with finding optimum production plans using specified quantities of some or all of the resources involved.

IV. ANALYSIS OF PRODUCTION WITH LIMITED FACTORS

The diagrams which we have developed are readily adaptable to the analysis of the consequences of limits on the factor supplies. Such limits are, of course, the heart of Figure 1, where the four principal lines represent limitations on the process levels which result from limits on the four factor quantities considered. But Figure 1 cannot be used when more than two processes have to be considered. For such problems diagrams like Figures 3, 4, and 5 have to be used.

Figure 6 reproduces the situation portrayed in Figure 5 with some additional data, to be explained below. Let *OF* represent the maximum amount of capital which can be used and thus show a factor limitation. The horizontal line through *F* divides the diagram into two sections: all points above the line correspond to programs which require more capital than is available; points on and below the line represent programs which do not have excessive capital requirements. This horizontal line will be called the capital limitation line. Points on or below it are called "feasible," points above it are called "infeasible."

The economic unit portrayed in Figure 6 has the choice of

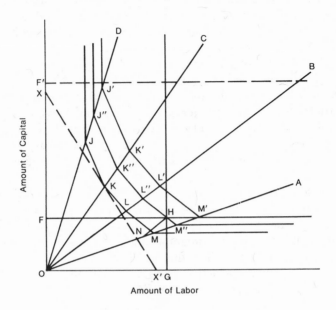

FIGURE 6

FOUR PROCESSES, WITH LIMITATIONS

operating at any feasible point. If maximum output is its objective, it will choose a point which lies on the highest possible isoquant, i.e., the highest isoquant which touches the capital limitation line. This is the one labeled $J'K'L'M'$, and the highest possible output is attained by using Process A.

Of course, maximum output may not be the objective. The objective may be, for example, to maximize the excess of the value of output over labor costs. We shall refer to such an excess as a "net value." The same kind of diagram can be used to solve for a net value provided that the value of each unit of output is independent of the number of units produced [9] and that the cost of each unit of labor is similarly constant. If these provisos are met, each point on a process ray will correspond to a certain physical output but also to a certain value of output, cost of la-

9. This is a particularly uncomfortable assumption. We use it here to explain the method in its least complicated form.

bor, and net value of output. Further, along any process ray the net value of output will equal the physical output times the net value per unit and will therefore be proportional to the physical output. We may thus use a diagram similar to Figure 6 except that we think of net value instead of physical output as measured along the process rays and we show isovalue lines instead of isoquants. This has been done on Figure 7, in which the maximum net value attainable is the one which corresponds to the isovalue contour through point *P*, and is attained by using Process C.

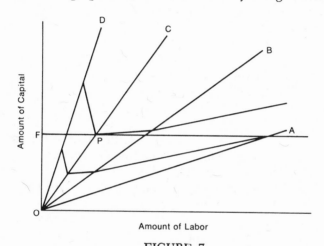

FIGURE 7

Four Processes with Isovalue Lines

It should be noted in both Figures 6 and 7 that the optimal program consisted of a single process, that shifts in the quantity of capital available would not affect the designation of the optimal process though they would change its level, and that the price lines, which are crucial in Figure 5, played no role.

The next complication, and the last one we shall be able to consider, is to assume that both factors are in limited supply. This situation is portrayed in Figure 6 by adding the vertical line through point *G* to represent a labor limitation. The available quantity of labor is shown, of course, by the length *OG*. Then the points inside the rectangle *OFHG* represent programs which can be implemented in the sense that they do not require more than the available supplies of either factor. This is the rectangle of feasible programs. The greatest achievable output is the one which corresponds to the highest isoquant which touches the rectangle of feasible programs. This is the isoquant $J''K''L''M''$, and furthermore, since the maximum isoquant touches the rectangle at H, H represents the program by which the maximum output can be produced.

This solution differs from the previous ones in that the solution point does not lie on any process ray but between the rays for Processes A and B. We have already seen that a point like H represents using Process A at level ON and Process B at level NH.

Two remarks are relevant to this solution. First: with the factor limitation lines as drawn, the maximum output requires two processes. If the factor limitation lines had been drawn so that they intersected exactly on one of the process rays, only one process would have been required. If the factor limitation lines had crossed to the left of Process D or to the right of Process A, the maximizing production plan would require only one process. But, no matter how the limitation lines be drawn, at most two processes are required to maximize output. We are led to an important generalization: maximum output may always be obtained by using a number of processes which does not exceed the number of factors in limited supply, if this number is greater than zero. The conclusions we drew from Figures 6 and 7 both conform to this rule, and it is one of the basic theorems of mathematical programming.

Second: although at most two processes are required to obtain the maximum output, which two depends on the location of the factor limits. As shown, the processes used for maximum output were Processes A and B. If somewhat more capital, represented by the amount OF', were available, the maximizing processes would have been Processes C and D. If two factors are limited, it is the ratio between their supplies rather than the absolute supplies of either which determines the processes in the optimum program. This contrasts with the case in which only one factor is limited. Just as the considerations which determine the optimum set of processes are more complicated when two factors are limited than when only one is, so with three or more limited factors the optimum conditions become more complicated still and soon pass the reach of intuition. This, indeed, is the *raison d'être* of the formidable apparatus of mathematical programming.

We can make these considerations more concrete by applying them to the automobile example. Referring to Figure 1, we note that the optimum production point, C, lay on the limitation lines for engine assembly and metal stamping, but well below the limits for automobile and truck assembly. The limitations on automobile and truck assembly capacity are, therefore, ineffective and can be disregarded. The situation in terms of the two effectively limiting types of capacity is shown in Figure 8.

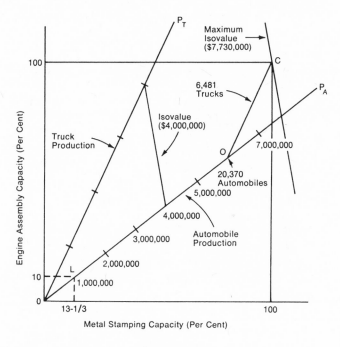

FIGURE 8

AUTOMOBILE EXAMPLE, OPTIMAL PLAN

In Figure 8 the ray P_A represents the process of producing automobiles and P_T the process for producing trucks. These two processes can be operated at any combination of levels which does not require the use of more than 100 percent of either metal stamping or engine assembly capacity. Thus the rectangle in the diagram is the region of feasible production programs. The optimal production program is the one in the feasible region which corresponds to the highest possible net revenue.[10] Thus it will be helpful to construct isorevenue lines, as we did in Figure 7. To do this, consider automobile production first. Each point on P_A corresponds to the production of a certain number of automobiles per month. Suppose, for example, that the scale is such that point L represents the production of 3,333 automobiles per month. It will be recalled that each automobile yields a net revenue of $300. Therefore, 3,333 automobiles yield a revenue of $1,000,000. Point L, then, corresponds to a net revenue of $1,000,000 as well as to an output of 3,333 automobiles per month. Since (see Figure 1) 3,333 automobiles require 13⅓ percent of metal stamping capacity and 10 percent of engine assembly capacity, the coordinates of the $1,000,000 net revenue point on P_A are established at once. By a similar argument, the point whose coordinates are 26⅔ percent of metal stamping capacity and 20 percent of engine capacity is the $2,000,000 net revenue point on P_A. In the same manner, the whole ray can be drawn and scaled off in terms of net revenue, and so can P_T, the process ray for truck production. The diagram is completed by connecting the $4,000,000 points on the two process lines in order to show the direction of the isorevenue lines.

The optimum program is at point C, where the two capacity limits intersect, because C lies on the highest isorevenue line which touches the feasible region. Through point C we have drawn a line parallel to the truck production line and meeting the automobile production line at D. By our previous argument, the length OD represents the net revenue from automobile production in the optimal program and the length DC represents the net revenue from trucks. If these lengths be scaled off, the result, of course, will be the same as the solution found previously.

V. IMPUTATION OF FACTOR VALUES

We have just noted that the major field of application of mathematical programming is to problems where the supply of

10. Since the objective of the firm is, by assumption, to maximize revenue rather than physical output, we may consider automobile and truck production as two alternative processes for producing revenue instead of as two processes with disparate outputs.

one or more factors of production is absolutely limited. Such scarcities are the genesis of value in ordinary analysis, and they generate values in mathematical programming too. In fact, in ordinary analysis the determination of outputs and the determination of prices are but two aspects of the same problem, the optimal allocation of scarce resources. The same is true in mathematical programming.

Heretofore we have encountered prices only as data for determining the direct costs of processes and the net value of output. But of course the limiting factors of production also have value although we have not assigned prices to them up to now. In this section we shall see that the solution of a mathematical programming problem implicitly assigns values to the limiting factors of production. Furthermore, the implicit pricing problem can be solved directly and, when so solved, constitutes a solution to the optimal allocation problem.

Consider the automobile example and ask: how much is a unit (1 percent) of each of the types of capacity worth to the firm? The approach to this question is similar in spirit to the familiar marginal analysis. With respect to each type of capacity we calculate how much the maximum revenue would increase if one more unit were added, or how much revenue would decrease if one unit were taken away. Since there is a surplus of automobile assembly capacity, neither the addition nor the subtraction of one unit of this type would affect the optimum program or the maximum net revenue. Hence the value of this type of capacity is nil. The analysis and result for truck assembly are the same.

We find, then, that these two types of capacity are free goods. This does not imply that an automobile assembly line is not worth having, any more than, to take a classic example, the fact that air is a free good means that it can be dispensed with. It means that it would not be worthwhile to increase this type of capacity at any positive price and that some units of these types could be disposed of without loss.

The valuation of the other types of capacity is not so trivial. In Figure 9 possible values per percent of engine assembly capacity are scaled along the horizontal axis and values per percent of metal stamping capacity are scaled along the vertical axis. Now consider any possible pair of values, say engine assembly capacity worth \$20,000 per unit and metal stamping

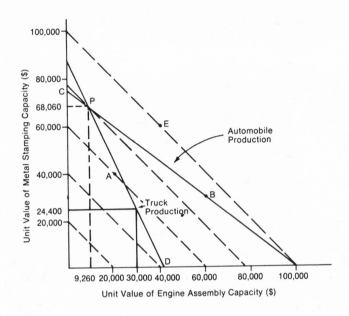

FIGURE 9

AUTOMOBILE EXAMPLE, IMPLICIT VALUES

worth $40,000. This is represented by point A on the figure. Applying these values to the data on pages 293–294, the values of capacity required for producing an automobile is found to be $(0.004 \times \$40,000) + (0.003 \times \$20,000) = \$220$ which is well under the value of producing an automobile, or $300.[11] In the same way, if engine assembly capacity is worth $60,000 per percent of capacity and metal stamping capacity is valued at $30,000 per unit (point B), the cost of scarce resources required to produce an automobile will be exactly equal to the value of the product. This is clearly not the only combination of resource values which will precisely absorb the value of output when the resources are used to produce automobiles. The automobile production line on the figure, which passes through point B, is the locus of all such value combinations. A similar

11. These unit values are also marginal values since costs of production are constant.

line has been drawn for truck production to represent those combinations of resource values for which the total value of resources used in producing trucks is equal to the value of output. The intersection of these two lines is obviously the only pair of resource values for which the marginal resource cost of producing an additional automobile is equal to the net value of an automobile and the same is true with respect to trucks. The pair can be found by plotting or, with more precision, by algebra. It is found that 1 percent of engine assembly capacity is worth $9,259 and 1 percent of metal stamping capacity is worth $68,056.

To each pair of values for the two types of capacity, there corresponds a value for the entire plant. Thus to the pair of values represented by point A there corresponds the plant value of $(100 \times \$20,000) + (100 \times \$40,000) = \$6,000,000$. This is not the only pair of resource values which give an aggregate plant value of $6,000,000. Indeed, any pair of resource values on the dotted line through A corresponds to the same aggregate plant value. (By this stage, Figure 9 should become strongly reminiscent of Figure 1.) We have drawn a number of lines parallel to the one just described, each corresponding to a specific aggregate plant value. The dashed line which passes through the intersection of the two production lines is of particular interest. By measurement or otherwise this line can be found to correspond to a plant value of $7,731,500 which, we recall, was found to be the maximum attainable net revenue.

Let us consider the implications of assigning values to the two limiting factors from a slightly different angle. We have seen that as soon as unit values have been assigned to the factors an aggregate value is assigned to the plant. We can make the aggregate plant value as low as we please, simply by assigning sufficiently low values to the various factors. But if the values assigned are too low, we have the unsatisfactory consequence that some of the processes will give rise to unimputed surpluses. We may, therefore, seek the lowest aggregate plant value which can be assigned and still have no process yield an unimputed surplus. In the automobile case, that value is $7,731,500. In the course of finding the lowest acceptable plant value we find specific unit values to be assigned to each of the resources.

In this example there are two processes and four limited resources. It turns out that only two of the resources were effectively limiting, the others being in relatively ample supply. In general, the characteristics of the solution to a programming problem depend on the relationship between the number of limited resources and the number of processes taken into consideration. If, as in the present instance, the number of limited resources exceeds the number of processes, it will usually turn out that some of the resources will have imputed values of zero and that the number of resources with positive imputed values will be equal to the number of processes.[12] If the number of limited resources equals the number of processes all resources will have positive imputed values. If, finally, the number of processes exceeds the number of limited resources, some of the processes will not be used in the optimal program. This situation, which is the usual one, was illustrated in Figure 6. In this case the total imputed value of resources absorbed will equal net revenue for some processes and will exceed it for others. The number of processes for which the imputed value of resources absorbed equals the net revenue will be just equal to the number of limited resources, and the processes for which the equality holds are the ones which will appear at positive levels in the optimal program. In brief, the determination of the minimum acceptable plant value amounts to the same thing as the determination of the optimal production program. The programming problem and the valuation problem are not only closely related they are basically the same.

This can be seen graphically by comparing Figures 1 and 9. Each figure contains two axes and two diagonal boundary lines. But the boundary lines in Figure 9 refer to the same processes as the axes in Figure 1, and the axes in Figure 9 refer to the same resources as the diagonal boundary lines in Figure 1. Furthermore, in using Figure 1 we sought the net revenue corresponding to the highest dashed line touched by the boundary; in using Figure 9 we sought the aggregate value corresponding to the lowest dashed line which has any points on or outside the boundary; and the two results turned out to be the same. Formally

12. We say "usually" in this sentence because in some special circumstances the number of resources with positive imputed values may exceed the number of processes.

stated, these two figures and the problems they represent are *duals* of each other.

The dualism feature is a very useful property in the solution of mathematical programming problems. The simplest way to see this is to note that when confronting a mathematical programming problem we have the choice of solving the problem or its dual, whichever is easier. Either way we can get the same results. We can use this feature now to generalize our discussion somewhat. Up to now when dealing with more than two processes we have had to use relatively complicated diagrams like Figure 6 because straightforward diagrams like Figure 1 did not contain enough axes to represent the levels of the processes. Now we can use diagrams modeled on Figure 9 to depict problems with any number of processes so long as they do not involve more than two scarce factors. Figure 10 illustrates a diagram for four pro-

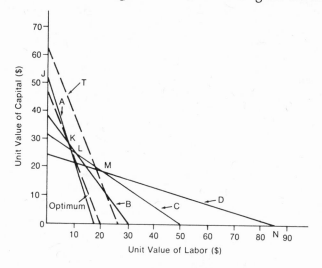

FIGURE 10

THE VALUATION PROBLEM, FOUR PROCESSES

cesses and is, indeed, derived from Figure 6. In Figure 10, line *A* represents all pairs of factor values such that Process A would yield neither a profit nor a loss. Lines *B*, *C*, and *D* are similarly interpreted. The dashed line *T* is a locus along which the aggregate value of the labor and capital available to the firm (or industry) is constant. Its position is not relevant to the analysis; its slope, which is simply the ratio of the quantity of available labor to that of capital, is all that is significant. The broken line $JKLMN$ divides the graph into two regions. All points on or above it represent pairs of resource values such that no process gives rise to an unimputed surplus. Let us call this the acceptable region. For each point below that broken line there is at least one process which does have an unimputed surplus. This is the unacceptable region. We then seek for that point in the acceptable region which corresponds to the lowest aggregate plant value. This point will, of course, give the set of resource values which makes the accounting profit of the firm as great as possible without giving rise to any unimputed income. The point which meets these requirements is K, and a dotted line parallel to T has been drawn through it to indicate the minimum acceptable aggregate plant value.

At point K, processes A and B yield zero profits, and processes C and D yield losses. Hence processes A and B are the ones which should be used, exactly as we found in Figure 6. To be sure, this diagram does not tell the levels at which A and B should be used, any more than Figure 6 tells the valuations to be placed on the two resources. But finding the levels after the processes have been selected is a comparatively trivial matter. All that is necesssary is to find the levels which will fully utilize the resources which are not free goods. This may be done algebraically or by means of a diagram like Figure 8.

VI. APPLICATIONS

In the first section we asserted that the principal motivation of mathematical programming was the need for a method of analysis which lent itself to the practical solution of the day-to-day problems of business and the economy in general. Immediately after making that claim we introduced a highly artificial problem followed by a rather extended discussion of abstract and formal relationships. The time has now come to indicate the basis for saying that mathematical programming is a practical method of analysis.

The essential simplification achieved in mathematical programming is the replacement of the notion of the production function by the notion of the process. The process is a highly observable unit of activity and the empirical constants which characterize it can be estimated without elaborate analysis. Furthermore in many industries the structure of production corresponds to operating a succession of processes, as we have conceived them. Many industrial decisions, like shutting down a bank of machines or operating an extra shift, correspond naturally to our concept of choosing the level of operation of a process. In brief, mathematical programming is modeled after the actual structure of production in the hope that thereby it will involve only observable constants and directly controllable variables.

Has this hope been justified? The literature already contains a report of a successful application to petroleum refining.[13] I have made a similar application which, perhaps, will bear description. The application was to a moderate-sized refinery which produces premium and regular grades of automotive gasoline. The essential operation studied was blending. In blending, ten chemically distinct kinds of semirefined oil, called blending stocks, are mixed together. The result is a salable gasoline whose characteristics are approximately the weighted average of the characteristics of the blending stocks. For example, if 500 gallons of a stock with octane rating of 80 are blended with 1,000 gallons of a stock with octane rating of 86 the result will be $500 + 1,000 = 1,500$ gallons of product with octane rating of $(\frac{1}{3} \times 80) + (\frac{2}{3} \times 86) = 84$.

The significant aspect of gasoline blending for our present purposes is that the major characteristics of the blend—its knock rating, its vapor pressure, its sulphur content, etc.—can be expressed as linear functions of the quantities of the various blending stocks used. So also can the cost of the blend if each of the blending stocks has a definite price per gallon. Thus the problem of finding the minimum cost blend which will meet given quality specifications is a problem in mathematical programming.

Furthermore, in this refinery the quantities of some of the blending stocks are definitely limited by contracts and by refining capacity. The problem then arises: what are the most profitable quantities of output of regular and premium gasoline, and how

13. A. Charnes, W. W. Cooper, and B. Mellon, "Blending Aviation Gasolines," *Econometrica,* Apr. 1952, pp. 135–59.

much of each blending stock should be used for each final product? This problem is analogous to the artificial automobile example, with the added complication of the quality specifications. The problem is too complicated for graphic analysis but was solved easily by arithmetical procedures. As far as is known, mathematical programming provides the only way for solving such problems. Charnes and Cooper have recently published the solution to a similar problem which arose in the operations of a metal-working firm.[14]

An entirely different kind of problem, also amenable to mathematical programming, arises in newsprint production. Freight is a major element in the cost of newsprint. One large newsprint company has six mills, widely scattered in Canada, and some two hundred customers, widely scattered in the United States. Its problem is to decide how much newsprint to ship from each mill to each customer so as, first, to meet the contract requirements of each customer, second, to stay within the capacity limits of each mill, and third, to keep the aggregate freight bill as small as possible. This problem involves 1,200 variables (6 mills × 200 customers), in contrast to the two- or four-variable problems we have been discussing. In the final solution most of these variables will turn out to be zero—the question is which ones. This problem is solved by mathematical programming and, though formidable, is not really as formidable as the count of variables might indicate.

These few illustrations should suffice to indicate that mathematical programming is a practical tool for business planning. They show, also, that it is a flexible tool because both examples deviated from the format of the example used in our expansion. The petroleum application had the added feature of quality specification. In the newsprint application there were limits on the quantity of output as well as on the quantities of the inputs. Nevertheless mathematical programming handled them both easily.

On the other hand, it should be noted that both of these were

14. A. Charnes, W. W. Cooper, and Donald Farr and Staff, "Linear Programming and Profit Preference Scheduling for a Manufacturing Firm," *Journal of the Operations Research Society of America,* May 1953, pp. 114–29.

small-scale applications, dealing with a single phase of the operation of a single firm. I believe that this has been true of all successful applications to date. Mathematical programmers are still a long way from solving the broad planning problems of entire industries or an entire economy. But many such broad problems are only enlarged versions of problems which have been met and solved in the context of the single firm. It is no longer premature to say that mathematical programming has proved its worth as a practical tool for finding optimal economic programs.

VII. CONCLUSION

Our objective has been only to introduce the basic notions of mathematical programming and to invest them with plausibility and meaning. The reader who would learn to solve a programming problem—even the simplest—will have to look elsewhere,[15] though this paper may serve as a useful background.

Although methods of solution have been omitted from this exposition, we must emphasize that these methods are fundamental to the whole concept of mathematical programming. Some eighty years ago Walras conceived of production in very much the same manner as mathematical programmers, and more recently A. Wald and J. von Neumann used this view of production and methods closely allied to those of mathematical programming to analyze the conditions of general economic equilibrium.[16] These developments, however, must be regarded merely as precursors of mathematical programming. Programming had no independent existence as a mode of economic analysis until 1947 when G. B.

15. The standard reference is T. C. Koopmans, ed., *Activity Analysis of Production and Allocation* (New York, 1951). Less advanced treatments may be found in A. Charnes, W. W. Cooper, and A. Henderson, *An Introduction to Linear Programming* (New York, 1953); and my own *Application of Linear Programming to the Theory of the Firm* (Berkeley, 1951).

16. Walras' formulation is in *Eléments d'économie politique pure ou théorie de la richesse sociale*, 2d ed. (Lausanne, 1889), 20e Leçon. The contributions of A. Wald and J. von Neumann appeared originally in *Ergebnisse eines mathematischen Kolloquiums*, Nos. 6, 7, 8. Wald's least technical paper appeared in *Zeitschrift für Nationalökonomie*, VII (1936) and has been translated as "On some Systems of Equations of Mathematical Economics," *Econometrica*, Oct. 1951, pp. 368–403. Von Neumann's basic paper appeared in translation as "A Model of General Economic Equilibrium," *Rev. Econ. Stud.*, 1945–46, pp. 1–9.

Dantzig announced the "simplex method" of solution which made practical application feasible.[17] The existence of a method whereby economic optima could be explicitly calculated stimulated research into the economic interpretation of mathematical programming and led also to the development of alternative methods of solution. The fact that economic and business problems when formulated in terms of mathematical programming can be solved numerically is the basis of the importance of the method. The omission of methods of solution from this discussion should not, therefore, be taken to indicate that they are of secondary interest.

We have considered only a few of the concepts used in mathematical programming and have dealt with only a single type of programming problem. The few notions we have considered, however, are the basic ones; all the rest of mathematical programming is elaboration and extension of them. It seems advisable to mention two directions of elaboration, for they remove or weaken two of the most restrictive assumptions which have here been imposed.

The first of these extensions is the introduction of time into the analysis. The present treatment has dealt with a single production period in isolation. But in many cases, successive production periods are interrelated. This is so, for example, in the case of a vertically integrated firm where the operation of some processes in one period is limited by the levels of operation in the preceding period of the processes which supply their raw materials. Efficient methods for analyzing such "dynamic" problems are being investigated, particularly by George Dantzig.[18] Although the present discussion has been static, the method of analysis can be applied to problems with a time dimension.

The second of these extensions is the allowance for changes in the prices of factors and final products. In our discussion we regarded all prices as unalterable and independent of the actions of the economic unit under consideration. Constant prices are, undeniably, a great convenience to the analyst, but the method

17. G. B. Dantzig, "Maximization of a Linear Function of Variables Subject to Linear Inequalities," T. C. Koopmans, ed., op. cit., pp. 339–47.

18. "A Note on a Dynamic Leontief Model with Substitution" (abstract), *Econometrica,* Jan. 1953, p. 179.

can transcend this assumption when necessary. The general mathematical theory of dealing with variable prices has been investigated [19] and practical methods of solution have been developed for problems where the demand and supply curves are linear.[20] The assumption of constant prices, perhaps the most restrictive assumption we have made, is adopted for convenience rather than from necessity.

Mathematical programming has been developed as a tool for economic and business planning and not primarily for the descriptive, and therefore predictive, purposes which gave rise to the marginal analysis. Nevertheless it does have predictive implications. In so far as firms operate under the conditions assumed in mathematical programming it would be unreasonable to assume that they acted as if they operated under the conditions assumed by the marginal analysis. Consider, for example, the automobile firm portrayed in Figure 1. How would it respond if the price of automobiles were to fall, say by $50 a unit? In that case the net revenue per automobile would be $250, the same as the net revenue per truck. Diagrammatically, the result would be to rotate the lines of equal revenue until their slope was 45 degrees. After this rotation, point C would still be optimum and this change in prices would cause no change in optimum output. Mathematical programming gives rise, thus, to a kinked supply curve.

On the other hand, suppose that the price of automobiles were to rise by $50. Diagrammatically this price change would decrease the steepness of the equal revenue lines until they were just parallel to the metal stamping line. The firm would then be in a position like that illustrated by the YY' line in Figure 5. The production plans corresponding to points on the line segment DC in Figure 1 would all yield the same net revenue, and all would be optimal. If the price of automobiles were to rise by more than $50 or if a $50 increase in the price of automobiles were accom-

19. See H. W. Kuhn and A. W. Tucker, "Non-Linear Programming," in J. Neyman, ed., *Proceedings of the Second Berkeley Symposium on Mathematical Statistics and Probability* (Berkeley, 1951), pp. 481–92.

20. I reported one solution of this problem to a seminar at the Massachusetts Institute of Technology in September 1952. Other solutions may be known.

panied by any decrease in the price of trucks, the point of optimal production would jump abruptly from point *C* to point *D*.

Thus mathematical programming indicates that firms whose choices are limited to distinct processes will respond discontinuously to price variations: they will be insensitive to price changes over a certain range and will change their levels of output sharply as soon as that range is passed. This theoretical deduction surely has real counterparts.

The relationship between mathematical programming and welfare economics is especially close. Welfare economics studies the optimal organization of economic effort; so does mathematical programming. This relationship has been investigated especially by Koopmans and Samuelson.[21] The finding, generally stated, is that the equilibrium position of a perfectly competitive economy is the same as the optimal solution of the mathematical programming problem embodying the same data.

Mathematical programming is closely allied mathematically to the methods of input-output analysis or interindustry analysis developed largely by W. W. Leontief.[22] The two methods were developed independently, however, and it is important to distinguish them conceptually. Input-output analysis finds its application almost exclusively in the study of general economic equilibrium. It conceives of an economy as divided into a number of industrial sectors each of which is analogous to a process as the term is used in mathematical programming. It then takes either of two forms. In "open models" an input-output analysis starts with some specified final demand for the products of each of the sectors and calculates the level at which each of the sector-processes must operate in order to meet this schedule of final demands. In "closed models" final demand does not appear but attention is concentrated on the fact that the inputs required by each sector-process must be supplied as outputs by some other sector-processes. Input-output analysis then calculates a mutually

21. T. C. Koopmans, "Analysis of Production as an Efficient Combination of Activities," in T. C. Koopmans, ed., op. cit., pp. 33–97; P. A. Samuelson, "Market Mechanisms and Maximization" (a paper prepared for the Rand Corp., 1949).

22. W. W. Leontief, *The Structure of American Economy 1919–1939*, 2nd. ed. (New York, 1951).

compatible set of output levels for the various sectors. By contrast with mathematical programming the conditions imposed in input-output analysis are sufficient to determine the levels of the processes and there is no scope for finding an optimal solution or a set of "best" levels. To be sure, input-output analysis can be regarded as a special case of mathematical programming in which the number of products is equal to the number of processes. On the other hand, the limitations on the supplies of resources which play so important a role in mathematical programming are not dealt with explicitly in input-output analysis. On the whole it seems best to regard these two techniques as allied but distinct methods of analysis addressed to different problems.

Mathematical programming, then, is of significance for economic thinking and theory as well as for business and economic planning. We have been able only to allude to this significance. Indeed, apart from the exploration of welfare implications, very little thought has been given to the consequences for economics of mathematical programming because most effort has been devoted to solving the numerous practical problems to which it gives rise. The outlook is for fruitful researches into both the implications and applications of mathematical programming.

Applications of Linear Programming in the Oil Industry

W. W. Garvin, H. W. Crandall, J. B. John, and R. A. Spellman

The authors of this article, which appeared in Management Science, *are executives of major oil companies.*

As technology advances and improves, problems become more interwoven and complex. The problems of the oil industry are no exception. They can logically be grouped into categories according to the different phases of our business as shown in Figure 1. An integrated oil company must first of all carry out exploration activities to determine the spots where oil is most likely to be found. The land must then be acquired or leased and an exploratory well or "wildcat" as it is called is drilled. If luck is with us, we hit oil. Additional wells are drilled to develop the field and production gets under way. The oil is transported by various means to the refinery, where a variety of products are manufactured from it. The products in turn leave the refinery, enter the distribution system, and are marketed.

Needless to say, each of the areas shown in Figure 1 is full of unanswered questions and problems. Different methods exist for exploring the oil potentialities of a region. How should they be combined for maximum effectiveness? An oil field can be produced in many different ways. Which is best? The complexity of a modern refinery is staggering. What is the best operating plan? And what precisely do we mean by "best"? Of course, not all the problems in these areas lend themselves to linear programming but some of them do. What we would like to do is to pick out a few representative *LP* type problems from each area, show how they were formulated, and, in some cases, discuss the results that were obtained.

FIGURE 1

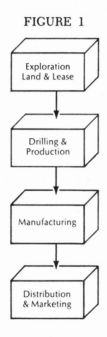

We had hoped to find applications [of linear programming] in all four of the areas shown in Figure 1. Unfortunately, we were successful only in three. We did not find any nonconfidential applications in the field of exploration. Exploration is one of the most confidential phases of our business and it is for that reason that oil companies are not very explicit about their studies in this field. We can state, however, from personal experience, that a number of applications to exploration are under investigation.

Let us therefore turn our attention to the remaining three areas of Drilling and Production, Manufacturing, and Distribution and Marketing. Out of the Drilling and Production area the problem of devising a model for a producing complex was selected. In the case of Manufacturing, the selection was difficult because historically this was the first area of application and much work has been done in this field. The problem of incremental product costs illustrates the technique of parametric programming and also shows what can happen if too many simplifications are introduced.

FIGURE 2

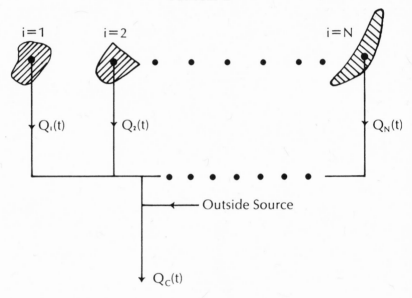

MODEL OF A PRODUCING COMPLEX

Let us now turn our attention to the model of a producing complex. We are indebted to the Field Research Laboratory of Magnolia Petroleum Company and to Arabian American Oil Company for contributing this application. Consider N oil fields or reservoirs ($i = 1, 2 \cdots N$), as shown in Figure 2, which are producing at rates $Q_i(t)$ where t is the time. The total production of the N reservoirs is to be adjusted to meet a commitment $Q_c(t)$ (such as keeping a pipe line full or a refinery supplied). An outside source of crude oil is also available. Let the profit realizable per barrel be $c_i(t)$ and consider that the operation is to be run on this basis for a period of T years. Production limitations exist which require that the $Q_i(t)$ do not exceed certain values and that the pressures in the reservoirs do not fall below certain values. These limits may be functions of time. We shall consider the case where these fields are relatively young so that development drilling activity will occur during the time period under consideration. The problem is to determine a schedule of $Q_i(t)$ such that the profit over T years is a maximum.

By splitting up the period T into time intervals $(k = 1, 2 \cdots K)$ and bringing in the physics of the problem, it can be shown that the condition that the field pressures are not to fall below certain minimum values assumes the form:

$$\sum_{j=1}^{k} (f_{i,k-j+1} - f_{i,k-j})Q_{ij} \leqq P_{i0} - P_{i \text{ min}} \tag{1}$$

for all i and k. The f's describe the characteristics of the fields and are known. The right-hand side is the difference between the initial and the minimum permissible pressure of the ith field. The variable is Q_{ij} which is the production rate of the ith field during the jth period. Additional constraints on the Q_{ij}'s are that the total production for any time period plus the crude oil possibly purchased from the outside source, Q_j, be equal to the commitment for that time period:

$$\sum_{i=1}^{N} Q_{ij} + Q_j = Q_{cj}, j = 1, 2 \cdots K \tag{2}$$

Furthermore, production limitations exist such that:

$$Q_{ij} \leqq Q_{ij \text{ max}} \tag{3}$$

which are simple under bound constraints. The objective function expressing profit over the time period considered is:

$$\sum_{j=1}^{K} \sum_{i=1}^{N} c_{ij}Q_{ij} + \sum_{j=1}^{K} c_j Q_j = \max \tag{4}$$

which completes the formulation of the linear programming problem. The coefficients c_{ij} and c_j are the profit per barrel of the ith reservoir at time j and correspondingly for purchased crude oil.

Thus far, everything has been rather straightforward. But now, the time has come to clutter up the theory with facts. Let us take a closer look at the coefficients c_{ij}. If we plot revenue versus a particular production rate Q_{ij}, we get a straight line passing through the origin as shown in Figure 3. Cost versus Q_{ij} is also more or less a straight line which, however, does not pass through the origin. The cost function is discontinuous at the origin, corresponding to a set-up charge such as building a road, a pipeline, or harbor facilities, or installing a gas-oil separator.

FIGURE 3

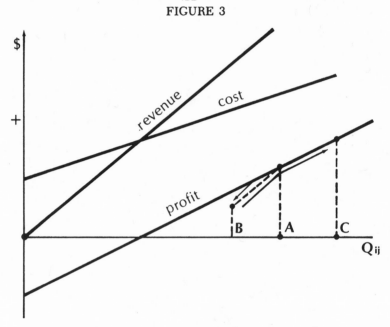

It drops to zero when $Q_{ij}=0$ because this corresponds to not yet developing the field. Also shown in Figure 3 is profit versus Q_{ij} which is the difference between revenue and cost. The profit function thus is the straight line shown plus the origin. Hence, we can say that profit from Q_{ij} production is $c_{ij}Q_{ij}-s_{ij}$ where s_{ij} is zero if Q_{ij} is zero and s_{ij} is a constant if $Q_{ij}>0$. This is a particularly difficult constraint. No general methods are available for handling this except a cut-and-try approach. This type of fixed set-up charge constraint occurs in many practical problems and we shall meet it again later on.

One other complicating feature should be mentioned. Consider that during a certain time period, Q_{ij} was at level "A" as shown in Figure 3 and that in the succeeding time period $Q_{i, j+1}$ has dropped to level "B." The profit at level "B" is not obtained by following the profit line to operating level "B" but rather by following a line as shown which is parallel to the revenue line. The reduction in level from "A" to "B" involves merely turning a few valves and essentially does not entail any reduction in operating costs. If, on the other hand, we go from "A" to "C" in succeeding time periods, then we do follow the profit line because an increase in production necessitates drilling additional wells assuming that all the wells at "A" are producing at maximum economic capacity. If we should go from "A" to "B" to "C" in succeeding time periods and if "A" was the maximum field development up to that time, then in going from "B" to "C" we would follow the broken path as shown in Figure 3.

This state of affairs can be handled by building the concept of "production capacity" into the model and requiring that production capacity never decreases with time. But this can be done only at the expense of enlarging the system appreciably.

There exist other factors and additional constraints which must be taken into account. As is so often the case, we are dealing here with a system which on the surface looks rather simple but which becomes considerably more complex as we get deeper into it to make it more realistic. Nevertheless, the simple system or modest extensions of it enables an entire producing complex to be studied, thus providing a good basis upon which to build more realistic models.

INCREMENTAL PRODUCT COSTS

Let us now leave the problems of petroleum production behind us and venture into the petroleum refinery. As was indicated before, a great deal of work has been done in this area. The few problems we shall discuss will be illustrative of what is going on in this field.

We shall consider at first a simple but nevertheless instructive example. A refinery produces gasoline, furnace oil and other products as shown in Figure 4. The refinery can be supplied with a fairly large number of crude oils. The available crude oils have different properties and yield different volumes of finished products. Some of these crudes must be refined because of long-term minimum volume commitments or because of requirements for specialty products. These crudes are considered fixed and yield

FIGURE 4

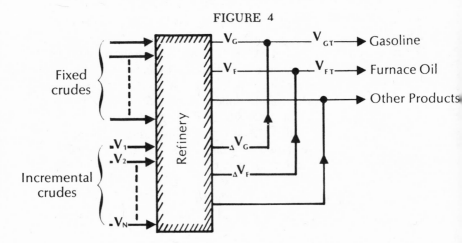

gasoline and furnace oil volumes V_G and V_F respectively. From the remaining crudes and from those crudes which are available in volumes greater than their minimum volume commitment must be selected those which can supply the required products most economically. These are the incremental crudes. Denote the gasoline and furnace oil volumes which result from the incremental crudes by ΔV_G and ΔV_F and the total volumes (fixed plus incremental) by V_{GT} and V_{FT}. The problem is to determine the minimum incremental cost of furnace oil as a function of incremental furnace oil production keeping gasoline production and general refinery operations fixed.

The formulation of this problem is straightforward:

$$\sum_1^N a_{Gi} V_i = V_{GT} - V_G = \Delta V_G \tag{5}$$

$$\sum_1^N a_{Fi} V_i = V_{FT} - V_F = \Delta V_F \tag{6}$$

$$V_i \leqq V_{i\,max} \tag{7}$$

$$\sum_{.1}^N c_i V_i = min \tag{8}$$

where a_{Gi} and a_{Fi} are the gasoline and furnace oil yields of the ith crude, V_i and $V_{i\,max}$ are the volume and availability of the ith incremental crude and c_i is the cost of producing incremental gasoline plus incremental furnace oil per barrel of the ith crude. This cost is made up of the cost of crude at the refinery, the incremental processing costs and a credit for the by-products produced at the same time.

The procedure now consists of assuming a value for ΔV_F and obtaining an optimal solution. The shadow price of equation (6) will then be equal to the incremental cost of furnace oil because it represents the change in the functional corresponding to a change of one barrel in ΔV_F. The incremental cost thus obtained, however, is valid only over ranges of variation of ΔV_F which are sufficiently small so that the optimum solution remains feasible. Beyond that permissible range of ΔV_F the basis must be changed with a resulting change in the shadow price. For problems of this type, the so-called "parametric programming" procedure can be used. This procedure has been incorporated into the IBM 704 LP code. It starts with an optimal solution and then varies in an arbitrary but preassigned manner the constants on the right-hand side until one of the basic variables becomes zero. The computer then prints out the optimal solution which exists at that time, changes the basis to an adjacent extreme point which is also optimum, and repeats this process until a termination is reached.

An actual problem was run with the model shown in Figure 4. Thirteen incremental crudes were available and incremental gasoline production was fixed at 14,600 barrels daily. The results are shown in Figure 5 which shows the minimum total incremental cost as a function of incremental furnace oil production. Ignore the dashed line for the moment. The circles represent points at which the optimum basis had to be changed. The functional is a straight line between these points. It turned out that incremental furnace-oil production was possible only in the range from about 7,100 bpd to about 11,200 bpd. Between the two extremes, the functional exhibits a minimum at about 8,000 bpd. The reason for the minimum is to be found in the fact that near the two extremes of furnace oil production, little choice exists in the composition of the crude slate. Volume is the limitation and economics plays a secondary part. Away from the two

FIGURE 5

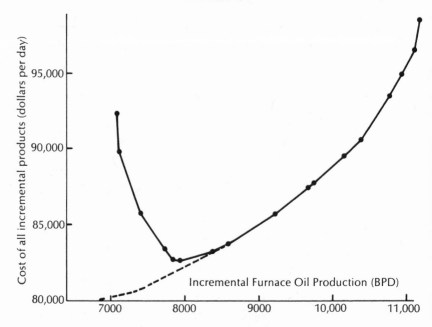

extremes, however, we have greater flexibility in crudes run and thus have the freedom to pick the cheapest crude combination. Figure 6 shows the incremental cost of furnace oil as a function of furnace oil production. It is a staircase type function because the shadow price remains unchanged as long as the optimum basis remains feasible and jumps discontinuously whenever the basis is changed. At low levels of incremental furnace oil production, the incremental cost becomes negative because in that region it is *more* expensive to make *less* furnace oil.

If we now were to show our model and our results to the refiner, he would immediately detect a fly in the ointment. The negative incremental cost at low furnace oil production runs counter to his intuitive feeling for the problem. He would point out, and rightly so, that the formulation of our model is not complete. Common sense would dictate the making of the larger volumes of furnace oil at lower cost and disposing of the excess furnace oil in some manner. For example, this excess can be mixed into heavy fuel production. If all the heavy fuel that is made can be sold, the net cost of the furnace oil overproduction

FIGURE 6

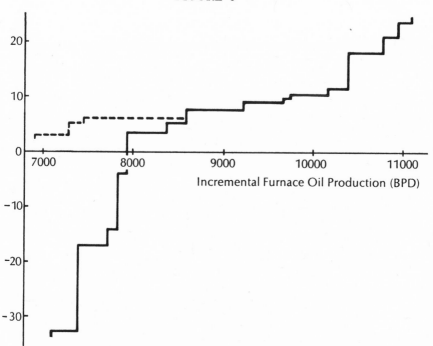

would be the negative of the value of heavy fuel indicating a credit we receive for increasing heavy fuel production.

We are tempted, therefore, to try the formulation shown in Figure 7 where we permit the diversion of some furnace oil to heavy fuel. The equation for gasoline production remains unchanged but the furnace oil equation now reads:

$$\sum_{1}^{N} a_{iF} V_i - s_1 = \Delta V_F \tag{9}$$

and the objective form is:

$$\sum_{1}^{N} c_i V_i - v_{HF} s_1 = \min \tag{10}$$

where s_1 is a slack variable indicating the volume of furnace oil diverted to heavy fuel and v_{HF} is the value per barrel of heavy fuel. It is not possible, however, to divert unlimited amounts of furnace oil into heavy fuel without violating heavy fuel's speci-

FIGURE 7

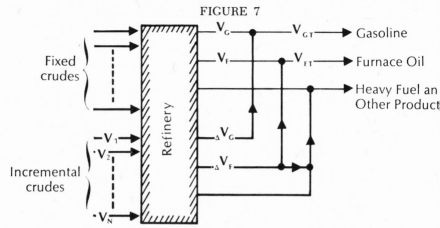

fications. The upper limit on how much furnace oil can be mixed into heavy fuel depends on the volume of heavy fuel produced which in turn is related to the crude slate, and would depend also on the specifications of heavy fuel. Furthermore, if we bring heavy fuel into the picture explicitly, the cost coefficients used before must be modified. The problem is beginning to become more complex. To take these effects into account would form the basis of an entirely new study. For purposes of the present illustration, however, the situation can be handled roughly as follows. It turns out from experience and by considering the volumes involved that the excess furnace oil production should be less than or at most equal to about 15 percent of the incremental furnace oil production if all the excess is to go to heavy fuel and specifications on heavy fuel are to be met. Therefore, the additional constraint

$$\sum_{1}^{N} a_{iF} V_i + s_2 = 1.15 \Delta V_F \tag{11}$$

was added to the system where s_2 is a slack variable. This constraint insures that no undue advantage is taken of the freedom introduced by excess furnace oil production.

The results for this second formulation of the problem are shown by the dashed lines in Figures 5 and 6. The abscissa now refers to that part of incremental furnace oil production which leaves the refinery as furnace oil. Excess furnace oil is produced below incremental furnace oil production of about 8,600 bpd.

FIGURE 8

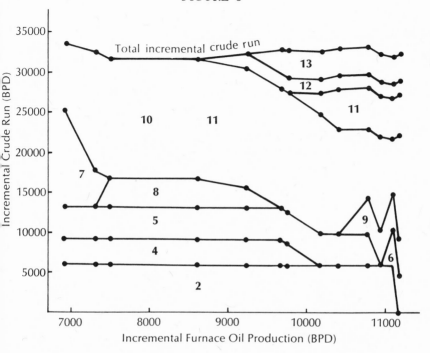

Above that level, it is not economic to produce more furnace oil than required and, consequently, there is no difference between the two formulations of the problem. Constraint (11) is limiting for incremental furnace oil production below about 7,500 bpd. Figure 8 shows the composition of the optimum crude slate for the second formulation as a function of incremental furnace oil production. This is useful information to have on hand. Note that no changes occur in the range of incremental furnace oil production from 7,500 to 8,600 bpd. In this range, actual incremental furnace oil production remains fixed at 8,600 bpd with any excess going into heavy fuel.

The modern refinery is a complicated system with strong interdependence among the activities within it. The example just described illustrates this point and shows the importance of the refiner's experience in correctly isolating portions of the refinery which can be separately considered.

Decision Analysis Comes
of Age

JACOB W. ULVILA AND
REX V. BROWN

Rex Brown is chairman of Decision Science Consortium, Inc. and Jacob W. Ulvila is vice president of this firm. The following paper was published in the Harvard Business Review *in 1982.*

In the early 1970s, C. Jackson Grayson, onetime head of the Wage and Price Commission and also author of one of the first books on applied decision analysis, urged analysts to "put people, time, power, data accessibility, and response time into models and create crude, workable solutions" if they wanted busy people like himself to use them.[1]

At the time, decision analysis was still an experimental management technique, a fairly straightforward application of statistical decision theory. The choice facing a decision maker was expressed as a mathematical function of probability and utility numbers, which measured the person's uncertainties and value judgments. (The best option was the one with the highest expected utility.) Although decision analysis was well established as a way to quantify logically the considerations that go into any choice among options, it had just

Note: Some footnotes have been omitted from the original article.

1. See C. Jackson Grayson, *Decisions Under Uncertainty* Boston: Division of Research, Harvard University Graduate School of Business Administration, 1960 and "Management Science and Business Practice," *HBR* July–August 1973, p. 41.

begun to move out of the business schools and into practical application in the business world. Only a handful of corporations provided inhouse expertise, and consultants specializing in decision analysis were rarely called on.

Now, after ten years of sometimes humbling feedback from the real world, analysts have learned to be more flexible and modest in how to make the basic decision theory formulation useful to managers. The technology has been enhanced to capture more considerations relevant to sound decision making, notably through multiattribute utility analysis and improved interaction with the user. Decision analysis has emerged as a complement to older decision-making techniques such as systems modeling and operations research. In addition to statistical decision theory, the new technology draws on psychology, economics, and social science.

What is retained and is distinctive about the approach is that the quantitative models incorporate personal judgments. To distinguish this approach from other ways of analyzing decisions in widespread use (such as those that depend only on "objective" inputs), we call it personalized decision analysis.

Analysts have learned to use the data and expertise that are immediately available to the decision maker and to play back conclusions to the manager in close to real time. In 1970, an analysis was rarely completed within three months. Now, meaningful analysis of a problem can be generated in an afternoon, and a succession of analyses can be presented in intervals of one or two days. Without greatly disturbing their schedule of meetings or reflective process, managers can now respond to these analyses and provide input for other rounds.

Although such decision analysis has not become the dominant analytic discipline that some people expected, its use has grown dramatically since 1970. Personalized decision analysis has become an accepted part of the staff services that major corporations draw on routinely, much as they do industrial psychology, cost analysis, marketing research, and economic analysis. And virtually all the major areas of government have adopted decision analysis in one form or another.

The case studies that we present in this article illustrate how managers use the three major variants of decision analysis currently in use—decision tree analysis, probabilistic forecasting, and multiattribute utility analysis.

DECISION TREE ANALYSIS

Decision tree analysis is the oldest and most widely used form of decision analysis. Managers have used it in making business decisions in uncertain conditions since the late 1950s, and its techniques are familiar. Over the past several years, however, the manner in which people conduct decision tree analysis has expanded. Today's analyst has at his or her disposal not only an array of computer supports that make quick turnaround possible but also the accumulated wisdom of analysts over the last 20 years. The following case illustrates some of the components of a successful decision tree analysis. They include the use of simple displays, sensitivity analysis to guide refinements, and subsidiary models to ensure completeness. Also important are the direction and integration the analysis gives to the contributions of experts as well as the involvement of top managers.

Should AIL Purchase Rights to a New Patent? · Late in 1974, the AIL Division of Cutler-Hammer, Inc. (now a division of Eaton Corporation) was offered the opportunity to acquire the defense market rights to a new flight-safety system patent. The inventor claimed he had a strong patent position as well as technical superiority, but the market for the product was very uncertain, mostly because of pending legislative action. Because the inventor wished to make an offer to other companies if AIL was not interested, he asked AIL to make the decision in a few weeks, a period of time clearly inadequate to resolve any uncertainties it was aware of.

AIL had not used formal decision analysis before. Top managers were, however, familiar with the theory and its typical applications through the literature and interested in trying these techniques on an actual decision to evaluate their worth. The patent decision appeared to be a good candidate for such a trial.

A team of AIL personnel and outside analysts spent two weeks developing an analysis of the patent idea. All the while, the team stayed in continual contact with top management.

Ail's Analysis · The analysts used standard decision tree techniques. Exhibit 1 shows the immediate choice, to purchase a six-month option on the patent rights or not, and the main uncertainties that affected the decision. The attractiveness of each outcome, or path through the tree, is represented by its present-value earnings.

EXHIBIT 1

AIL's Decision Tree

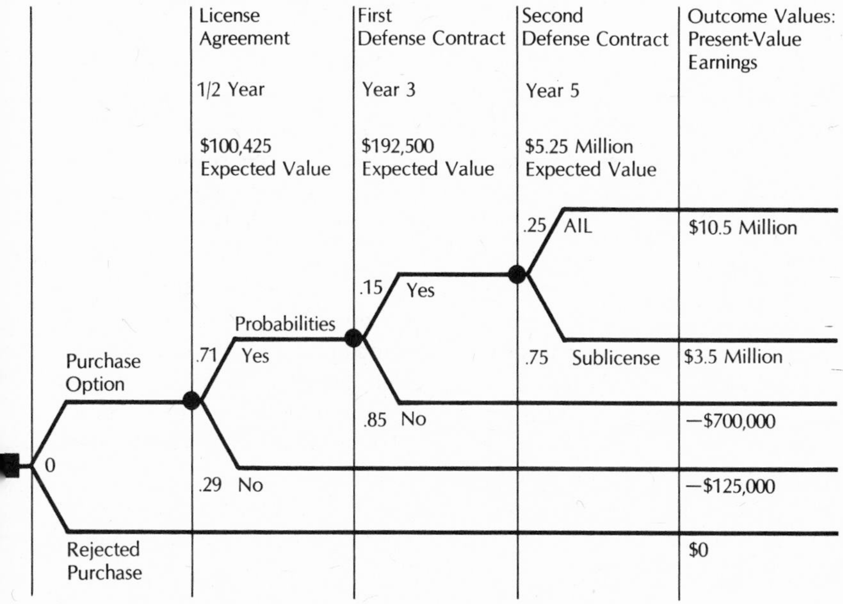

License Agreement	First Defense Contract	Second Defense Contract	Outcome Values: Present-Value Earnings
1/2 Year	Year 3	Year 5	
$100,425 Expected Value	$192,500 Expected Value	$5.25 Million Expected Value	

```
                                          .25  AIL        $10.5 Million
                              .15  Yes  ●
               Probabilities
Purchase  .71  Yes  ●                     .75  Sublicense  $3.5 Million
Option
         ●                    .85  No                     -$700,000

0  ●           .29  No                                     -$125,000

Rejected                                                   $0
Purchase
```

These range from a loss of $700,000 to a gain of $10.5 million. The expected value at each node in the tree is calculated by taking a probability-weighted average of its branches. Working these values gives an expected value of $100,425. That is, AIL could expect to be better off by $100,425 if it purchased the six-month option.

The mechanics of the analysis—specifying the tree, assigning values, and calculating results—are straightforward. The usefulness of the analysis, however, depends more on how the analysis process is managed than on the mechanics. Five features that are often absent in unsuccessful attempts to apply decision analysis marked this implementation as a success.

A Simple Display The focus of the analysis was the simple tree shown in Exhibit 1. The most common mistake that a beginner at decision analysis makes is to include everything the choice involves in the tree. This is a sure way to end up with a mess, which only the analyst, if anyone, can understand. Such a tree is unlikely to influence any manager's decision.

The trick is to design a simple tree that captures the essence of the problem by including its most important elements. In this case, the most important elements affecting earnings were the probabilities of exercising the option, receiving an initial contract, and continuing on a second contract.

Refining the Elements   By means of an interactive computer program, the analysts determined how sensitive the results were to changes in the inputs to the tree. The analysis was then expanded in a way that would be most responsive to what the decision maker needed to know.

Use of Subsidiary Models   The analysts at AIL developed models to refine estimates of the most sensitive inputs. Using a simple tree does not make the analysis coarse or incomplete; subsidiary models can ensure any desired level of detail and sophistication. In this case, the analysts used three subsidiary models. They used one to determine yearly earnings and calculate present values and another to assess the probability of receiving a contract.

The latter model reflected important factors such as the timing and terms of a possible legislative mandate for the system, the strength of possible competitive systems, and the likelihood of a crash or near crash of a plane within the next several months. The analysts used a third model to assess probability distributions of earnings from the contracts that reflected uncertainties in the number of units, the price per unit, and the profit margin. Each subsidiary model was compact and could be displayed on a single chart, which the analysts used to answer top managers' questions about how the figures in the main model had been determined.

Team Input   At AIL various people were involved with each aspect of the model, so that each expert could focus on the area of his expertise. Those most knowledgeable about the chances of winning the second contract, for example, addressed this aspect of the problem but did not consider other aspects. The combined contributions of all the experts formed a unified picture for top management.

Contact with Top Management   The most important factor was the close work of top management with the analysis team throughout the analysis. This interaction ensured that:

1. The choices modeled were in fact the choices under consideration. (In this case, as a result of the modeling, the analysts identified a new choice—waiting and seeking a sublicense.)
2. All important concerns were addressed. For AIL, the issues included the impact that decision factors other than direct earnings have (in this case, return on capital).
3. The level of modeling was right. That is, some aspects were modeled formally, but others were left to informal consideration. For example, the analysts explored AIL's attitude toward risk taking by displaying risk profiles of the choices rather than by assessing and using a utility function. (Because answering the hypothetical questions about preferences for uncertain returns that are required to establish a utility function strikes many managers as gambling, many of them are reluctant to do it. In this case, the uncertainties of the decision could be sufficiently characterized in simple risk profiles.)

Exhibit 2 shows the risk profiles of the alternatives AIL faced. Purchasing the option would give an expected net present value of earnings of about $100,000, a 60 percent chance of losing about

EXHIBIT 2

RISK PROFILES FOR AIL's PATENT PURCHASING DECISION
(Distribution of incremental discounted earnings in millions of dollars)

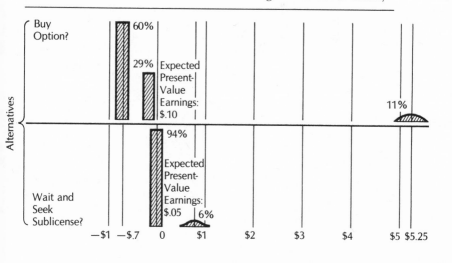

$700,000, a 29 percent chance of losing about $125,000, and an 11 percent chance of having a positive return from a distribution with an expectation of about $5.25 million. (This picture corresponds to a more detailed analysis of the earnings from a defense contract.)

The alternative, waiting and seeking a sublicense, would have a 94 percent chance of producing no gain (or loss) and a 6 percent chance of producing a distribution with an expectation of about $830,000 and would result in an expected value of about $50,000. This display facilitated a unanimous decision by the decision-making group (the president and his vice presidents for business development and operations) to go with the less risky strategy even though it offered a slightly lower expected value.

Other Companies' Experiences · Companies in a wide range of industries are using decision tree analysis to make a variety of decisions. For example:

• Through this kind of analysis, Ford has determined whether to produce its own tires and whether to stop producing convertibles.

• The defense systems division of Honeywell uses decision tree analysis to evaluate the attractiveness of new weapons programs. On a regular basis, program managers and the director of planning develop models to help decide which programs to pursue and how they should allocate internal research and development funds.

• With decision tree analysis, Pillsbury's grocery products division has evaluated major decisions, such as whether to switch from a box to a bag for a certain grocery product. In this case, even when analysts used pessimistic assessments expressed by a manager who initially recommended remaining with the box, the analysis showed that the profitability would be greater with the bag. The analysis also showed that the value of making a market test, as urged by some executives, could not remotely approach its cost. The bag was introduced, and the profits on the product climbed.

• Faced with a decision to electrify part of its system, which would involve capital expenditures of several hundred million dollars, Southern Railway carried out an analysis that gave managers a better understanding of the interactions of variables influencing the decision.

• Many major oil and gas companies, such as Union Texas Petroleum, the Champlin oil and gas subsidiary of Union Pacific, and Gulf Oil, apply decision analysis regularly to choose appropriate sites for exploration and evaluate the economics of field development.

• ITT uses decision analysis at many levels of the company, especially for capital investment decisions.

PROBABILISTIC FORECASTING

The previous section illustrates how personalized decision analysis can capture all the thinking that goes into a particular decision. The technique has other uses as well. Analysts can develop certain aspects of decision analysis into analytic tools that can be used in a variety of contexts. Analysts can use the probabilistic modeling aspects of decision analysis to develop forecasts of, for instance, future sales and profits, which in turn can be used to support decisions about planning, investment, and marketing. Developing a single aspect of personalized decision analysis to support decisions in a variety of contexts is likely to become very popular. Because its cost can be spread over many uses, a company can afford to use enough computerization and staff time to do this type of analysis properly.

The following example illustrates how personalized decision analysis can be used for forecasting. Of course, this kind of analysis is not the only way to carry out quantitative forecasting. What is distinctive about this approach's contribution to the problem is that, rather than limit a forecast to statistical extrapolation from the past, it can combine assessments of judgment with data. In cases where little or no relevant history is available on which to base a forecast and where each product's success depends on a combination of events about which personal judgment is virtually the only source of information, this form of analysis is particularly helpful.

How Will Honeywell's Defense Division Grow? · In late 1979, the manager of planning for the defense systems division of Honeywell, Inc. faced the task of planning for division's growth over the next ten years. A major part of the work involved finding how to stay within the R&D budget and yet pursue new product opportunities to increase the division's sales and profits.

After he screened the new product opportunities according to their fit with the rest of the division, the manager needed forecasts of the products' sales, profits, and investment requirements. The products' successful development, the strength of competition, and their eventual market success were all uncertain. In addition, the chances for success of some of the products were interrelated, and several products offered the chance of significant collateral business.

The approach the analysts took was to build a composite forecast for the division by combining decision tree analyses of individual products. During the project, Honeywell's planners worked closely with decision analysis consultants and, by the time they had finished, had acquired the skills needed to carry out the analyses in-house. This type of analysis is now a regular part of Honeywell's project evaluation, planning, and forecasting activity.

The analysts developed a model for each product along lines similar to AIL's. The analysis team worked closely with each project manager and his staff to build the decision tree, assess probabilities and values, and discuss results and sensitivities.

The two analyses differed significantly, however, in a number of ways. First, the results of Honeywell's analysis were to be used for forecasting as well as for decision making. This use meant that the analysts would need to model additional factors and would have to make the form the outputs took suitable for forecasting.

Second, because the success of some products was related to the the success of others, the analysts had to include in the analysis such factors as common investments, collateral business opportunities, and marketing interactions.

Third, Honeywell's problem presented no clear single criterion according to which management could make a decision. Honeywell considered several financial criteria such as internal rate of return, net present value, and yearly streams of profits, investments, and return on investment.

Honeywell's Forecasts · Exhibit 3 shows the probabilistic sales forecast for one group of interrelated products. This forecast is based on decision tree analyses of three main products and two collateral business opportunities. The analysts first developed decision trees for each product to determine the distributions of sales in the event that a market sufficient to support full production both did and did not emerge. Then they developed a second level of analysis to model the key interdependencies among the products; specifically, the probability of any particular product being in full production depended on which other products were also in full production.

The forecast shows that low sales are expected from the products for the first seven years. After that, sales for the next six years are expected to be about $75 million per year. This amount is not cer-

EXHIBIT 3

DISTRIBUTION OF SALES FOR A GROUP OF INTERRELATED PRODUCTS

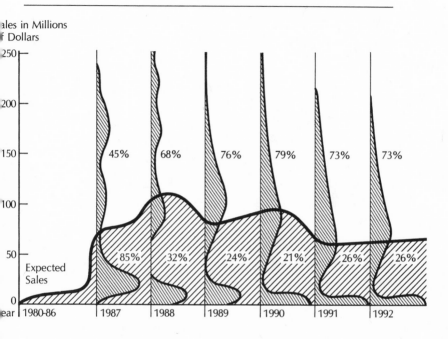

tain, however. The forecast, for instance, shows a 24 percent chance of sales being below $25 million in 1989.

The supporting decision tree analyses were useful for explaining the shape of each year's forecast. Exhibit 4 shows that because of uncertainty about which products would have sufficient markets to support full production by 1988, the forecast for sales is "lumpy." The reasons for these uncertainties are detailed in the decision tree analyses.

This analysis helped Honeywell to assess the chances that these products would meet sales goals, the uncertainties in the assessment, and the reasons for the uncertainties. By detailing the chain of events that would produce different levels of sales, it also identified points of leverage—places where Honeywell could take action to change probabilities and improve sales.

EXHIBIT 4

DETAILED FORECAST OF SALES IN 1988

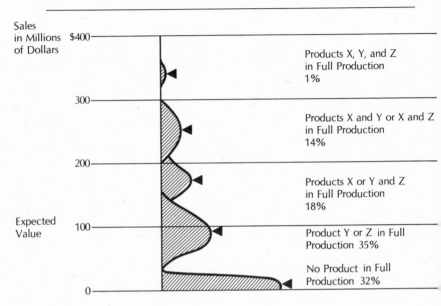

The analysts also used the decision trees to forecast yearly profits, fund flows, assets, research and development investments, and the related financial quantities of net present value, internal rate of return, and annual return on investment. Their forecasts indicated that these products could be expected to exceed requirements on all factors and that, unless Honeywell was very risk averse, they were attractive.

Honeywell's managers compared forecasts to decide which product opportunities to pursue. These comparisons provided an additional screen since some products were clearly worse than others on *all* factors. But because the analysis didn't show the relative importance of each factor—some products were projected to perform better on certain factors (for example, internal rate of return and net present value) and other products were projected to perform better on other factors (for example, return on investment)—an unambiguous ordering of the products was impossible. Honeywell's managers might have had such an ordering if their analysts had used some of the newer techniques of multiattribute utility.

MULTIATTRIBUTE UTILITY ANALYSIS

In trying to determine where to place its European subsidiary, the top management of one company completely ignored a decision tree analysis that showed careful consideration of the financial implications of possible locations. When pressed for an explanation, top management confided that the choice was dominated by the fact that key personnel wanted to be near the International School in Geneva. Somehow, that consideration seemed too noneconomical and nonrational to be included in the analysis—yet it did dominate the decision. At the time the decision was made, the technology of decision analysis was ill equipped to handle the trade-offs between financial effects and intangibles. A new technique, multiattribute utility analysis, makes such modeling possible by precisely specifying the factors that affect the choice, making trade-offs among the factors, and choosing the alternative that offers the best balance.

Multiattribute utility analysis evolved out of decision analysis that supported government decisions, in which the need to balance multiple objectives is most obvious. As the case of the company deciding where to put its plant shows, however, its usefulness for business decision making is evident. For example, plant sites usually differ in such intangibles as the skill of the local work force, the ability of local management, and the management problems of operating plants in the locations under consideration. These are important factors to consider in the decision of where to locate the plant, yet it is virtually impossible to specify their impact on profit with any precision.

Many factors also arise in strategic decisions. For example, Michael E. Porter has argued that, when considering the strategic decisions of vertical integration, major capacity expansion, and entry into new businesses, managers should go beyond cost and investment analyses to consider broad strategic issues and perplexing administrative problems and that these are very hard to quantify. Multiattribute utility analysis, which is illustrated in the following case, provides a way to quantify and trade off such factors.

Which Bomb-Detection System Should the FAA Choose? · Over the past few years, the Federal Aviation Administration has been supporting research and development on a system to detect bombs in airplane baggage. In early 1980, the program manager for this project had to decide which of several candidate systems to continue funding. The candidates differed greatly in their potential performance and technical characteristics. Since none was clearly superior in all respects, the program manager sought a method for weighing the various characteristics to arrive at a measure of overall value.

A team of outside analysts worked closely with the program manager and other FAA personnel to develop a comprehensive model of the value of each system. To determine an efficient allocation of budgeted funds, they combined these values with assessments of the probabilities of success and development costs.

The FAA's Analysis · The analysts' primary goal was to develop a comprehensive model for evaluating and comparing candidates. This development involved four activities—defining attributes of value, assessing performance of the candidates on each attribute, determining trade-offs across attributes, and calculating overall values.

Defining Preference Attributes The analysts sought to define attributes with four characteristics. The attributes were to be comprehensive enough to account for most of what is important in evaluating the candidates, to highlight the differences among the candidates, to reflect separate, nonoverlapping values to avoid double counting, and to be independent of each other.

When the analysts had identified attributes that satisfied these four requirements, they then arranged the attributes in a hierarchy showing the logical relationships among attributes. This is shown in Exhibit 5.

The first main attribute is the effectiveness of the device at detecting bombs. This is subdivided into the type of explosive, the size of the bomb, and the detection-false alarm ratio.

The second main attribute, development considerations, is divided into four subcategories—time to develop a prototype, production lead time, operating size (which would determine a system's location in an airport), and transportability.

Cost to employ the system in an airport, the third main attribute, is divided into initial costs and recurring costs. Initial costs reflect a basic cost estimate based on technical considerations and an estimate of the effects of competition. Recurring costs include mainte-

EXHIBIT 5

Hierarchy of Attributes in the FAA's Analysis
(In Preference Weights)

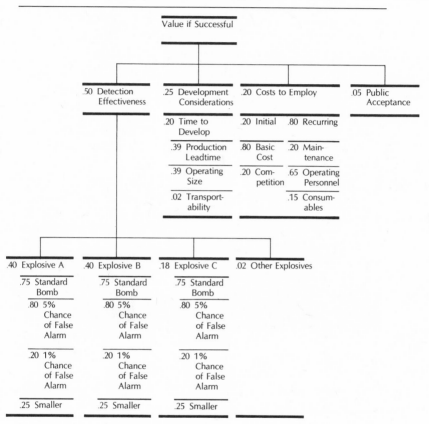

nance, operating personnel, and material consumed during operation.

The fourth main attribute is the system's acceptability to passengers.

Assessing Performance of Candidates on Each Attribute   To assess preference, the analysts required scales for all attributes. They used two types of measure—scales with natural standard units (including dollars for costs, months or hours for time, and percentages for detection rates) and relative scales. Wherever possible, the performance of a candidate was first assessed in natural units. These assessments were then transformed into 0-to-100-point scales for standardization. The candidate with the best performance (the lowest cost, for example) received a score of 100; the one with the worst performance (the highest cost, for instance) received a score of 0; and the others received intermediate scores.

Where no natural measure existed (for example, for "public acceptance"), performance was assessed directly on a 0-to-100-point scale. Again, a score of 100 was assigned to the candidate with the best performance, 0 to the worst performance, and so forth.

Exhibit 6 shows, for instance, the scores for the six candidates on each development consideration. Candidate A was assessed to have the best "time to develop" since it was fully developed at the time of the analysis. It was assigned a value of 100. Candidate C would take the longest time to develop—four years. It received a value of 0. Other candidates would take intermediate amounts of time to develop and thus received intermediate scores.

EXHIBIT 6

PERFORMANCE OF THE FAA'S BOMB DETECTION CANDIDATES ON
DEVELOPMENT CONSIDERATIONS ON A SCALE OF 0 TO 100

Developmental considerations	Candidates					
	A	B	C	D	E	F
Time to develop	100	50	0	62	50	25
Production leadtime	50	100	75	50	0	50
Operating size	100	100	50	100	0	100
Transportability	100	100	100	100	0	60

Determining Trade-Offs Across Attributes   By assessing a set of weights to represent the decision maker's judgment about the relative importance of improving performance from the worst to the best level for each attribute, analysts could determine trade-offs across attributes. The analysts assessed the weights by referring to the range of performance the scales reflected instead of to abstract notions of importance.

Consider, for example, the weights of the development considerations shown in Exhibit 5. For these attributes, the ranges of possible variation in "production lead time" (18 months) and in "operating size" were considered most important. The variation of "time to develop" (4 years) was assessed to be half as important (as important as a variation of 9 months on "production lead time"). Finally, the variation of "transportability" (32 hours) was assessed to be one-tenth as important as "time to develop" (or about as important as 5 months of development time). These assessments are represented by weights that are in the ratios of .5:1:1:.05 for time to develop, production lead time, operating size, and transportability. Normalized weights of .20:.39:.39:.02 (which retain these ratios) were used for standardization.

The analysts assessed weights both directly, as we explained earlier, and indirectly. They used an indirect method to assess the weight between initial and recurring costs. This method determined weights that were consistent with a 10 percent discount rate and a ten-year operating horizon.

Calculating Overall Values   The fourth modeling activity was to calculate a weighted-average score for each candidate by working up through the hierarchy. Thus, using the values in Exhibit 6 and the weights in Exhibit 5, analysts calculated the value of candidate A on "development considerations" as:

$$(100)(.20) + (50)(.39) + (100)(.39) + (100)(.02) \simeq 80.$$

Similar calculations produced the values for the candidates on each main attribute that are shown in Exhibit 7. The analysts next calcu-

EXHIBIT 7

OVERALL VALUE OF CANDIDATES ON A SCALE OF 0 TO 100

		Candidates					
Attribute category	Preference weight	A	B	C	D	E	F
Detection effectiveness	.50	57	72	88	62	39	0
Other development considerations	.25	80	90	51	73	10	85
Costs to employ	.20	82	91	88	87	39	70
Public acceptance	.05	70	90	90	85	0	100
	Overall value	68	81	79	71	30	35

lated the overall value of each candidate by taking a weighted average of these scores. For example, the overall value of candidate A is:

$$(57)(.50) + (80)(.25) + (82)(.20) + (70)(0.5) \simeq 68.$$

Overall value is a measure of the attractiveness of each candidate that can be compared with measures for other candidates. The result of the analysis shows that candidate B offers the best balance of characteristics, that candidates C and D are almost as attractive, and that candidates E and F offer the worst balances.

The Value of the Analysis · The FAA's primary use of the analysis was to quantify each candidate's value in a way that permitted comparison. To determine an efficient allocation of R&D funds, the analysts combined these evaluations with estimates of each candidate's probability of success and cost of development.

The FAA's analysis also facilitated several aspects of the decision-making process. First, it helped resolve disagreements. The disaggregation of the elements of the decision clarified the source of a disagreement—was it about facts (for example, the cost of a system) or a difference in judgment (for instance, the relative importance of cost in comparison with detection performance)? Once the disagreements were clear, managers could deal with them by, for example, gathering additional supporting information. If the disagreement persisted, the model could determine its importance. For each input, the model could show whether the disagreement significantly affected the overall evaluation. Even if a disagreement was significant, the model at least isolated its cause. This clarification enabled the ultimate decision maker to make a better judgment.

The disaggregation also allowed the analyst to make a comprehensive analysis of the candidates. The team could investigate each attribute thoroughly yet keep its contribution to the overall evaluation in perspective. This arrangement prevented the analysts from wasting attention on unimportant issues.

To give a balanced picture of the whole, the multiattribute analysis synthesized the various pieces of the assessment. The analysts considered the impact of all important factors before they came up with a recommendation.

Business Use of Multiattribute Utility Analysis · Multiattribute utility analysis has been used widely to aid government decision makers. For instance, it has been used to select military systems, set water-supply policy, site nuclear facilities, allocate nuclear inspection resources, determine fire department operations, evaluate crime-prevention programs, and prepare international negotiators.

Its use as an aid in making business decisions has not been as widespread, but the next few years should see a dramatic increase. Multiattribute analysis is useful for any decision in which multiple factors are important, no alternative is clearly best on all factors, and some factors are difficult to quantify. Several business decisions have these characteristics:

Where to Put a Plant Sites often differ in many important aspects. Some factors, such as differences in capital costs (land, plant, and equipment) and in operating revenue and expenses (access to markets, labor rates, tax benefits, shipping costs), are easily reduced to financial terms. Other factors that may be crucial to the decision are more difficult to reduce to dollars. These include the availability and skill of local labor, the degree of unionization, the difficulty of managing geographically dispersed units, and legal restrictions on operations. Multiattribute analysis can highlight the sources of differences and enable managers to make quantitative trade-offs between financial factors and "intangibles."

Whether to Integrate Vertically A decision to integrate an operation or not requires that management consider a multitude of factors, many of which are difficult to quantify with standard financial techniques: access to new information, access to new technologies, ability to control specifications of products or raw materials, economies of combined operations, difficulty in balancing "upstream" and "downstream" units, and increased fixed costs of doing business.

Whether and How to Enter A New Business · This decision can involve considerations that are often ignored in capital budgeting: (*a*) the production or marketing "fit" between new and existing businesses or technologies; (*b*) Special skills or technologies required to operate the new business; (*c*) "Cultural fit" between new and old businesses (especially important if entry is by acquisition); (*d*) Relative strengths of competitors in the new business. By using multiattribute utility analysis, managers can balance these factors against financial considerations to derive a comprehensive evaluation of alternatives.

What and Whether to Negotiate   Many negotiations—labor, real estate, and sales, for example—may involve several issues. A labor negotiation could include issues of wage rates, length of agreement, grievance procedures, work rules, seniority, job security, union security, vacations, fringe benefits, and pension fund contributions. Both sides' opening positions on the issues are often clear, but how they view the trade-offs across issues is not. Using multiattribute analyses of their own preferences and trade-offs and those of the other side, negotiators can uncover opportunities to give a small concession in return for a large benefit.

How to Allocate Research and Development Budgets   Research and development projects often exhibit a variety of performance characteristics that managers may need to balance to determine the best project. Multiattribute utility analysis can help them do this. They can also combine such an analysis with a decision tree analysis to address uncertainties and risks.

THE FORECAST FOR DECISION ANALYSIS

If the trends of the past decade continue at their present rate, then over the next decade we can certainly expect to see personalized decision analysis spread and become firmly established as a staff function throughout industry. Virtually all corporations of any substance will have in-house staffs or outside consultants to analyze decisions and report findings to top management.

The big question is, however, whether decision analysis will become an integrated part of management's decision making. As C. Jackson Grayson has persuasively argued, the integration requires that the cultural gap between management scientists and managers be bridged. Without the bridge, personalized decision analysis, like operations research and other analytic techniques, may never be more than an optional aid, albeit interesting.

For the integration to take place, managers will have to become more skilled at using decision analysis and its practitioners more effective than they are now. In other words, analysts and managers-to-be need to undergo extensive training in the integration of decision analysis with existing organizational and personal decision processes. (This training would go far beyond the teaching of particular techniques, which is as far as most business schools go now.) The integration may also require organizational changes in control and reward structures in business.

At present, appropriate professional training is not readily available to either the manager or the specialized decision analyst. What is needed is a course of study (and supporting research) that integrates the logical, the psychological, and the organizational aspects of applied subjective decision analysis. This will probably not become available until there is at least one institute of research and teaching devoted to all aspects of decision-aiding technology (including personalized analysis) and to their integration.

This training would require overcoming the institutional rigidities associated with partitioning universities along such traditional departmental lines as engineering, psychology, business, and statistics. Even within single departments such as business, the feeder disciplines—organizational behavior, applied mathematics, finance, business policy, and marketing—are usually kept jealously apart. If these can be adequately synthesized, management science in general, and personalized decision analysis in particular, can at last achieve full-fledged assimilation into the day-to-day business of management.

Introduction to Statistical
Decision Theory

John Pratt, Howard Raiffa,
and Robert Schlaifer

*John Pratt, Howard Raiffa, and Robert Schlaifer
are professors in the Graduate School of Business
Administration at Harvard University. This article is taken from their book,* Introduction to Statistical Decision Theory.

THE PROBLEM OF DECISION UNDER UNCERTAINTY

When all of the facts bearing on a business decision are accurately known—when the decision is made "under certainty"—
careless thinking or excessive computational difficulty are the
only reasons why the decision should turn out, after the fact,
to have been wrong. But when the relevant facts are not all
known—when the decision is made "under uncertainty"—it is
impossible to make sure that every decision will turn out to have
been right in this same sense. Under uncertainty, the businessman is forced, in effect, to gamble. His previous actions have
put him in a position where he must place bets, hoping that he
will win but knowing that he may lose. Under such circumstances, a right decision consists in the choice of the best possible
bet, whether it is won or lost after the fact. A businessman who
buys fire insurance does not censure himself if his plant has not

burned down by the time the insurance expires, and the following example is typical of other decisions which must be made and judged in this way.

An oil wildcatter who holds an option on a plot of land in an oil-producing region must decide whether to drill on the site before the option expires or to abandon his rights. The profitability of drilling will depend on a large number of unknowns— the cost of drilling, the amount of oil or gas discovered, the price at which the oil or gas can be sold, and so forth—none of which can be predicted with certainty. His problem is further complicated by the fact that it is possible to perform various tests or experiments that will yield a certain amount of information on the geophysical structure below the land on which he has an option. Since some structures are more favorable to the existence of oil than others, this information would be of considerable help in deciding whether or not to drill; but the various tests cost a substantial amount of money, and hence it is not at all obvious that any of the available tests should be performed. The wildcatter must nevertheless decide which if any of the tests are to be performed, and ultimately, if not now, he must decide whether or not to drill.

Decision Trees · The essential characteristics of this example are two in number:

1. A *choice* or in some cases a sequence of choices must be made among various possible courses of action.
2. This choice or sequence of choices will ultimately lead to some *consequence*, but the decision maker cannot be sure in advance what this consequence will be because it depends not only on his choice or choices but on an unpredictable *event* or sequence of events.

The essence of any such problem can be brought out very clearly by a type of diagram known as a *decision tree.*

As an example that will illustrate all the essential points involved in the construction of a decision tree without useless complexities, we shall take a somewhat simplified version of the oil-drilling problem described just above. For our present purpose we shall assume that:

1. If the well is drilled at all, it will be drilled on a fixed-price contract for $100,000;

2. If oil is struck, the wildcatter will immediately sell out to a major producer for $450,000;

3. Only one type of test or experiment, namely a seismic sounding, can be performed before deciding whether or not to drill. This experiment costs $10,000; if it is performed, it will reveal with certainty whether the structure is of Type *A* (very favorable to the existence of oil), Type *B* (less favorable), or Type *C* (very unfavorable).

On these assumptions the wildcatter's decision problem can be represented by the tree shown as Figure 1. We imagine the decision-maker as standing at the base of the tree (the left side of the diagram) and as being obliged to choose first between having the seismic sounding made and not having it made. If the wildcatter's choice is to have the sounding made, one of three events will occur: the subsurface structure will be revealed to be of Type *A*, *B*, or *C*. If the wildcatter's choice is not to have the sounding made, then only one event can occur: no information.

Whatever the wildcatter's first-stage choice may be and whatever the first-stage event, the wildcatter must now enter a second stage by making a choice between drilling and abandoning the option. If he drills, then one or the other of two events will occur: oil or dry hole; if he chooses to abandon the option, the only possible "event" is "option rights lost."

Finally, at the end (right) of the tree we write down a description of the consequence of each possible sequence of choices and events. If the wildcatter chooses not to have the sounding made and to abandon his option, the consequence is simply $0—we neglect whatever he may originally have paid for the option because this is a sunk cost that cannot be affected by any present decision and therefore is irrelevant to the decision problem. Suppose, on the contrary, he decides to drill even though he has learned nothing about the subsurface structure; if he strikes a dry hole, he loses the $100,000 drilling cost, whereas if he strikes oil, his profit is the $450,000 for which he sells the rights less the $100,000 cost of drilling. If in the first stage he decides to have the sounding made, then the consequences of abandoning the option, drilling a dry hole, or striking oil are all reduced by the $10,000 cost of the sounding.

FIGURE 1

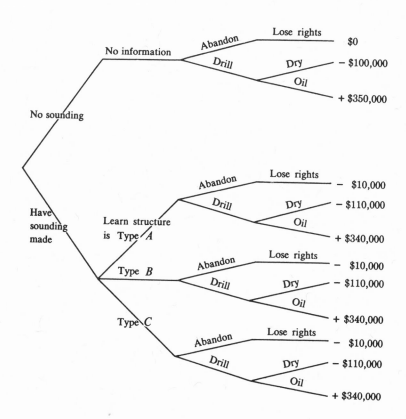

THE PROBLEM OF ANALYSIS

Analysis of the Simplest Problems · Before we even try to say what we mean by a "reasoned solution" of a complex decision problem of the kind we have just described, let us try to get a start by seeing what a sensible businessman might do when he solves a much simpler problem.

We consider an example. A manufacturer, Mr. L. K. Jones, has recently experienced a serious decline in demand for his product and as a result will be forced to lay off a substantial portion of his work force, spend money for protective treatment of idle machinery, and so forth, unless he can obtain a large order which the XYZ Company is about to place with some supplier. To have a chance at obtaining this order, Jones will have to incur considerable expense both for the making of samples and for sending a team of sales engineers to visit the XYZ Company; he must now decide whether or not to incur this expense. Formally, his problem can be described by the tree shown in Figure 2, where the three possible consequences of the two possible acts are represented by symbols:

C_1 = layoff of substantial part of work force, cost of protecting machinery;

C_2 = same as C_1, and in addition the cost of unsuccessful attempt to obtain order;

C_3 = substantial monetary profit on order, less cost of obtaining it.

FIGURE 2

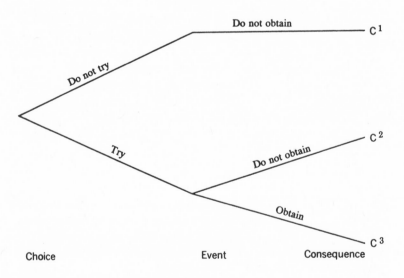

The structure of *this* problem is simple enough to make quite clear to anyone the issues that are involved in its solution. Jones (or any other sensible businessman faced with a problem of this sort) will feel that his decision will depend on two separate considerations: (1) his judgment concerning his chances of getting the order if he tries, and (2) a comparison of the cost of trying with the advantages which will accrue to him if he succeeds. If the cost is quite small relative to the advantages which would accompany success, he will make the attempt even if he thinks the chances of success are quite small; if, on the other hand, the cost of trying to get the order is so large that it would eat up most of the profits, he will not make the attempt unless he feels virtually sure that the attempt will succeed.

Sometimes a businessman who is thinking about a problem of this kind will go even further and *quantify* some if not all of his reasoning. He may say, for example, that there is so much to be gained by obtaining the order that he would try to obtain it even if there were only 1 chance in 3 of success; he may then conclude either (*a*) that he *will* make the attempt because in his opinion the chances are at least as good as 1 in 3, or else (*b*) that he *will not* make the effort because in his opinion the chances of success are less than 1 in 3. Alternatively, the businessman may start from the other side of the problem, say that in his opinion he has about 1 chance in 3 of getting the order if he tries, and then conclude either (*a*) that he *will* make the attempt because the gains which would accrue from success are so great that a 1/3 chance of obtaining them is well worth the cost of trying, or else (*b*) that he *will not* make the attempt because the gains are too small to warrant the cost when there is only 1 chance in 3 of success.

THE BASES OF DECISION: PREFERENCE AND JUDGMENT

The problem we have just discussed suffices to make it quite clear that there is in general no "objectively correct" solution to *any* decision problem. Since Jones is personally responsible for the decision to try or not to try to get the order, his decision must *necessarily* rest on:

1. How good *he feels* the chances of obtaining the order would have to be to make it worth his while to try;

2. How good *in his opinion* the chances of obtaining the order actually are.

What the businessman actually does when he answers questions of type 1 is quantify his *personal preference* for C_1 relative to C_2 and C_3; what he does when he answers questions of type 2 is quantify his *personal judgment* concerning the relative strengths of the factors that favor and oppose certain events. If he behaves reasonably, he then chooses the solution of the problem which is *consistent* with this personal preference and this personal judgment.

ANALYSIS OF COMPLEX PROBLEMS;
THE ROLE OF FORMAL ANALYSIS

Since reasonable decisions in even the simplest problems must rest necessarily on the responsible decision maker's personal judgments and personal preferences, it is intuitively quite clear that these same elements must be involved in the solution of complex problems represented by decision trees with many levels and many branches at each level. It would be folly, in other words, to look for a method of analysis that will lead to an "objectively correct" solution of the oil-drilling problem we have used. A reasonable decision-maker wants his decision to agree with his preferences and his best judgments, and he will have (and should have) no use for any proposal that purports to solve his problem by some "formula" that does *not* incorporate his preferences and judgments. This assertion does not of course imply that the decision-maker should ignore objective evidence that is relevant and available.

Stated in another way, the reason why a decision-maker might want help in analyzing a decision problem like our oil-drilling example, when Jones needed no help in deciding whether or not to try for the order from the XYZ Company, is that Jones could easily see the *implications* of his preferences and judgments whereas the wildcatter cannot. The wildcatter may feel quite sure that, for example, he would decide to drill if he knew that the structure was of Type *A* or *B* and would decide not to drill if he knew that the structure was of Type *C*; however, his immediate problem is to decide whether or not to spend $10,000 in order to learn what the structure is, and while it is obvious that this information has value, it is not at all clear whether the value is greater or less than the $10,000 the information will cost.

Any decision problem, no matter how complex, can in principle be reduced to a number of problems each of which individually has the same simple structure as the problem described by the tree of Figure 2.

If, in each of these simple problems, the decision-maker will

1. Quantify his *preference* by telling us how good the chances of obtaining C_3 *would have to be* to make him willing to gamble on C_2 or C_3 rather than to take C_1 for certain, and

2. Quantify his *judgment* by telling us how good in his opinion the chances of obtaining C_3 *actually are,*

and if, in addition, he accepts certain simple principles of "reasonable," "consistent," or "coherent" behavior, then it is possible by purely logical deduction to find that solution of the complex problem which is *logically consistent with the decision-maker's own preferences and judgments.*

Naturally we are concerned with decision problems where this kind of analysis by decomposition and evaluation produces fruitful results. There are, of course, many problems—some would say "most problems"—where although in principle such an analysis could be made it would not be profitable to do so. In many situations, the incremental advantage to be gained from formal analysis cannot be expected to repay the effort, time, and cost of the analysis; in others, the decision maker may not be able, especially without training, to quantify his preference and judgments in the way required for a formal analysis; in still others, the decision problem may be faithfully abstracted into the proper form only to prove to be too complicated for the analytical tools we have available. Even after granting all these exceptions, however, there remain many problems in which formal analysis can be of considerable help to a businessman who wishes to take advantage of it.

A Note on Decision-making under Uncertainty

MARTIN SHUBIK

*Martin Shubik is Professor of Industrial Admin-
istration at Yale University. This is an excerpt of
his article in* The Journal of Business.

By introducing considerations of probability, an attempt can be
made to extend the economic theory of choice to conditions involving uncertainty. The heroic assumption must be made that
the situations to be modeled are such that it is valid and useful
to utilize the theory of probability. This has given rise to discussions concerning subjective probability and a large literature on
probabilistic preferences and the theory of utility. Problems concerning gambling and risk preference have been examined, and
several alternatives for optimal behavior have been suggested.
For example, Savage has offered a man who wishes to minimize
regret. In other words, after the event, when he looks back, he
wishes to have acted in such a manner that he will be least sorry
concerning the outcome.

Bayesian and "maximin" principles[1] have also been suggested
as manners in which the individual should cope with lack of

1. [The "maximin" principle is often called the "minimax" principle.
Editor]

knowledge. The simple examples given here illustrate the behaviors manifested in following these different principles. In Figure 1 a simple 2×2 payoff matrix is presented. The decision-maker must choose between one of two actions, knowing that "Nature," or the environment, may also make a choice which affects him. For example, if both select their second alternative, the payoff is 7 to the decision-maker. The principle he follows will depend upon his view of the forces and motivations present in his environment.

"Nature"

The Decision-maker

	1	2
1	1	9
2	2	7

FIGURE 1

The Bayesian assumption says that all the actions of "Nature" are equiprobable, and thus the optimal behavior under this assumption will be to select the first alternative, with an expected payoff of:

$$\tfrac{1}{2}\,(1) + \tfrac{1}{2}\,(9) = 5.$$

The maximin assumption has the decision-maker believe that the environment is "out to get him." In this case he will select his second alternative, assuming that, since the worst will happen, he can at least guarantee 2 for himself.

"Nature"

The Decision-maker

	1	2
1	1	0
2	0	2

FIGURE 2

The "regret payoff" is illustrated in Figure 2 for the same situation. If he selected his second alternative and the environment did likewise, he would obtain 7 (Fig. 1) but could have obtained 9 (by selecting his first alternative); hence his regret is 2.

Shackle has constructed a "potential surprise function" which he feels dominates many major decisions which must be made in face of uncertainty which cannot be adequately portrayed by considerations of probability. All the methods noted above depend upon assumptions as to how to deal with uncertainty. Which is the "best" assumption depends upon the application and knowledge of human behavior.

In spite of the limitations of models of probability, operations research and industrial statistics have, however, flourished by applying normative models of economic man acting under probabilistically portrayed uncertainty. Theoretical models of inventory, sequential sampling, and various queueing problems have been actively applied. These have already influenced the inventory levels of the whole economy and have had an effect on the understanding of reliability and risk in areas as diverse as individual credit risks, quality control in production, and stockpiling for emergency.

One area in which the applications have been fewer but the implications deeper is that of dynamic programming. This methodology deals with situations where at each period the decision-maker chooses an action which influences a sequence of events stretching off into the possibly indefinite future. In subsequent periods he has the opportunity to modify the effects of previous decisions by current action. Although this theory still deals with statistical uncertainty and mathematical expectations, the rules of decision generated as dynamic program solutions have more of the flavor of over-all long-range strategic decisions. Dividend and investment policies can be studied as dynamic programs. However, the mathematics of functional equations used in dynamic programming is, unfortunately, difficult and still relatively underdeveloped.

Decision Theory: An Example

A. A. WALTERS

A. A. Walters is Professor of Economics at Johns Hopkins University. This piece comes from his book, Introduction to Econometrics.

It is often claimed that the ultimate purpose of any investigation is to enable us to make better decisions. From a judgment of the state of the world we evaluate the consequences of each potential course of action. We then decide to pursue one of these courses of action according to our view of the attractiveness of the consequences. For example, suppose we are concerned with finding the optimum tax to impose on confectionery and that we know that the elasticity of supply is infinite; then the question turns on the elasticity of demand. With the traditional approach we would either estimate the elasticity of demand or examine certain hypotheses about the elasticity. Let us suppose, for simplicity, that the elasticity of demand is *either* unity *or* 0.5. We might then set up our experiment to discover which hypothesis has the highest likelihood—using either Bayesian methods or the traditional methods of hypothesis testing. At this stage the statistician's job *per se* is completed and the decision-maker takes over.

With decision theory, however, the statistical problem is extended to consider the costs of making various decisions if certain hypotheses hold. Again let us simplify and assume that there are only two possible courses of action—to tax at 10 percent or not to tax at all. Then we can characterize the four outcomes by the following costs:

Elasticity

	1	0.5
Tax	$10 million	0
No tax	0	$5 million

Now if the main purpose of the tax is to raise revenue, it is clear that taxing confectionery when the elasticity is unity involves expense and no tax revenue—so we have supposed that the cost is $10 million which has been entered in the appropriate box of the table of outcomes. If, on the other hand, we impose a tax and the elasticity is only 0.5, we have taxed 'correctly' and we reckon the cost at zero. Similarly, if we do not tax when we should not, the cost can be taken as zero. If we miss an opportunity for taxing, i.e. no tax when the elasticity is 0.5, we incur a cost of $5 million.

Now let us suppose that we have *already carried out the survey* and found that the chance of unit elasticity is 0.2 and the likelihood of 0.5 elasticity is 0.8. Then we can find the expected costs of adopting the tax as

$$[(\$10 \text{ million}) \times 0.2] + [(\$0 \text{ million}) \times 0.8] = \$2 \text{ million}.$$

This is simply the sum of the outcome multiplied by the likelihood of that outcome. Similarly, the expected costs of not adopting the tax is

$$[(\$0 \text{ million}) \times 0.2] + [(\$5 \text{ million}) \times 0.8] = \$4 \text{ million}.$$

So we have

Strategy	*Expected costs*
Tax	$2 million
No tax	$4 million

and it is clearly the best strategy to tax confectionery.

This result is, however, critically dependent on the criteria we have adopted—that is, the minimizing of expected costs. There is nothing sacrosanct about this aim; and it is natural to consider alternative approaches. One such is to find the strategy which results in as low a value as possible for the *maximum* loss. In short the strategy is concerned with minimizing the maximum loss—or even shorter "minimax."

In our table we see that, if we tax, the maximum possible loss is \$10 million. If we do not tax, the maximum possible loss is \$5 million. Clearly the maximum loss is minimized if we then choose not to tax confectionery—and we are ensured that the maximum loss is \$5 million. This is a different solution from that developed for the "expected loss" criterion. The minimax strategy represents a "safety-first" attitude to decision-making. In this strategy the numerical value of the likelihoods, provided they exceed zero, do not play a part—whereas in the "expected loss" case they play a critical role.

There are, of course, many other criteria for decision-making. But there is no obvious rule for choosing between the criteria available. Each must be chosen according to the "utility function" of the decision-maker. An ultra-cautious individual may choose "minimax," a less cautious man the "expected loss" criterion. If it is possible to describe each situation by means of a utility function we can generalise the choice criterion to one of maximizing expected utility (or minimizing expected disutility). This will then enable us to take account of the fact that a large loss, for example, has enormous disutility, while a small loss has proportionately less disutility. For example, we may assume that the disutility function is simply the *square* of the loss so that we have the disutility table in "utils":

	Elasticity	
	1	0
Tax	100	0
No tax	0	25

Units: utils.

And now calculating expected disutility

for tax $(100 \times 0.2) + (0 \times 0.8) = 20$ utils;

for no tax $(0 \times 0.2) + (25 \times 0.8) = 20$ utils.

There is a tie! It does not matter whether we choose to tax confectionery or not—they have equal disutility. If the disutility function had been the *cube* of the loss, then we should have been better off *not* introducing a tax. For the rest of this discussion we shall adopt only one of the various criteria discussed above—we shall use the simple "expected loss" formulation.

Up to now we have supposed that the experiment (the survey) had already taken place and that we were concerned with making a decision on the basis of its results about the likelihoods. But frequently we find ourselves in the situation where *whether to do a survey or not is actually part of the decision-making procedure*. In other words we start our decision-making process *before* the sample; we ask whether it is worthwhile sampling or not. This is a question in addition to those about choosing an action strategy, i.e. whether to tax or not.

Obviously the question of whether to sample or not will depend on two things: first the cost of the sample itself and secondly our ideas about how the sample result is likely to affect our views about the likelihoods of the elasticities. To develop the latter point suppose that *if the elasticity is actually unity* there is a very high chance (say 0.9) that the experiment will produce the correct result (elasticity = 1.0), and only a low chance (0.1) that the experiment will produce the wrong result, i.e. falsely allege that the elasticity is 0.5.

Now let us suppose that, as before, we can, before we decide whether or not to sample, ascribe probabilities to the hypotheses elasticity = 1, and 0.5, and let us suppose that these are respectively 0.3 and 0.7. These figures measure our degree of belief in the validity of the hypothesis before the sample is carried out. (They correspond to the values of 0.8 and 0.2 which we assumed in the previous example, when we assumed that we had already sampled and incorporated the results in these two likelihoods.) We can now calculate the chances of *both* the elasticity being unity *and* the experiment producing evidence showing that it is unity (and we use the mnemonic "prob" for probability):

$$\text{prob}\left[\quad\text{elasticity}=1,\quad \begin{matrix}\text{sample}\\ \text{indicates unity}\end{matrix}\right]$$
$$=\text{prob}\left[\begin{matrix}\text{sample}\\ \text{indicates unity}\end{matrix}\,\middle|\,\begin{matrix}\text{elasticity}\\ =1\end{matrix}\right]\cdot\ \text{prob[elasticity}=1]$$

by the ordinary laws of conditional probability.[1]

---

1. Prob [event x | event y] is the probability that event x occurs *given that event y occurs:* it is a conditional probability. On the other hand, prob [event x, event y] is the probability that *both* event x and event y occur. Clearly, prob [event x, event y] = prob [event x | event y] · prob [event y] · [*Editor.*]

Numerically

$$\text{prob}\left[\text{elasticity}=1, \begin{array}{l}\text{sample}\\\text{indicates unity}\end{array}\right]=0.9\times0.3$$
$$=0.27.$$

Similarly

$$\text{prob}\left[\text{elasticity}=1, \begin{array}{l}\text{sample}\\\text{indicates }0.5\end{array}\right]=0.1\times0.3$$
$$=0.03$$

—this shows the likelihood that *both* the elasticity is unity *and* the sample evidence indicated that it is (wrongly) 0.5.

We have dealt with the case when the elasticity is unity; now we examine the case when the elasticity is 0.5. Suppose now that in fact the elasticity were 0.5. Then let us assume that the likelihood of the sample survey pointing to the correct result (i.e. elasticity $=0.5$) is 0.6, and the likelihood of it indicating the wrong result (unity) is 0.4. One can then construct the chances of the outcomes:

$$\text{prob}\left[\text{elasticity}=0.5, \begin{array}{l}\text{sample indicates}\\\text{elasticity}=0.5\end{array}\right]$$

$$=\text{prob}\left[\begin{array}{l}\text{sample indicates}\\\text{elasticity}=0.5\end{array}\middle|\text{elasticity}=0.5\right]\cdot\text{prob}\left[\text{elasticity}=0.5\right]$$

$$=0.6\times0.7=0.42.$$

Similarly

$$\text{prob}\left[\text{elasticity}=0.5, \begin{array}{l}\text{sample indicates}\\\text{elasticity}=1\end{array}\right]$$

$$=\text{prob}\left[\begin{array}{l}\text{sample indicates}\\\text{elasticity}=1\end{array}\middle|\text{elasticity}=0.5\right]\cdot\text{prob}\left[\text{elasticity}=0.5\right]$$

$$=0.4\times0.7=0.28.$$

These chances give us a measure of how the sample is likely to influence our views of the elasticity. We can portray them in a table which gives us the chances of outcomes when it is *assumed that we have decided to sample*. Notice that the sum of the joint chances over the sample outcomes gives us the prior probabilities

TABLE 1

Joint Chance of Sample Outcome and Actual Elasticity

		Actual elasticity:		Sum Prior probability of sample outcomes
		0.5	1.0	
Sample indicates elasticity to be	0.5	0.42	0.03	0.45
	1.0	0.28	0.27	0.55
Sum	Prior probability of actual elasticity	0.70	0.30	1.00

of the elasticities, 0.7 and 0.3. The sum horizontally gives the prior probabilities of the sample outcomes.

Now we can specify the decisions open to us and the costs associated with each eventuality. Let us assume that the survey costs \$2 million. The costs of the various outcomes can be tabulated as follows:

Costs in \$ million

Strategy	Elasticity	
	0.5	1.0
Sample and tax	2	12
Sample and no tax	7	2
No sample and tax	0	10
No sample and no tax	5	0

We have simply incorporated the cost of the sample in this Table. Thus when we sample and tax and the elasticity is actually unity we incur the total cost of \$12 million, of which \$2 million was spent on the sample.

We might set out the process of decision-making in the form of a "tree." We begin on the left with the problem whether or not to sample—and there are two branches, the upper one representing no sample and the bottom one representing the decision to sample. The bottom branch is then split into two according to the results of the sample—the upper one indicating the sample outcome favorable to the elasticity being 0.5, and the lower one favorable to the elasticity being 1.0. To each of these outcomes of the sample we can attach the prior probabilities (given that the sample has been carried out) indicated in the last column of Table 1—0.45 for the elasticity $=0.5$, and 0.55 for the elasticity $=1.0$. We then continue our tree with the *action* branch—to tax or not to tax. The two sample branches, as well as the upper "do not-sample" branch, are each split into two, so that we have six possible positions at the end of the action stage. Note that there are no probabilities attached to the action stage—we choose one course or another, just as we choose whether or not to sample. The last stage is the actual *realization* of the elasticity, i.e. whether it is 0.5 or 1.0. The costs of each of the outcomes, as described in the table above, is now attached to each of the final branch-ends. (Note that we have assumed that the outcome of the sample makes no difference to the branch-end costs.)

The problem is now tackled in reverse. We start at the branch-ends and work backwards to the root of the tree. Consider, for example, the topmost action branch—(do not sample)→(tax). Now we know that two possibilities arise—the elasticity may be 0.5 with prior probability 0.7 and the elasticity may be 1.0 with prior probability 0.3. So we can find the expected costs as

$$(\$0 \text{ million}) \times 0.7 + (\$10 \text{ million}) \times 0.3 = \$3 \text{ million.}$$

Now consider the "no tax" strategy, the second action branch, and we calculate expected costs as

$$(\$5 \text{ million}) \times 0.7 + (\$0 \text{ million}) \times 0.3 = \$3.5 \text{ million.}$$

We insert these values on the diagram at the appropriate junctions and encircle them. Clearly this calculation makes the no-tax strategy (when we have already decided *not* to sample) redundant—the expected costs of taxing are $0.5 *less*. Thus, effectively, the expected costs of not sampling—and then following the best policy of taxing—are $3 million, so enter that value, duly encircled at the junction at the beginning of the action branch.

More difficulties are involved with the sampling branches. Again let us start at the top branch-end—the process of: (sample) —(outcome favorable to elasticity $=0.5$—(tax)—(elasticity $=0.5$). Working backwards from the branch-ends we see that the final process is the probabilistic realization that the elasticity is either

ACTION	PROBABILITY	ACTION	PROBABILITY	COSTS
To sample or not to sample	Outcome of sample	To tax or not to tax	Realized elasticity	

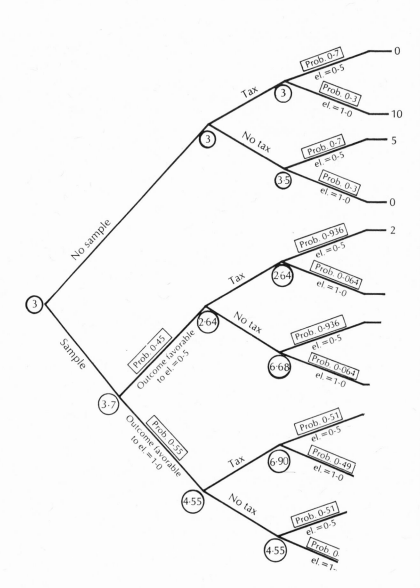

0.5 (1st branch) or 1.0 (2nd branch), each of which has associated costs \$2 million and \$12 million. These probabilities are conditional upon the fact that we (i) chose to sample; (ii) observed an outcome of the sample favorable to elasticity $= 0.5$; (iii) chose to tax. On (ii) looking back to Table 1 we can see that the prior probability of the sample indicating an elasticity of 0.5 is given as 0.45. (And if we get a sample which indicates this elasticity we would choose to tax.) So we can write

$$\text{prob}\left[\text{ elasticity} = 0.5 \left| \begin{array}{l} \text{(i) sample} \\ \text{(ii) outcome of sample} \\ \text{\quad favorable to } 0.5 \end{array} \right.\right]$$

$$= \text{prob}\left[\text{ elasticity} = 0.5 \left| \begin{array}{l} \text{outcome of} \\ \text{sample favorable} \\ \text{to } 0.5 \end{array} \right.\right],$$

since (i) sampling is already implied in (ii) the particular sample outcome favorable to 0.5. So we can construct:

$$\text{prob}\left[\text{ elasticity} = 0.5 \left| \begin{array}{l} \text{outcome of} \\ \text{sample favorable} \\ \text{to } 0.5 \end{array} \right.\right]$$

$$= \frac{\text{prob}\left[\text{ elasticity} = 0.5, \begin{array}{l} \text{outcome of} \\ \text{sample favorable} \\ \text{to elasticity} = 0.5 \end{array} \right]}{\text{prob}\left[\begin{array}{l} \text{outcome of} \\ \text{sample favorable} \\ \text{to elasticity} = 0.5 \end{array}\right]},$$

by the ordinary rules of conditional probability. Returning to Table 1 we see that this is

$$\text{prob}\left[\text{ elasticity} = 0.5 \left| \begin{array}{l} \text{outcome of sample} \\ \text{favorable to elasticity} = 0.5 \end{array} \right.\right] = \frac{0.42}{0.45}$$

$$= 0.936,$$

and

$$\text{prob}\left[\text{ elasticity} = 1.0 \left| \begin{array}{l} \text{outcome of sample} \\ \text{favorable to elasticity} = 0.5 \end{array} \right.\right] = \frac{0.03}{0.45}$$

$$= 0.064.$$

One can now calculate the expected costs of the strategy of sampling and taxing if the outcome is favorable to 0.5. We have, as expected, costs

$$(\$2 \text{ million}) \times 0.936 + (\$12 \text{ million}) \times 0.064 = \$2.64 \text{ million},$$

which we enter, duly encircled, at the appropriate junction. Secondly let us examine the no-tax branch of the "outcome-favorable-to-0.5" case. This, of course, should be the same as the case considered immediately above. Only the decision tax or no tax differs.

Now consider the other main branch of the sample result where the evidence favors an elasticity of 1.0. Taking the "tax" branch first, we calculate the probability of an elasticity of 0.5 emerging, given that the sample outcome favored 1.0.

$$\text{prob}\left[\text{elasticity}=0.5 \,\middle|\, \begin{array}{l}\text{outcome of sample}\\\text{is favorable to 1.0}\end{array}\right]$$

$$= \frac{\text{prob}\left[\text{elasticity}=0.5, \begin{array}{l}\text{outcome of sample is}\\\text{favorable to 1.0}\end{array}\right]}{\text{prob}\left[\begin{array}{l}\text{outcome of sample is}\\\text{favorable to 1.0}\end{array}\right]},$$

which from Table 1 is

$$\frac{0.28}{0.55} = 0.51.$$

The probability of the other branch where elasticity is unity is then $1 - 0.51 = 0.49$. These two probabilities are repeated for the last "no tax" branches. To find the expected costs at this last stage we repeat the operation—for example, for the last two branches

$$\{(7 \text{ million}) \text{ with prob} = 0.51\} + \{(\$2 \text{ million}) \text{ with prob} =$$
$$0.49\} = 3.57 + 0.98 = \$4.55 \text{ million}$$

which we enter in a circle at the junction.

In the action of choosing to tax or not we clearly wish to consider only those which have the lowest cost. Thus if we find ourselves at the point of having sampled and found that the evidence favored the elasticity of 0.5 we should clearly tax, since the expected cost $2.64 million would be lower than not taxing. We enter then $2.64 million at the junction of sample outcome and tax. Similarly if the sample outcome were favorable to elasticity = 1.0, then the choice is clearly "no tax" with an expected cost of $4.55 million.

Lastly we see whether it is worth while sampling. From the sample branch there are two outcomes:

(i) an expected cost of $2.64 million with an associated probability of 0.45;

(ii) an expected cost of $4.55 million with an associated probability of 0.55.

We then form the expected costs of sampling as

($2.64 million) × 0.45 + ($4.55 million) × 0.55 = $3.7 million.

Now it is clearly not efficient to sample the population since the expected costs of sampling are $3.7 million whereas, in the no-sample branch the expected costs are only $3 million. The optimum policy, therefore, is *not* to sample, and to introduce the tax. This completes the analysis of the decision-making process.

One of the results of this example is that it is not worth while to sample. We can get a more direct measure of why this is the case. The sample, we assumed, costs us $2 million, and if we sampled the minimum costs, including the sample costs, are $3.7 million, i.e.

Sample costs	$2 million
Other expected costs	$1.7 million
Total	$3.7 million

To be worth while the sample would have to cost less than $1.3 million; this would give a total cost less than $3 million—so it would be then preferable to sample before making the decision. As it stands, however, the sample information is worth less than it costs to acquire it.

We must now touch on some of the problems of the decision-theory approach. One which will certainly have occurred to the reader is that of attributing costs to each possible outcome. Often one just cannot formulate what the costs are likely to be. It is, however, a compelling argument that one always in fact behaves *as if* there were costs attributable to every outcome. Surely it is a good discipline to have to formulate them explicitly. In practice one often uses useful shortcuts; one commonly used rule is to use the square of the deviation of the estimate of the unknown parameter from its true value as the "loss function." Thus in our example the relative 'loss' would be measured by the square of the estimated elasticity from its true value, e.g.

Loss when elasticity $= 1.0$ and we judge it to be $0.5 = (0.5 - 1.0)^2$

$$= 0.25.$$

When the elasticity is estimated at its correct value, the loss is zero. This loss function is, of course, quite arbitrary, but statisticians have found in practice that this is a useful loss function to use in the absence of any detailed cost specification.

Another major difficulty lies in attaching values to the probabilities which need to be quantified in using decision functions. This involves specifying the prior probabilities of the elasticities assuming certain values, and the more complex task of stating the probabilities of the sample indicating the correct and incorrect elasticities. This is merely a way of evaluating what the sample is going to tell us—but it is not at all easy to put quantities on the probability of the sample results revealing the true facts.

Our example is extremely simple. We have not considered the enormous number of opportunities which occur in practical cases. For example, we might consider many samples of various size, complexity and cost. Formally it is easy to extend the theory to deal with multiple opportunities, but the problems of specifying the probabilities of the outcomes are not simplified! Even so, it is often useful to draw a decision tree, or at least certain of the main branches, to clear one's mind about the decision problem.

Heuristic Programs for Decision-making

JEROME D. WIEST

*Jerome D. Wiest is Professor of Management at
the University of Utah. This article appeared in
the* Harvard Business Review.

In an age of rapidly expanding technology and methodology,
the language of science has inevitably crept into the vocabulary
of the business world, with the result that the businessman has
ceased to be surprised (though he is still slightly perplexed, perhaps) by strange words like cybernetics and cryogenics. Sometimes (as with cybernetics) the words are new; sometimes they
are old with new or expanded meanings. An example of the
latter kind—one that is appearing with increasing frequency in
literature of interest to the thoughtful businessman—is *heuristic.*
Often it appears in such terms as *heuristic programming* or
heuristic problem-solving.

The word has an old and venerable meaning; as used recently,
however, it refers to a particular approach to decision-making
that is rapidly growing in application and importance. In recent

years, for example, heuristic programs have been applied with varying degrees of success to such problems as:

- Assembly line balancing.
- Facilities layout.
- Portfolio selection.
- Job shop scheduling.
- Electric motor design.
- Warehouse location.
- Inventory control.
- Resource allocation to large projects.

Although notable in their own right, these programs are just forerunners of what promises to be a significant new development in programmed decision-making—a development with which the informed businessman will want to keep abreast.

In order to better understand the significance of heuristic problem-solving, let us first examine the traditional meaning of the word *heuristic,* and then note the developments which have expanded this meaning and led to the current interest in heuristic problem-solving. Actually, the basic notion of heuristic problem-solving is not new, and a mere definition of the term is likely to leave most managers with the impression that the notion is trivial. But some rather sophisticated extensions of a basically simple concept, when combined with the computational power of a computer, enable the problem-solver to deal successfully with many problems that have not yielded previously to established problem-solving techniques. As we shall see, it is this combination of ideas and developments that gives significance to the concept.

MEANING AND SIGNIFICANCE

Anciently, *heuristic* (as a noun) was the name of a branch of study belonging to logic or philosophy, the aim of which was to investigate the methods of discovery and invention.[1] In present usage the meaning has expanded somewhat. A *heuristic* is itself an aid to discovery—especially the discovery of a solution to a problem. Going one step further, we may describe a heuristic

1. See György Polya, *How To Solve It* (Garden City, New York: Doubleday & Co., Inc., 1957).

as any device or procedure used to reduce problem-solving effort
—in short, a rule of thumb used to solve a particular problem.

Familiar Examples · We all use heuristics in our daily living,
drawing them from our knowledge and experience. To help us
face the countless problem-solving situations that confront us
each day, we devise simple rules of thumb that free us from the
task of solving the same or similar problems over and over again.
For example, consider the rule, "When the sky is cloudy, take an
umbrella to work." The problem at hand is how to defend one-
self against the potential discomforts of the weather. This simple
heuristic avoids more complicated problem-solving procedures
such as reading the weather report, calling the weather bureau,
analyzing barometer readings, and so forth. For many problems
of this kind, we lack the time or inclination to employ more
thorough problem-solving procedures. A simple (if not infalli-
ble) rule serves us best.

Businessmen frequently develop and follow various heuristics
in their own operations, perhaps without realizing that they are
employing a type of heuristic problem-solving. The following
examples should be familiar:

• *Stock market investing*—"Buy when prices move rapidly in one
direction with heavy volume." Or, "Sell when the good news is out."
• *Inventory control*—"When the stock gets down to four, that's the
time to buy some more." (Such heuristics are called "trigger-level"
rules.)
• *Accounting*—"Value at cost or market, whichever is lower." Or,
"First in, first out."
• *Job scheduling*—"First come, first served. Or, "Schedule the red-
flag jobs first."
• *Management*—"Handle only the exceptional problems; let subordinates decide routine matters."

I could cite other and more complex examples of heuristics, but
these should suffice to indicate their general nature. While
heuristics may not lead to the best solution in a particular case,
experience over time has proved their general usefulness in finding good solutions to recurring problems with a minimum of
effort.

All of the above heuristics could be improved by further

elaboration to take into account exceptional circumstances or additional information. Thus the inventory control rule might also take into consideration recent trends in usage rates and expectations of future demand for a stocked item. Instead of a simple rule of thumb, a combination of rules might be better. This leads us to the heuristic program.

HEURISTIC PROGRAMMING

In simplest terms a heuristic program is a collection or combination of heuristics used for solving a particular problem. If the program is sufficiently complex, it may require a computer for its solution. As a matter of fact, most of the interesting developments in heuristic programming that have appeared in the literature recently have relied on computers. Such heuristic programs take the form of a set of instructions for directing the computer to solve a problem—the way a manager might do it if he had enough time. To cover all contingencies likely to occur in a difficult problem setting, a group of heuristics may become quite complicated—too difficult to follow through at man's pace of problem-solving. Hence the need for a computer.

Why resort to heuristic programming in the first place? Why not use other techniques that mathematicians and operations researchers have devised in recent years? There seems to be no end to their bag of tools—many of them highly acclaimed and of proved usefulness, such as linear programming, waiting-line models, statistical decision theory, linear decision rules, and so on. There are essentially two answers to these questions.

Large Problems · Some problems—although they can be reduced to numbers and equations—are too large to solve by analytical techniques, even with the aid of a computer. Linear programming, for instance, has been widely used to solve many problems of resource allocation (transportation routing, machine scheduling, product mix, oil refinery operations, and so forth); but some problems are just too large for it—job shop scheduling, for instance. Conceptually, linear programming could lead to an optimum assignment of start times for the thousands of jobs to be scheduled in a large shop, given some criterion like "minimize idle machine time"; but the number of steps necessary to reach the optimum solution—though finite—is so large as to render the method useless. In this application, linear programming is computationally inefficient.

Heuristic programming, on the other hand, attempts to short-cut computations. It is not so concerned with finding the one best answer after a lengthy search as with rapidly reaching a satisfactory one. In other words, it is willing to trade a guaranteed optimum solution for a "good" one if it can do so with considerably less computational effort.

Ill-Structured · The other reason for employing heuristic programming is that some problems are "ill structured"—they cannot be expressed in mathematical terms. Judgment, intuition, creativity, and learning are important elements of the problem and its solution, and these variables are qualitative rather than numerical. Quantitative techniques are not available or are not suitable for solving such problems.

Heuristic means of dealing with ill-structured problems have been explored by a number of researchers in the field of "artificial intelligence." Their object has been to develop computer programs that imitate certain human problem-solving processes. Among their efforts have been programs which prove mathematical theorems, play chess, write music, and solve problems like the "cannibal and missionary" problem.

A business manager may ask: What relevance do chess-playing and theorem-proving programs have to solutions of ill-structured business problems? None of the programs of the foregoing type have a business orientation; but if the programs were successful, they would indeed have implicit relevance, for they deal with problem-solving situations in which judgment, intuition, and even creativity play an important part. If a computer could be "taught" to exercise these qualities in a game context, it might be programmed to display them when dealing with the ill-structured problems so ubiquitous in the manager's world.

Results to date, however, are mixed. While there are some programs that have demonstrated these human-like qualities to some degree, the problems with which they have dealt differ in complexity by several orders of magnitude from typical ill-structured managerial problems. It is not clear that a straightforward extension of these programming concepts plus an increase in computer size and speed is all that is needed to bridge the gap. We need to learn much more about the brain and cognitive processes before we can claim success in dealing with such problems mechanically. Accomplishments in artificial intelligence, while substantial, seem not to have kept pace with early successes and hopes, as the complexity of problems facing researchers has become more apparent. For example:

• Language translation programs, after early apparent gains, have experienced considerable difficulties and are far from being generally useful.

• Pattern-recognition programs, despite much excellent work, do not even approach the flexibility of human pattern-recognition processes. Automatic reading devices are able to handle only typed or handprinted material of great uniformity in type and layout. A person's tolerance for ambiguity and his ability to decipher various styles of type and handwriting seem even further beyond mechanical duplication than they did a few years ago when early successes led to high optimism.

• Even chess-playing programs are still poor novices at the game, despite some predictions in the late 1950's that a computer would be the world's champion chess player in 1967.

Nevertheless, these efforts are increasing our ability to understand and to deal with qualitative phenomena. It is reasonable to suppose that the boundary between what we consider structured and ill-structured problems—between problems which have yielded to programmed solutions and those which have not—will continue to change. Such developments are still in the future, however, and must await the researcher's exploration of human thinking and complex problem-solving processes. Whether these can be efficiently imitated or simulated by digital computers remains to be proved.

Thus we come back to the application of heuristic programming to problems which are too large (or not suitable) for solution by analytical means. It is this area that is of current interest to businessmen. An idea of the kinds of problems which have yielded—or conceivably might yield—to solution by heuristic techniques should indicate the range of their usefulness as well as their limitations.

WIDE-RANGING USES

Most business-oriented heuristic programs apply to what may be characterized as combinatorial problems because of the extremely large number of ways in which a series of decisions can be made. A problem may be likened to a maze consisting of a sequence of decision points; at each point a number of paths are available, but only one can be chosen. Thus, as illustrated schematically in the "tree diagram" shown in Exhibit 1, there are numerous combinations of paths which lead from the initial point to some terminal point.

Each node represents a decision point; lines represent various possible decisions that could be made, and lead either to another decision point or to a terminal node. The heavy line indicates a path, or series of decisions, leading to a particular solution to the problem. Thus each terminal node represents a possible solution —a plan of action.

One method of finding the optimum solution is to enumerate each possible path, evaluate the end result according to some criteria, and select the best path. Obviously, if the problem contains many decision points and various paths at each of these points, the number of possible combinations becomes enormous. For example, a series of ten distinct decisions, each of which could be made in five different ways, leads to almost ten million different solutions or combinations of decisions. (Since the decisions at each step are considered to differ from decisions at previous or subsequent steps, the number of branches at each decision point is raised to the power of the number of decision points. In this example, $5^{10} = 9,765,625$.)

Most of the combinatorial-type decisions to which heuristic programming has been applied are actually much larger than this. Even with the aid of a high-speed computer, enumeration is not a feasible solution method for large problems. Accordingly, the heuristic technique is to prune the tree—eliminate some branches from the start so a much smaller maze remains to be searched. This is illustrated in the "pruned" tree diagram in Part B of Exhibit 1.

The danger in pruning the tree, of course, is that a good branch may be cut off by mistake. A path that appears to be

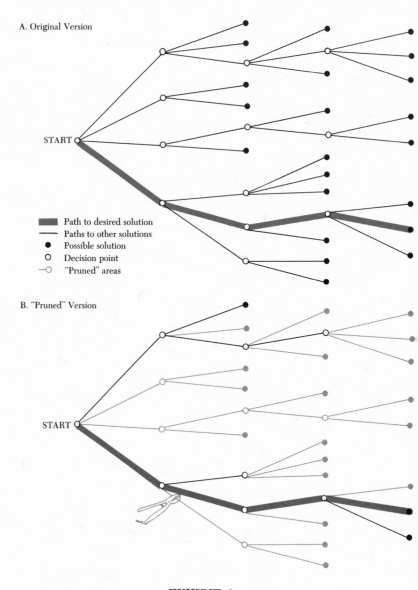

A. Original Version

START

Path to desired solution
Paths to other solutions
● Possible solution
○ Decision point
─○ "Pruned" areas

B. "Pruned" Version

START

EXHIBIT 1

REPRESENTATION OF A PROBLEM

of doubtful value may later lead to a desirable outcome. A given heuristic may eliminate that path—perhaps the one that leads to the optimum solution. However, as noted before, sacrifice of a guaranteed optimum solution is the price paid for the reduction in search effort that heuristics provide. (But, then, a guarantee is of little real value if the price of reaching the optimum solution is prohibitive.)

Now that we have considered rather abstractly the kinds of problems that may yield to heuristic approaches, let us next examine some particular cases of managerial decision-making for which heuristic programs have been written.

Portfolio Selection · In some instances, heuristic programs have been written to simulate the existing decision-making activities of an individual; in other cases, attempts have been made to go beyond what is presently feasible for humans. An example of the former is a heuristic approach to the investment of trust funds held by banks.[2] The program simulates the decision-making (in this case a particular trust investment officer) in his selection of a portfolio, based on information available to him at the time he makes a decision. In brief, the program operates as follows:

• A preference list of stocks is established and stored in the computer memory. It includes some eighty issues, categorized by industry and representing the working list of stocks from which the investment officer will make all his portfolio selections. The preference list, designed to cover various economic conditions and updated by the officer periodically, is taken as a given by the program.

• Various data associated with each of the companies represented in the list (such as price, growth rate, dividend rate, price-earnings ratio, expected earnings, and so forth) are also stored.

• From this list a portfolio is generated, based on rules of thumb (heuristics) which relate information about the client, the securities market, and the economy to the selection of particular stocks in the list. The heuristics were compiled from a study of past decisions of the trust officer and "protocols" or verbalizations of his decision processes.

• The program keeps a history (in memory) of its past decisions and their outcomes and modifies its future behavior by eliminating unsuccessful procedures. For instance, if a certain stock were more volatile than originally believed, the selling rate might be increased

2. See Geoffrey P. Clarkson and Allan H. Meltzer, "Portfolio Selection: A Heuristic Approach," *Journal of Finance*, December 1960, p. 465.

in a falling market. Thus the program "learns" from its previous experience—paralleling to some degree human learning processes.

Two things should be noted about this kind of program:

(1) It simulates the decisions of a *particular* investment officer. No attempt is made to determine if some other person in this position has superior heuristics. Thus the program is not prescriptive in nature; it is descriptive, and only in a narrow sense (i.e., it describes only one person rather than trust officers in general).

(2) The human activity described is sufficiently simple to be formalized. The portfolio selection rules followed by the trust officer are explicable to a large degree and can be set down in terms of unambiguous rules (and hence can be programmed for a computer). The determination and translation of these rules are not perfect, as the computer-produced portfolios have differed slightly from the trust officer's, but they are remarkably close.

Many business decision processes are of this type; that is, the decision rules may be clearly identified and formalized. In all such cases the process may be simulated by means of heuristic programming. We should note that, in some of these instances, a computer is not a necessary adjunct to the process. A human can follow the programming instructions and perform each step as required. If the heuristics are numerous and complicated, however, humans are much less efficient at the task than computers are.

Assembly Line Balancing · A production management problem that occurs frequently in industries where products are assembled on a conveyor line is balancing the line—assigning elemental assembly tasks to work stations situated along the line. In general, each work station is manned by a single operator. Ideally, the sum of task times at each station is the same as that at all other stations; the line is then said to be perfectly balanced. An out-of-balance line requires more operators than the ideal line, since operators are idle during part of each work cycle at some of the stations and the lost time has to be compensated for by additional work stations.

The assignment of elementary tasks to work stations is an example of the combinatorial type of problem which I described earlier. There are many ways of combining tasks—too many to enumerate for large, real-life problems. Several heuristic approaches have been suggested, however, which attempt to narrow in on some smaller set of "good" combinations.[3] Some of the heuristics employed are quite sophisticated and are not necessarily attempts to duplicate the procedures a human line balancer would go through. One technique, for example, capitalizes on the speed of a computer in order to rapidly generate many solutions on a trial-and-error basis—a process for which a human, at his plodding pace, would be grossly inefficient. The solutions are not completely random samples from the set of all possible combinations, however, but are biased (this is where the heuristics come into play) in favor of more promising combinations. In one application the program was able to find an optimum balance of 1,000 elemental tasks distributed to 200 work stations—all in three minutes of computer time.[4]

Job Shop Scheduling · The problem of job shop scheduling appears in many guises outside of the typical machine shop, but it is most familiar in that setting. It may be characterized as a continuous inflow of jobs, each of which requires one or more operations (perhaps in a given sequence) to be performed on one or more machines. The problem is to schedule the operations on the machines in such a way as to minimize idle machine time or total time of jobs in the system, or to meet some other criterion. A similar problem exists in many office operations, where letters or other paperwork (jobs) are assigned to secretaries or clerks or other "processors." Engineering departments, drafting rooms, mail-order operations, printing shops, computer centers, and

3. See Fred M. Tonge, *A Heuristic Program for Assembly Line Balancing* (Englewood Cliffs, New Jersey: Prentice-Hall, Inc., 1961); Maurice Kilbridge and Leon Wester, "A Heuristic Method of Assembly Line Balancing," *Journal of Industrial Engineering*, July–August 1961, p. 292; W. B. Helgeson and D. P. Birnie, "Assembly Line Balancing Using the Ranked Positional Weight Technique," *Journal of Industrial Engineering*, November–December 1961, p. 394; and Albert Arcus, *An Analysis of a Computer Method of Sequencing Assembly Line Operations* (unpublished doctoral dissertation, University of California, Berkeley, September 1963).
4. See Albert Arcus, op. cit.

surgery wards—to name just a few examples—all have scheduling problems characteristic of job shop operations.

When the number of operations to be completed is large, the number of possible solutions (different schedules, in this case) is enormous. Before the advent of the computer, job-shop scheduling for large operations had to be decentralized. Due dates for jobs were established by the production control office (with plenty of slack time allowed), but it was the foreman—or workers—who decided on the start time of each job operation. High in-process inventories, delays in schedules, and broken promises to customers were all common management problems.

Heuristic techniques, aided by the use of a computer, permit greater centralization of job-shop scheduling, and thus enable the manager of the operation to exercise more effective control. At the heart of heuristic scheduling programs are rules for deciding which jobs will be scheduled on particular machines and when. Each machine may be viewed as a service facility with a waiting line of jobs to be serviced. The simplest heuristic for determining the order in which the waiting jobs will be taken is "first come, first served," but many others are possible—for instance, "schedule first the job which can be finished first," and "schedule the longest jobs first." Scheduling programs use these rules, or some combination of them, modified as necessary to take into account sequencing constraints, machine capabilities, special priority jobs, and so forth—all integrated in a program which specifies unambiguously the order in which jobs are to be processed and on what facilities.[5]

At least one large-scale installation of a heuristic-based job shop scheduling program has been reported:

The shop, a gear producer with 1,000 machine tools handling up to 2,000 orders at any one time, found that the computerized scheduling program increased production 5 percent to 10 percent, decreased lead time up to three months, and boosted on-time deliveries by 30 percent. Top managers feel that they are finally "in control" of the operations of the plant; the project schedule enables them to predict order delivery dates more confidently, as well as plan purchases of new equipment. Foremen like the program because it frees them from the

5. William S. Gere, Jr., "A Heuristic Approach to Job Shop Scheduling" (unpublished doctoral dissertation, Carnegie Institute of Technology, 1962).

responsibility of scheduling jobs (and the frequent negotiation of schedule changes with other foremen) and allows them to devote more time to quality control and supervision of employees.[6]

Facilities Location · In the same context as the job shop scheduling problem is the facilities location problem. When the nature of products and demand patterns suggests a process-controlled (or functional) layout, then the relative location of various machine groups or types of equipment is an important problem for management to solve. That arrangement which leads to the lowest costs for moving all orders through the shop is generally regarded as the best solution (assuming, of course, that other constraints, such as necessary adjacent locations of related facilities, can be observed).

Again, the problem is a large combinatorial one. Just twelve departments can be arranged in over a million non-redundant patterns of relative location. The problem may be conceptualized analytically, but there is no way to promise the best possible solution. However, a heuristic program has been written for successively exchanging pairs of departments in a given location pattern until no further reductions in transportation costs can be obtained.[7] An optimum pattern is not assured, but the solutions reached have been better than those obtained by other techniques.

Inventory Control · Numerous mathematical techniques for minimizing costs in an inventory system are available for use by the inventory manager. The techniques start with the simple economic lot-size formulas and proceed through highly sophisticated models. Many companies—especially those whose inventory stock includes thousands of different items—find it difficult to fit the models to their own requirements and conditions. Assumptions of the model are not met in practice, demand patterns are unpredictable, cost data are unavailable, or the sheer size of the problem frustrates attempts at analytical solutions.

6. See "Computer Planning Unsnarls the Job Shop," *Business Week,* April 2, 1966, p. 60.

7. See, for example, Elwood S. Buffa, Gordon C. Armour, and Thomas E. Vollmann, "Allocating Facilities With CRAFT," *Harvard Business Review,* March–April 1964, p. 136.

As a result, heuristic inventory rules are widely used by business managers, whether in the form of trigger-level rules or more complex procedures. Computerized systems containing both analytical and heuristic elements are used by a number of companies for purposes of inventory control.[8] The problem, especially when considered in the larger context of an operational system, is exceedingly complex, somewhat ill structured, and a likely candidate for solution by heuristic programming techniques. Since inventory decisions have implications for marketing and finance functions as well as for production, top managers in these areas should be aware of, and have some part in establishing, the heuristics which underlie the inventory control system.

Warehouse Sites · Business or government operations which require large-scale distribution networks face the problem of determining the number and location of regional warehouses. The geographical pattern of locations which just matches the expense of establishing and operating warehouses with the resulting savings in transportation costs and incremental profits from more rapid delivery is most profitable. The number of possible patterns and the complexity of the problem (as exemplified by transportation rate structures) rule out the feasibility of mathematical solutions. As a result, most distribution systems have grown, not toward some optimal pattern, but one warehouse at a time, each located at what appears to be the best site at the particular moment. This is clearly not the way to maximize profits in the long run.

Various heuristic approaches to the problem have been suggested.[9] One of these selects from all possible sites the relatively few that appear promising, calculates the net savings that would result from locating a warehouse at each of these sites, adds warehouses one at a time to the best of these until no

8. For several examples, see Joseph Buchan and Ernest Koenigsberg, *Scientific Inventory Management* (Englewood Cliffs, New Jersey: Prentice-Hall, Inc., 1963).

9. See Alfred A. Kuehn and Michael J. Hamburger, "A Heuristic Program for Locating Warehouses," *Management Science*, July 1963, p. 643; and Leon Cooper, "Location-Allocation Problems," *Operations Research*, May–June 1963, p. 331.

further savings result, and then "bumps and shifts" warehouses in the selected sites until no further improvement is apparent. Kuehn and Hamburger report that the program can handle several hundred sites and several thousand shipment destinations. Results from trials on small-scale problems have been equal to or better than those from alternative methods available.

Engineering Design · Heuristic programs have also been reported which can solve certain engineering design problems that lend themselves to formal structuring. The design of electric motors is a case in point. Because of the great range of customer specifications for voltage, power, size, metallurgical properties, environmental conditions, and so forth, large electrical equipment manufacturers will build hundreds of motors and transformers whose designs differ from basic types in varying degrees. Heuristic programs, with the help of a computer, relieve engineers of the rather tedious task of designing a motor for each new customer order that differs from a standard design.

Large-Project Scheduling · Large projects, such as the construction of buildings and plants, missile development programs, large-scale maintenance projects, and so forth, present scheduling problems similar to those for job shop scheduling except that the activities (jobs) which comprise a large project have more complex sequencing relationships and the project has an end point. The project manager must be able to schedule, with some degree of precision, the start and completion dates for all of the major activities. Also, he must have a workable means of measuring ongoing progress for purposes of control and for redirecting resources to activities which are behind schedule.

Such planning and scheduling techniques as PERT and CPM have been widely used by large-project managers in recent years, but in their conventional form they fail to consider the constraints imposed on activity scheduling when resources are limited. The usual problem facing project managers is allocating scarce resources among the various activities to be scheduled in such a way as to keep the project on schedule and to minimize costs of resources used. The number of possible schedules for activity start and completion times and for resource use, given sequencing relationships, estimated durations, and limited resources, is enormously large for all but the smallest projects. No manager even with the aid of a computer, could enumerate them all and find the best one.

Because of the great interest in large-project management during recent years much research effort has been devoted to the problem of resource scheduling; and most of the suggested scheduling techniques are based on heuristic programming. The programs in general are quite flexible. They enable the manager to ask questions such as:

• What if we double the number of engineers assigned to propulsion system design in the next six months? '
• What if we lease five additional earth-movers during the summer season?
• What if the funding of the new by-pass highway system is decreased 10 percent beginning January?
• How would these changes in resource availabilities affect the progress and anticipated finish date of the project?

Heuristic programs can be used to generate project schedules under varying conditions, simulating for the manager the anticipated effects of proposed resource changes or other scheduling constraints.

As a further illustration of heuristic programming and how heuristics are combined to make decisions, an example of a project scheduling program is developed in the Appendix. Some of the basic scheduling heuristics and their interrelationships are displayed in a simplified flow diagram.

CURRENT USEFULNESS

The foregoing illustrations of heuristic programs, while not exhaustive, indicate the range of current applications and suggest in part the kinds of problems that might be solved by this technique. There remains the practical question: Has heuristic problem-solving developed to the point where it is really useful for the businessman today?

The question cannot be given an unqualified answer because the evidence is mixed and subject to at least some controversy. Several heuristic programs have proved to be feasible and efficient, and they are in use today. For instance, the program for designing electric motors was first reported to be in use eight years ago and presumably is still functional. And at least one machine shop is scheduling job operations by an extensive heuristic program, apparently with considerable success. Several other companies are in the process of installing similar systems. Large-project scheduling programs also have been used by many firms. One proprietary program has been available for over three years; other programs have been or are in the process of being developed by several companies to match their own particular requirements. Line-balancing programs have been tested by a number of companies, notably those in the automobile industry, with results as yet unpublished. Likewise, no report has been made of a large-scale application of a warehouse location program. The process-layout program has been utilized in a variety of firms—from factories to movie studios to engineering departments—with reported success.

The problem of evaluating heuristic programs is twofold. First, much of the work in the field has been done by researchers who are primarily concerned with conceptualizing a problem and its heuristic solution. Testing a model in the "real world" and subjecting it to the mundane problems (often unanticipated by the researcher) that inevitably complicate matters require time and often different talents. Thus real-world applications and evaluation quite naturally lag behind research developments.

Secondly, there is the problem of standards. How does a manager determine what is a "good" heuristic program? In most instances, results cannot be compared to an optimal solution because the latter is generally not available. The minimum-length schedule for a large project with limited resources, for example, is frequently incalculable. The relevant and, in most cases, the only comparison that can be made is with results from traditional techniques. A manager should examine the output of a heuristic program with the following four questions in mind:

• Does it produce better results than our present methods do?
• Are there incremental savings in resources?
• Are computational effort and expense reduced without sacrificing the quality of work?
• Is the information produced more timely, and are decisions reached earlier, than by present methods?

In summary, a few existing programs have been tried and have passed the above test; some have not been tried at all; and the evidence on others has not come in yet. We should note that in all cases heuristic programs which have been applied to problems of business decision-making are *special-purpose* programs; they have been designed specifically to solve a particular problem. None of them are general problem solvers in the sense that the procedures used adapt to the particular tasks given to them.

EFFECT ON MANAGEMENT

Last rites have been pronounced more than once for the middle manager since the advent of the computer, while his health and resilience in an age of change have been praised by others. Most of the disagreement is based on differences of opinion about the proportion of his job that is well structured (i.e., has clear-cut objectives and straightforward decision procedures) and that which is ill structured (i.e., concerns vaguely defined problems) and thus not as susceptible to programming.

It is not my purpose here to enter into that debate, except to note that heuristic methods of decision-making have made some inroads into the ill-structured problems or at least have changed our minds about what should be considered ill structured. In any event it is apparent that the role of the middle manager is changing as methods are found of programming more and more problem-solving activities. In view of the total scope of his activities, however, the inroads appear relatively minor.

What seems relevant is not how much of his job will be taken away, but how the remaining activities will change. Heuristic as well as analytic techniques of decision-making yield computer outputs which in most cases have to be combined and tempered with managerial judgment and acumen. The computer is a partner of, rather than replacement for, the manager. Instead of trying to replace the human decision maker *in toto,* we should concentrate on discovering which elements of a manager's task are best handled by him and which by the computer. As Hubert L. Dreyfus suggests:

> We must couple [the computer's] capacity for fast and accurate calculation with the [human's] short-cut processing made possible by the fringes of consciousness and ambiguity tolerance. . . . In problem solving once the problem is structured and planned, a machine could take over to work out the details (as in the case of machine shop allocation or investment banking). A mechanical dictionary would be useful in translation. In pattern recognition, machines are able to recognize certain complex patterns that the natural prominences in our experience force us to exclude.[10]

In short, the combination of man and computer can lead to accomplishments that neither is capable of alone.

Beyond the technological capabilities of computers and heuristic programs is the question of economics. Sunlight is free, and we know how to convert it into electricity; but it has not replaced coal as a source of energy for generating power. Likewise, computer technology has outpaced its economic feasibility in some applications. Humans are still less expensive decision-makers than computers are for many problems that both are capable of solving. We should add, however, that computers are decreasing in cost (per computation) while humans are increasing in cost. The break-even point is changing continually.

CONCLUSION

Surveying the field of heuristic programming, we may summarize progress to date by noting that several programs have proved the usefulness of a heuristic approach to decision-making when applied to certain problems that we have characterized as large combinatorial types. Some programs are in actual operation; others are being developed. Additionally, researchers are extending the boundaries of programmable decision-making into the area of ill-structured problems. They are showing that some decision processes can be formalized and described in terms of heuristic decision rules. All heuristic programs that have been applied to business problems, I again emphasize, have been

10. "Alchemy and Artificial Intelligence," The RAND Corporation, Vol. P–3244, December 1965, p. 82.

special-purpose programs, tailored to a specific and narrowly defined problem.

Some early successes in heuristic programs—computer programs that played chess, recognized patterns, and proved mathematical theorems—led many competent researchers to conclude that human decision-making involving judgment, intuition, and creativity could be simulated by a computer and that decision-making by mechanical means was no longer confined to well-structured problems. The view has been well stated by Herbert A. Simon and Allen Newell:

"With recent developments in our understanding of heuristic processes and their simulation by digital computers, the way is open to deal scientifically with ill-structured problems—to make the computer co-extensive with the human mind." [11]

Though widely supported, this view has been subjected to some recent debate. Skeptics have noted that recent progress in artificial intelligence has failed to match the rate of early successes, as the complexities of problems facing researchers have become apparent. Dreyfus recently observed:

There is . . . evidence that human and mechanical information processing proceed in entirely different ways. At best, research in artificial intelligence can write programs which allow the digital computer to *approximate,* by means of discrete [stepwise] operations, the results which human beings achieve [by much more efficient techniques]. . . .[12]

Because of this, Dreyfus sees a limit to how far we can go in cognitive simulation using the present heuristic approach, even with newer and faster machines, better programming languages, and more clever heuristics.

A new appreciation for the human being as a problem-solver has resulted. It now appears that radical advances in programmed solution procedures for most ill-structured management problems are not just around the corner, as supposed, or even yet on the horizon, and that advancements will be made more slowly than earlier supposed. Meanwhile, however, there

11. "Heuristic Problem Solving: The Next Advance in Operations Research," *Operations Research,* January–February 1958, p. 9.

12. Dreyfus, op. cit., p. 63.

are many opportunities for applying heuristic problem-solving techniques. They can be used on well-structured but difficult-to-solve problems and also on problems which, though apparently not well structured, may yield to formalization with careful analysis and some degree of ingenuity. Business managers can profitably search for opportunities of these kinds.

APPENDIX. SCHEDULING PROJECTS

A simplified version of a heuristic program for scheduling a large project is shown in the flow diagram in Figure A. The program is based essentially on three heuristics:

(1) Allocate resources serially in time. That is, start on the first day and schedule all jobs possible, then do the same for the second day, and so on.
(2) When several jobs compete for the same resources, give preference to the jobs with the least slack.
(3) Reschedule non-critical jobs, if possible, in order to free resources for scheduling critical (non-slack) jobs.

To illustrate how these heuristics operate in the program, let us apply them to one part of the main project. This smaller project consists of ten jobs, each of which requires a certain amount of time and a given number of men (crew). For simplicity, let us assume that all the men are interchangeable. In practical situations, however, the various jobs may require men of different skills as well as other resources such as machines, materials, money, and so forth.

For technological reasons, some jobs must be completed before others can begin. Thus in the project list in Figure B, Job 9 cannot begin until Jobs 2 and 6 have been completed. To simplify this exposition, I have chosen a crew size for each job which is identical to its job number. Thus Job 1 requires one man, Job 5 requires five men, and so forth.

The small project is best visualized as a network diagram in which each job appears as an arrow, and the connections of arrows indicate the predecessor relationships. The arrow for Job 9, for example, is directly preceded by the arrows for Jobs 2 and 6. (See Figure C.) If we draw the diagram on a horizontal time scale in such a way that a job arrow's placement and

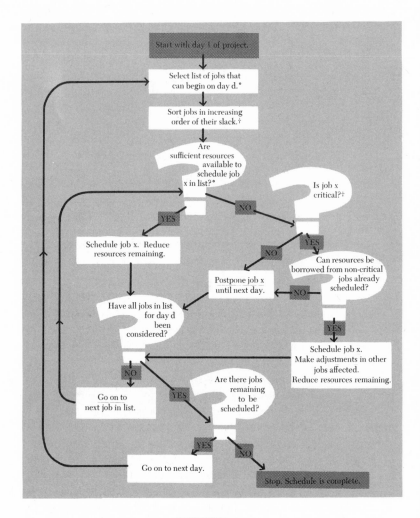

FIGURE A

° Day d is day under consideration; Job x is job under consideration.
† *Slack* is a measure of the number of days a job may be delayed without
delaying the project as a whole. A job is *critical* if it has no slack.

FIGURE B

Job number	Predecessor jobs	Length (days)	Crew size
1	7	3	1
2	4	2	2
3	7	2	3
4	7	3	4
5	7	2	5
6	3	3	6
7	(none)	1	7
8	1	2	8
9	2,6	1	9
10	9,5	3	10

horizontal length indicate the period during which the job is active, then we can illustrate both the project and its time schedule. Figure C shows a schedule for our project in which all jobs have been started as early as their predecessors will

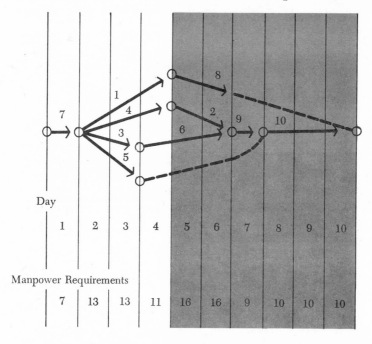

FIGURE C

allow. (Dashed lines indicate ordering relationships and are necessary when a job's successors do not begin immediately following its completion.) The number above each arrow identifies the job and its crew size. Job 4, for example, requires four men on each of Days 2, 3, and 4. Thus we can calculate daily manpower requirements for the schedule by summarizing vertically the crew sizes of all jobs active on a given day. In the schedule graph in Figure C, manpower requirements start at seven on Day 1, climb to thirteen on Days 2 and 3, and so on.

Suppose, however, that only ten men are available to assign to the project on any one day. How should the project be scheduled in order not to exceed this constraint but still to complete it as soon as possible? One way to find the shortest feasible schedule would be to enumerate all possible schedules. For example, on the first day there is just one possible choice of jobs (Job 7). On the second day, with four jobs available, there are thirteen feasible combinations: four consisting of a single job, six consisting of pairs of jobs, and three consisting of triples of jobs. (The remaining combinations exceed the manpower limit of ten.) Each of these thirteen choices represents a branch on a tree diagram, and multiple choices fan out from each of these on succeeding days. The tree of all possible schedules is very large, even for this small project.

DAY-TO DAY DECISIONS

The heuristic program diagrammed in Figure C trims the tree drastically; it selects just one branch at each decision point (one combination of jobs each day), only occasionally retracing its steps to see if a better branch could be found. Scheduling day by day (as required by the first heuristic mentioned earlier), the program would make the following decisions.

Day 1 · Only one job (7) is available to start in this period, and there are sufficient men to schedule it.

Schedule Job 7 (slack = 0, as it is calculated relative to jobs on the critical path, which are defined to have no slack); three men remain.

Day 2 · Four jobs (1, 3, 4, and 5) can be started on Day 2, but there are not enough men to schedule them all. The second heuristic calls for scheduling the jobs with the least slack first.

Schedule Job 3 (slack = 0); seven men remain.
Schedule Job 4 (slack = 0); three men remain.

Jobs 1 and 5 both have four days slack; but since there are just 3 men unassigned, Job 5 must be delayed.

Schedule Job 1 (slack = 4); two men remain.
Postpone Job 5 (slack = 4).

Day 3 · We assume that jobs cannot be interrupted once started; partially completed jobs have first call on the available resources.

Continue Job 3 (slack = 0); seven men remain.
Continue Job 4 (slack = 0); three men remain.
Continue Job 1 (slack = 1); two men remain;

Since there are still not enough men for Job 5, it must be delayed again.

Postpone Job 5 (slack = 3).

At this point the schedule graph appears as shown in Figure D. Heavy lines indicate jobs already scheduled; light lines are projected schedules—which still must be checked for feasibility.

Note that Job 5, which has been postponed two days, now has only two days slack (possible slippage) remaining.

Day 4 ·

Continue Job 4 (slack = 0); six men remain.
Continue Job 1 (slack = 4); five men remain.

Job 6 has no slack and hence is critical, but only five men are still unassigned. The third heuristic is now brought into play: Are there non-critical jobs still active which could be postponed without delaying the project? Job 1 satisfies this requirement and hence is reassigned to begin later.

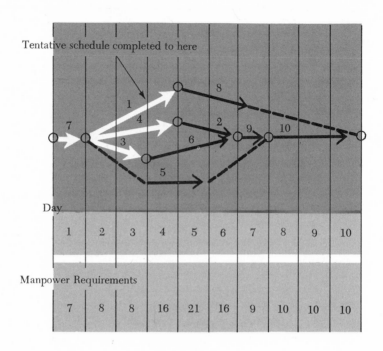

FIGURE D

Reschedule Job 1; six men remain.
Schedule Job 6 (slack = 0); zero men remain.
Postpone Job 5 (slack = 2).

The schedule graph at the end of Day 4 is shown in Figure E.

Day 5 ·

Continue Job 6 (slack = 0); four men remain.
Schedule Job 2 (slack = 0); two men remain.
Schedule Job 1 (slack = 1); one man remains.
Postpone Job 5 (slack = 1).

Day 6 ·

Continue Job 6 (slack = 0); four men remain.
Schedule Job 2 (slack = 0); two men remain.

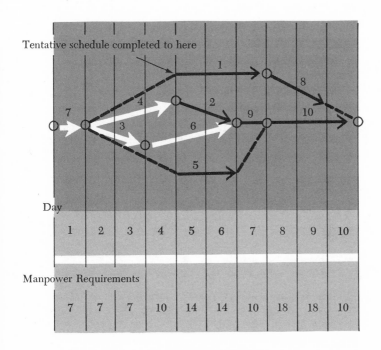

FIGURE E

Schedule Job 1 (slack = 1); one man remains.
Postpone Job 5 (slack = 0).

Job 5 has now become critical, as shown in Figure F. Note that the projected finish date has been delayed a day.

Day 7 ·

Continue Job 1 (slack = 2); nine men remain.
Schedule Job 5 (slack = 0); four men remain.
Postpone Job 9 (slack = 1).

Day 8 ·

Continue Job 5 (slack = 0); five men remain.
Postpone Job 9 (slack = 0); no non-critical jobs can be rescheduled).
Postpone Job 8 (slack = 2).

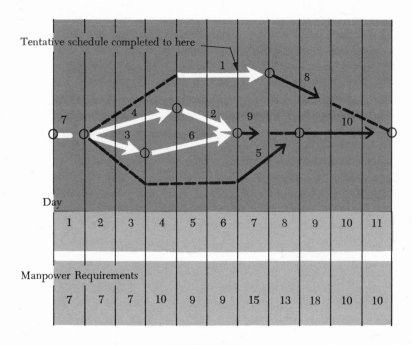

FIGURE F

At the end of Day 8, the schedule graph appears as shown in Figure G.

Remaining Period · The program decisions for the remaining six days are as follows:

Day 9—Schedule Job 9 (slack = 0); one man remains. Postpone Job 8 (slack = 2).
Day 10—Schedule Job 10 (slack = 0); no men remain. Postpone Job 8 (slack = 1).
Day 11—Continue Job 10 (slack = 0); no men remain. Postpone Job 8 (slack = 0).
Day 12—Continue Job 10 (slack = 1); no men remain. Postpone Job 8 (slack = 0).
Day 13—Schedule Job 8 (slack = 0); two men remain.
Day 14—Continue Job 8 (slack = 0); two men remain.

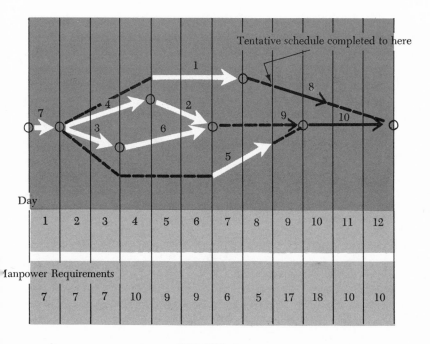

FIGURE G

All jobs are now scheduled. The final schedule graph appears in Figure H.

Thus the manpower limit of ten men per day has resulted in a four-day increase in the project length, compared with the unlimited resource schedule. In this application the heuristic program has found an optimal schedule. There are other feasible schedules, but none shorter than fourteen days.

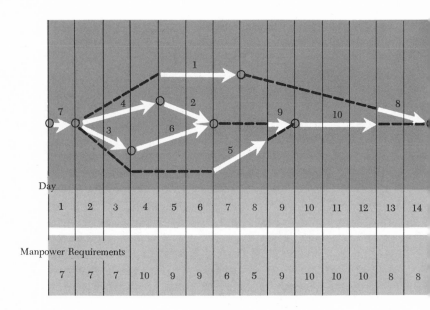

FIGURE H

Part Seven

Game Theory, Inventory Policy, and Queuing Analysis

GAME THEORY, inventory models, and queuing analysis are all important tools of managerial economics. The first two papers of Part Seven are concerned with the theory of games. John McDonald discusses one-person, two-person, and three-person games, using the liquor industry to illustrate games with more than two persons. J. D. Williams shows how conflict situations must be described in order to be amenable to game-theory analyses; the basic elements are the number of persons, the payoff, the strategy, and the game matrix.

The next three papers in this part are an introduction to inventory theory. The short piece by Thomson M. Whitin introduces the reader to the lot-size formula used to calculate economical purchase quantities. As Whitin points out, this formula is by no means new. The following paper by John F. Magee provides a very readable and useful account of the basic inventory techniques in use; the discussion is sprinkled liberally with references to particular cases. Finally, William J. Baumol describes the salient characteristics of queuing problems, which have received a great deal of attention from managerial economists and operations researchers, and shows how Monte Carlo techniques can be used to solve them.

The "Game" of Business

JOHN MCDONALD

John McDonald was an editor of Fortune Maga-
zine. This article is taken from his book, Strategy
in Poker, Business, and War.

The core of business is the market. The core of the market is
the relationship of buyer and seller, whether either is an individual or a corporation. The theory of games investigates the interior
of this relationship with game models.

From the standpoint of the individual there are three possible
economic situations on earth: one man alone, two men, or three
or more men. One man is Robinson Crusoe alone on an island.
He plays there the game of solitaire, maximizing his gain uncom-
plicated by anything but the forces of nature, which are predictable, at least in such terms as probable rainfall and the probability
of a tornado.

If there are two men on earth, the individual enters into the
relation of exchange (buyer-seller), in which the problem of the
other fellow appears; he can no longer maximize his gain but
must seek a limitation of the possibilities in an optimum. But if
there are three men, the novelty occurs that two of them may
gain more by combining against the third (e.g., two sellers against
a buyer, or vice versa). These three situations are the same as
those found in games.

Any industry serves as an example of strategical game play. Take the liquor industry, which like steel, oil or automobiles has only a few sellers. The following story was told at length in *Fortune* magazine. Samuel Bronfman of Seagram had come down from Canada at the time of repeal and built his organization on blended whiskey in the tradition of Canadian and Scotch whiskeys. U.S. distillers, slow to adopt blends, preferred to sell the traditional American rye and bourbon. But blended whiskey could be nationally advertised to better advantage (rye and bourbon being largely regional); and Bronfman made the most of it. His marketing strategy consisted of blends, brand names and mild taste. Eventually there was a contest for leadership in the industry between Seagram and Schenley. Lewis Rosenstiel of Schenley, an old-school U.S. distiller, divided his attention between blends and straights. Now whiskey is made at one time to be sold four or more years later, and there is a corresponding risk in the inventory. Keep too little and you may run short. Keep too much and you may get stuck (whiskey consumption roughly follows the income curve; and as in any industry total inventories can get out of hand, resulting, in the absence of mandatory fair trade laws, in occasional price wars). "Holidays" during World War II had eliminated several crops of whiskey and inventories generally were low. Rosenstiel is known as an inventory strategist. He came out of the war period with brand sales off but with perhaps half of the remaining aged whiskey inventory in the U.S. Bronfman of Seagram had used up a large part of his whiskey inventory in gaining record brand sales. In this situation, they had a contest for the leadership, a kind of two-man game within the industry.

Facing a forthcoming shortage, Bronfman could either buy scarce bulk whiskey at a losing price and maintain Seagram's brand sales with a decline in profits, or maintain his rate of profit out of his remaining inventory with a decline in brand sales—or follow a mixed policy. In any event he could not maximize both brand sales and profits. Rosenstiel could sell the inventory to Bronfman at high bulk prices and no sales cost and thus maximize profits in the immediate circumstance; or he could put the inventory into Schenley brands with an expensive and risky sales campaign to raise brand sales at less profit. Like Bronfman, but for different reasons, he could not maximize both brand sales and profits.

Nor could the policies of the antagonists fail to conflict; for Rosenstiel, who, having the better inventory, had the dominant choice, could reconcile their difference only by taking profit and giving Bronfman the market (brand sales), i.e., take short-term gains at the cost of long-term losses. Within limits, Bronfman would have been glad to buy the market (take short-term losses with long-term gains)—if Rosenstiel would let him. But Rosenstiel wouldn't. Each sought an optimum move on a strategical basis. The game broadened out with larger numbers as Bronfman got some whiskey from another source. Rosenstiel opened a "back-label" campaign to make his aged stocks pay off. The consequences of the struggle have not been told, but whatever they are, they are the consequences of conscious strategy. Theoretically, Seagram and Schenley had another alternative, namely, to combine. There are good reasons why they would not, yet each of these corporate individuals like so many others in industry had grown large through combination.

The three-man coalition game can be played as an auction with one seller and two buyers. The seller has a reserve price of, say, $10 on the object to be sold. The first buyer is willing to go to not more than $15; the second buyer to not more than $20. Clearly the second buyer being the stronger will get the object. Ordinarily he is expected to get it for something over $15. But suppose the second buyer approaches the first and makes a deal to eliminate competitive bidding. He can then get the object for something over $10. The deal, however, requires a division of the spoils. The second, stronger buyer must pay the first, weaker buyer something for making the coalition. That payment must be enough to yield the second buyer the "best" profit, and yet enough to ensure that his partner will remain in the coalition: two maximums which must be resolved. For another, rival deal is possible —in game theory but not in classical economics—namely this: The seller may cross the market and break up the coalition by paying something to the second buyer to restore the bidding and thereby push the selling price back above $15. Thus each two-man game in this three-man game is under the influence of the other possible two-man games, in arriving at the distribution payment.

In the theory of games a number of solutions, i.e., distribution schemes, are possible, some of which are enforceable and therefore dominate others. In classical theory the weaker buyer gets nothing; in game theory he gets a bribe, and the bribe will be expressed in the price. Here the difference between classical economics and game theory can be shown with simple numbers. In classical theory the price is between $15 and $20 (all going to the seller). In game theory it is between $10 and $20, depending on the bargaining ability of the players.

The basic strategy of organizers of industry from the beginning has been to substitute combination for large-number competition. The value which J. P. Morgan put on combination was indicated in the capitalization of the United States Steel Corporation in 1901. The Corporation, which brought together about 65 percent of the steel capacity of the United States, was capitalized at about twice the tangible value given to its separate properties before combination. The specific combinative value (about three-quarters of a billion dollars minus an unknown value put on "good will") was expressed in the new common stock—attacked as "watered stock"—which eventually paid off as the technical and strategical market advantages of combination were realized. The Corporation later met rivalry from other combinations which were organized in opposition to it.

Rockefeller's genius similarly expressed itself in combinations. But some of these early combinations, as they were organized, were unwieldy. Standard Oil stockholders probably benefited from the trust's court-ordered dissolution in 1911. It became impolitic thereafter, under the Sherman Act, for one organization to hold an overwhelming share of the market. For that reason or because its ability to compete against counter-combinations was injured by organizational and management defects, the Steel Corporation retreated to its present holdings of about one-third of the industry's ingot capacity. Its present leadership of the industry is maintained by modern market techniques described in oligopoly and game theory.

Introduction to Game Theory

J. D. WILLIAMS

J. D. Williams was head of the mathematics department at the RAND Corporation. This article comes from his book, The Compleat Strategyst.

The number of persons involved is one of the important criteria for classifying and studying games, 'person' meaning a distinct set of interests. Another criterion has to do with the payoff: What happens at the end of the game? Say at the end of the hand in poker? Well, in poker there is usually just an exchange of assets. If there are two persons, say you (Blue) and we (Red), then if you should win $10, we would lose $10. In other words,

$$\text{Blue winnings} = \text{Red losses}$$

or, stated otherwise,

$$\text{Blue winnings} - \text{Red losses} = 0$$

We may also write it as

$$\text{Blue payoff} + \text{Red payoff} = \$10 - \$10 = 0$$

by adopting the convention that winnings are positive numbers and that losses are negative numbers.

It needn't have turned out just that way; i.e., that the sum of the payoffs is zero. For instance, if the person who wins the pot has to contribute 10 percent toward the drinks and other

incidentals, as to the cop on the corner, then the sum of the payoffs is not zero; in fact

$$\text{Blue payoff} + \text{Red payoff} = \$9 - \$10 = -\$1$$

The above two cases illustrate a fundamental distinction among
games: It is important to know whether or not the sum of the
payoffs, counting winnings as positive and losses as negative, to
all players is zero. If it is, the game is known as a *zero-sum
game*. If it is not, the game is known (mathematicians are not
very imaginative at times) as a *non-zero-sum game*. The importance of the distinction is easy to see: In the zero-sum case, we
are dealing with a good, clean, closed system; the two players
and the valuables are locked in the room. It will require a certain effort to specify and to analyze such a game. On the other
hand, the non-zero-sum game contains all the difficulties of the
zero-sum game, plus additional troubles due to the need to incorporate new factors. This can be appreciated by noting that we
can restore the situation by adding a fictitious player—Nature,
say, or the cop. Then we have

$$\text{Blue payoff} = \$9$$
$$\text{Red payoff} = -\$10$$
$$\text{Cop payoff} = \$1$$

so now

$$\text{Blue payoff} + \text{Red payoff} + \text{Cop payoff} = \$9 - \$10 + \$1 = 0$$

which is a *three-person zero-sum* game, of sorts, where the third
player has some of the characteristics of a millstone around the
neck. But recall that we don't like three-person games so well as
we do two-person games, because they contain the vagaries of
coalitions. So non-zero-sum games offer real difficulties not present in zero-sum games, particularly if the latter are two-person
games.

Parlor games, such as poker, bridge, and chess, are usually
zero-sum games, and many other conflict situations may be
treated as if they were. Most of the development of game theory
to date has been on this type of game. Some work on non-zero-
sum games has been done, and more is in progress, but the subject is beyond our scope. A troublesome case of particular interest
is the two-person game in which the nominally equal payoffs

differ in utility to the players; this situation occurs often even in parlor games.

Just as the word "person" has a meaning in game theory somewhat different from everyday usage, the word 'strategy' does too. This word, as used in its everyday sense, carries the connotation of a particularly skillful or adroit plan, whereas in game theory it designates any *complete* plan. *A strategy is a plan so complete that it cannot be upset by enemy action or Nature;* for everything that the enemy or Nature may choose to do, together with a set of possible actions for yourself, is just part of the description of the strategy.

So the strategy of game theory differs in two important respects from the conventional meaning: It must be utterly complete, and it may be utterly bad; for nothing is required of it except completeness. Thus, in poker, all strategies must make provision for your being dealt a royal flush in spades, and some of them will require that you fold instantly. The latter are not very glamorous strategies, but they are still strategies—after all, a bridge player once bid 7 no-trump while holding 13 spades. In a game which is completely amenable to analysis, we are able—conceptually, if not actually—to foresee all eventualities and hence are able to catalogue all possible strategies.

We are now able to mention still another criterion according to which games may be classified for study, namely, the number of strategies available to each player. Thus, if Blue and Red are the players, Blue may have three strategies and Red may have five; this would be called a 3×5 game (read 'three-by-five game').

When the number of players was discussed, you will recall that certain numbers—namely, one, two, and more-than-two—were especially significant. Similarly, there are critical values in the number of strategies; and it turns out to be important to distinguish two major categories. In the first are games in which the player having the *greatest* number of strategies still has a finite number; this means that he can count them, and finish the task within some time limit. The second major category is that in which at least one player has infinitely many strategies, or, if the word 'infinitely' disturbs you, in which at least one player has a number of strategies which is larger than any definite number you can name. (This, incidentally, is just precisely what 'infinitely large' means to a mathematician.)

While infinite games (as the latter are called) cover many interesting and useful applications, the theory of such games is difficult. 'Difficult' here means that there are at least some problems the mathematician doesn't know how to solve, and further that we don't know how to present any of it within friendly pedagogical limits; such games require mathematics at the level of the calculus and beyond—mostly beyond. Therefore we here resolve to confine our attention to finite games.

THE GAME MATRIX

We are now in a position to complete the description of games, i.e., conflict situations, in the form required for game theory analysis. We will freely invoke all the restrictions developed so far. Hence our remarks will primarily apply to finite, zero-sum, two-person games.

The players are Blue and Red. Each has several potential strategies which we assume are known; let them be numbered just for identification. Blue's strategies will then bear names, such as Blue 1, Blue 2, and so on; perhaps, in a specific case, up to Blue 9; and Red's might range from Red 1 through Red 5. We would call this a nine-by-five game and write it as '9 × 5 game.' Just to demonstrate that it is possible to have a 9 × 5 game, we shall state one (or enough of it to make the point). Consider a game played on the following page.

The rules require that Blue travel from B to R, following the system of roads, without returning to B or using the same segment twice during the trip. The rules are different for Red, who must travel from R to B, always moving toward the west. Perhaps Blue doesn't want to meet Red, and has fewer inhibitions about behavior. You may verify that there are nine routes for Blue and five for Red.[1]

1. To avoid even the possiblity of frustrating you this early in the game,

The rules must also contain information from which we can determine what happens at the end of any play of the game: What is the payoff when, say, Blue uses the strategy Blue 7 (the northern route, perhaps) and Red uses Red 3 (the southern route, perhaps)? There will be $9 \times 5 = 45$ of these pairs and hence that number of possible values for the payoff; and these must be known. Whatever the values are, it is surely possible to arrange the information on the kind of bookkeeping form shown on Chart 1, page 188.

Such an array of boxes, each containing a payoff number, is called a *game matrix*. We shall adopt the convention that a positive number in the matrix represents a gain for Blue and hence a loss for Red, and vice versa. Thus if two of the values in the game matrix are 3 and -8, as shown in Chart 2 (page 188), the

we itemize the routes. Blue may visit any of the following sets of road junctions (beginning with *B* and ending with *R* in each case):

b, bac, bacd, ab, ac, acd, dcab, dc, d

Red may visit

b, ba, ca, cd, d

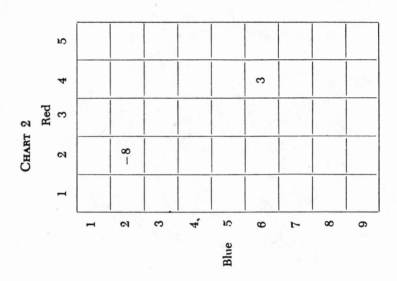

CHART 2

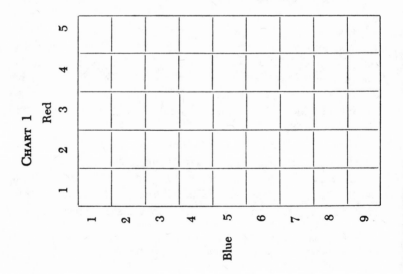

CHART 1

meaning is: When Blue uses Blue 6 and Red uses Red 4, Blue wins 3 units, whereas when Blue 2 is used vs. Red 2, Red wins 8 units.

When the original problem has been brought to this form, a game theory analysis may begin, for all the relevant information is represented in the descriptions of the strategies whose signatures border the matrix and in the payoff boxes. This is the game theory model of the conflict, and the applicability of the subsequent analysis will depend completely on the adequacy of this form of representation—a set of strategies and a payoff matrix.

THE CRITERION

A perennial difficulty in modelmaking of the analytical (as opposed to wooden) variety is the illness which might well be known as criterion-trouble. What is the criterion in terms of which the outcome of the game is judged? Or should be judged?

To illustrate the wealth of possible criteria in a homely example, consider a housewife who has $5 to spend on meat. What should she buy? If her criterion is simply quantity, she should buy the cheapest kind and measure the payoff in pounds. If it is variety, she should buy minimum, useful quantities of several kinds, beginning with the cheapest kinds; she measures the payoff by the number of kinds she buys. Or she may be interested in protein, fat, or calories. She may have to satisfy various side conditions, or work within certain constraints, such as allergies, tastes, or taboos. She may be interested in least total effort, in which case she may say, "I want five dollars worth of cooked meat—the nearest, of course—and deliver it sometime when you happen to be down our way."

Generally speaking, criterion-trouble is the problem of what to measure and how to base behavior on the measurements. Game Theory has nothing to say on the first topic, but it advocates a very explicit and definite behavior-pattern based on the measurements.

It takes the position that there is a definite way that rational people should behave, if they believe in the game matrix. The notion that there is some way people ought to behave does not refer to an obligation based on law or ethics. Rather it refers to a kind of mathematical morality, or at least frugality, which claims that the *sensible object of the player is to gain as much from the game as he can, safely, in the face of a skillful opponent who is pursuing an antithetical goal.* This is our model of rational behavior. As with all models, the shoe has to be tried on each time an application comes along to see whether the fit is tolerable; but it is well known in the Military Establishment, for instance, that a lot of ground can be covered in shoes that do not fit perfectly.

Let us follow up the consequences of this model in a zero-sum game, which, you will recall, is a closed system in which assets are merely passed back and forth between the players. It won't affect anything adversely (except Red), and it will simplify the discussion, if we assume for a moment that all payoffs in the game matrix are *positive;* this means that the strategy options available to the players only affect how many valuables Red must give to Blue at the end of a play of the game; this isn't a fair game for Red, but we will let him suffer for the common weal.

Now the viewpoint in game theory is that *Blue wishes to act in such a manner that the least number he can win is as great as possible, irrespective of what Red does;* this takes care of the safety requirement. *Red's comparable desire is to make the greatest number of valuables that he must relinquish as small as possible, irrespective of Blue's action.* This philosophy, if held by the players, is sufficient to specify their choices of strategy. If Blue departs from it, he does so at the risk of getting less than he might have received; and if Red departs from it, he may have to pay more than he could have settled for.

The above argument is the central one in game theory. There is a way to play every two-person game that will satisfy this criterion. However, as in the case of the housewife buying meat, it is not the only possible criterion; for example, by attributing to the enemy various degrees of ignorance or stupidity, one could devise many others. Since game theory does not attribute these attractive qualities to the enemy, it is a conservative theory.

You will note an apparent disparity in the aims of Blue and Red as stated above; Blue's aims are expressed in terms of winning and Red's in terms of losing. This difference is not a real one, as both have precisely the same philosophy. Rather, it is a consequence of our convention regarding the meaning of positive and negative numbers in the game matrix. The adoption of a uniform convention, to the effect that Blue is always the maximizing player and Red the minimizing player, will reduce technical confusion (once it becomes fixed in your mind); but let's not pay for this mnemonic by coming to believe that there is an essential lack of symmetry in the game treatment of Blue and Red.

Introduction to the Lot-Size Formula

Thomson M. Whitin

Thomson M. Whitin is Professor of Economics at Wesleyan University. This is an excerpt from his article in the Quarterly Journal of Economics.

The best known "scientific" inventory control system involves the calculation of economical purchase quantities and reorder point quantities. Several authors independently arrived at the same basic formula for determining economical purchase quantities in the 1920s. A number of different factors contributed to the development of such formulas.

First of all, the increasing size of business establishments has played an important role. It was possible for most firms in the past to make use of highly inefficient inventory control methods and yet still maintain profit margins. Modern large-scale enterprises often operate with small profit margins which might well be eliminated by poor inventory control methods. Furthermore, size in itself makes obvious the existence of possibilities of substantial savings through improvement in inventory control.

Secondly, during the past century, there has been an enormous increase in the amount of business training. High schools now offer some business preparatory courses, and the growth of business administration colleges has been extremely rapid. This additional training has made recent generations of businessmen more aware of improvement possibilities. Also, trade publications on market research, purchasing, retailing, standardization, and many other topics have contributed much to businessmen's understanding of the various problems which confront them.

A third factor that has aided the transition to modern inventory control methods is the increased emphasis that has been placed on the importance of engineers in business. The entrance of many trained engineers into business has brought with it the "scientific" approach, including scientific methods of production control, factory layout, standardization, etc. Also, cost accounting has helped entrepreneurs to evaluate the performance of various departments of their establishments, thus indicating specific areas where better control may be needed.

A final factor that gave impetus to research on inventory control was the "inventory depression" of 1921, which taught businessmen to be extremely wary of inventory accumulation. As a result of these factors, formulas for determining economic purchase quantities have been derived. These formulas involve a simple application of elementary differential calculus to inventory control.

The economic purchase quantity may be determined in the following manner. Two different sets of cost factors must be considered, namely, those which increase as purchase quantities increase and those which decrease as purchase quantities increase. Among those costs which increase are interest, obsolescence, risk, depreciation, storage, etc., while the forces making for decreasing costs include such items as quantity discounts, freight differentials, and procurement costs. In the following example, assume that the expense of procurement is constant and that interest, risk, depreciation, obsolescence, etc., may be lumped into one percentage figure (I). Let Y designate expected yearly sales (in \$), Q be the economic purchase quantity (in \$) and S be the procurement expense (in \$). Then total annual variable costs involved in ordering and carrying purchase quantities may be expressed as follows: $TVC = \dfrac{Q}{2}I + \dfrac{Y}{Q}S$. Differentiating with respect to the purchase quantity, Q, and setting the derivative equal to zero, the solution

$$Q = \sqrt{\frac{2YS}{I}}$$

results, where Q is the purchase quantity that minimizes combined ordering costs and carrying charges. This economical purchase quantity is thus seen to vary with the square root of sales and inversely with the square root of the carrying charges. This formula has been used in business and its use has been accompanied by good results.

Guides to Inventory Policy: Functions and Lot Sizes

JOHN F. MAGEE

John F. Magee is President of Arthur D. Little, Inc. This article appeared in the Harvard Business Review.

"Why are we always out of stock?" So goes the complaint of great numbers of businessmen faced with the dilemmas and frustrations of attempting simultaneously to maintain stable production operations, provide customers with adequate service, and keep investment in stocks and equipment at reasonable levels.

But this is only one of the characteristic problems business managers face in dealing with production planning, scheduling, keeping inventories in hand, and expediting. Other questions— just as perplexing and baffling when managers approach them on the basis of intuition and pencil work alone—are: How often should we reorder, or how should we adjust production, when sales are uncertain? What capacity levels should we set for job-shop operations? How do we plan production and procurement for seasonal sales? And so on, and so on.

In this series of articles, I will describe some of the technical developments which aim at giving the business manager better control over inventory and scheduling policy. While these techniques sometimes employ concepts and language foreign to the line executive, they are far from being either academic exercises or mere clerical devices. They are designed to help the business manager make better policy decisions and get his people to follow policy more closely.

As such, these techniques are worth some time and thought, commensurate with the central importance of production planning and inventory policy in business operations. Indeed, many companies have found that analysis of the functions of inventories, measurement of the proper level of stocks, and development of inventory and production control systems based on the sorts of techniques described in this and following sections can be very profitable. For example:

• Johnson & Johnson has used these techniques for studying inventory requirements for products with seasonally changing demand, and also to set economical inventory goals balancing investment requirements against additional training and overtime costs.

• The American Thread Company, as a supplier to the fashion goods industry, plagued with large in-process inventories, day-to-day imbalances among production departments, labor turnover, and customer service difficulties, found these methods the key to improved scheduling and control procedures. Now these improved procedures help keep an inventory of tens of thousands of items in balance and smooth out production operations even in the face of demand showing extremely erratic fluctuations due to fashion changes.

• The Lamp Division of the General Electric Company has reported using these methods to survey its finished inventory functions and stock requirements in view of operating conditions and costs. This survey indicated how an improved warehouse reorder system would yield inventory cuts at both factories and warehouses, and pointed to the reorder system characteristics that were needed; it led to the installation of a new reorder and stock control system offering substantial opportunities for stock reduction. The analytic approach can also be used to show clearly what the cost in inventory investment and schedule changes is to achieve a given level of customer service.

• An industrial equipment manufacturer used these methods to investigate inventory and scheduling practices and to clear up policy ambiguities in this area, as a prelude to installing an electronic computer system to handle inventory control, scheduling, and purchase requisitions. In general, the analytic approach has proved a valuable help in bringing disagreements over inventory policy into the open, helping each side to recognize its own and the others' hidden assumptions, and to reach a common agreement more quickly.

• The Procter & Gamble Company recently described how analysis of its factory inventory functions and requirements, using these methods, has pointed out means for improved scheduling and more efficient use of finished stock. The analysis indicated how the company could take advantage of certain particular characteristics of its factories to cut stocks needed to meet sales fluctuations while still maintaining its long-standing policy of guaranteed annual employment.

These are only a few instances of applications. Numerous others could be drawn from the experience of companies ranging from moderate to large size, selling consumer goods or industrial products, with thousands of items or only a few, and distribution in highly stable, predictable markets or in erratically changing and unpredictable circumstances.

In the present article major attention will be devoted to (a) the conceptual framework of the analytic approach, including the definition of inventory function and the measurement of operational costs; and (b) the problem of optimum lot size, with a detailed case illustration showing how the techniques are applied.

This case reveals that the appropriate order quantity and the average inventory maintained do not vary directly with sales, and that a good answer to the lot-size question can be obtained with fairly crude cost data, provided that a sound analytical approach is used. The case also shows that the businessman does not need calculus to solve many inventory problems (although use has to be made of it when certain complications arise).

INVENTORY PROBLEMS

The question before management is: How big should inventories be? The answer to this is obvious—they should be just big enough. But what is big enough?

This question is made more difficult by the fact that generally each individual within a management group tends to answer the question from his own point of view. He fails to recognize costs outside his usual framework. He tends to think of inventories in isolation from other operations. The sales manager commonly says that the company must never make a customer wait; the production manager says there must be long manufacturing runs for lower costs and steady employment; the treasurer says that large inventories are draining off cash which could be used to make a profit.

Such a situation occurs all the time. The task of all production planning, scheduling, or control functions, in fact, is typically to balance conflicting objectives such as those of minimum purchase or production cost, minimum inventory investment, minimum storage and distribution cost, and maximum service to customers.

Production vs. Time · Often businessmen blame their inventory and scheduling difficulties on small orders and product diversity: "You can't keep track of 100,000 items. Forecasts mean nothing. We're just a job shop." Many businessmen seem to feel that their problems in this respect are unusual, whereas actually the problems faced by a moderate-size manufacturer with a widely diversified product line are almost typical of business today.

The fact is, simply, that under present methods of organization the costs of paper work, setup, and control, in view of the diversity of products sold, represent an extremely heavy drain on many a company's profit and a severe cost to its customers. The superficial variety of output has often blinded management to the opportunities for more systematic production flow and for the elimination of many of the curses of job-shop operation by better organization and planning.

The problem of planning and scheduling production or inventories pervades all operations concerned with the matter of production versus time—i.e., the interaction between production, distribution, and the location and size of physical stocks. It occurs at almost every step in the production process: purchasing, production of in-process materials, finished production, distribution of finished product, and service to customers. In multiplant operations, the problem becomes compounded because decisions must be made with reference to the amount of each item to be produced in each factory; management must also specify how the warehouses should be served by the plants.

Action vs. Analysis · The questions businessmen raise in connection with management and control of inventories are basically aimed at action, not at arriving at answers. The questions are stated, unsurprisingly, in the characteristic terms of decisions to be made: "Where shall we maintain how much stock?" "Who will be responsible for it?" "What shall we do to control balances or set proper schedules?" A manager necessarily thinks of problems in production planning in terms of centers of responsibility.

However, action questions are not enough by themselves. In order to get at the answers to these questions as a basis for taking action, it is necessary to back off and ask some rather different kinds of questions: "Why do we have inventories?" "What affects the inventory balances we maintain?" "How do these effects take place?" From these questions, a picture of the inventory problem can be built up which shows the influence on inventories and costs of the various alternative decisions which the management may ultimately want to consider.

This type of analytic or functional question has been answered intuitively by businessmen with considerable success in the past. Consequently, most of the effort toward improved inventory management has been spent in other directions; it has been aimed at better means for recording, filing, or displaying information and at better ways of doing the necessary clerical work. This is all to the good, for efficient data-handling helps. However, it does not lessen the need for a more systematic approach to inventory problems that can take the place of, or at least supplement, intuition.

As business has grown, it has become more complex, and as business executives have become more and more specialized in their jobs or farther removed from direct operations, the task of achieving an economical balance intuitively has become increasingly difficult. That is why more businessmen are finding the concepts and mathematics of the growing field of inventory theory to be of direct practical help.

One of the principal difficulties in the intuitive approach is that the types and definitions of cost which influence appropriate inventory policy are not those characteristically found on the books of a company. Many costs, such as setup or purchasing costs, are hidden in the accounting records. Others, such as inventory capital costs, may never appear at all. Each cost may be clear to the operating head primarily responsible for its control;

since it is a "hidden" cost, however, its importance may not be clear at all to other operating executives concerned. The resulting confusion may make it difficult to arrive at anything like a consistent policy.

In the last five years in particular, operations research teams have succeeded in using techniques of research scientists to develop a practical analytic approach to inventory questions, despite growing business size, complexity, and division of management responsibility.

INVENTORY FUNCTIONS

To understand the principles of the analytic approach, we must have some idea of the basic functions of inventories.

Fundamentally, inventories serve to uncouple successive operations in the process of making a product and getting it to consumers. For example, inventories make it possible to process a product at a distance from customers or from raw material supplies or to do two operations at a distance from one another (perhaps only across the plant). Inventories make it unnecessary to gear production directly to consumption or, alternatively, to force consumption to adapt to the necessities of production. In these and similar ways, inventories free one stage in the production-distribution process from the next, permitting each to operate more economically.

The essential question is: At what point does the uncoupling function of inventory stop earning enough advantage to justify the investment required? To arrive at a satisfactory answer we must first distinguish between (a) inventories necessary because it takes time to complete an operation and to move the product from one stage to another; and (b) inventories employed for organizational reasons, i.e., to let one unit schedule its operations more or less independently of another.

Movement Inventories · Inventory balances needed because of the time required to move stocks from one place to another are often not recognized, or are confused with inventories resulting from other needs—e.g., economical shipping quantities (to be discussed in a later section).

The average amount of movement inventory can be determined from the mathematical expression $I = S \times T$ in which S

represents the average sales rate, T the transit time from one stage to the next, and I the movement inventory needed. For example, if it takes two weeks to move materials from the plant to a warehouse, and the warehouse sells 100 units per week, the average inventory in movement is 100 units per week times 2 weeks, or 200 units. From a different point of view, when a unit is manufactured and ready for use at the plant, it must sit idle for two weeks while being moved to the next station (the warehouse); so, on the average, stocks equal to two weeks' sales will be in movement.

Movement inventories are usually thought of in connection with movement between distant points—plant to warehouse. However, any plant may contain substantial stocks in movement from one operation to another—for example, the product moving along an assembly line. Movement stock is one component of the "float" or in-process inventory in a manufacturing operation.

The amount of movement stock changes only when sales or the time in transit is changed. Time in transit is largely a result of method of transportation, although improvements in loading or dispatching practices may cut transit time by eliminating unnecessary delays. Other somewhat more subtle influences of time in transit on total inventories will be described in connection with safety stocks.

Organization Inventories · Management's most difficult problems are with the inventories that "buy" organization in the sense that the more of them management carries between stages in the manufacturing-distribution process, the less coordination is required to keep the process running smoothly. Contrariwise, if inventories are already being used efficiently, they can be cut only at the expense of greater organization effort—e.g., greater scheduling effort to keep successive stages in balance, and greater expediting effort to work out of the difficulties which unforeseen disruptions at one point or another may cause in the whole process.

Despite superficial differences among businesses in the nature and characteristics of the organization inventory they maintain, the following three functions are basic:

business. They are maintained wherever the user makes or purchases material in larger lots than are needed for his immediate purposes. For example, it is common practice to buy raw materials in relatively large quantities to order to obtain quantity price discounts, keep shipping costs in balance, and hold down clerical costs connected with making out requisitions, checking receipts, and handling accounts payable. Similar reasons lead to long production runs on equipment calling for expensive setup, or to sizable replenishment orders placed on factories by field warehouses.

(2) *Fluctuation stocks,* also very common in business, are held to cushion the shocks arising basically from unpredictable fluctuations in consumer demand. For example, warehouses and retail outlets maintain stocks to be able to supply consumers on demand, even when the rate of consumer demand may show quite irregular and unpredictable fluctuations. In turn, factories maintain stocks to be in a position to replenish retail and field warehouse stocks in line with customer demands.

Short-term fluctuations in the mix of orders on a plant often make it necessary to carry stocks of parts of subassemblies, in order to give assembly operations flexibility in meeting orders as they arise while freeing earlier operations (e.g., machining) from the need to make momentary adjustments in schedules to meet assembly requirements. Fluctuation stocks may also be carried in semifinished form in order to balance out the load among manufacturing departments when orders received during the current day, week, or month may put a load on individual departments which is out of balance with long-run requirements.

In most cases, anticipating all fluctuations is uneconomical, if not impossible. But a business cannot get along without some fluctuation stocks unless it is willing and able always to make its customers wait until the material needed can be purchased conveniently or until their orders can be scheduled into production conveniently. Fluctuation stocks are part of the price we pay for our general business philosophy of serving the consumers' wants (and whims) rather than having them take what they can get. The queues before Russian retail stores illustrate a different point of view.

(3) *Anticipation stocks* are needed where goods or materials

are consumed on a predictable but changing pattern through the year, and where it is desirable to absorb some of these changes by building and depleting inventories rather than by changing production rates with attendant fluctuations in employment and additional capital capacity requirements. For example, inventories may be built up in anticipation of a special sale or to fill needs during a plant shutdown.

The need for seasonal stocks may also arise where materials (e.g., agricultural products) are *produced* at seasonally fluctuating rates but where consumption is reasonably uniform; here the problems connected with producing and storing tomato catsup are a prime example.[1]

Striking a Balance · The joker is that the gains which these organization inventories achieve in the way of less need for coordination and planning, less clerical effort to handle orders, and greater economies in manufacturing and shipping are not in direct proportion to the size of inventory. Even if the additional stocks are kept well balanced and properly located, the gains become smaller, while at the same time the warehouse, obsolescence, and capital costs associated with maintaining inventories rise in proportion to, or perhaps even at a faster rate than, the inventories themselves. To illustrate:

Suppose a plant needs 2,000 units of a specially machined part in a year. If these are made in runs of 100 units each, then twenty runs with attendant setup costs will be required each year.

If the production quantity were increased from 100 to 200 units, only ten runs would be required—a 50 percent reduction in setup costs, but a 100 percent increase in the size of a run and in the resulting inventory balance carried.

If the runs were further increased in length to 400 units each, only five production runs during the year would be required—only 25 percent more reduction in setup costs, but 200 percent more increase in run length and inventory balances.

The basic problem of inventory policy connected with the three types of inventories which "buy" organization is to strike

1. See Alexander Henderson and Robert Schlaifer, "Mathematical Programing: Better Information for Better Decision-making," *Harvard Business Review*, May–June 1954, p. 73. [This paper also appears in this volume.— Ed.]

a balance between the increasing costs and the declining return earned from additional stocks. It is because striking this balance is easier to say than to do, and because it is a problem that defies solution through an intuitive understanding alone, that the new analytical concepts are necessary.

INVENTORY COSTS

This brings us face to face with the question of the costs that influence inventory policy, and the fact, noted earlier, that they are characteristically not those recorded, at least not in directly available form, in the usual industrial accounting system. Accounting costs are derived under principles developed over many years and strongly influenced by tradition. The specific methods and degree of skill and refinement may be better in particular companies, but in all of them the basic objective of accounting procedures is to provide a fair, consistent, and conservative valuation of assets and a picture of the flow of values in the business.

In contrast to the principles and search for consistency underlying accounting costs, the definition of costs for production and inventory control will vary from time to time—even in the same company—according to the circumstances and the length of the period being planned for. The following criteria apply:

(1) *The costs shall represent "out-of-pocket" expenditures, i.e., cash actually paid out or opportunities for profit foregone.* Overtime premium payments are out-of-pocket; depreciation on equipment on hand is not. To the extent that storage space is available and cannot be used for other productive purposes, no out-of-pocket cost of space is incurred; but to the extent that storage space is rented (out-of-pocket) or could be used for other productive purposes (foregone opportunity), a suitable charge is justified. The charge for investment is based on the out-of-pocket investment in inventories or added facilities, not on the "book" or accounting value of the investment.

The rate of interest charged on out-of-pocket investment may be based either on the rate paid banks (out-of-pocket) or on the rate of profit that might reasonably be earned by alternative uses of investment (foregone opportunity), depending on the financial policies of the business. In some cases, a bank rate may be used on short-term seasonal inventories and an internal rate for long-term, minimum requirements.

Obviously, much depends on the time scale in classifying a given item. In the short run, few costs are controllable out-of-pocket costs; in the long run, all are.

(2) *The costs shall represent only those out-of-pocket expenditures or foregone opportunities for profit whose magnitude is affected by the schedule or plan.* Many overhead costs, such as supervision costs, are out-of-pocket, but neither the timing nor the size is affected by the schedule. Normal material and direct labor costs are unaffected in total and so are not considered directly; however, these as well as some components of overhead cost do represent out-of-pocket investments, and accordingly enter the picture indirectly through any charge for capital.

Direct Influence · Among the costs which directly influence inventory policy are (a) costs depending on the amount ordered, (b) production costs, and (c) costs of storing and handling inventory.

Costs that depend on the amount ordered—These include, for example, quantity discounts offered by vendors; setup costs in internal manufacturing operations and clerical costs of making out a purchase order; and, when capacity is pressed, the profit on production lost during downtime for setup. Shipping costs represent another factor to the extent that they influence the quantity of raw materials purchased and resulting raw stock levels, the size of intraplant or plant-warehouse shipments, or the size and the frequency of shipments to customers.

Production costs—Beyond setup or change-over costs, which are included in the preceding category, there are the abnormal or non-routine costs of production whose size may be affected by the policies or control methods used. (Normal or standard raw material and direct labor costs are not significant in inventory control; these relate to the total quantity sold rather than to the amount stocked.) Overtime, shakedown, hiring, and training represent costs that have a direct bearing on inventory policy.

To illustrate, shakedown or learning costs show up wherever

output during the early part of a new run is below standard in quantity or quality.[2] A cost of undercapacity operation may also be encountered—for example, where a basic labor force must be maintained regardless of volume (although sometimes this can be looked on as part of the fixed facility cost, despite the fact that it is accounted for as a directly variable labor cost).

Costs of handling and storing inventory—In this group of costs affected by control methods and inventory policies are expenses of handling products in and out of stock, storage costs such as rent and heat, insurance and taxes, obsolescence and spoilage costs, and capital costs (which will receive detailed examination in the next section).

Inventory obsolescence and spoilage costs may take several forms, including (1) outright spoilage after a more or less fixed period; (2) risk that a particular unit in stock or a particular product number will (a) become technologically unsalable, except perhaps at a discount or as spare parts, (b) go out of style, or (c) spoil.

Certain food and drug products, for example, have specified maximum shelf lives and must either be used within a fixed period of time or be dumped. Some kinds of style goods, such as many lines of toys, Christmas novelties, or women's clothes, may effectively "spoil" at the end of a season, with only reclaim or dump value. Some kinds of technical equipment undergo almost constant engineering change during their production life; thus component stocks may suddenly and unexpectedly be made obsolete.

Capital Investment · Evaluating the effect of inventory and scheduling policy upon capital investment and the worth of capital tied up in inventories is one of the most difficult problems in resolving inventory policy questions.

Think for a moment of the amount of capital invested in inventory. This is the out-of-pocket, or avoidable, cash cost for material, labor, and overhead of goods in inventory (as distinguished from the "book" or accounting value of inventory).

2. See Frank J. Andress, "The Learning Curve as a Production Tool," *Harvard Business Review,* January–February 1954, p. 87.

For example, raw materials are normally purchased in accordance with production schedules; and if the production of an item can be postponed, buying and paying for raw materials can likewise be put off.

Usually, then, the raw material cost component represents a part of the out-of-pocket inventory investment in finished goods. However, if raw materials must be purchased when available (e.g., agricultural crops) regardless of the production schedule, the raw material component of finished product cost does not represent avoidable investment and therefore should be struck from the computation of inventory value for planning purposes.

As for maintenance and similar factory overhead items, they are usually paid for the year round, regardless of the timing of production scheduled; therefore these elements of burden should not be counted as part of the product investment for planning purposes. (One exception: if, as sometimes happens, the maintenance costs actually vary directly with the production rate as, for example, in the case of supplies, they should of course be included.)

Again, supervision, at least general supervision, is usually a fixed monthly cost which the schedule will not influence, and hence should not be included. Depreciation is another type of burden item representing a charge for equipment and facilities already bought and paid for; the timing of the production schedule cannot influence these past investments and, while they represent a legitimate cost for accounting purposes, they should not be counted as part of the inventory investment for inventory and production planning purposes.

In sum, the rule is this: for production planning and inventory management purposes, the investment value of goods in inventory should be taken as the cash outlay made at the time of production that could have been delayed if the goods were not made then but at a later time, closer to the time of sale.

Cost of Capital Invested. This item is the product of three factors: (a) the capital value of a unit of inventory, (b) the time a unit of product is in inventory, and (c) the charge or imputed interest rate placed against a dollar of invested cash. The first factor was mentioned above. As for the second, it is fixed by management's inventory policy decisions. But these decisions can be made economically only in view of the third factor. This factor depends directly on the financial policy of the business.

Sometimes businessmen make the mistake of thinking that cash tied up in inventories costs nothing, especially if the cash to finance inventory is generated internally through profits and depreciation. However, this implies that the cash in inventories would otherwise sit idle. In fact, the cash could, at least, be invested in government bonds if not in inventories. And if it were really idle, the cash very likely should be released to stockholders for profitable investment elsewhere.

Moreover, it is dangerous to assume that, as a "short-term" investment, inventory is relatively liquid and riskless. Businessmen say, "After all, we turn our inventory investment over six times a year." But, in reality, inventory investment may or may not be short-term and riskless, depending on circumstances. No broad generalization is possible, and each case must be decided on its own merits. For example:

• A great deal of inventory carried in business is as much a part of the permanent investment as the machinery and buildings. The inventory must be maintained to make operations possible as long as the business is a going concern. The cash investment released by the sale of one item from stock must be promptly reinvested in new stock, and the inventory can be liquidated only when the company is closed. How much more riskless is this than other fixed manufacturing assets?

• To take an extreme case, inventory in fashion lines or other types of products having high obsolescence carries a definite risk. Its value depends wholly on the company's ability to sell it. If sales are insufficient to liquidate the inventory built up, considerable losses may result.

• At the other extreme, inventory in stable product lines built up to absorb short-term seasonal fluctuations might be thought of as bearing the least risk, since this type of investment is characteristically short-term. But even in these cases there can be losses. Suppose, for instance, that peak seasonal sales do not reach anticipated levels and substantially increased costs of storage and obsolescence have to be incurred before the excess inventory can be liquidated.

Finally, it might be pointed out that the cost of the dollars invested in inventory may be underestimated if bank interest rate is used as the basis, ignoring the risk-bearing or entrepreneur's compensation. How many businessmen are actually satisfied with uses of their companies' capital funds which do not earn more than a lender's rate of return? In choosing a truly appropriate rate—a matter of financial policy—the executive must answer some questions:

1. Where is the cash coming from—inside earnings or outside financing?
2. What else could we do with the funds, and what could we earn?
3. When can we get the investment back out, if ever?
4. How much risk of sales disappointment and obsolescence is really connected with this inventory?
5. How much of a return do we want, in view of what we could earn elsewhere or in view of the cost of money to us and the risk the inventory investment entails?

Investment in Facilities. Valuation of investment in facilities is generally important only in long-run planning problems—as, for example, when increases in productive or warehouse capacity are being considered. (Where facilities already exist and are not usable for other purposes, and where planning or scheduling do not contemplate changing these existing facilities, investment is not affected.)

Facilities investment may also be important where productive capacity is taxed, and where the form of the plan or schedule will determine the amount of added capacity which must be installed either to meet the plan itself or for alternative uses. In such cases, considerable care is necessary in defining the facilities investment in order to be consistent with the principles noted above: i.e., that facilities investment should represent out-of-pocket investment, or, alternatively, foregone opportunities to make out-of-pocket investment elsewhere.

Customer Service · An important objective in most production planning and inventory control systems is maintenance of reasonable customer service. An evaluation of the worth of customer service, or the loss suffered through poor service, is an important part of the problem of arriving at a reasonable inventory policy. This cost is typically very difficult to arrive at, including as it does the paper-work costs of rehandling back orders and, usually much more important, the effect that dissatisfaction of customers may have on future profits.

In some cases it may be possible to limit consideration to the cost of producing the needed material on overtime or of purchasing it from the outside and losing the contribution to profit which it would have made. On the other hand, sometimes the possible loss of customers and their sales over a substantial time may outweigh the cost of direct loss in immediate business, and it may be necessary to arrive at a statement of a "reasonable" level of customer service—i.e., the degree of risk of running out of stock, or perhaps the number of times a year the management is willing to run out of an item. In other cases, it may be possible to arrive at a reasonable maximum level of sales which the company is prepared to meet with 100 percent reliability, being reconciled to have service suffer if sales exceed this level.

One of the uses of the analytic techniques described below is to help management arrive at a realistic view of the cost of poor service, or of the value of building high service, by laying out clearly what the cost in inventory investment and schedule changes is to achieve this degree of customer service. Sometimes when these costs are clearly brought home, even a 100 percent service-minded management is willing to settle for a more realistic, "excellent" service at moderate cost, instead of striving for "perfect" service entailing extreme cost.

OPTIMUM LOT SIZE

Now, with this background, let us examine in some detail one of the inventory problems which plague businessmen the most —that of the optimum size of lot to purchase or produce for stock. This happens also to be one of the oldest problems discussed in the industrial engineering texts—but this does not lessen the fact that it is one of the most profitable for a great many companies to attack today with new analytic techniques.

Common Practices · This problem arises, as mentioned earlier, because of the need to purchase or produce in quantities greater than will be used or sold. Thus, specifically, businessmen buy raw materials in sizable quantities—carloads, or even trainloads —in order to reduce the costs connected with purchasing and control, to obtain a favorable price, and to minimize handling and transportation costs. They replenish factory in-process stocks of parts in sizable quantities to avoid, where possible, the costs of equipment setups and clerical routines. Likewise, finished stocks maintained in warehouses usually come in shipments substantially greater than the typical amount sold at once, the motive again being, in part, to avoid equipment setup and paperwork costs and, in the case of field warehouses, to minimize shipping costs.

Where the same equipment is used for a variety of items, the equipment will be devoted first to one item and then to another in sequence, with the length of the run in any individual item to be chosen, as far as is economically possible, to minimize change-over cost from one item to another and to reduce the production time lost because of clean-out requirements during change-overs. Blocked operations of this sort are seen frequently, for example, in the petroleum industry, on packaging lines, or on assembly lines where change-overs from one model to another may require adjustment in feed speeds and settings and change of components.

In all these cases, the practice of replenishing stocks in sizable quantities compared with the typical usage quantity means that inventory has to be carried; it makes it possible to spread fixed costs (e.g., setup and clerical costs) over many units and thus to reduce the unit cost. However, one can carry this principle only so far, for if the replenishment orders become too large, the resulting inventories get out of line, and the capital and handling costs of carrying these inventories more than offset the possible savings in production, transportation, and clerical costs. Here is the matter, again, of striking a balance between these conflicting considerations.

Even though formulas for selecting the optimum lot size are presented in many industrial engineering texts,[3] few companies make any attempt to arrive at an explicit quantitative balance of inventory and change-over or setup costs. Why?

For one thing, the cost elements which enter into an explicit solution frequently are very difficult to measure, or are only very hazily defined. For example, it may be possible to get a fairly accurate measure of the cost of setting up a particular machine,

3. See, for example, Raymond E. Fairfield, *Quantity and Economy in Manufacture* (New York, D. Van Nostrand Company, Inc., 1931).

but it may be almost impossible to derive a precise measure of the cost of making out a new production order. Again, warehouse costs may be accumulated separately on the accounting records, but these rarely show what the cost of housing an *additional* unit of material may be. In my experience the capital cost, or imputed interest cost, connected with inventory investment never appears on the company's accounting records.

Furthermore, the inventory is traditionally valued in such a way that the true incremental investment is difficult to measure for scheduling purposes. Oftentimes companies therefore attempt to strike only a qualitative balance of these costs to arrive at something like an optimum or minimum-cost reorder quantity.

Despite the difficulty in measuring costs—and indeed because of such difficulty—it is eminently worthwhile to look at the lot-size problem explicitly formulated. The value of an analytic solution does not rest solely on one's ability to plug in precise cost data to get an answer. An analytic solution often helps clarify questions of principle, even with only crude data available for use. Moreover, it appears that many companies today still have not accepted the philosophy of optimum reorder quantities from the over-all company standpoint; instead, decisions are dominated from the standpoint of some particular interest such as production or traffic and transportation. Here too the analytic solution can be of help, even when the cost data are incomplete or imperfect.

Case Example · To illustrate how the lot-size problem can be attacked analytically—and what some of the problems and advantages of such an attack are—let us take a fictitious example. The situation is greatly oversimplified on purpose to get quickly to the heart of the analytic approach.

Elements of the Problem. Brown and Brown, Inc., an automotive parts supplier, produces a simple patented electric switch on long-term contracts. The covering is purchased on the outside at $0.01 each, and 1,000 are used regularly each day, 250 days per year.

The castings are made in a nearby plant, and B. and B. sends its own truck to pick them up. The cost of truck operation, maintenance, and the driver amounts to $10 per trip.

The company can send the truck once a day to bring back 1,000 casings for that day's requirements, but this makes the cost of a casing rather high. The truck can go less frequently, but this means that it has to bring back more than the company needs for its immediate day-to-day purposes.

The characteristic "saw-tooth" inventory pattern which will result in shown in Exhibit 1, where 1,000 Q casings are picked up each trip (Q being whatever number of days' supply is obtained per replenishment trip). These are used up over a period of Q days. When the inventory is depleted again, another trip is made to pick up Q days' supply or 1,000 Q casings once more, and so on.

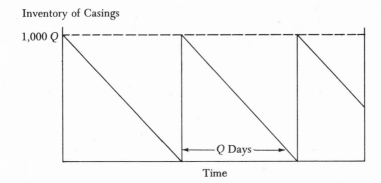

Inventory of Casings

1,000 Q

Q Days

Time

EXHIBIT 1

PATTERN OF INVENTORY BALANCE
(1,000 Q CASINGS OBTAINED PER REPLENISHMENT TRIP;
1,000 CASINGS USED PER DAY)

B. and B. estimates that the cost of storing casings under properly controlled humidity conditions is $1 per 1,000 casings per year. The company wants to obtain a 10 percent return on its inventory investment of $10 (1,000 times $0.01), which means that it should properly charge an additional $1 (10 percent of $10), making a total inventory cost of $2 per 1,000 casings per year.

(Note that, in order to avoid undue complications, the inventory investment charge is made here only against the purchase price of the casings and not against the total delivery cost including transportation. Where transportation is a major component of total cost, it is of course possible and desirable to include it in the base for the inventory charge.)

Graphic Solution. Brown and Brown, Inc., can find what it should do by means of a graph (see Exhibit 2) showing the annual cost of buying, moving, and sorting casings:

Cost (dollars)

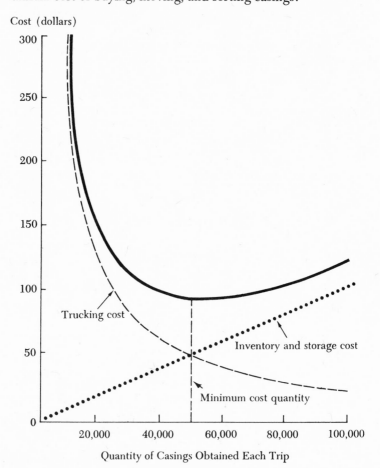

Quantity of Casings Obtained Each Trip

EXHIBIT 2

ANNUAL COST OF BUYING, MOVING, AND STORING CASINGS
COMPARED WITH REORDER QUANTITY

The broken line shows total trucking costs versus the size of the individual purchase quantity:

- If 1,000 casings are purchased at a time, the total cost is $10 times 250 trips, or $2,500 per year.
- If 10,000 casings are purchased at one time, only 25 trips need be made, for a total cost of $250 per year.
- If 100,000 casings are purchased, only 2½ trips, on the average, have to be taken each year, for a total of $25.

The dotted line shows the inventory cost compared with the size of the purchased quantity:

- If 10,000 casings are purchased at one time, the inventory at purchase will contain 10,000, and it will gradually be depleted until none are on hand, when a new purchase will be made. The average inventory on hand will thus be 5,000 casings. The cost per year will be $2 times 5,000 casings, or $10.
- Similarly, if 100,000 casings are purchased at one time, the average inventory will be 50,000 casings, and the total inventory and storage cost will be $100.

The solid line is the total cost, including both trucking and inventory and storage costs. The total cost is at a minimum when 50,000 casings are purchased on each trip and five trips are made each year.

The solution to B. and B.'s problem can be reached algebraically as well as graphically. Exhibit 3 shows how the approach works in this very simple case.

Similar Cases The problem of Brown and Brown, Inc., though artificial, is not too far from the questions many businesses face in fixing reorder quantities.

Despite the simplifications introduced—for example, the assumption that usage is known in advance—the method of solution has been found widely useful in industries ranging from mail order merchandising (replenishing staple lines), through electrical equipment manufacturing (ordering machined parts to replenish stockrooms), to shoe manufacturing (ordering findings and other purchased supplies). In particular, the approach

---

EXHIBIT 3

EXAMPLE OF ALGEBRAIC SOLUTION OF SAME INVENTORY
PROBLEM AS EXHIBIT 2

The total annual cost of supplying casings is equal to the sum of the direct cost of the casings, plus the trucking cost, plus the inventory and storage cost.

Let:

T = total annual cost

b = unit purchase price, $10 per 1,000 casings

s = annual usage, 250,000 casings

A = trucking cost, $10 per trip

N = number of trips per year

i = cost of carrying casings in inventory at the annual rate of $2 per 1,000, or $0.002 per casing

x = size of an individual purchase ($x/2$ = average inventory)

Then the basic equation will be:

$$T = bs + AN + ix/2$$

The problem is to choose the minimum-cost value of x (or, if desired, N). Since x is the same as s/N, N can be expressed as s/x. Substituting s/x for N in the above equation, we get:

$$T = bs + As/x + ix/2$$

From this point on we shall use differential calculus. The derivative of total cost, T, with respect to x will be expressed as:

$$dT/dx = -As/x^2 + i/2$$

And the minimum-cost value of x is that for which the derivative of total cost with respect to x equals zero. This is true when:

$$x = \sqrt{2As/i}$$

Substituting the known values for A, s, and i:

$$x = \sqrt{2 \cdot 10 \cdot 250,000/.002} = 50,000 \text{ casings}$$

---

has been found helpful in controlling stocks made up of many low-value items used regularly in large quantities.

A number of realistic complications might have been introduced into the Brown and Brown, Inc., problem. For example:

• In determining the size of a manufacturing run, it sometimes is important to account explicitly for the production and sales rate. In this case, the inventory balance pattern looks like Exhibit 4 instead of the saw-tooth design in Exhibit 1. The maximum inventory point is not equal to the amount produced in an individual run, but to that quantity less the amount sold during the course of the run. The maximum inventory equals $Q(1 - S/P)$, where Q is the amount produced in a single run, and S and P are the daily sales and production rates respectively.

Inventory of Casings

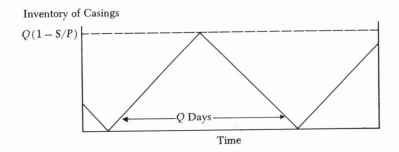

EXHIBIT 4

INFLUENCE OF PRODUCTION AND SALES RATE ON
PRODUCTION CYCLE INVENTORY

This refinement can be important, particularly if the sales rate is fairly large compared with the production rate. Thus, if the sales rate is half the production rate, then the maximum inventory is only half the quantity made in one run, and the average inventory equals only one-fourth the individual run quantity. This means that substantially more inventory can be carried—in fact, about 40 percent more.

• When a number of products are made on a regular cycle, one after another, with the sequence in the cycle established by economy in change-over cost, the total cycle length can be obtained in the same ways as described above. Of course, it sometimes happens that there is a periodic breach in the cycle, either to make an occasional run of a product with very low sales or to allow for planned maintenance of equipment; the very simple run-length formulas can be adjusted to allow for this.

• Other kinds of costs can also be included, such as different sorts of handling costs. Or the inventory cost can be defined in such a way as to include transportation, obsolescence, or even capital and storage cost as part of the unit value of the product against which a charge for capital is made. When a charge for capital is included as part of the base value in computing the cost of capital, this is equivalent to requiring that capital earnings be compounded; this can have an important bearing on decisions connected with very low volume items which might be purchased in relatively large, long-lasting quantities.

Complications such as the foregoing, while important in practice, represent changes in arithmetic rather than in basic concept.

Significant Conclusions · When the analytic approach is applied to Brown and Brown's problem and similar cases, it reveals certain relationships which are significant and useful to executives concerned with inventory management:

(1) *The appropriate order quantity and the average inventory maintained do not vary directly with sales.* In fact, both of these quantities vary with the square root of sales. This means that with the same ordering and setup cost characteristics, the larger the volume of sales of an item, the less inventory per unit of sales is required. One of the sources of inefficiency in many inventory control systems is the rigid adoption of a rule for ordering or carrying inventory equivalent to, say, one month's sales.

(2) *The total cost in the neighborhood of the optimum order quantity is relatively insensitive to moderately small changes in the amount ordered.* Exhibit 2 illustrates this proposition. Thus, all that is needed is just to get in the "right ball park," and a good answer can be obtained even with fairly crude cost data. For example, suppose the company had estimated that its total cost of holding 1,000 casings in inventory for a year was $1 when it actually was $2 (as in our illustration). Working through the same arithmetic, the company would have arrived at an optimum order quantity of 70,000 casings instead of 50,000. Even so, the total cost would have been (using the correct $2 annual carrying cost):

3.6 trips per year @ $10	=	$36
35,000 casings average inventory @ $0.002	=	70
Total annual cost	=	$106

Thus, an error of a factor of 2 in one cost results in only 6 percent difference in total cost.

In summary, Brown and Brown's problem, despite its oversimplification, provides an introduction to the analytic approach to inventory problems.

In particular, it illustrates the first essential in such an approach—i.e., defining an inventory function. In this case the function is to permit purchase or manufacture in economical order quantities or run lengths; in other cases it may be different. The important point is that this basic function can be identified wherever it may be found—in manufacturing, purchasing, or warehouse operation.

The only way to cut inventories is to organize operations so that they are tied more closely together. For example, a company can cut its raw materials inventory by buying in smaller quantities closer to needs, but it does so at a cost; this cost results from the increased clerical operations needed to tie the purchasing function more closely to manufacturing and to keep it more fully informed of manufacturing's plans and operation. The right inventory level is reached when the cost of maintaining any additional inventory cushion offsets the saving that the additional inventory earns by permitting the plant to operate in a somewhat less fully organized fashion.

B. and B.'s problem also illustrates problems and questions connected with defining and making costs explicit. The inventory capital cost is usually not found on a company's books, but it is implied in some of the disagreements over inventory policy. Here, again, bringing the matter into the open may help each side in a discussion to recognize its own and the others' hidden assumptions, and thus more quickly to reach a common agreement.

Queuing Analysis and
Monte Carlo Methods

WILLIAM J. BAUMOL

William J. Baumol is Professor of Economics at Princeton and New York Universities. This article is taken from his book, Economic Theory and Operations Analysis.

QUEUING ANALYSIS

Queuing theory is one of the subjects which has loomed large in the literature of operations research. Any operation in which the objects to be dealt with arrive at irregular intervals, and in which the operating facilities are of limited capacity, is a queuing problem. Automobiles waiting to be serviced in a garage, subway riders waiting to get through a turnstile, and telephone callers waiting for a clear line all constitute queues. Among the real problems to which queuing theory has been applied are the landing of aircraft, the parking of automobiles, the timing of traffic lights, the processing of films, and the servicing of travelers through customs.

One of the key characteristics of a queue is the random pattern of arrivals, which can therefore only be described in probabilistic terms. There will be times, which cannot be predicted precisely, when the number of arrivals will be unusually large, and as a result, it will then take longer to be serviced. For example, in a supermarket, customer delays at the checkout counters may be caused by the arrival of a large number of customers at the same time, or by the coincidental arrival of several customers each of whom has many groceries in her shopping basket, so that the average checkout time is materially increased.

Suppose the manager of the supermarket wishes to know what sort of delays his customers are likely to encounter. The analyst requires information about two frequency distributions, one describing customer arrivals and the other the length of time it takes a clerk to handle a customer's purchases. Once both of these have been found, mathematical analysis permits us, in many cases, to find out such things as the expected average customer waiting time, the expected length of the waiting lines at different times of the day or week, etc.

The basic idea of the calculation is relatively simple, although the details are ingenious and complicated. The probability that there will be, say, 25 customers waiting now is equal to the sum of probabilities of the several alternative series of events which can produce this result. For example, there would now be 25 customers in line if 24 customers were there one minute ago, none has since been serviced, and one more customer has just arrived. Since we know the probability of a customer's having been serviced during any one minute and of a customer's arriving during any one minute, we can find out the relationship between the probability that there were 24 customers a minute ago and the probability that there are 25 customers in line now. Similarly, we can find the probability that the lines will grow from 25 to 26 customers in this way; and we can trace, customer by customer, the expected growth of the queues in the supermarket from the time it opens in the morning with zero customers.

One of the most interesting results of the theory states, in effect, that service facilities must have excess capacity built into them if service is not to break down altogether. More specifically, suppose the service facilities, if they were always kept fully occupied, were just sufficient to meet the needs of all the store's customers. Then queues would just grow longer and longer, without limit, and ultimately the operations would collapse. The basic reason for this result is, of course, that customer arrivals are *not* spread evenly in time, and so during some periods the facility will temporarily be idle whereas at other times it will be overcrowded. But, by assumption, the facilities would be of sufficient capacity only if there were no such oscillations in customer arrival time. To permit them to cope with bunched arrivals, therefore, the capacity of service facilities must be increased.

The theory also permits us, at least in principle, to investigate how much the expected length of queue lines will be reduced when a number of new checkout counters are added in our supermarket. This immediately raises an optimality question— just how many checkout counters should the supermarket have? More counters cost money to install and operate. Too many counters will therefore be wasteful, but too small a number of counters will slow down service and lose customers. The optimality problem, then, is to determine the intermediate number of counters which best serves management's purposes. Unfortunately, these probabilistic optimality calculations are often likely to grow very complex; therefore, instead of a direct approach to the problem, the operations researcher frequently resorts to the methods described in the following section.

ARTIFICIAL EXPERIMENTATION: MONTE CARLO TECHNIQUES

Before we can hope to find out the consequences of a course of action, it is necessary to have some sort of data. For example, suppose, as before, that it is desired to test some proposed service facilities to see how often customers will be kept waiting, and how long they will have to wait, on the average. These figures, of course, depend on the fluctuations in the number of customer arrivals—how frequently their number will exceed a particular magnitude.

In solving such a problem, experimentation is not a real possibility. It can be costly in customer relations to try very much more meager service facilities just to see what will happen. It may be that some information can be obtained from the experience of other supermarkets. But this may be too limited in range and in quantity to be of much assistance.

The operations researcher has, however, invented another very effective way to gather the relevant data: that is, to make them up himself, or rather to let the mathematical statistician make them up for him! But one may well ask, how can improvised statistics help us to foresee what will happen in the real world?

The answer is that the numbers are invented in a manner which carefully employs the analytical methods of mathematical statistics in order to stretch as far as possible such few actual data as are available to begin with. At some particular moment in the week we may assume that customers will arrive randomly, in a pattern somewhat similar to outcomes in successive throws of a pair of dice. The pattern of customer arrivals may then be described in terms of a frequency distribution, which indicates how many weeks in a year customer arrivals per hour can be expected to fall between 100 and 110 units, how often the number will lie in the 110 to 120 range, etc.

Now, from the available information *and the nature of the problem,* the statistician can often decide which frequency distribution best describes the pattern of expected customer arrivals. From this frequency distribution it is then possible to construct an artificial history of customer arrivals by choosing randomly among all the possibilities, but in a way which is "loaded" to produce the right frequencies. To give a very simple illustration, suppose we consider two possibilities: A, fewer than 100 arrivals per hour and B, at least 100 arrivals. If, on some basis, the odds are computed to be 2 to 1 in favor of A, we can generate an artificial demand history as follows: Toss the (unbiased) die. If it falls, 1, 2, 3, or 4, put down an A; if it falls 5 or 6, put down a B. This might yield a pattern for weekly demands such as the following:

TABLE 1

| | | Arrival "history" | |
"Week"	Face of die	Under 100	100 or more
First	3	A	
Second	1	A	
Third	3	A	
Fourth	5		B
Fifth	6		B
Sixth	2	A	
Seventh	2	A	

This, incidentally, indicates the reason for the term "Monte Carlo method."

In practice, it is not actually necessary to toss any dice. Instead, we can use tables called "tables of random numbers" which have been worked out in advance. Moreover, the computations can be made by high-speed electronic computers which are able, in a few minutes or hours, to run off thousands of cases and manufacture data whose collection would, otherwise, require many years. But although this method is economical and powerful, it must be used only with the greatest care and caution. As we have seen, everything depends on the choice of frequency distribution (i.e., the odds of the various outcomes), and unless there is some assurance that these have been picked well, the entire calculation can be worthless.

Once this artificial experience has been generated, it can be used to find approximate solutions to optimality problems such as that of determining the number of checkout counters which was described in the last section—problems where straightforward computational methods are too complex. To illustrate the approach, consider the (unrelated) problem of finding an approximate root of the equation

$$X^2 - 6X + 9.1 = 0.$$

Instead of using the standard formula, we can go about it indirectly by trial and error, first, say, substituting $X = 1$ to find that the expression takes the value

$$(1)^2 - 6(1) + 9.1 = 4.1.$$

Clearly, $X = 1$ is not our root. So we try again, this time using, say, $X = 0$, and we see that this value of X makes the expression equal 9.1—i.e., it has only made things worse. We therefore infer that we have been going in the wrong direction, so this time we go up and try $X = 2$, etc. The results of several such trials can be tabulated as follows:

Trial value of X	1	0	2	3	4
Value of $X^2 - 6X + 9.1$	4.1	9.1	1.1	0.1	1.1

Clearly, this suggests that there is a root located very close to $X = 3$, at which the value of the expression is very close to zero, and we can take this as the approximate value of the root we are seeking.

The finding of optimal solutions in queuing problems and many other difficult operations problems can be approached in somewhat the same spirit with the aid of Monte Carlo methods. A number of alternative possibilities (number of possible checkout counters) can be postulated, and their consequences over a long period can then be simulated and reported on by the computer with the aid of Monte Carlo predictions of customer arrivals. If our objective is to minimize some sort of over-all cost function (which includes the costs of operating additional checkout counters as well as the costs of customer delays), we would take the optimal solution to be approximated by that trial (number of checkout counters) for which the machine reported the lowest over-all expected costs.

Unfortunately, this description, although correct in essence, is somewhat misleading in its simplicity. Particularly where decisions involve the assignment of values to a number of interrelated variables and where the ranges of possible values are considerable, there are difficult problems in deciding on what combination of values to try out next. It is by no means easy to design a procedure which converges with reasonable rapidity toward an optimal solution.

It is to be emphasized that the use of Monte Carlo methods is not limited to queuing problems. They can be used in inventory analysis, replacement analysis (when to stop repairing a piece of equipment and replace it with a new one), and a wide variety of other situations in which a prominent role is played by probabilistic elements such as the timing and magnitudes of customer demands or of the need for repairs.

Part Eight

Business, Government, and Public-Sector Decision Making

BUSINESS decisions are circumscribed and regulated by the government. In recent years, with the increased competition from foreign producers, there has been considerable pressure for, and controversy over, quotas and other government policies designed to protect American industry. The opening article, by the editor, analyzes the economic effects of steel import quotas. The following item, which is taken from the opinion of the U.S. Court of Appeals, relates to the case in which International Business Machines Corporation appealed a judgment in favor of Telex Computer Products. This was one of the most important cases in the antitrust field in recent years.

Modern economic analysis and operations research have come to play a significant role in the public sector of the economy as well as in private business. In the next article, E. S. Savas shows how some relatively simple analytical techniques were used to help New York City do a better job of coping with snow emergencies. The following paper, by Howard, Matheson, and North, describes how decision theory has been used to analyze whether or not the federal government should seed hurricanes.

Next, we discuss cost-benefit analysis, an important tool of applied economics that has been employed frequently to help improve decision making in the public sector of the economy. Roland N. McKean describes the nature and limitations of cost-benefit analyses, such analyses being "attempts to estimate certain costs and gains that would result from alternative courses of action." McKean points out the common elements in all such analyses and cites some pitfalls that may lie in wait for the unwary analyst. Hirshleifer, De Haven, and Milliman discuss the economic aspects of the utilization of existing water supplies. They show various ways that economic analysis can be useful in formulating public policy in this area. Finally, the Congressional Budget Office analyzes the cost and pricing of the space shuttle.

The Economic Effects of
Steel Import Quotas

EDWIN MANSFIELD

*Edwin Mansfield is Director of the Center for
Economics and Technology at the University of
Pennsylvania. This is an excerpt from the fifth
edition of his book,* Microeconomics: Theory and
Applications, *published in 1985.*

During the early 1980s, the system of free trade that helped to
bring about the economic prosperity of the 1960s and 1970s came
under increasing attack. The recession of 1981–82 resulted in serious unemployment in many nations of the world. With over 20 million people out of work in 1983 in the United States and Western
Europe alone, a growing number of businessmen, labor leaders,
and politicians raised their voices to demand protectionist barriers
against foreign competition. Nowhere was there more concern over
foreign competition than in the American steel industry, which rolled
up an impressive record of losses in the early 1980s. (For example,
Bethlehem Steel Corporation lost about $1.5 billion in 1982.) Faced
with great difficulties in competing with Japanese and other foreign
steelmakers, American steel firms pleaded with the government to
set quotas limiting the quantity of steel that could be imported into
the United States, and their petitions were heard. The European
Community promised to hold the amount of steel it exported to the
United States to an average of only 5.4 percent of the American
market. And in May 1983, the International Trade Commission
unanimously recommended that the United States establish quotas

on the amount of some steel products that could be imported for three years.

An enormous amount of controversy resulted among economists and others. Traditionally, most economists have argued against quotas of this sort on the grounds that they reduce trade, raise prices, protect domestic industry at the expense of consumers, and reduce the standard of living of the nation as a whole. To estimate the effects of such a quota, the staff of the Federal Trade Commission (FTC) carried out a detailed economic study,[1] which is useful in demonstrating how microeconomic theory can contribute to the analysis of major public policies. To begin with, the FTC economists estimated the demand curve for steel in the United States and the supply curve for U.S.-produced steel, both shown in Figure 1. The supply curve for foreign-produced steel was a horizontal line at $311. Thus, adding horizontally the supply curve for U.S. steel and the supply curve for foreign steel, we get the supply curve of all steel in the United States, which is SGW. Since this supply curve intersects the demand curve at point A, the equilibrium price is $311 per ton and the equilibrium quantity is 91.7 million tons of steel. The U.S. steel industry supplies 78.1 million tons, and foreigners supply 13.6 million tons.

What is the effect if the U.S. government imposes a quota which limits imports to 11 million tons? In other words, what would happen if American steel imports could not exceed 11 million tons? The demand and supply curves show that, if the price is $322, American demand will exceed American supply by 11 million tons. Thus, once the quota is imposed, the price will rise to $322, since this is the price that will reduce our imports to the amount of the quota. Consequently, the equilibrium will be at point B, where price is $322 per ton and the equilibrium quantity is 90.8 million tons of steel. The U.S. steel industry supplies 79.8 million tons, and foreigners supply 11 million tons.

Who gains and who loses from this quota? American consumers lose an amount equal to the shaded area in Figure 1. Before the imposition of the quota, consumer's surplus in the United States equals the area under the demand curve above the price of $311 (that is, it equals the area of triangle DCA). After the imposition of

1. Federal Trade Commission, *Staff Report on the United States Steel Industry and Its International Rivals*, November 1977.

FIGURE 1

EFFECTS OF A STEEL IMPORT QUOTA

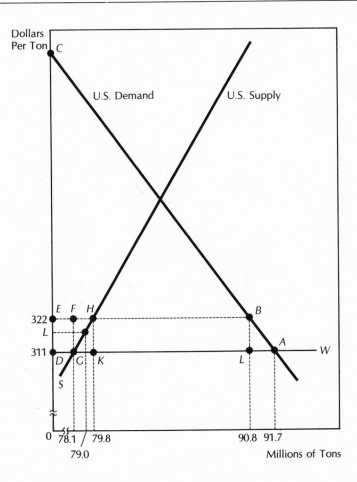

the quota, consumer's surplus in the United States equals the area of triangle *ECB*). The reduction in consumer's surplus due to the imposition of the quota is area *DCA* minus *ECB*, or area *DEBA* (which is shaded). This area equals ½(322 − 311)(90.8 + 91.7) = 1,003.75 millions of dollars. Thus consumers stand to lose about $1 billion per year from the quota.

American steel producers gain from the quota, their gain being of two types. First, they are able sell the 78.1 million tons that they would have sold without the quota at a higher price ($322 rather than $311). The extra profit equals the area of rectangle *DEFG*, or $(322 - 311)$ $(78.1) = 859.1$ millions of dollars. Second, they are able to sell 79.8, rather than 78.1 million tons. Their profit from the extra 1.7 million tons equals the area of triangle *GFH*, or $\frac{1}{2}(322 - 311)$ $(79.8 - 78.1) = 9.4$ millions of dollars. (Why is this their profit? Because the supply curve shows the industry's marginal cost at each level of output. For example, the marginal cost of the 79-millionth ton of U.S.-produced steel equals *OL*. Thus the profit earned from the 79-millionth ton equals its price minus *OL*, or $322 - OL$. If we add up the difference between price and marginal cost for all of the extra 1.7 million tons, we get the area of triangle *GFH*.) Adding the two types of gain, American steel producers increase their profits by $859.1 + 9.4 = 868.5$ millions of dollars per year.

Part of U.S. consumers' losses find their way into the pockets of foreign steelmakers. After the imposition of the quota, U.S. consumers buy 11 million tons of foreign steel products, which cost $322 - 311 = 11$ dollars per ton more than before the imposition of the quota. Thus $11 \times 11 = 121$ millions of dollars per year (the area of rectangle *KHBL*) of U.S. consumers' losses are transferred to foreign steelmakers.[2]

In addition, part of U.S. consumers' losses is due to their consuming 90.8 rather than 91.7 million tons of steel products. The loss in consumer's surplus arising from their forgoing the consumption of these 0.9 million tons equals the area of triangle *LBA*, or $\frac{1}{2}(322 - 311)$ $(91.7 - 90.8) = 5.0$ millions of dollars. The area of this triangle equals the consumer's surplus from the consumption of these 0.9 million tons.

Finally, part of U.S. consumers' losses is due to the fact that more costly U.S. steel is being substituted for less costly foreign steel. After the quota is introduced, U.S. steel firms produce 79.8 million tons, in contrast to 78.1 million tons before the imposition of the

---

2. This assumes that foreign exporters would be called upon to monitor exports to comply with the quota. Alternatively, with restrictive licensing of domestic importers, the importers extract this profit. According to the FTC economists, the former assumption is more likely.

quota. The extra $79.8 - 78.1 = 1.7$ million tons could be obtained more cheaply from foreign producers. The total extra amount that U.S. consumers pay for this 1.7 million tons equals the area of triangle GHK, or $\frac{1}{2}(322 - 311)(79.8 - 78.1) = 9.4$ millions of dollars. (Why is this the correct measure? Because the extra amount paid for each ton is the difference between the marginal cost of producing it in the U.S. and the cost of obtaining it from abroad. For example, for the 79-millionth ton produced in the United States this difference equals $OL - \$311$, since its marginal cost equals OL and the cost of obtaining it from abroad is $311. Thus, if we sum up the differences for all 1.7 million extra tons, the total extra amount that consumers pay for this reason equals the area of triangle GHK.)

To sum up, this analysis indicates that U.S. steel producers gain \$868.5 million per year from the quota, while U.S. consumers lose \$1,003.75 million per year. Thus consumers lose more than producers gain. Part of the difference goes to foreign producers; the rest is due to lower consumption of steel products and the substitution of high-cost U.S. steel for cheaper foreign steel.

It is important to note the limitations as well as the usefulness of these results. Because of the roughness of the data, figures like \$868.5 million are spuriously accurate. More important, the analysis, by looking simply at how all U.S. consumers and all U.S. steel producers are affected, evades many issues. For example, once one recognizes that we cannot make interpersonal comparisons of utility, the interpretation of the results is clouded. Also, the simple demand-and-supply analysis in Figure 1 may not be appropriate, given the market structure in the steel industry. Nonetheless, economists find it worthwhile to make studies of this sort. . . . Although the importance of political factors is obvious, microeconomic investigations of this sort have had an important influence on policy-makers inside and outside the government who are concerned with protectionist barriers, here and abroad, against free trade.

Telex Corporation *v.* International Business Machines Corporation

U.S. COURT OF APPEALS

This case, decided in 1975, was one of the most important in the antitrust field in recent years. It was held before Circuit Judges Seth, McWilliams, and Doyle. The following passages are taken from the opinion. [510 F.2d 814 (1975)]

COMPLAINT AND DISCOVERY PROCEEDINGS

The appellant, International Business Machines Corporation (IBM), here appeals a judgment in favor of Telex Computer Products, Inc. (Telex), appellee, in the total amount of $259.5 million, plus $1.2 million in attorney's fees and costs (this latter amount was stipulated by the parties). Actual damages were determined to be in the amount of $117.5 million. This amount was reduced substantially before trebling so as to prevent Telex from profiting as a result of certain advantages obtained from unlawful competitive activities and its illegal obtaining of trade secrets of IBM. Originally the trial court had ordered damages in favor of Telex in the amount of $352.5 million, but in amended findings and judgment this was reduced as stated above.

Telex has alleged in the complaint that IBM violated sections 1 and 2 of the Sherman Act, 15 U.S.C. §§ 1, 2, and section 2 of the

Clayton Act, 15 U.S. C. § 13, in that IBM had monopolized and attempted to monopolize the manufacture, distribution, sale, and leasing of electronic data processing equipment. The complaint was later amended to charge IBM in more specific terms with monopolization in the manufacture, distribution, sale, and leasing of plug compatible peripheral products which are attached to IBM central processing units.

IBM in turn filed a counterclaim against Telex in which the latter is charged with unfair competition, theft of trade secrets, and copyright infringement pursuant to both state law and 17 U.S. C. § 101. . . .

EVIDENCE PRESENTED AT THE TRIAL

The evidence established that IBM was first incorporated in 1924 and operated as a producer of office machinery and equipment. However, in the early 1950's it entered the electronic data processing industry. It produced a research computer in 1953 and installed its first computer for use in commercial work in 1955. Telex began manufacturing electronic data processing products in the year 1959. The evidence established in the court found that the electronic data processing industry was a young, dynamic one with a tremendous amount of revenue. In 1952 its total revenues were $48 million. By 1970 its total revenues equalled $10.2 billion. The number of companies in the electronic data processing business grew from thirteen in 1952 to 1,773 in 1970. Nevertheless, IBM, although originally dominant, steadily declined. It had 64.1 percent of the electronic data processing revenues in 1952, but only 35.1 percent of the total revenue in the year 1970. Although IBM was recognized as an industry leader, having more revenue from the industry than any other company, it did not, according to the finding of the trial court, have monopoly power or status in the industry as a whole.

At the outset it is necessary to distinguish between the general systems portion of the industry which encompasses the manufacture of the basic electronic data processing system, the essential equipment being a central processing unit. The number of manufacturers engaged in the manufacturing of the processing units increased dramatically, from three in 1952 to ninety-six in 1972. The court found that about eight or nine of these were considered principal manufacturers. In the segment of the industry involving the manufacture of the central processing units, IBM did not have monopoly power, although it was estimated by the court that its market share was about thirty-five percent.

In addition to the central processing unit, a data processing system also has a number of so-called peripheral devices which are connected with the central processing unit and which perform various special functions in the data processing system. These include information storage components like magnetic tape drives, magnetic disk drives, magnetic drums, and magnetic strip files; terminal devices such as printers; memory units, which are specialized storage units, and other similar types of peripheral components. Sometimes these devices are included in the central processing unit, that is, do not exist as external components. It is these peripheral components with which we are primarily concerned in this lawsuit. The importance of these can be judged from the fact that the court found that they constitute 50 to 75 percent of the total price of an electronic data processing system. The term "plug compatible peripheral device" is the specific class of equipment that enters into this case. What is meant is that a producer of a complete electronic processing unit manufactures, as noted, the central processing unit and peripheral components which are geared to use on that central processing unit. Many manufacturers produce peripheral components primarily for attachment to central processing units of a particular manufacturer and so, therefore, the plug compatible peripheral device refers to a component which is functionally equivalent to the manufacturer's peripheral device and can be readily plugged into that central processing unit. Undoubtedly it is the wide use of the IBM central processing unit that caused Telex and others to market peripheral devices which were plug compatible with the IBM unit and which could replace IBM peripheral devices which had been made for the IBM central system.

The Relevant Market · The District Court found that there existed a definable market for all peripheral devices plug compatible with IBM processing units. The court further found that there were individual submarkets for each particular type of peripheral product.

In making its finding as to the scope and extent of the plug compatible peripheral, the trial court used IBM documents which found that the original entry into the market was relatively simple and easy because the manufacturer needed only to produce the peripheral device and he could copy test IBM peripheral products. The number of manufacturers of IBM peripherals rose from two or three in 1966 to approximately 100 as of the time of trial. Telex and some eleven others were the major manufacturers of IBM plug compatible products.

Originally, of course, IBM, being the only manufacturer of peripheral products plug compatible with its system, had 100 percent of the market. The court found that as other manufacturers entered the plug compatible market with IBM, the IBM share became substantially eroded and this is particularly true starting in 1968, at which time market erosion occurred first in the tape drive line followed by the disk drive line in 1969 and with continued erosion into 1970.

The court considered the erosion of IBM's market in this area as appropriate background for consideration of the IBM antitrust violations which the court concluded had occurred. The primary determination was that IBM was guilty of monopolization or attempting to monopolize, contrary to section 2 of the Sherman Act in five specific respects:

1. Announcement and institution of the 2319A disk storage facility in September 1970.
2. The announcement of the 2319B disk storage facility in December 1970.
3. The announcement of the Fixed Term Plan long term leasing program in May 1971.
4. The announcement and implementation of the Extended Term Plan, which was also a leasing plan, in March 1972.
5. IBM's pricing policies with regard to its memory products during 1970 and 1971. . . .

CONSIDERATION OF THE ISSUES

The Relevant Market · The threshold issue is whether the court erred in its findings as to the scope and extent of the relevant product market for determination whether there existed power to control prices or to exclude competition, that is, whether there was monopoly power. As heretofore pointed out, the court determined that the relevant product market was limited to peripheral devices plug compatible with IBM central processing units together with particular product submarkets; magnetic tape products, direct access storage products, memory products, impact printer products, and communication controllers, all of which were plug compatible with an IBM CPU. IBM had sought a determination that the relevant product market consisted of electronic data processing systems together with the products which are part of such systems or at least that the relevant product market should consist of all peripheral products and not be limited to those currently attached to IBM systems.

The trial court's initial approach to the problem was restricted to consideration of whether the market "may be realistically subdivided in the time frame 1969–1972 to focus on and encompass only those parts of current product lines which are respectively attached to IBM systems rather than all those products which actually have similar uses in connection with other systems." The court recognized that inasmuch as every manufacturer, originally at least, has 100 percent of its own product, including the peripherals, the likelihood of finding monopolization in this area increases as the circumscribing products market is more circumscribed.

The trial court also recognized that the cost of adaptation of peripherals to the CPUs of other systems is roughly the same with respect to every system, that is, the cost of the interface, the attachment which allows the use of peripherals manufactured by one system to be used on another central processing unit is generally about the same. But these practical interchange possibilities did not deter the court in reaching a conclusion that the products market was practically restricted. A factor which influenced the trial court was the commitment of Telex to supplying peripherals plug compatible with IBM systems. The court appeared to disregard the interchangeability aspect of the peripherals manufactured by companies other than IBM, giving emphasis to the fact that Telex, for example, had not chosen to manufacture such peripheral products of the kind and character manufactured by companies other than IBM. The trial court did, however, recognize the presence of interchangeability of use and the presence of cross-elasticity of demand. The court thought, however, that the presence of these factors was not sufficiently immediate.

(1) We recognize that market definition is generally treated as a matter of fact and that findings on this subject are not to be overturned unless clearly erroneous. Our question is, therefore, whether it was clearly erroneous for the court to exclude peripheral products of systems other than IBM such as Honeywell, Univac, Burroughs, Control Data Corp. and others, together with peripheral products plug compatible with the systems and, indeed, whether the systems themselves manufactured by the companies are to be taken into account. It is significant, of course, that peripheral products constitute a large percentage of the entire data processing system, somewhere between 50 and 75 percent.

Inasmuch as IBM's share of the data processing industry as a whole is insufficient to justify any inference or conclusion of market power in IBM, the exclusion from the defined market of those products which are not plug compatible with IBM central processing units has a significant impact on the court's decision that IBM possessed monopoly power.

We then must inquire whether this market definition was correct in light of the following factors:

1. Should peripheral products not plug compatible with IBM systems be considered part of the relevant market in view of the existence of easy and practicable interchange of these products by use of interfaces designed for this purpose?

2. Should not the peripheral products plug compatible with systems other than IBM be considered part of the relevant market because of the admitted competition existing between system manufacturers on a system by system basis in which the peripherals are a significant part of the system?

In dealing with the issue whether peripheral products non-compatible with IBM systems ought to be considered, the court said in Finding 47 that as a *practical* matter there is no direct competition between IBM peripherals and the peripherals of other systems manufacturers. However, this finding is out of harmony with other findings which the court made. *See*, for example, Finding 38, wherein the court said that "It cannot be gainsaid that indirectly at least and to some degree the peripheral products attached to non-IBM systems necessarily compete with and constrain IBM's power with respect to peripherals attached to IBM systems." The court also stated in Finding 38 that:

[S]uppliers of peripherals plug compatible with non-IBM systems could in various instances shift to the production of IBM plug compatible peripherals, and vice versa, should the economic rewards in the realities of the market become sufficiently attractive and if predatory practices of others did not dissuade them. In the absence of defensive tactics on the part of manufacturers of CPU's, the cost of developing an interface for a peripheral device would generally be about the same regardless of the system to which it would be attached, and such cost has not constituted a substantial portion of the development cost of the peripheral device.

The factor of ease of designing interfaces to allow interchange of peripherals was obviously troublesome to the court and this trouble continued after the court had rendered its decision. He was still treating the issue on October 17, 1973, in the posttrial hearing. *See* Court Papers, 445–446. The court's final words on the subject were:

I'm down to the edge lawn, and I think the best service I can do is to speed the matter to that final determination. If I'm wrong on my market definition, then you did what you had a right to do.

In essence, [a] witness said that the engineering costs of developing interfaces was minimal and that he had advocated modifying interfaces so that Telex products could be used with systems other than IBM. Another example of ease of interface design is shown by the fact that following RCA's decision to abandon the computer systems business and turn it over to Univac, Telex recognized a marketing opportunity and it began marketing its 6420 tape unit, the plug compatible equivalent of IBM's 3420 Aspen tape unit, as a plug compatible unit with RCA CPUs. The documents sought to emphasize the ease of use in the RCA system of this peripheral equipment designed for IBM equipment originally.

Still another exhibit in the record recognizing the practicability of interface change on peripheral equipment is a February 4, 1972, memorandum of R. M. Wheeler, Chairman of the Board of Telex, requesting a letter or his signature which could be sent to systems manufacturers. This letter was to be sent to systems manufacturers. It offered to sell peripheral equipment plug compatible with the central processing units of the manufacturers. Specific reference was made to the 6420 tape unit, among others, which would normally be compatible to IBM's central processing unit. The Wheeler letter stated that Telex would be willing to interface their equipment at no cost to the purchaser.

Manufacturers of peripherals were not limited to those which were plug compatible with IBM CPU's. These manufacturers were free to adapt their products through interface changes to plug into non-IBM systems. It also followed that systems manufacturers could modify interfaces so that their own peripheral products could plug into IBM CPUs. Factually, then, there existed peripheral products of other CPU manufacturers which were competitive with IBM peripherals and unquestionably other IBM peripherals were capable of having their interfaces modified so that their peripheral products would plug into non-IBM's CPU.

(2) The fact that Telex had substantially devoted itself to the manufacture of peripheral products which were used in IBM CPUs and which competed with IBM peripheral products cannot control in determining product market since the legal standard is whether the product is reasonably interchangeable.

This standard was laid down by the Supreme Court in the famous case of *United States* v. *E. I. DuPont de Nemours & Co.*, 351 U.S. 377, 76 S.Ct. 994, 100 L.Ed. 1264 (1956). In this case, as in the case at bar, the scope of the products market was crucial. The Supreme Court determined that if one product may substitute for another in the market it is "reasonably interchangeable." It was applied there even though DuPont largely controlled the production of cellophane. It was held to be not guilty of monopolization simply because the relevant market included cellophane as well as other flexible wrapping materials. On this the Court stated:

[W]here there are market alternatives that buyers may readily use for their purposes, illegal monopoly does not exist because the product said to be monopolized differs from others. If it were not so, only physically identical products would be a part of the market. [351 U.S. at 394, 76 S.Ct. at 1006–1007.]

(3) One evidence of cross-elasticity is the responsiveness of sales of one product to price changes of another. But a finding of actual fungibility is not necessary to a conclusion that products have potential substitutability. In this respect the Court said:

Every manufacturer is the sole producer of the particular commodity it makes but its control in the above sense of the relevant market depends upon the availability of alternative commodities for buyers: i.e., whether there is a cross-elasticity of demand between cellophane and the other wrappings. This interchangeability is largely gauged by the purchase of competing products for similar uses considering the price, characteristics and adaptability of the competing commodities. [351 U.S. at 380, 76 S.Ct. at 999.]

The Court's further rendition of examples clarified its ruling:

Determination of the competitive market for commodities depends on how different from one another are the offered commodities in character or use, how far buyers will go to substitute one commodity for another.

The Court then turned its attention to the analogy of building materials and said:

For example, one can think of building materials as in commodity competition but one could hardly say that brick competed with steel or wood or cement or stone in the meaning of Sherman Act litigation; the products are too different. . . .

The Court continued:

On the other hand, there are certain differences in the formulae for soft drinks but one can hardly say that each one is an illegal monopoly. [351 U.S. at 393, 76 S.Ct. at 1006.]

It is helpful to consider the rulings of lower courts based on the *DuPont* decision. An example is *United States* v. *Charles Pfizer & Co.*, 246 F.Supp. 464 (D.C.N.Y.1965), where the court applied the ruling of *DuPont* that complete identity of use is not a prerequisite to a finding of interchangeability. The government had argued that the defendant had a monopoly in the citric acid market. The record, however, disclosed that citric acid was in competition with lactic acid, tartaric acid, phosphoric acid, and fumaric acid in its uses in the food and beverage industry. Since these different products were functionally interchangeable, the court decided that the relevant market included all such acidic products, and on that account the government was held to have not proven that the relevant market was solely the citric acid market. . . .

The consequences of the Court's holding are very clear; there can be no ruling of monopolization where the issue is judged on the basis of the entire market rather than a small segment of it. . . .

(4) It seems clear that reasonable interchangeability is proven in the case at bar and hence the market should include not only peripheral products plug compatible with IBM CPUs, but all peripheral products, those compatible not only with IBM CPUs but those compatible with non-IBM systems. This is wholly justifiable because the record shows that these products, although not fungible, are fully interchangeable and may be interchanged with minimal financial outlay, and so cross-elasticity exists within meaning of the *DuPont* decision.

(5) The court's very restrictive definition of the product market in the face of evidence which established the interchangeable quality of the products in question, together with the existence of cross-elasticity of demand, must be regarded as plain error. . . .

The Political Properties of Crystalline H₂O: Planning for Snow Emergencies in New York

E. S. SAVAS

E. S. Savas is Professor of Public Systems Management at Columbia University. This paper appeared in Management Science *in 1973.*

It was on Sunday, February 9, 1969, that a malevolent god of weather deposited a goodly amount of snow upon New York City —this in spite of repeated forecasts by the official U.S. weather seers that nothing of the sort was going to happen. By the time the Department of Sanitation realized that the city was in for a real humdinger and called in additional men to augment its skeletal Sunday work force, many men could not reach their work stations because traffic arteries were impassable and public transit was reduced to spasmodic operation. Those who managed to report to work found that their equipment frequently could not cope with the deep drifts that had accumulated, and broke down. Or, they looked back on their freshly plowed swath and watched the wind undo their work. Others could not proceed because abandoned cars blocked their paths. Some succeeded in finishing their plowing assignments, only to discover later that what they had plowed turned out to be an isolated street segment because the abutting, complementary plow routes fore and aft of their stretch, lying within adjacent districts, could not be completed.

Late Sunday the city was a winter wonderland. Families tumbled out of the canyons and frolicked together in the snow, while some skiers were sighted ostentatiously poling along the truly Great White Way. By mid-week however, with only scant progress evident in the mammoth task of clearing away the snow, the brief holiday mood had long since given way to denunciations by assorted politicians, labor leaders, businessmen, and a high United Nations official, complaints from the public, critical editorials, calls for resignations, City Council hearings—and loud, prolonged jeering with pointed, indelicate suggestions during a visit to Queens—all directed at Mayor John V. Lindsay. In particular, many self-professed "little people" living in the "outer boroughs" of Queens, Brooklyn, the Bronx, and Staten Island resented what they felt was an undue concentration on cleaning up the snow in Manhattan, where the sophisticated smart set is reputed to live, while Mayor Lindsay, as usual in their eyes, ignored them and their simple, middle-class needs in favor of the rest of the city. That the mayoral election later in the year would afford a splendid opportunity for retribution did not entirely escape the attention of the mayor's angry critics.

Every special interest group had its own diagnosis of the problem and its own preferred solution. Surprisingly enough, each solution that was offered usually meant more money for the offerer. For example, one proffered solution was to have more sanitation workers on duty around the clock during the winter, at overtime rates. Another was to buy more snow-removal equipment. Yet another was to hire more mechanics to maintain the existing equipment. Still another was to allow sanitation workers to report for snow-removal duty wherever they found it convenient, presumably near their homes. Finally, owners of large bulldozers thought that the problem would be substantially alleviated if the city would merely agree to pay usurious rates to hire their equipment during snow emergencies.

It was in such harried, emotional, and politically charged circumstances, eight days after the storm, that Mayor Lindsay directed the systems analysis unit in his office to undertake a thorough study of the city's snow-fighting capability. The analysts pounced upon the problem like dogs presented with a choice T-bone steak, delighted at the opportunity to gnaw on such a fresh and meaty morsel.

The analysis was not to be an inquisition to find a culprit or a scapegoat. Its objective was to find out what went wrong and to prevent its recurrence. Realistically, the project could not be expected to produce meaningful results soon enough to be useful during the remaining few weeks of the current snow season. In fact, Deputy Mayor Timothy W. Costello, to whom the unit reported, cautioned them against excessive enthusiasm and subsequent disappointment by suggesting that it would be a warm day in New York when the study was finished, with interest in the problem having melted away with the snows of yesteryear.

STRUCTURING THE PROBLEM

A review of the literature and a survey of practices in other cities, together with an examination of the written procedures in New York City, proved generally informative but failed to provide a methodology suitable for the task at hand. Accordingly, it was necessary to create an original approach to the problem and after some initial groping the effort gradually crystallized about four fundamental, strategic questions:

(1) How much snow falls on New York City?

(2) How much work has to be done to clean it up?

(3) What is the city's capacity for performing this work?

(4) What improvements are needed to eliminate any imbalances between work load and work capacity?

How Much Snow Falls on New York? · To answer the first question required a methodical search of U.S. Weather Bureau records back to 1910, which revealed that a storm matching or exceeding the February storm's depth of fifteen inches occurs once in twelve years, on the average. This means that such a storm will occur "at the wrong time"—i.e., when only a minimal (Sunday) force is on duty—once in 84 years, and, if the weather forecasters are credited with merely 50 percent accuracy, such an unfortunate episode will occur "unexpectedly and at the wrong time" no more than once in 168 years, on the average. (To spin this out further, the better part of a millennium is likely to pass before a recurrence in an election year!) When the analysts presented the statistics, with the wry remark that we were fortunate to have observed such a rare event during our lifetimes, Mayor Lindsay, to his credit, mustered a wan smile.

More constructively, inspection of snow records disclosed that:

(a) Snowfall in New York City averages 33 inches annually.

(b) An average season has two storms greater than four inches (see Figure 1).

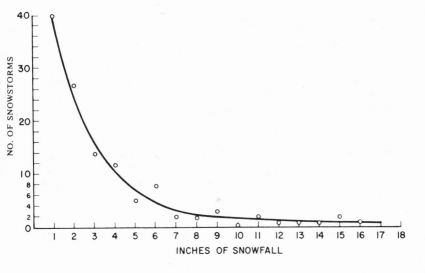

FIGURE 1

FREQUENCY DISTRIBUTION OF SNOWSTORMS, BY DEPTH, 1948–1967
(FOR SNOWFALLS OF AT LEAST ONE INCH)

(c) An average season has six to seven snowstorms of an inch or more (see Figure 2).

(d) The rate of accumulation of snow during a snowstorm was as high as 10.4 inches in eight hours, as shown in Table 1.

How Much Work Has to Be Done? Coping with a snowstorm in New York involves up to three sequential activities:

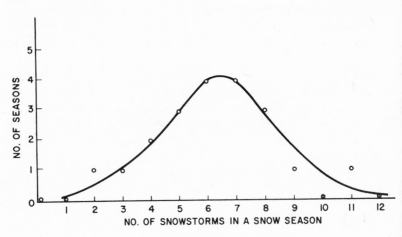

FIGURE 2

Frequency Distribution of Snow Seasons by
Number of Snowstorms, 1948–1967
(for snowfalls of at least one inch)

spreading salt, plowing, and hauling away snow. Spreading salt, which is done by special-purpose vehicles, is the routine, first line of defense and is usually done perhaps twelve times a year; that is, not only for the six or seven snowfalls which turn out to be greater than one inch, but also for others which appear threatening but ultimately deposit less than an inch, and for freezing rain. Plowing is done three or four times an average year, as depths approach four inches or so. (Specific decisions about plowing will depend on such factors as current ground temperature, predicted air temperature, wind, and traffic conditions—because spreading salt is more effective for melting snow when traffic is relatively heavy.) Removal of snow by hauling is relatively rare, being reserved generally for snowfalls greater than six inches when the temperature is expected to remain below freezing for an appreciable period of time. The study addressed all three activities—spreading, plowing, and hauling—but only the first two will be discussed here.

The data on snowfalls, and the work activity dictated in response to snow, confirm that a comprehensive snow plan is necessary, for it will be exercised about a dozen times a year even though incapacitating storms, such as the one which triggered the propect, are quite rare.

TABLE 1

PEAK ACCUMULATION RATES FOR SNOWFALLS[1]

*A. Average accumulation during the peak period
of indicated duration [2]*

Final depth	No. of storms	1 hr.	2 hrs.	3 hrs.	4 hrs.	5 hrs.	6 hrs.	7 hrs.	8 hrs.
4"–9"	14	1.0"	1.7"	2.4"	2.9"	3.3"	3.6"	4.0"	4.3"
9"+	9	1.7"	2.9"	3.9"	4.8"	5.6"	6.3"	6.9"	7.4"

*B. Maximum accumulation during the peak period
of indicated duration [3]*

Final depth	No. of storms	1 hr.	2 hrs.	3 hrs.	4 hrs.	5 hrs.	6 hrs.	7 hrs.	8 hrs.
4"–9"	1	1.4"	2.6"	3.3"	4.2"	4.7"	5.2"	5.5"	5.6"
9"+	1	2.5"	4.1"	5.4"	6.7"	7.6"	8.6"	9.5"	10.4"

[1] Based on the 23 storms greater than or equal to four inches during the period 1958–1967.

[2] For example, if one looks at the 3-hour period of heaviest snowfall for each of the 14 storms whose final depth was 4"–9", the average accumulation during those 3-hour periods was 2.4".

[3] For example, the greatest 5-hour accumulation for any storm was 7.6"; this occurred for a storm whose final depth was greater than 9".

To determine the amount of cleanup work called for by a snowstorm, it was necessary to analyze the street system. The Department of Sanitation, which is responsible for snow removal, divides the streets into three priority classes, primary, secondary and tertiary, corresponding to the relative importance of the streets. As shown in Table 2A, primary streets comprised 43 percent of the linear street mileage, but 45 percent of the spreader miles, 53 percent of the plow miles in the city. (Depending on the width of the street, a vehicle may have to traverse it more than once in order to salt it or plow it, while spreaders and plows have different effective widths.) Clearly, a ranking system which was so undiscriminating as to assign more than half the total plowing work an equally high priority left something to be desired.

TABLE 2

Street Mileage

A. Existing street network

Class of street	Linear miles		Spreader miles		Plow miles	
	Number	Percent	Number	Percent	Number	Percent
Primary	2530	43	2733	45	6755	53
Secondary	1978	34	1978	33	3500	28
Tertiary	1331	23	1331	22	2444	19
Total	5839	100	6042	100	12,699	100

B. Recommended street network

	Number	Percent	Number	Percent	Number	Percent
Primary						
Emergency	1600	27	1730	28	4272	33
Other	930	16	1003	17	2483	20
Secondary	1978	34	1978	33	3500	28
Tertiary	1331	23	1331	22	2444	19
Total	5839	100	6042	100	12,699	100

There did exist within the primary streets a category labeled Snow Emergency Streets, which totaled only 428 miles, some 7 percent of the total street mileage. However, this distinction was not used in actual operations, and furthermore an inquiry concluded that much of this street network was originally devised as the best way to flee the city in the event of a nuclear holocaust, rather than as a network which, if cleared, would enable the city to function adequately after a major snowfall. Therefore, a new high-priority network was designed during this study; it included all parkways and bus routes, and the streets which connect hospitals, police stations, fire houses, bus garages, and fuel depots to those arteries. It represents 1,600 linear miles, or 33 percent of the city's total plow miles. Clearing these streets represents the minimum work that has to be done to permit the city to function during a snow emergency. Table 2B defines the work load, in terms of the number of miles to be covered, given a policy determination that only primary, or primary and secondary, or all streets are to be cleared.

What Is the Capacity for Performing This Work? · In order to estimate the city's capacity for snow removal work, it was necessary to look at the type, amount, and productivity of equipment.

The principal snow fighting equipment consists of spreaders and plows, for which a conservatively high down-time figure of 40 percent was assumed in the analysis; that is, it was assumed that 40 percent of the spreaders and plows would be out of commission, so that only 134 spreaders and 1,050 plows would be available for work. (Actual down time was on the order of 30 to 35 percent.) Productive time was estimated by making allowance for meal time, rest breaks, refueling time, travel time to and from routes, etc., and from this it was concluded that about 12 hours of productive time on the route is available during the two-shift, 22-hour winter work day. Furthermore, it was assumed that

TABLE 3

PLOWING CAPABILITY

	Snow emergency streets	All primary streets	Primary and secondary streets	All streets
Plow miles	4,272	6,755	10,255	12,699
Max. hrs. to plow	2.75	3.65	4.85	5.70
Avg. peak accumulation °	3.7″	4.5″	5.5″	6.1″
Max. peak accumulation °	5.0″	6.3″	7.5″	8.3″

° Derived from Table 1, for storms greater than 9″ for the indicated "Max hrs. to plow."

up to 1.25 hours would be needed to start up and reach the beginning of a route. Finally, an extremely conservative figure of only 5 mph was assumed for the vehicles while on their routes. (This is the average auto speed in mid-Manhattan at noon on weekdays; plow speeds at midnight in Staten Island are obviously much higher.)

Putting together all these productivity figures and the street mileages leads to the striking conclusion that there is sufficient equipment available, in the aggregate, to plow *every* mile of *every* street in the city in only six hours, and to plow the high-priority streets in less than two hours! Based on the snow-accumulation rates of Table 1, and the above productivity estimates, Table 3 is derived. Recognizing that plows can work in depths up to about eight inches, it can confidently be concluded that the high-priority network can "always" be kept plowed.

That is, the plowing force can "always" complete plowing those streets well before eight inches of snow would accumulate, and they could keep those streets open during the remainder of "any" snowstorm by repeatedly traversing those routes.

A corresponding analysis shows that the salt-spreading capability was inadequate, for it would take seven hours to spread salt on all primary streets, during which time (see Table 1) 9.5 inches has been observed to accumulate and the spreaders would therefore be unable to complete their work. Additional spreaders are needed in order to assert with confidence that the high-priority streets could "always" be salted before the snow becomes too deep for the spreaders to negotiate.

From the foregoing analysis of work loads and equipment capability, and contrary to some of the touted "solutions," the inexorable conclusion was that aside from additional spreaders, neither more plows nor improved maintenance was necessary; the plowing problem lay elsewhere. Indeed, if the available equipment could, in principle, plow the entire street network so quickly, where was the problem?

What Improvements Are Needed? · The answer was to be found in the geographic deployment of equipment and the rate of mobilization of manpower to man the equipment.

The matter of equipment deployment is an interesting one. Most of the plowing vehicles are simply refuse-collection trucks fitted with plows. The trucks may have been satisfactorily distributed throughout the boroughs for their primary function, collection, but they were not properly distributed for plowing. (See Table 4.) The reason is obvious: a one-mile street segment in a bucolic area of Richmond will generate much less refuse than will a one-mile street segment in densely populated Manhattan, but it will have just as much snow to be plowed. In other words the public, without benefit of systems analysis, perceived the situation quite correctly: Manhattan did indeed receive better snow-cleaning service. But this was a direct, technical consequence of Manhattan's high population density rather than a deliberate decision to withhold services from the other boroughs.

In order to satisfy these widely differing needs, for refuse collection and for plowing, one is faced with the necessity of pro-

TABLE 4

GEOGRAPHICAL DEPLOYMENT OF PLOWS
IN RELATION TO NEED

Area	Plow-miles of primary streets (%)	Distribution of plows (%)
Manhattan West	8.6	9.2
Manhattan East	6.5	10.7
Bronx West	6.6	8.9
Bronx East	9.9	8.4
Brooklyn West	9.6	11.0
Brooklyn North	7.5	11.5
Brooklyn East	6.8	9.8
Queens West	14.7	12.8
Queens East	20.8	13.5
Richmond	9.2	4.0
Total	100.2%	99.8%

viding two widely differing truck allocation patterns. This dilemma was ultimately resolved by taking advantage of vehicles such as flushers, on which plows can be mounted. During the winter, when these see little use for flushing, they are to be relocated in such a way that, together with its normal complement of refuse-collection trucks, each borough will have a plowing capability proportional to the number of plow miles of high-priority streets in that borough. The few remaining disparities can be eliminated by directing certain truck-rich areas to send the desired number of trucks to certain truck-poor areas at the start of a snowstorm. This final distribution is designed to equalize the time it takes for each borough to clean its high-priority streets.

In a completely analogous way, the spreaders were shown to be distributed inappropriately, leading to disparities between areas of up to 3:1 in the amount of time needed to spread salt on their primary streets. Because spreaders are single-purpose vehicles, unlike plows, it was possible to deploy them in such a way as to equalize spreading time for all areas of the city. (It should be noted that reported productivity differences between different parts of the city were used to "fine tune" the recommended deployment of plows and spreaders; however, because of reporting uncertainties, the allocation ultimately was made based on the distribution of plow-miles and spreader-miles among areas.)

Another finding worth noting concerns the distance between garages and the plow routes. In deriving Table 3, a startup delay of 1.25 hours was allowed as a conservative city-wide average. Again, however, looking at geographic variations proved useful, for in eastern Queens the travel time from the garage to the routes was as much as two or three hours during a snowstorm. This study confirmed the previously perceived need for a new garage in that area, and it was eventually acquired and put into operation.

Given sufficient equipment properly allocated throughout the city, with a rational set of priorities for work assignments, the only remaining need is for a good mobilization plan, i.e., a plan which provides the right number of workers at the right place and at the right time.

Ordinarily, the more than 9,000 uniformed members of the department's work force are easily sufficient to man all the snow equipment. However, manpower mobilization was a problem on Sunday, when for a 24-hour period the field force was insufficient to man even the full complement of spreaders, let alone any plows. Now this staffing problem can easily be solved with money. More men could be assigned routinely to Sunday duty or called up on short notice and at premium rates. In fact, two weeks after this famous storm, when another storm threatened and no one was taking any chances, the city spent one-third of a million dollars mobilizing and not a flake fell. The issue was how to provide, in effect, low-cost insurance against a serious snow emergency. The solution was to devise operating procedures which would increase the rate of mobilization and thereby decrease the elapsed time needed to have an adequate number of men and machines out on the streets.

This was accomplished by mounting plows on one-fifth of the trucks just before winter weekends. By doing this in advance, a critical time advantage is gained, for it takes almost two man-hours to prepare a truck in this way. In addition, some of the spreaders are loaded with salt just prior to winter weekends, even though unused salt will have to be unloaded on Monday to prevent caking and flat tires. Finally, in cooperation with the union, a special Sunday roster was developed, a snow emergency force which had agreed to respond to a telephone callup and to report promptly to their assigned posts. This agreement was encouraged by making more attractive arrangements for compensatory time off.

Implementation · The analysis was completed in June and then presented to Mayor Lindsay. By that time the mayoral campaign was in full swing and it was clear that the snow of February was gone but not forgotten; it had become a very lively campaign issue, with many candidates emphasizing it in speeches and in their TV advertisements.

In this environment, implementing the recommendations proved relatively easy; for once, a management science unit was in the right place at the right time with the right answers to an important problem—and without even a written report in hand.

The word went forth to put the findings into practice promptly, viz., before election day in November.

Week-long work sessions and regular reviews with the commissioner and the mayor's assistant gradually generated modifications, improvements, unanimous acceptance, budget alterations—and visible changes. Finally, the effort culminated in the preparation of a detailed briefing report, for issuance at a major press conference. The process of writing this press release was itself salutary, for it served to crystallize some hitherto unresolved areas, and clear up some lingering ambiguities. The final document described quite specifically the changes and improvements made in the city's snow-fighting tactics since the disastrous snowstorm, as evidence that the administration had learned from its experiences and that the problems would not recur. This candor was in keeping with the dominant motif of the mayoral campaign, the theme of chastened wisdom gained from experience in the second toughest job in America.

Near the start of the next snow season, just a few weeks before election day, a major press conference was held—at the famous corner in Queens where there was much ado nine months earlier. Mayor Lindsay announced the various changes and improvements made since then and was able to state with confidence that the problem would not recur.

Because the news photographers and TV cameramen would have found nothing very photogenic about allocation charts and tables, and lists of names, some of the city's new snow-fighting equipment was put on display for the occasion. In other words, for the results of urban systems analysis to be published in the right journals—*The New York Times* and the *Post*—the skills of a public relations expert in the City Hall Press Office were indispensable.

The city's new Snow Emergency Plan went into effect. Mayor Lindsay was re-elected. (No causal relationship is implied.) A report documenting the work was finally written and issued.

In the ensuing four years only one storm represented any sort of practical test of the system, an eight-inch storm on a holiday, January 1, 1971. Everything went smoothly and the city was cleaned up within a few hours, with credit properly going to the Mayor, the Department of Sanitation, and the new plan.

The Decision to Seed
Hurricanes

R. A. Howard, J. E. Matheson, and D. W. North

R. A. Howard is Professor of Engineering-Eco-
nomic Systems at Stanford University. Together
with J. E. Matheson and D. W. North, he wrote
an article in Science from which this piece is condensed. Some of the substantiating technical
analysis, as well as extensive discussion of the
evaluation of additional seedings, are excluded
here.

The possibility of mitigating the destructive force of hurricanes by seeding them with silver iodide was suggested by R. H. Simpson in 1961. Early experiments on hurricanes Esther (1961) and Beulah (1963) were encouraging, but strong evidence for the effectiveness of seeding was not obtained until the 1969 experiments on Hurricane Debbie. Debbie was seeded with massive amounts of silver iodide on 18 and 20 August 1969. Reductions of 31 and 15 percent in peak wind speed were observed after the seedings.

Over the last ten years property damage caused by hurricanes has averaged $440 million annually. Hurricane Betsy (1965) and Hurricane Camille (1969) each caused property damage of approximately $1.5 billion. Any means of reducing the destructive force of hurricanes would therefore have great economic implications.

DECISION TO PERMIT OPERATIONAL SEEDING

In the spring of 1970 Stanford Research Institute began a small study for the Environmental Science Service Administration (ESSA) to explore areas in which decision analysis might make significant contributions to ESSA, both in its technical operations and in its management and planning function. At the suggestion of Myron Tribus, Assistant Secretary of Commerce for Science and Technology, we decided to focus the study on the decision problems inherent in hurricane modification.[1]

The objective of the present U.S. government program in hurricane modification, Project Stormfury, is strictly scientific: to add to man's knowledge about hurricanes. Any seeding of hurricanes that threaten inhabited coastal areas is prohibited. According to the policy currently in force, seeding will be carried out only if there is less than a 10 percent chance of the hurricane center coming within fifty miles of a populated land area within eighteen hours after seeding.

If the seeding of hurricanes threatening inhabited coastal areas is to be undertaken, it will be necessary to modify the existing policies. The purpose of our analysis is to examine the circumstances that bear on the decision to change or not to change these existing policies.

The decision to seed a hurricane threatening a coastal area should therefore be viewed as a two-stage process: (i) a decision is taken to lift the present prohibition against seeding threatening hurricanes, and (ii) a decision is taken to seed a particular hurricane a few hours before that hurricane is expected to strike the coast. Our study is concentrated on the policy decision rather than on the tactical decision to seed a particular hurricane at a particular time. It is also addressed to the experimental question:

1. A detailed discussion of the research is to be found in the project's final report (D. W. Boyd, R. A. Howard, J. E. Matheson, D. W. North, Decision Analysis of Hurricane Modification [Project 8503, Stanford Research Institute, Menlo Park, California, 1971]). This report is available through the National Technical Information Service, U.S. Department of Commerce, Washington, D.C., accession number COM-71-00784.

What would be the value of expanding research in hurricane modification, and, specifically, what would be the value of conducting additional field experiments such as the seedings of Hurricane Debbie in 1969?

Our approach was to consider a representative severe hurricane bearing down on a coastal area and to analyze the decision to seed or not to seed this "nominal" hurricane. The level of the analysis was relatively coarse, because for the policy decision we did not have to consider many geographical and meteorological details that might influence the tactical decision to seed. We described the hurricane by a single measure of intensity, its maximum sustained surface wind speed, since it is this characteristic that seeding is expected to influence. The surface winds, directly and indirectly (through the storm tide), are the primary cause of the destruction wrought by most hurricanes. The direct consequence of a decision for or against seeding a hurricane is considered to be the property damage caused by that hurricane. (Injuries and loss of life are often dependent on the issuance and effectiveness of storm warnings; they were not explicitly included in our analysis.)

However, property damage alone is not sufficient to describe the consequence of the decision. There are indirect legal and social effects that arise from the fact that the hurricane is known to have been seeded. For example, the government might have some legal responsibility for the damage caused by a seeded hurricane. Even if legal action against the government were not possible, a strong public outcry might result if a seeded hurricane caused an unusual amount of damage. Nearly all the government hurricane meteorologists that we questioned said they would seed a hurricane threatening their homes and families—if they could be freed from professional liability.

The importance of the indirect effects stems in large part from uncertainty about the consequences of taking either decision. A hurricane is complex and highly variable, and at present meteorologists cannot predict accurately how the behavior of a hurricane will evolve over time. The effect of seeding is uncertain also; consequently, the behavior of a hurricane that is seeded will be a combination of two uncertain effects: natural changes and the changes induced by seeding.

❋   ❋   ❋

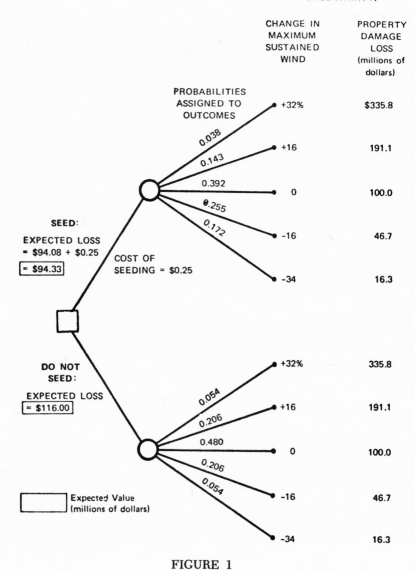

FIGURE 1

THE SEEDING DECISION FOR THE NOMINAL HURRICANE

THE DECISION TO SEED

The decision to seed is shown in the form of a decision tree in Figure 1. The decision to seed or not to seed is shown at the decision node denoted by the small square box; the consequent resolution of the uncertainty about wind change is indicated at the chance nodes denoted by open circles. For expository clarity and convenience, especially in the later stages of the analysis, it is convenient to use discrete approximations to the probability distributions for wind change (Table 1).

TABLE 1

PROBABILITIES ASSIGNED TO WIND CHANGES OCCURRING IN THE 12 HOURS BEFORE HURRICANE LANDFALL. DISCRETE APPROXIMATION FOR FIVE OUTCOMES.

Interval of changes in maximum sustained wind	Representative value in discrete approximation (%)	Probability that wind change will be within interval	
		If seeded	If not seeded
Increase of 25% or more	+32	.038	.054
Increase of 10 to 25%	+16	.143	.206
Little change, +10 to −10%	0	.392	.480
Reduction of 10 to 25%	−16	.255	.206
Reduction of 25% or more	−34	.172	.054

As a measure of the worth of each alternative we can compute the expected loss for each alternative by multiplying the property damage for each of the five possible outcomes by the probability that the outcome will be achieved and summing over the possible consequences. The expected loss for the seeding alternative is $94.33 million (including a cost of $0.25 million to carry out the seeding); the expected loss for the not-seeding alternative is $116 million; the difference is $21.67 million or 18.7 percent.

❂   ❂   ❂

GOVERNMENT RESPONSIBILITY

The analysis in the section above indicates that, if minimizing the expected loss in terms of property damage (and the cost of seeding) is the only criterion, then seeding is preferred. However, an important aspect of the decision—the matter of government responsibility—has not yet been included in the analysis. We have calculated a probability of .36 that a seeded hurricane will intensify between seeding and landfall and a probability of .18 that this intensification will be at least 10 percent. This high probability is largely the result of the great natural variability in hurricane intensity. It is advisable to consider both the legal and the social consequences that might occur if a seeded hurricane intensified.

The crucial issue in the decision to seed a hurricane threatening a coastal area is the relative desirability of reducing the expected property damage and assuming the responsibility for a dangerous and erratic natural phenomenon. This is difficult to assess, and to have a simple way of regarding it we use the concept of a government responsibility cost, defined as follows. The government is faced with a choice between assuming the responsibility for a hurricane and accepting higher probabilities of property damage. This situation is comparable to one of haggling over price: What increment of property-damage reduction justifies the assumption of responsibility entailed by seeding a hurricane? This increment of property damage is defined as the government responsibility cost. The government responsibility cost is a means of quantifying the indirect social, legal, and political factors related to seeding a hurricane. It is distinguished from the direct measure—property damage—that is assumed to be the same for both modified and natural hurricanes with the same maximum sustained wind speed.

We define the government responsibility cost so that it is incurred only if the hurricane is seeded. It is conceivable that the public may hold the government responsible for not seeding a severe hurricane, which implies that a responsibility cost should also be attached to the alternative of not seeding. Such a cost would strengthen the implication of the analysis in favor of permitting seeding.

The assessment of government responsibility cost is made by considering the seeding decision in a hypothetical situation in which no uncertainty is present. Suppose the government must choose between two outcomes:

(1) A seeded hurricane that intensifies 16 percent between the time of seeding and landfall.

(2) An unseeded hurricane that intensifies more than 16 percent between the time of seeding and landfall. The property damage from outcome 2 is x percent more than the property damage from outcome 1.

If x is near zero, the government will choose outcome 2. If x is large, the government will prefer outcome 1. We then adjust x until the choice becomes very difficult; that is, the government is indifferent to which outcome it receives. For example, the indifference point might occur when x is 30 percent. An increase of 16 percent in the intensity of the nominal hurricane corresponds to property damage of $191 million, so that the corresponding responsibility cost defined by the indifference point at 30 percent is (.30) ($191 million), or $57.3 million. The responsibility cost is then assessed for other possible changes in hurricane intensity.

The assessment of government responsibility costs entails considerable introspective effort on the part of the decision-maker who represents the government. The difficulty of determining the numbers does not provide an excuse to avoid the issue. Any decision or policy prohibiting seeding implicitly determines a set of government responsibility costs. As shown in the last section, seeding is the preferred decision unless the government responsibility costs are high.

Let us consider an illustrative set of responsibility costs. The government is indifferent, if the choice is between:

(1) A seeded hurricane that intensifies 32 percent and an unseeded hurricane that intensifies even more, causing 50 percent more property damage.

(2) A seeded hurricane that intensifies 16 percent and an unseeded hurricane that causes 30 percent more property damage.

(3) A seeded hurricane that neither intensifies nor diminishes (0 percent change in the maximum sustained wind speed after the seeding) and an unseeded hurricane that intensifies slightly, causing 5 percent more property damage.

(4) A seeded hurricane that diminishes by more than 10 percent and an unseeded hurricane that diminishes by the same amount. (If the hurricane diminishes after seeding, everyone agrees that the government acted wisely; thus, responsibility costs are set at zero.)

The analysis of the seeding decision with these government responsibility costs included is diagramed in Figure 2. Even with these large responsibility costs, the preferred decision is still to seed.

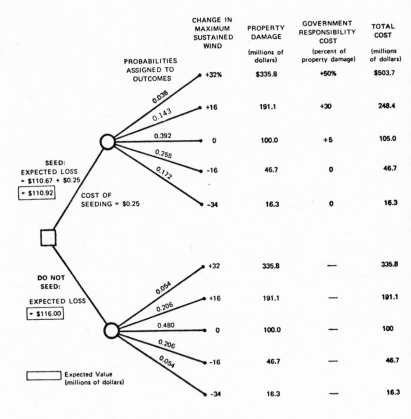

FIGURE 2

The Seeding Decision for the Nominal Hurricane
(government responsibility cost included)

The responsibility costs needed to change the decision are a substantial fraction of the property damage caused by the hurricane. For the $100-million hurricane chosen as the example for this section, the average responsibility cost must be about $22 million to change the decision. If the hurricane were in the $1-billion class, as Camille (1969) and Betsy (1965) were, an average responsibility cost of $200 million would be needed. In other words, an expected reduction of $200 million in property damage would be foregone if the government decided not to accept the responsibility of seeding the hurricane.

The importance of the responsibility issue led us to investigate the legal basis for hurricane seeding in some detail. These investigations were carried out by Gary Widman, Hastings College of the Law, University of California. A firm legal basis for operational seeding apparently does not now exist. The doctrine of sovereign immunity provides the government only partial and unpredictable protection against lawsuits, and substantial grounds for bringing such lawsuits might exist. A better legal basis for government seeding activities is needed before hurricane seeding could be considered other than as an extraordinary emergency action. Specific congressional legislation may be the best means of investing a government agency with the authority to seed hurricanes threatening the coast of the United States.

* * *

EXPERIMENTAL CAPABILITY DECISION

The occurrence of hurricanes is a random phenomenon. Therefore, it is uncertain whether there will be an opportunity for an experimental seeding before the arrival of a threatening storm that might be operationally seeded. Opportunities for experimental seeding have been scarce. In the last few years there have been only six experimental seedings, and these have ben conducted on three hurricanes, Esther (1961), Beulah (1963), and Debbie (1969). Experimental seedings have been limited to a small region of the Atlantic Ocean accessible to aircraft bases in Puerto Rico, and few hurricanes have passed through this region.

There are many other regions of the ocean where hurricanes might be found that satisfy the present criterion for experimental seeding—that is, the hurricane will be seeded only if the probability is less than .10 that it will come within 50 miles of a populated land area within 18 hours after seeding. However, a decision to expand the present experimental capability of Project Stormfury would need to be made well before the experiment itself. Whereas the seeding itself requires only that an aircraft be fitted with silver iodide pyrotechnic generators, the monitoring of the subsequent development of the hurricane requires other aircraft fitted with the appropriate instrumentation. The requirements in equipment, crew training, and communications and support facilities are substantial. In addition, permission may be needed from nations whose shores might be threatened by the seeded hurricane. The experimental decision, then, involves an investment in the capability to perform an experimental seeding. Whether an experiment is performed depends on the uncertain occurrences of hurricanes in the experimental areas.

The expected time before another experimental opportunity for Project Stormfury's present capability is about one full hurricane season. There was no opportunity during 1970. Preliminary estimates of the cost of a capability to seed hurricanes in the Pacific are about $1 million. The incidence of experimentally seedable hurricanes in the Pacific appears to be more than twice that in the Atlantic. Therefore, it appears advisable to develop a capability to conduct experimental hurricane seeding in the Pacific Ocean since the benefits expected from this capability outweigh the costs by a factor of at least 5.

CONCLUSIONS FROM THE ANALYSIS

The decision to seed a hurricane imposes a great responsibility on public officials. This decision cannot be avoided because inaction is equivalent to a decision not to permit seeding. Either the government must accept the responsibility of a seeding that may be perceived by the public as deleterious, or it must accept the responsibility for not seeding and thereby exposing the public to higher probabilities of severe storm damage.

Our report to the National Oceanic and Atmospheric Administration recommended that seeding be permitted on an emergency basis. We hope that further experimental results and a formal analysis of the tactical decision to seed a particular hurricane will precede the emergency. However, a decision may be required before additional experimental or analytical results are available. A hurricane with the intensity of Camille threatening a populous coastal area of the United States would confront public officials with an agonizing but unavoidable choice.

The decision to seed hurricanes can not be resolved on strictly scientific grounds. It is a complex decision whose uncertain consequences affect many people. Appropriate legal and political institutions should be designated for making the hurricane-seeding decision, and further analysis should be conducted to support these institutions in carrying out their work.

✿   ✿   ✿

Cost-Benefit Analysis

ROLAND N. McKEAN

Roland N. McKean is Professor of Economics at the University of Virginia. This selection is taken from his book, Public Spending

"Cost-benefit analyses" are attempts to estimate certain costs and gains that would result from alternative courses of action. For different applications, other names are often used: "cost-effectiveness analysis" when courses of action in defense planning are compared; "systems analysis" when the alternatives are relatively complex collections of interrelated parts; "operations research" when the alternatives are modes of operation with more or less given equipment and resources; or "economic analysis" when the alternatives are rival price-support or other economic policies. The term "cost-benefit analysis" was originally associated with natural-resource projects but has gradually come to be used for numerous other applications. The basic idea is not new: individuals have presumably been weighing the pros and cons of alternative actions ever since man appeared on earth; and in the early part of the nineteenth century, Albert Gallatin and others put together remarkably sophisticated studies of proposed U.S. government canals and turnpikes. But techniques have improved, and interest has been growing. All these studies might well be called economic analyses. This does not mean that the economist's skills are the only ones needed in making such analyses or, indeed, that economists are very good at making them. It merely means that this analytical tool is aimed at helping decision makers—consumers, businessmen, or government officials—economize.

In recent years, the Bureau of the Budget, the National Bureau of Standards, many other U.S. agencies, and governments and agencies in other nations have been exploring possible uses of cost-benefit analysis. Sometimes the analyses are essentially simple arithmetic. Sometimes high-speed computers are used—as they were, for instance, in the search by a Harvard group for the best way to use water in the Indus River basin in Pakistan. One of the major applications of cost-benefit analysis will continue to be the comparison of alternative natural-resources policies—proposals to reduce air and water pollution, to divert water from the Yukon to regions further south, to do something about the rapidly declining water level in the Great Lakes, and so on. But other applications are appearing with growing frequency—comparisons of such things as alternative health measures, personnel policies, airport facilities, education practices, transportation systems, choices about the management of governmental properties, and antipoverty proposals.

All such analyses involve working with certain common elements: (1) objectives, or the beneficial things to be achieved; (2) alternatives, or the possible systems or arrangements for achieving the objectives; (3) costs, or the benefits that have to be foregone if one of the alternatives is adopted; (4) models, or the sets of relationships that help one trace out the impacts of each alternative on achievements (in other words, on benefits) and costs; and (5) a criterion, involving both costs and benefits, to identify the preferred alternative. In connection with each of these elements there are major difficulties. Consider a personal problem of choice that an individual might try to analyze—selecting the best arrangements for his family's transportation. Spelling out the relevant objectives, that is, the kind of achievements that would yield significant benefits, is no simple task. The objectives may include commuting to work, getting the children to school, travel in connection with shopping, cross-country trips, and so on. Part of this travel may be across deserts, along mountain roads, in rainy or icy or foggy conditions. The family may attach a high value to the prestige of traveling in style (or of being austere, or of simply being different from most other people). Another objective that is neglected all too often is a hard-to-specify degree of flexibility to deal with uncertainties. Adaptability and flexibility are particularly important objectives if one is examining alternative educational programs, exploratory research projects, or R&D policies. Overlooking any of the relevant objectives could lead to poor choices.

The second element, the alternative ways of achieving the benefits, also deserves careful thought, for selecting the best of an unnecessarily bad lot is a poor procedure. In choosing a family's transportation system, the alternatives might include various combinations of a compact automobile, a luxury automobile, a pickup truck, a jeep, a motor scooter, an airplane, a bicycle, the use of a bus system, and the use of taxicabs.

In many problems of choice, the alternatives are called "systems," and the analyses are called "systems analyses." This terminology is quite appropriate, because the word "system" means a set of interrelated parts, and the alternative ways of achieving objectives usually are sets of interrelated parts. At the same time, the word "system" is so general that this usage is often confusing. In defense planning, for example, the term "system" can be used to refer to such sets of interrelated parts as the following:

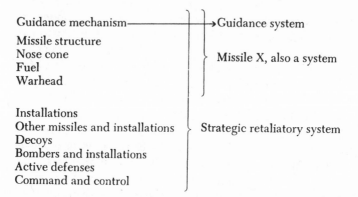

All three of these systems are collections of interrelated parts. How large should systems be for their comparison to be called a "systems analysis" or for their comparison to be a useful aid?

There are no correct answers; one must exercise judgment in deciding how large the systems should be to provide worthwhile assistance in tracing out the costs and benefits. (In effect, one must weigh the costs against the benefits of preparing alternative cost-benefit analyses.) Where interrelationships are relatively important, one is usually driven to consider large systems. Thus to choose between two engines for a supersonic airliner, one can hardly compare thrusts alone and make an intelligent selection, for weight, reliability, cost, noise, etc., may have diverse effects on overall desirability. The power plants must be fitted (at least on paper) into rival aircraft designs, and thence into airline and airport systems to see their net impact on the real objectives and the full costs. Moreover, other components of the projected systems may have to be modified so as not to use either engine stupidly. Suppose one engine would make possible the use of relatively short runways. To use an aircraft with this power plant in an intelligent way, one might have to modify many parts of the proposed airports, traffic patterns, ground installations for instrument-landing systems, and even proposed airline schedules. Hence one would end up comparing rather broad systems having many common components but also having several components that differed.

So much for the alternative systems to be compared. The third element of cost-benefit analysis, cost, is crucial because it really reflects the alternative benefits that one might obtain from the resources. It is just as foolish to measure costs incorrectly or to neglect part of them as it is to measure benefits incorrectly or neglect part of them. If selecting a luxury car entails building a new garage or paying higher insurance premiums, these are part of the costs of choosing that alternative. If one already has an adequate garage, the value foregone by using it (but *not* the cost of building a garage) is the relevant cost.

"Models," the fourth element of cost-benefit analysis, are simply crude representations of reality that enable one to estimate costs and benefits. If a person figures, "With the bus I could average ten miles per hour, traverse the five miles to work in one-half hour, spend five hours per week commuting to work, and would stand up 50 percent of the distance on 50 percent of the trips," he is using a model. If he says, "With Automobile X, I would get a motor tune-up every 5,000 miles and would therefore spend $50 per year on that item," he visualizes these events and uses a set of relationships, that is, a model, to estimate this cost. When one tries to perceive how something would work, it has become convenient and fashionable to say, "Let's build a model," though one could simply say, "Let's devise a way to predict what would happen (or a new way to estimate costs and benefits)."

The fifth element of cost-benefit analysis is the criterion or test of preferredness by means of which one points to the best choice. People tend to make a variety of criterion errors. One error, the use of the ratio of benefits to costs, is such a perennial favorite that it merits a brief discussion. Suppose at first that both benefits and costs can be measured *fully and correctly* in monetary terms and that one must choose among the following three discrete (and not mutually exclusive) alternatives:

	A	B	C
Cost	$100	$100	$200
Benefit one year later	$150	$105	$220
Ratio of benefits to costs	1.5	1.05	1.10

Suppose further that the constraint is that funds can be borrowed at 6 percent. Which projects should be undertaken, and what is the criterion? A and C, both of which yield more than 6 percent, should be undertaken, and the proper criterion is to maximize the present value of net worth or, its surrogate, to undertake projects wherever the marginal benefit exceeds the marginal cost. Note that the criterion is *not* to maximize the ratio of benefits to costs, which would restrict one to Project A. If the constraint is a fixed budget of $200, Projects A and B should be selected. Again, maximizing the ratio of benefits to costs would limit one to Project A.

Or consider two discrete and mutually exclusive alternatives (for example, two sizes of a dam):

	A	B
Cost	$100	$200
Benefit one year later	$150	$260
Ratio of benefits to costs	1.50	1.30

If funds can be borrowed at 6 percent, Project B should be undertaken. One should not choose A simply because the benefit-cost ratio is larger. Ratios are not irrelevant—every marginal productivity is a ratio—for one often seeks to *equalize* certain ratios as a condition for achieving a desired maximum. But the ratio itself is not the thing to be maximized.

The issue takes on a good deal of importance when the benefits can only be suggested by physical products or capabilities. In these circumstances, presumably in desperation, people frequently adopt as a criterion the maximization of some such ratio as satellite payload per dollar, hours of student instruction per dollar, or target-destruction capability per dollar. But the benefit-cost ratios of rival proposals simply cover up the relevant information. Take another example from the choices that confront the individual. If one is selecting a hose with which to sprinkle his lawn, one may have the following options:

	⅝-IN DIAMETER	1-IN. DIAMETER
Cost	$3	$5
Benefit (water put on lawn per hour)	108 gallons	150 gallons
Ratio of benefits to costs	36/1	30/1

The ratios are irrelevant. The pertinent question is whether or not the extra capability is worth the extra $2. Less misleading than showing the ratio would be showing the physical capabilities and the costs à la consumers' research. Or, where it makes sense to do so, one can adjust the scale of the alternatives so that each costs the same or achieves the same objectives. Then one can see which system achieves a specified objective at minimum cost, or achieves the greatest benefit for a specified budget. This is not a perfect criterion, for someone has to decide if the specified budget (or objective) is appropriate. But at least this sort of test is less misleading than a benefit-cost ratio.

With regard to this fifth element of cost-benefit analysis, discussing the correct way to design criteria may seem like discussing the correct way to find the Holy Grail. In a world of uncertainty and individual utility functions, judgments must help shape choices, and no operational test of preferredness can be above suspicion. Moreover, analyses vary in their quality, which is hard to appraise, and in their applicability to different decisions. For these reasons, responsible decision makers must treat cost-benefit analyses as "consumers' research" and introduce heroic judgments in reaching final decisions. In a sense, then, it may be both presumptuous and erroneous to discuss having a test of preferredness in these quantitative analyses.

Criteria should be considered, nonetheless, in connection with such analysis. First, cost-benefit analysts do apply criteria, especially in designing and redesigning the alternatives to be compared. They delete features that appear to be inefficient, add features that appear to be improvements, and probe for alternative combinations that are worth considering. This screening of possibilities and redesign of alternative systems entails the use of criteria, and these should be explicitly considered and exhibited. Second, whether or not they ought to, analysts often present the final comparisons in terms of a criterion. Thus while it may be wrong to talk as if a definitive criterion is an element of every analysis, these warnings about criterion selection should be emphasized.

Needless to say, in reaching decisions, one should attempt to take into account *all* gains and *all* costs. Some people feel that there are two types of gain or cost, economic and noneconomic, and that economic analysis has nothing to do with the latter. This distinction is neither very sound nor very useful. People pay for—that is, they value—music as well as food, beauty or quiet as well as aluminum pans, a lower probability of death as well as garbage disposal. The significant categories are not economic and noneconomic items but (1) gains and costs that can be measured in monetary units (for example, the use of items like typewriters that have market prices reflecting the marginal evaluations of all users); (2) other commensurable effects (impacts of higher teacher salaries, on the one hand, and of teaching machines, on the other hand, on students' test scores); (3) incommensurable effects that can be quantified but not in terms of a common denominator (capability of improving science test scores and capability of reducing the incidence of ulcers among students); and (4) nonquantifiable effects. Examples of the last category are impacts of alternative policies on the morale and happiness of students, on the probability of racial conflicts, and on the probability of protecting individual rights. In taking a position on an issue, each of us implicitly quantifies such considerations. But there is no way to make quantifications that would necessarily be valid for other persons. This sort of distinction between types of effects does serve a useful purpose, especially in warning us of the limitations of cost-benefit analysis.

One should recognize, too, that cost-benefit analysis necessarily involves groping and the making of subjective judgments, not just briskly proceeding with dispassionate scientific measurements. Consider the preparation of such analyses to aid educational choices. No one says, "This is the educational objective, and here are the three alternative systems to be compared. Now trace out the impacts of each on cost and on achievement of the objective, and indicate the preferred system." What happens is that those making the analysis spend much time groping for an *operational* statement of the objective, such as a designated improvement in specific test scores without an increase in the number of dropouts or nervous breakdowns. A first attempt is made at designing the alternative ways of realizing this objective. Preliminary costs are estimated. Members of the research team perceive that the systems have differential impacts on other objectives, such as flexibility, or student performance on tests two years later, or student interest in literature. Or the rival arrangements may elicit different reactions from teachers, parents, and school boards, affecting the achievement of other objectives. The analysts redesign the alternatives in the light of these impacts, perhaps so that each alternative performs at least "acceptably" with respect to each objective. Next it appears that certain additional features such as extra English-composition courses might add greatly to capability but not much to cost. Or the research team's cost group reports that certain facilities are extremely expensive and that eliminating them might reduce costs greatly with little impairment of effectiveness. In both cases the systems have to be modified again. This cut-and-try procedure is essential. Indeed, this process of redesigning the alternatives is probably a more important contribution than the final cost-effectiveness exhibits. In any event, the preparation of such an analysis is a process of probing—and not at all a methodical scientific comparison following prescribed procedures.

An appreciation of cost-benefit analysis also requires an awareness that incommensurables and uncertainties are pervasive. Consider the impacts of alternative educational policies that were mentioned above. These effects can perhaps be described, but not expressed in terms of a common denominator. Judgments about the extent of these effects and their worth have to be made. Some costs, such as the monetary measures of foregone benefits, perhaps additional sacrifices in terms of personality adjustment and ultimate effectiveness, or undesirable political repercussions that yield costs, cannot validly be put in terms of a common denominator. Furthermore, because of uncertainties, whatever estimates can be prepared should in principle be probability distributions rather than unique figures for costs and gains. The system that performs best in one contingency may perform worst in another contingency. Finally, costs and gains occur over a period of time, not at a single point in time, and there is no fully acceptable means of handling these streams of costs and gains in analyzing many options.

These difficulties are present because life is complex, and there is no unique correct choice. The difficulties are not created by cost-benefit analysis. Moreover, they do not render quantitative economic analysis useless. They simply mean that one has to be discriminating about when and how to use various tools. In general, the broader choices made by higher-level officials pose relatively great difficulties regarding what value judgments to make and what the physical and social consequences of alternative actions would be. Consider, for example, the allocation of the U.S. budget among various departments or the allocation of funds among such functions as the improvement of health, education, or postal service. Cost-benefit analysis gives relatively little guidance in making these choices, for in the end the decision maker's task is dominated by difficult personal judgments. Cost-benefit analysis may help somewhat, for it is the appropriate framework in terms of which to *think* about these broad choices, and it can usually provide *some* improved information. When personal judgments must play such a huge role, however, the improved information may not be worth much.

Consider another example of such broad choices: the government's allocation of its R&D effort between basic research and applied development. To choose between these two alternatives, officials must rely heavily on personal judgments about the consequences and judgments concerning the value of those consequences. Values cannot be taken as agreed upon, and physical-sociological effects cannot be predicted with confidence. Quantitative analysis can probably contribute only a little toward the sharpening of intuition here. Or consider the allocation of effort between improving medical care for the aged and improving it for the young. Suppose one could make extremely good predictions of the effects, which would of course aid decision makers. The final choice would be dominated in this instance by value judgments about the worth of prolonging the lives of elderly persons, the worth of lengthening the lives of persons in great pain, the worth of saving the lives of weakened or physically handicapped children, the relief of different kinds of distress, and so on.

Another broad or high-level choice that brings out these difficulties is the allocation of funds to, or for that matter within, the State Department. In the tasks of diplomacy it is hard to visualize taking a set of value tags as being clearly stated, let alone agreed upon. And disagreement is quite understandable in predicting the effects of alternative courses of action on the probabilities of stable alliances, provocations, little wars, nuclear wars, and so on. Positive science has provided few tested hypotheses about these relationships.

As one proceeds to narrower or lower-level problems of choice, these difficulties frequently, though not always, become less severe. (Actual decisions, of course, vary continuously in the extent to which they present these difficulties, but it is often economical to think in terms of such categories as broad and narrow or high-level and low-level choices). Within such tasks as education and health improvement, there are lower-level choices for which quantitative analysis may be very helpful, but there are also many middle-level choices that are fraught with difficulties. Should more effort be placed on the improvement of mental health even if it means less emphasis on the treatment of conventional ailments? Should effort be reallocated from higher education toward the improvement of elementary-school training, or vice versa? Or, as an alternative policy, should government

leave such allocative decisions more than at present to the uninfluenced choices of individuals families? Cost-benefit analysis
cannot do much to resolve the uncertainties about the consequences of such decisions, about their relative worths to individual citizens, or about whose value judgments should be given
what weights.

Within applied research and development, a choice between
specific projects might appear to be a low-level choice that economic analysis could greatly assist. In such instances, it is true
that values can sometimes be taken as agreed upon. In selecting
research and development projects for new fuels, for instance,
the values to be attached to various outcomes are not obvious,
yet they are probably not major sources of divergent views.
Perhaps the principal difficulty is the inability to predict the
physical consequences, including "side effects," of alternative
proposals. Here too, cost-benefit analysis may be destined to
play a comparatively small role.

One can list many problems of choice that seem to fall somewhere in this middle ground—that is, where cost-benefit analysis
can be helpful but not enormously so. It would appear, for
instance, that the selection of antipoverty and welfare programs
depends heavily on consequences that one cannot predict with
confidence and on value judgments about which there is much
disagreement. Similar statements apply also to the selection of
foreign-aid programs, urban-development proposals, or law-
enforcement programs—the comparison of different methods of
curbing the use of narcotics, say, or of different penal institutions
and procedures. In education, many decisions that may appear
to be low-level or relatively simple—for example, the selection
among alternative curricula or teaching methods or disciplinary
rules—are inevitably dominated by judgments about the consequences of these policies and about the value tags to be attached
to those consequences.

It is in connection with comparatively narrow problems of
choice that cost-benefit analysis can sometimes play a more
significant role. In these instances, as might be expected, the
alternatives are usually rather close substitutes. Science can often
predict the consequences of govenmental natural-resource in-

vestments or choices affecting the utilization of water or land, and people can often agree on the values at stake—at least to a sufficient extent to render analyses highly useful. Competing irrigation plans, flood-control projects, swamp drainage and land reclamation ventures, and water-pollution control measures are examples of narrow problems of choice in which cost-benefit analysis can help.

Cost-benefit analysis also promises to be helpful in comparing certain transportation arrangements. The interdependencies of transportation networks with other aspects of life are formidable, yet with ingenuity extremely useful studies of some transportation alternatives can be produced. Numerous transportation alternatives have been the subject of such studies: highways, urban systems, inland waterways, modified railway networks, the utilization of a given amount of sea transport, air transport fleets, and of course many lower-level choices, such as alternative road materials, construction practices, airport facilities, and loading arrangements. In some instances, of course, the interdependencies may be too complex for analyses to be very valuable; transportation alternatives that affect a large region and its development yield chains of consequences that are extremely difficult to trace out.

At best, the difficulties of providing *valuable* information are awesome. There can always be legitimate disagreement about any of these policy decisions, and analyses must be regarded as inputs to decisions, not as oracular touchstones. Nonetheless, to think systematically about the costs and gains from alternative policies is surely more sensible than to rely on haphazard thought or intuition. Such analyses can bring out the areas of disagreement so that people can see where their differences lie. Even with considerable divergence in judgments, they can screen out the absurdly inferior alternatives, focusing the debate on subsets of relatively good alternatives. For some choices, cost-benefit analysis provides information that can help officials agree upon a course of action that is preferred or accepted by most citizens. And for all choices, it is the right framework to use in organizing the evidence and one's thoughts and intuitions regarding alternatives. Even in deciding which research project to undertake, or how much time to spend on it, a researcher consults rough cost-benefit T-accounts. In deciding anything, a person should weigh costs and gains. Preliminary weighing may suggest that the use of a tentative rule of thumb or "requirement" is preferable to further or repeated analyses, but he should not initially pull some mythical requirement out of the air.

The Utilization of Existing
Water Supplies

JACK HIRSHLEIFER, JAMES
DE HAVEN, AND JEROME MILLIMAN

Jack Hirshleifer is Professor of Economics at the
University of California at Los Angeles. Together
with James DeHaven and Jerome Milliman, he
wrote Water Supply *from which the following*
excerpt is taken.

1. EFFICIENCY EFFECTS AND DISTRIBUTION EFFECTS

The economic effects of any proposed policy can be divided
under two headings: the effects on *efficiency* and the effects on
distribution. Efficiency questions relate to the size of the pie
available; distribution questions, to who gets what share. More
formally, we can think of the pie as representing the national
income or community income. Someone may propose reducing
income taxes in the upper brackets on the ground that the high
rates now effective there seriously deter initiative and enterprise
and so reduce national income; he is making an efficiency argument that the present taxes reduce the size of the national pie.
Someone else may point out that such a change will help large
taxpayers as against small—a distributional consideration. In
the field of water supply it is possible to find examples in the West
where a certain amount of water could produce goods and
services more highly valued in the market place if it were shifted

from agricultural to industrial uses—this is an efficiency argument. On the other hand, this shift may hurt the interests of farmers or of their customers, employees, or suppliers while helping industrial interests—all distributional considerations.

Now economics can say something of the distributional consequences of alternative possible policies, but what it says stops short of any assertion that any man's interests or well-being can be preferred to another's. The fact that economics has nothing to say on such matters does not mean, of course, that nothing important can be said. Ethics as a branch of philosophy and the entire structure of law (which to some extent embodies or applies ethical thought) are devoted to the consideration of the rights and duties of man against man, and many propositions arising out of such thought may well command almost unanimous consent in our society. Ethics may say that no one should be permitted to starve, and law that no one should be deprived of property without due process, but these are propositions outside economics.

Most of what the existing body of economic thought has to say concerns the *efficiency* effects—the effects on size of the pie—of alternative possible policies or institutional arrangements. There is, of course, a sense in which enlarging the size of the pie may be said to be good for the eaters as a group irrespective of the distribution of shares. This sense turns upon the *possibility* of dividing the enlarged pie in such a way that everybody benefits. If such a distribution of the gain is not adopted, there may or may not be good reason for the failure to do so, but the reason is presumed to be legal or ethical and so outside the sphere of economic analysis. Economics alone cannot give us answers to policy problems; it can show us how to attain efficiency and what the distributional consequences are of attaining efficiency in alternative possible ways, but it does not tell us how to distribute the gain from increased efficiency.

It is true that it is often the case that the efficiency and distributional consequences of a proposed change cannot be so neatly separated. Any particular change in the direction of efficiency will involve a certain intrinsic distribution of gains and losses, and in practice it may be unfeasible to effect a redistribution such that everyone gains. Nevertheless, we feel that a presumption in favor of changes increasing the national income is justified, while conceding that this presumption can be defeated if there are irreparable distributive consequences that are sufficiently offensive on ethical or legal grounds.

Nothing is more common in public discussions of economic affairs, however, than a consideration of distributive effects of any change to the utter exclusion of the efficiency question. The agricultural price-support policy, for example, is usually and fruitlessly discussed pro and con in terms of the interests of farmers versus the interests of consumers and taxpayers. But a policy of expensive storage of perishing commodities to hold them out of human consumption is, obviously, inefficient. Concentration upon the efficiency question might readily suggest solutions that would increase the national income and would help consumers and taxpayers a great deal while hurting farmers relatively little or not at all.

2. THE PRINCIPLE OF EQUIMARGINAL VALUE IN USE

Suppose for simplicity we first assume that the stock or the annual flow of a resource like water becomes available without cost, the only problem being to allocate the supply among the competing uses and users who desire it. Economic theory asserts one almost universal principle which characterizes a good or efficient allocation—the principle we shall here call "equimarginal value in use." The *value in use* of any unit of water, whether purchased by an ultimate or an intermediate consumer, is essentially measured by the *maximum* amount of resources (dollars) which the consumer would be willing to pay for that unit. *Marginal* value in use is the value in use of the last unit consumed, and for any consumer marginal value in use will ordinarily decline as the quantity of water consumed in any period increases. The principle, then, is that the resource should be so allocated that all consumers or users derive equal value in use from the marginal unit consumed or used.

An example of the process of equating marginal values in use may be more illuminating than an abstract proof that this principle characterizes efficient allocations. Suppose that my neighbor and I are both given rights (ration coupons, perhaps) to certain volumes of water, and we wish to consider whether it might be in our mutual interest to trade these water rights between us for other resources—we might as well say for dollars, which we can think of as a generalized claim on other resources like clam chowders, baby-sitting services, acres of land, or yachts. My neighbor might be a farmer and I an industrialist, or we might both be just retired homeowners; to make the quantities interesting, we will assume that both individuals are rather big operators. Now suppose that the last acre-foot of my periodic entitlement is worth $10 at most to me, but my neighbor would be willing to pay anything up to $50 for that right—a disparity of $40 between our marginal values in use. Evidently, if I transfer the right to him for any compensation between $10 and $50, we will both be better off in terms of our own preferences; in other words, the size of the pie measured in terms of the satisfactions yielded to both of us has increased. (Note, however, that the question of whether the compensation should be $11 or $49 is purely distributional.)

But this is not yet the end. Having given up one acre-foot, I will not be inclined to give up another on such easy terms— water has become scarcer for me, so that an additional amount given up means foregoing a somewhat more urgent use. Conversely, my neighbor is no longer quite so anxious to buy as he was before, since his most urgent need for one more acre-foot has been satisfied, and an additional unit must be applied to less urgent uses. That is, for both of us marginal values in use decline with increases of consumption (or, equivalently, marginal value in use rises if consumption is cut back). Suppose he is now willing to pay up to $45, while I am willing to sell for anything over $15. Evidently, we should trade again. Obviously, the stopping point is where the last (or marginal) unit of water is valued equally (in terms of the greatest amount of dollars we would be willing to pay) by the two of us, based on the use we can make of or the benefit we can derive from the last or marginal unit. At this point no more mutually advantageous trades are available—efficiency has been attained.

Generalizing from the illustration just given, we may say that the principle of equimarginal value in use asserts that an efficient allocation of water has been attained when no mutually advantageous exchanges are possible between any pair of claimants, which can only mean that each claimant values his last or marginal unit of water equally with the others, measured in terms of the quantity of other resources (or dollars) that he is willing to trade for an additional unit of water.

What institutional arrangements are available for achieving water allocations that meet the principle of equimarginal value in use? Our example suggests that rationing out rights to the available supply will tend to lead to an efficient result if trading of the ration coupons is freely permitted; this is true so long as it can be assumed that third parties are unaffected by the trades. More generally, any such vesting of property rights, whether originally administrative, inherited, or purchased, will tend to an efficient solution if trading is permitted. (The question of the basis underlying the original vesting of rights is a serious and important one, but it is a distributional question.) A rather important practical result is derived from this conclusion if we put the argument another way: however rights are vested, we are effectively *preventing* efficiency from being attained if the law forbids free trading of those rights. Thus, if our ration coupons are not transferable, efficiency can be achieved only if the original distribution of rights was so nicely calculated that equimarginal value in use prevailed to begin with and that thenceforth no forces operated to change these values in use. As a practical matter, these conditions could never be satisfied. Nevertheless, legal limitations on the owner's ability to sell or otherwise transfer vested water rights are very common. While at times valid justification at least in part may exist for such limitations (one example is where third parties are injured by such transfers), it seems often to be the case that these prohibitions simply inflict a loss upon all for no justifiable reason. We shall examine some instances of limitations on freedom of transfer in a later section.

It is important to note here that the market price of water rights or ration coupons, if these can be freely traded, will tend to settle at (and so to measure) the marginal value in use of the consumers in the market. Any consumer who found himself with so many coupons that the marginal value in use to him was less than market price would be trying to sell some of his rights, while anyone with marginal value in use greater than market price former holder of the privilege will lose as compared with all others. The attainment of efficiency in the new situation means that it is *possible* to insure that everyone is better off. But whether it is or is not desirable to provide the compensation required to balance the loss of the formerly preferred customers is a distributional question.

Our discussion of the principle of equimarginal value in use has led to two rules of behavior necessary if efficiency is to be achieved in different institutional contexts: (1) If rights to water are vested as property, there should be no restrictions on the purchase and sale of such rights, so long as third parties are un-affected. (2) If water is being sold, the price should be equal to all customers. This second rule was derived, however, under a special assumption that the water became available without cost. More generally, there will be costs incurred in the acquisition and transport of water supplies to customers; taking costs into account requires a second principle for pricing of water in addition to the principle of equimarginal value in use.

3. THE PRINCIPLE OF MARGINAL-COST PRICING

In our previous discussion we assumed that a certain volume or flow of water became available without cost, the problem being to distribute just that amount among the potential customers. Normally, there will not be such a definite fixed amount but rather a situation in which another unit could always be made available by expending more resources to acquire and transport it, that is, at a certain additional or marginal cost. The question of where to stop in increasing the supplies made available is then added to the question just discussed of how to arrange for the allocation of the supplies in hand at any moment of time.

From the argument developed earlier about the allocation of a certain given supply, we can infer that, whatever the price may be, it should be equal to all users (since otherwise employ-ments with higher marginal values in use are being foregone in favor of employments with lower values). Suppose that at a certain moment of time this price is $30 per unit. Then, if the community as a whole can acquire and transport another unit of water for, say, $20, it would clearly be desirable to do so;

in fact, any of the individual customers to whom the unit of water is worth $30 would be happy to pay the $20 cost, and none of the other members of the community is made worse off thereby. We may say that, on efficiency grounds, additional units should be made available so long as any members of the community are willing to pay the additional or marginal costs incurred. To meet the criterion of equimarginal value in use, however, the price should be made equal for all customers. So the combined rule is to make the price equal to the marginal cost and equal for all customers.

One important practical consideration is that, because of differing locations, use patterns, types of services, etc., the marginal costs of serving different customers will vary. It is of some interest to know in principle how this problem should be handled. The correct solution is to arrange matters so that for each class of customers (where the classes are so grouped that all customers *within* any single class can be served under identical cost conditions) the prices should be the same and equal to marginal cost. *Between* classes, however, prices should differ, and the difference should be precisely the difference in marginal costs involved in serving the two.

Consider, for example, a situation in which there are two customers, identical in all respects except that one can be served at a marginal cost of $10 per unit and the other at $40—perhaps because the latter has a hilltop location and requires pumped rather than gravity service. If they are both charged $10, the community will be expending $40 in resources to supply a marginal unit which the latter customer values at $10; if they both are charged $40, the former customer would be happy to lay out the $10 it costs to bring him another unit. The principle of equimarginal value in use which dictates equal prices was based on the assumption that costless transfers could take place between customers, but in this case any transfer from the gravity to the pumped customer involves a cost of $30. Another way to look at the matter is to say that the commodity provided is not the same: the customer who requires pumped water is demanding a more costly commodity than the gravity customer.

Where water is sold to customers, therefore, the principles we have developed indicate that customers served under identical cost conditions should be charged equal prices and that the commodity should be supplied and priced in such a way that the price for each class of service should equal the marginal cost of serving that class. Where marginal costs differ, therefore, prices should differ similarly.

4. LIMITATIONS ON VOLUNTARY EXCHANGE OF WATER RIGHTS

In our theoretical discussion we saw that, given any particular vesting of water rights an efficient allocation will tend to come about if free exchange of these rights between users is permitted. There is in practice, however, a wide variety of limitations upon the free exchange of water rights. Water rights are sometimes attached to particular tracts of land (i.e., the water cannot be transferred except as a package deal with the land), especially under the "riparian" principle; transfers of water rights or of uses within water rights also often must in a number of jurisdictions meet approval of some administrative agency. Some legal codes grant certain "higher" users priority or preference over other, "lower" users, transfers from "higher" to "lower" uses being hindered thereby. As a related point, "higher" uses sometimes have a right of seizure. While voluntary transfers can usually be presumed to make both parties better off, and so be in the direction of increased efficiency, no such presumption applies for compelled transfers through seizure.

The above are all instances of violation of a general proposition about property rights. If property is to be put to its most efficient use, there should be no uncertainty of tenure and no restrictions upon the use to which it may be put. When this is the case, voluntary exchange tends to make the property find the use where it is valued the highest, since this use can outbid all others on the market. Uncertainty of tenure interferes with this process, because people will be unwilling to pay much for property, however valuable, if a perfect right cannot be conveyed, and the existing holder will be wary about making those investments necessary to exploit the full value of the property if there is a risk of seizure. All restrictions upon free choice of use, whether the restriction is upon place, purpose, or transfers to other persons, obviously interfere with the market processes which tend to shift the resource to its most productive use.

The reasons underlying adoption of restrictions like those mentioned above are probably mixed, but at least one of them may have some validity: changes in water use may conceivably affect adversely the interests of third parties, such as complementary users downstream, for whom some protection seems needed. This protection should not, as it usually does, go beyond what is necessary to insure preservation of the rights of the third parties. Under California law, for example, a riparian user might attempt to sell water to a non-riparian user who can use the water more productively, none of the other riparian users being harmed thereby. However, the nonriparian purchaser gains no rights against the other riparian users, who can simply increase their diversions, leaving none for the would-be purchaser. Again, a holder of certain appropriate rights might attempt to sell his rights to another. This transfer in some cases requires approval of an administrative board which protects the rights of third parties but whose latitude goes beyond this and permits disapproval on essentially arbitrary grounds as well.

We may comment here that the growing trend to limitation of water rights to "reasonable use" is by no means a wholly obvious or desirable restriction. We might reflect on the desirability of legislation depriving people of their automobiles or their houses when it is determined in some administrative or judicial process that their use was "unreasonable." The purpose of such legislation is the prevention of certain wastes which, if only free voluntary exchange of water rights without unnecessary restrictions were permitted, would tend naturally to be eliminated by market processes (since efficient users can afford to pay more for water than it is worth to wasteful users).

The question of "higher" and "lower" uses has an interesting history. The California Water Code declares that the use of water for domestic purposes is the highest use of water and that the next highest use is for irrigation. Essentially the same statement has been attributed to the emperor Hammurabi (2250 B.C.), a remarkable demonstration of the persistence of error.

The correct idea underlying this thought seems to be that, if we had to do almost entirely without water, we would use the first little bit available for human consumption directly, and then, as more became available, the next use we would want to consider is providing food through irrigation. Where this argument goes wrong is in failing to appreciate that what we want to achieve is to make the *marginal* values in use (the values of the last units applied to any purpose) equal. It would obviously be mistaken to starve to death for lack of irrigation water applied to crops while using water domestically for elaborate baths and air conditioning; the domestic marginal value in use in such a case would be lower. Similar imbalances can make the marginal value in use in industry higher than it is in either domestic or irrigation uses. Actually, the principle of higher and lower uses is so defective that no one would for a moment consider using it consistently (first saturating domestic uses before using any water for other uses, then saturating irrigation uses, etc.). Rather, the principle enters erratically or capriciously in limiting the perfection of property rights in water applied to "lower" uses, however productive such uses may be.

5. EXISTING PRICING PRACTICES IN WATER SUPPLY

Our analysis of the principles of efficient allocation among competitive users led to the conclusion that prices should be equal for all customers served under equivalent cost conditions and that the price should be set at the marginal cost or the cost of delivering the last unit. Alternatively, we may say that the amount supplied should be such that the marginal cost equals the amount the customer is willing to pay for the marginal unit. There are considerable theoretical and practical complications in this connection which we are reserving for discussion in later chapters, but a general survey of the existing situation will be useful here for contrasting practice with the theoretical principles.

Examination of the allocation arrangements of local systems for domestic, commercial, and industrial water supply (primarily municipally owned) reveals that the great majority allocate water by charging a price for its use. The leading exceptions are in unmetered municipalities where, since water bills are not a function of consumption, water *deliveries* may be considered free to the consumer. While a certain amount is ordinarily charged as a water bill in such cities, this is a fixed sum (or "flat rate") and does not operate as a price does in leading consumers to balance the value of use against the cost of use. According to a report published by the *American City Magazine*, a survey made in 1949 of seventy-two cities discovered that 97.7 percent of the services in those cities were metered. The survey excluded, however, several of the largest cities which were partially under flat rates—New York, Chicago, Philadelphia, Buffalo, and others. Since that time, according to the report, Philadelphia has abandoned the fixed-bill system, and generally it may be said that in the United States a condition of universal metering has been approached. As of 1954, the report estimates that metering covered from 90 to 95 percent of all services. Since unmetered services usually represent the smaller domestic users, the proportion of *use* that is metered is even greater than the proportion of *services*.

In those cases, such as New York City, where some users (primarily domestic) are unmetered while others users are charged a price per unit of water used, our rule of prices equal to marginal cost is violated. An unmetered consumer will proceed to use water until its marginal value in use to him is nil to correspond to its zero price to him. This is of course wasteful, because the water system cannot provide the commodity costlessly, and hence society will lose (setting distributional considerations aside) by the excess of the cost of delivery over the value in use for such units of consumption.

It might be thought that the domestic consumers, who are the unmetered customers almost always (the only other substantial classes of use frequently unmetered are public agencies, such as park, sanitation and especially fire departments), somehow deserve a priority or preference as compared with "intermediate" economic customers like industrial or commercial services. But an intermediate consumer is essentially a final consumer once removed. If consumers are required to pay more for water used in the production of food, clothing, and other items of value than they pay for water for direct consumption, an inefficient disparity in marginal values in use between the different uses will be created. Conversely, on efficiency grounds consumers should not be required to pay *more* for domestic water and for water used in industry than for water used to grow crops, such being the effect of existing policies which commonly grant the irrigation use of water a subsidy over all other uses.

A situation in which different prices are charged to different users, or to the same user for varying quantities of the same commodity, is called one of "price discrimination." While discrimination may under certain conditions be justified on one ground or another, it has the defect of preventing the marginal values in use from being made equal between the favored and the penalized uses or users. The only exception to this statement is where discrimination is applied within the purchases of a single individual—by, for example, a declining block rate. If there are no restrictions on use, the individual concerned will continue to equate all his marginal values in the various uses to the *marginal* price (the price for the last unit or for an additional unit) he must pay for the commodity purchased. So far as his own purchases are concerned, therefore, he will still equalize his marginal values in use for all his different uses. If such a block system is used for a number of individuals, however, marginal values in use will not in general be equated between individuals; some will tend to consume an amount such that they end up in the higher-priced block, and others will end up in the lower.

All price differences for the "same" commodity are not, however, evidence of price discrimination. In fact, there should be some difference of price where an extra delivery cost or processing cost must be incurred in serving certain users. These users can be considered as buying two commodities together—the basic commodity and the special delivery or processing. If the basic commodity is to be equally priced to all users, uses requiring such additional services must be charged more.

Turning to the practical side, we should mention at once that our earlier metering discussion neglected one important consideration: the cost of metering and the associated increase in billing costs. It is clear that the additional cost of meters (especially for a great many small users) may well exceed the possible gains from the rationalization of use which would follow metering. (There would, in general, be an aggregate reduction of use as well.) While this question bears further investigation, the dominant opinion in the field of municipal water supply seems to be that universal metering produces gains that are worth the cost. By way of contrast, it appears that in Great Britain domestic use is never metered.

Even if we turn, however, to a consideration of that part of water supply that is metered, or to systems that are completely metered, we find that some non-uniform pattern of prices typically exists. There are some exceptions. In Chicago, for example, all metered users pay the same price per unit of water delivered. A more typical rate system is that of Los Angeles, where rates vary by type of use and also by amount of use (a declining or "promotional" block rate), with a service charge independent of use but based on size of connection. A rate distinction is also made in Los Angeles between firm service and service that the water department may at its convenience provide or refuse, and in some cases between gravity and pumped services.

Some of these rate differences may not be inconsistent with our theoretical discussion. The rate differential may reflect an extra cost or difficulty of delivering to the customer (or customer class, where it is not worthwhile distinguishing between individual customers) charged the higher price.

Where customers' demands vary in the degree to which they impose a peak load on the system, some differential service or demand charge can be justified. In a sense, the commodity delivered off-peak is not the same as that delivered on-peak. The common system of basing a fixed-sum demand charge on the size of service connection is, however, very crude; it provides no deterrent to the customer's contributing to the peak load. Charging a lower rate for interruptible service is somewhat more reasonable. Ideally, the situation might be handled by having differing on-peak and off-peak prices. In water enterprises storage in the distribution system usually smooths out diurnal and weekly peaks. The seasonal peak in the summer is important, however. The Metropolitan Water District of Southern California has at times charged a premium price for summer deliveries.

Other differentiations can be justified by increased delivery costs necessary to reach certain classes of customers. A difference in rate between pumped and gravity service, for example, is eminently reasonable. We have not gone into the question of just how great the differences should be, but for the present we shall not consider such differences as violations of the principle of a common per-unit price to all.

Certain frequently encountered differences, which we may now properly call "price discrimination," are not based on any special cost of providing the service in question. In Los Angeles, for example, there is an exceptionally low rate for irrigation use. Domestic, commercial, and industrial services are not distinguished as such, but they are differentially affected by the promotional volume rates. More serious, because much more common, is the system of block rates, with reductions for larger quantities used. There is typically some saving in piping costs to large customers, since a main can be run directly to the service connection, whereas the same volume sold to many small customers would require a distribution network of pipes. Ideally, the cost of laying down the pipes to connect customers to the system should be assessed as one-time charge against the outlet served—or the lump sum could be converted into an annual charge independent of the amount of water consumed, to represent the interest and depreciation on the capital invested by the water system to serve the customer. The point is that, once the pipes are in, the unit marginal cost of serving customers is almost independent of the volume taken. A lower block rate leads therefore to wasteful use of water by large users, since small users would value the same marginal unit of water more highly if delivered to them. We may say that the promotional or block-rate system in the case of water leads to a discrimination in favor of users of water that happen to find it convenient to use a great deal of the commodity and against users that do not need as much water. The customer paying the lower price will on the margin be utilizing water for less valuable purposes than it could serve if transferred to the customer paying the higher price.

Because of the enormous fraction of water being used for irrigational purposes unusual interest attaches to the method by which water supplies of such projects are allocated to individual users. Not all irrigation water, of course, is distributed through an irrigation district or enterprise, a great deal being simply pumped or diverted by individual users. Such individual users can be considered to pay a price for water in the form of the costs actually incurred in its acquisition for irrigation purposes.

Reliable information is not available on the cost of water to irrigators, partly because of the differing methods of charging for water. The 1950 Census presented an over-all national average of $1.66 per acre-foot in 1949. This figure is not very meaningful, since it is the result of dividing water charges *per acre* by an estimate of average deliveries of water per acre. But the water charges per acre depend, for farmers served by an irrigation district or other supply enterprise, upon the terms of the "payment complex," which may include taxes and assessments, acreage charge, and service fees in addition to the water price.

Unfortunately, there do not seem to be any nationally compiled data on the methods used by irrigation enterprises to charge for water supplied. A tabulation by the Irrigation Districts Association of California indicates considerable variation in practice: some districts make no charge except by assessment of property; others charge a flat rate, either (1) a fixed amount per acre or (2), depending upon the crop, a variable amount per acre; still others charge a price per unit of water, either on a fixed or on a declining block (promotional) basis; still others have a mixture of pricing methods. Where no charge or only a flat-rate charge is made for water, the marginal price of water to the user would be zero if in fact the user can take unlimited quantities as a domestic consumer normally can (subject only to the limited size of his connection). But it seems to be fairly common practice in irrigation districts that the water is more or less rationed to the user; any "price" set is a fiscal measure to cover the operating and maintenance costs of the district and not a market price in the ordinary sense. We have seen that, with rationing of rights, efficiency can be achieved when trading is permitted. Purchase of water rights in irrigation districts normally takes place through purchase of land, which is usually freely possible (except for the so-called 160-acre limitation in Bureau of Reclamation projects), or through purchase of stock in mutual water companies. It may be remarked that a flat rate per acre varying by the type of crop grown is a kind of crude price, the higher flat rate generally corresponding to the more water-intensive crop. Irrigation districts may achieve reasonably efficient water allocations, but perhaps more often through the purchase of rights rather than the correct pricing of water itself. Where the water right cannot be detached from the land, this limitation on sale will create some inefficiency.

Pricing and Costs of the Space Shuttle

CONGRESSIONAL BUDGET OFFICE

The following article is an excerpt from Pricing
Options for the Space Shuttle, *published by the
Congressional Budget Office in 1985. Given the
recent controversy over the shuttle, it is particularly interesting.*

Since 1972 the National Aeronautics and Space Administration
(NASA) has spent $25.7 billion to develop, build, and operate the
space shuttle and its support facilities.[1] Through fiscal year 1990,
the annual shuttle budget is projected to be about $2 billion. The
shuttle system, called the Space Transportation System (STS) by
NASA, is a significant public investment designed to serve the space
transportation needs of the federal government, private firms, and
foreign governments. In order to recoup at least part of this cost,
NASA must charge for the use of the shuttle. Prices, which must
be set well ahead of actual launch, can be based on a variety of costs.
This paper investigates the alternative cost bases and discusses how
the different prices NASA might charge would achieve the nation's
space policy goals.

The space shuttle program was approved for development in 1972
as the nation's major effort in manned space operations, following
the successful completion of the Apollo Program. NASA originally
proposed to build both a fully reusable shuttle (technically called an
orbiter) and a permanently manned space station. Largely because

1. Unless otherwise stated, all dollar amounts in this report are expressed in 1982
dollars.

of budgetary concerns, this proposal was cut back to developing a partially reusable shuttle, which would serve as a first step toward building a space station.[2] Because the shuttle would be reusable, NASA originally thought it would be a cheaper means of transportation than traditional rockets, also called expendable launch vehicles (ELVs). In turn, these lower prices would help encourage commercial development of space.

NASA divides shuttle users into three major groups: U.S. civilian research agencies, including NASA itself; the Department of Defense (DoD); and foreign governments and commercial users.[3] A further distinction could be made between foreign and commercial users that are already mature commercial enterprises—communications satellites and remote-sensing satellites—and so-called "infant industries," such as materials processing and pharmaceutical manufacture. In this study, the term foreign and commercial market will be applied to the mature technologies only.[4] Most of these commercial payloads can also use ELVs, the only alternative to the shuttle for placing satellites in orbit. Because of this competitive means of transport, most commercial payloads are sensitive to the price charged for shuttle services.

In 1977, four years before the first flight and six years before the shuttle entered commercial operations, NASA issued its first pricing policy for shuttle launch services. Because of the long lead time required to design a satellite and integrate it with a launch vehicle— generally two to four years—pricing policies must be established well in advance of launch dates. The base price of $38 million per flight and additional user fees and insurance charges established at that time covered flights from 1983 through 1985. Customers paid a portion of the base price, depending on the share of the orbiter's capacity taken up by their cargo. Because the price was derived from NASA's projected total costs, it also was used to value the launch services provided to DoD.

2. The shuttle design was also modified to accommodate the needs of the Department of Defense (primarily a wider shuttle payload bay and greater maneuverability in landing).

3. Both foreign governments (except for European governments which use Arianespace) and foreign enterprises use the shuttle. Hereafter, "foreign" will encompass both these users.

4. NASA subsidizes flights for the infant industries through Joint Endeavor Agreements, which outline cost sharing between NASA and private firms and anticipate future full-price launch services if the new technologies prove viable.

In 1986 a higher, Phase II price of $71 million per flight will take effect. This price, however, reflects only part of the system's operating costs and none of its capital depreciation. . . .

WHY IS THE PRICE IMPORTANT?

The price NASA charges for shuttle services is important because of its effects on the budget and its influences on the success of the shuttle program in meeting its major objectives. The shuttle price determines how much, if any, of private-sector shuttle costs are subsidized by the general taxpayer. Less directly, it helps to determine what costs are charged to the DoD budget function.

More important, the shuttle price is a key factor in determining the resources the nation devotes to space, and whether these are provided by the public or private sector. For example, while a high price will discourage the shuttle's full use, it can also encourage private firms to provide competing services. Further, by influencing how often the shuttle system is used, the price will affect the decision to expand the system in the future (for example, by investing $1.7 billion to build an additional orbiter). In the long run, the resource allocation role played by the shuttle price will help to determine how and when the commercial development of space occurs. . . .

The shuttle price is particularly significant with regard to the objectives of cost recovery and space commercialization.[5] The effect of any particular shuttle price on either objective not only is difficult to gauge, but also is the substance of the current policy debate. For instance, it can be argued that a substantial price increase could encourage private U.S. companies to enter the market and push the U.S. government out of the commercial launch business. On the other hand, a very high NASA price could turn the launch market over to the shuttle's major current competitor, the European-backed Arianespace, and to such potential foreign competitors as the Japanese.

This analysis of shuttle costs and their relation to price illustrates the trade-offs that exist among a variety of space policy goals—

5. Cost recovery was a criterion in both the 1977 and 1982 pricing policies. National Security Directive 94, "Commercialization of Expendable Launch Vehicles," (May 16, 1983), indicated that full cost recovery should be the cost base for shuttle prices after 1988. NASA views its Phase III pricing policy as consistent with that directive.

encouraging the commercialization of space, recovering shuttle costs, and efficiently using the shuttle system, for example. In selecting a shuttle pricing policy, the Congress and the Administration also will be setting priorities among space policy objectives.

History of NASA Pricing · The cost and engineering analysis undertaken by NASA to develop the first shuttle pricing policy suggested that a single price could satisfy the whole array of budgetary, commercialization, and efficiency objectives. The Phase I price was calculated by estimating the average total operating cost for the 572 shuttle flights that NASA predicted would be flown from 1980 through 1991, and then adding 50 percent to the result as a contingency. Additional fees were added for insurance and ". . . a pro rata share of the depreciation of facilities and equipment and the amortization of the investment in the orbiter fleet."[6] This Phase I price was in NASA's estimation high enough to cover operational, capital and insurance costs, but low enough to attract foreign and commercial users. In fact, rather than subsidizing space transportation for private interests, the first analysis of price and cost indicated that the shuttle price, $38 million per flight plus a user fee and an insurance charge, would generate revenues in excess of its cost. In turn, this could have allowed the system to be expanded at private, rather than public, expense.

As unforeseen technical problems developed, the shuttle program met neither its cost nor flight-rate goals. By 1980 NASA's estimate of the number of flights through 1991 had fallen from 572 to 487 and, in combination with design changes and inaccurate cost estimates, this drove the per flight cost up by 73 percent.[7] NASA now estimates that the demand for the shuttle from 1980 through 1991 will be only 165 flights, or 30 percent of the 1977 estimate. The flight rate continues to be a key uncertainty because both the physical capability of the shuttle fleet to fly 24 times a year and the existence of sufficient demand to require 24 flights have been questioned.

6. C.M Lee and B. Stone, "STS Pricing Policy," *The Space Transportation System: A Review of its Present Capability and Probable Evolution*, AIAA/DGLR/BIS Space Systems Conference, Washington, D.C., October 18–20, 1982, p. 1.

7. See the Comptroller General, *NASA Must Reconsider Operation Pricing Policy to Compensate for Cost Growth on the Space Transportation System*, Report to the Congress of the United States (February 23, 1982), p. 7.

Higher shuttle costs increase the difficulties of achieving particular objectives with any specific shuttle launch price. The first analysis of shuttle prices foresaw a definite and substantial cost advantage for the shuttle compared with ELV's. Once this advantage was lost, a low (below average cost) shuttle price could be criticized for subsidizing the public-sector in competition with private interests, while a high shuttle price could be faulted for discouraging full use of an important national asset. Although the original shuttle pricing policy seemed to rule out a conflict between cost recovery and competitive pricing, the current debate focuses on precisely this point.

The Phase II price increase for flights from 1986 through 1988, formulated in 1982, reflected the strains caused by cost increases above the 1977 estimates. The price of $71 million per flight accounted for the increased cost of some shuttle components and a lower flight rate, 311 as opposed to 572. To offset these increases and to meet increasing domestic and foreign competition, this price was based on what NASA termed "out-of-pocket" costs (the average cost of hardware consumed in the launch process plus marginal service costs but excluding capital costs). Thus, in its Phase II pricing policy, NASA retained the goal of cost recovery, but changed its definition of costs.

The Worldwide ELV Industry · The resilience of ELVs as a competitive launch alternative to the shuttle is also an important consideration in setting shuttle prices. The viability of ELVs stems more from increased shuttle costs than from technical developments in rocketry or investment in new facilities. ELV competitors include Arianespace (the operator of Ariane, the European ELV) and several domestic ELV firms, including those that use the Delta and the Atlas–Centaur rockets. Technically, these rockets are very similar, although the American ELVs evolved from rockets built in the 1960s while Ariane was developed in recent years. The Ariane, which is launched from French Guyana, has a 12 percent to 15 percent performance advantage compared with launches from Florida, because its location near the equator provides a faster launch velocity as a result of the earth's rotation. Although the stated long-term goal for Ariane is a one-third share of the non-Communist world's market for space payloads, it now carries close to 40 percent of recent commercial launches, thanks to aggressive pricing and continued technical improvements.

The private domestic ELV industry has yet to win a launch bid. According to these firms, the major obstacle impeding their success is subsidized public sector competition, namely NASA and Arianespace.[8] NASA, for its part, responds that the technologies likely to be employed by domestic ELV firms have already been deeply subsidized, and that these firms should either be forced to pay for past government support or to compete with the shuttle as currently priced. Moreover, NASA and a different group of domestic private firms contend that the real investment in space commercialization is occuring in technologies which complement rather than compete with the shuttle. According to this view, private firms and space commercialization would be hurt rather than helped by a high shuttle price.

The conflicts surrounding the Phase II policy discussion have increased as the pricing policy for the 1989–1991 period is being formulated. A high shuttle price might better serve some policy objectives—such as cost recovery, encouraging private entrants to the domestic launch industry, and ensuring that the public sector does not overinvest in additional capacity. Other objectives, such as encouraging the use of the shuttle's unique capabilities and ensuring full use of the shuttle system's capacity, could be better served by a lower shuttle price. The optimism of the 1977 pricing policy analysis and the possibility it offered of a single price to meet a diverse set of general and specific objectives is all but gone. Instead, in choosing among different pricing policies, a choice must be made among different policy objectives. . . .

EXPENDITURES ON THE SHUTTLE SYSTEM: PAST AND PROJECTED

Past and projected spending for the shuttle system can be divided into four major categories: *(a)* design, development, testing and evaluation, which ended in 1983; *(b)* construction of facilities; *(c)* production of the orbiter and system capability; and *(d)* operations, which began in 1981.

Table 1 shows actual spending on these categories from fiscal years 1972 through 1984, and projected spending from fiscal years 1985

---

8. American ELV firms have been active in presenting their view of shuttle pricing to the public. Transpace Carriers Inc., the operator of the Delta rocket, has initiated a formal trade complaint currently being pursued by the U.S. Special Trade Representative.

TABLE 1

ACTUAL AND PROJECTED SPENDING ON THE SHUTTLE SYSTEM
(By fiscal year, in thousands of 1982 dollars)

Fiscal year	DDT&E[a]	Construction	Production	Operations	Total
Actual					
1972	0	40,481	0	0	40,481
1973	0	58,368	0	0	58,368
1974	216,393	108,897	0	0	325,290
1975	1,406,526	136,129	0	0	1,542,655
1976	2,540,765	78,586	0	0	2,619,351
1977	2,088,802	60,365	108,865	0	2,258,032
1978	1,898,462	103,469	60,522	0	2,062,453
1979	1,712,918	41,896	496,224	0	2,251,038
1980	1,339,136	42,017	906,963	462,768	2,750,884
1981	1,040,642	12,532	1,093,048	577,968	2,724,189
1982	894,000	20,050	1,282,750	734,860	2,931,600
1983	0	25,700	1,634,629	1,354,000	3,014,329
1984	0	73,300	689,815	2,364,167	3,127,282
Projected					
1985	0	37,900	556,545	1,934,105	2,528,550
1986	0	39,200	325,000	1,935,720	2,299,920
1987	0	40,700	175,000	1,937,113	2,152,813
1988	0	42,100	65,000	1,930,973	2,038,073
1989	0	43,700	25,000	1,930,483	1,999,183
1990	0	45,200	25,000	1,929,170	1,999,370

SOURCE: Congressional Budget Office based on NASA data.

[a] Design, development, testing, and evaluation.

through 1990. Before shuttle operations began in 1983, outlays in the above first three categories accounted for $17.8 billion. Of this total, 75 percent went to design, development, testing, and evaluation (DDT&E). These expenditures ended in 1983 when the shuttle became operational. Operational expenditures began in 1981 for flights to be undertaken in 1983 and beyond. On average for 1983 through 1985, the Congress authorized $3 billion annually for the shuttle system, divided equally between operations and capital spending to improve capabilities. By 1990 the operations portion of the shuttle system budget will dominate, accounting for more than 95 percent of the projected budget of $2 billion.

FROM BUDGET EXPENDITURE TO ECONOMIC COSTS

These budget numbers cannot be used alone to estimate the cost of the shuttle. Only operating expenditures correspond to an annual cost in the economic sense, and even these estimates require adjustment for the three-year period over which the cost of a shuttle flight is incurred and reimbursements for the flight are received. For example, the fiscal year 1983 budget included $1.4 billion (in 1983 dollars) for shuttle operations. This expenditure did not, however, represent the economic cost of the shuttle flights undertaken in 1983. The long lead times necessary to plan a flight and integrate payloads with the orbiter required expenditures as early as 1981. For the same reason, the 1983 budget for shuttle operations included funding for flights to be flown as late as 1985. Thus, an additional step in establishing the cost of the shuttle in any one year is to identify the operational costs for that particular year's flights. This analysis relies on NASA cost estimates for these data.

A more significant problem of translating budgetary outlays into economic costs arises because $20 billion, or 79 percent of the cumulative spending on the shuttle system through fiscal year 1984, was invested in capital assets (through the DDT&E, construction, and production accounts). For an economic analysis of cost, this investment must be translated into an annual capital charge, in contrast with budgetary authorizations in the year the investments were made.

If the shuttle were operated as a private business or a regulated utility, the annual cost of service would include a capital charge, which would be included in the price paid by customers. Without inclusion of this charge, the owners of the asset would not receive an adequate return on their investment. The shuttle is not strictly comparable to a private enterprise or a regulated utility because it is a very high-risk venture, generates social benefits that are difficult to anticipate or quantify, and has been designed to accommodate a set of needs—such as those required by the Defense Department— rot required by commercial users. Nevertheless, one view of the annual cost of the shuttle would capitalize—that is, include as capital costs—all preoperational and ongoing investments in the shuttle, including research and development spending. It would also include the cost of funds or interest costs tied up in the system before its commercial operation began. This last point, the cost of funds, is also pertinent to investments made since 1983 in assets that will become operational in several years.[9]

The capital charges estimated in this analysis need to be examined carefully on their own terms and in comparison with corresponding estimates for actual and potential shuttle competitors. The Arianespace cost data do not include a capital charge, nor is it clear that the rough order-of-magnitude estimates for the capital costs of private domestic ELV entrants incorporate the value of past or ongoing public investments made in their behalf, such as R&D expenditures on the Delta rocket.

9. The shuttle system orbiters are the best example to illustrate this point. NASA currently estimates that, if a new orbiter were to be built—an expenditure opposed by NASA—seven years would pass between the time spending began and the orbiter became operational. But a dollar spent on a new orbiter could have been used in some alternative way. Thus, while this "interest" on funds used to build the shuttle system is not included in NASA budgets, it is a legitimate "cost" of the shuttle program.